The Working Class in American History

Editorial Advisors

David Brody
Herbert G. Gutman
David Montgomery

D0890661

A list of books in the series appears at the end of this book.

A Generation of Boomers

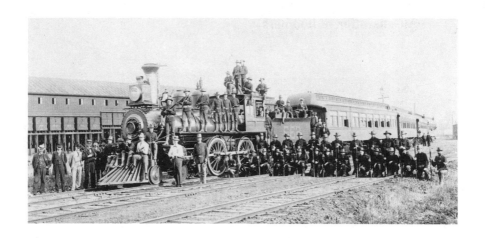

Shelton Stromquist

A Generation of Boomers:

The Pattern of

Railroad Labor Conflict

in Nineteenth-Century America

University of Illinois Press

URBANA AND CHICAGO

Publication of this work was supported in part by a grant from the Andrew W. Mellon Foundation.

Illini Books edition, 1993
©1987 by the Board of Trustees of the University of Illinois
Manufactured in the United States of America
1 2 3 4 5 C P 5 4 3 2 1

This book is printed on acid-free paper.

Library of Congress Cataloging-in-Publication Data

Stromquist, Shelton, 1943–
    A generation of boomers.

    (Working class in American history)
    Based on the author's thesis.
    Bibliography: p.
    Includes index.
    1. Strikes and lockouts—Railroads—United States—History— 19th century.   2. Railroads—United States—Employees—History— 19th century.   I. Title.
II. Series.
HD5325.R1S77   1987   331.89′281385′0973   85-29017
ISBN 0-252-01302-6 (cl : alk. paper)
ISBN 0-252-06344-9 (pb : alk. paper)

For Ann, Christopher, Matthew, and Elizabeth

Contents

Figures

Tables

Preface

Been on the hummer since ninety-four
Last job I had was on the Lake Shore,
Lost my office in the A. R. U.
And I won't get it back till nineteen-two,
And I'm still on the hog train flagging my meals,
Ridin' the brake beams close to the wheels.
                    —Anonymous railroad bard

"Boomer" railroad men have a cherished place in the popular imagination. Although the romance of their vocations and the itinerancy of their lives have been exaggerated, the term "Boomer" fittingly characterizes a significant portion of the generation of workers that built and operated the railroads during the expansive years of the late nineteenth century.

The scarcity of labor on the frontier of railroad expansion encouraged high turnover. Economist Victor Clark noted in his report to the Eight-Hour Commission that "train hands who drift about the country, working first for one road and then for another, are called 'boomers.' " While some railroad men settled in one place and worked for a single road for years, many did not. "During the era of rapid railway construction in the West, they formed a large part of the force in that section, because the roads had not been in existence long enough to create their own employees."

Railroad boomtowns, particularly in their first years of spectacular growth, reflected the life-style of the railroad men who settled or passed through them. The extraordinary expectation of town promoters that such growth could be sustained matched the faith of many railroad men that the high wages and privileges accorded their scarce skills were inviolable. A sense of craft pride was nourished by the central role that railroad workers played in the social and civic life of such communities.

The term *boomer* fits this period in still another sense. The relations between railroad management and labor were more volatile during the years from 1877 to 1894 than at any other time in the industry's history. The soaring expectations of railroad workers collided with the economizing proclivities of managers to produce explosions of industrial conflict that rattled the American social order. The cumulative strike experience and the repeated attempts to forge industrial organizations capable of confronting management as equals and arresting the erosion of wages and work rules produced a generation of boomers whose class consciousness was embodied in the American Railway Union.

The magnitude of these struggles has tended to capture the attention of historians as it did of contemporaries and to overshadow the underlying changes that they reflected. There are numerous excellent accounts of the major railroad strikes for this period.[1] There is also a rich literature of local studies that focus primarily on changes in working class culture and community in a variety of industrial settings.[2] But we lack a framework for integrating the local analysis of social and cultural patterns with changes in the political economy of nineteenth-century American capitalism, and we lack an analysis of strikes that locates episodes within broader patterns of emerging class conflict.

This volume is an attempt to build such a larger framework. Three aspects of this task should be mentioned at the outset. First, the starting point in this analysis is the behavioral record of strike activity between 1877 and 1894. That record reveals complex patterns in the incidence and location of strikes, the issues that precipitated them, the breadth of participation, and the success achieved. These patterns require explanation. A focus on the handful of major national strikes of the period neither reveals nor explains the wider patterns of conflict. Furthermore, railroad strikes directly influenced the institutional innovations of workers *and* managers as they sought to consolidate or extend their advantages, and to limit the damage their interests might suffer from the conflict.

Second, this is a study in the *political economy* of railroad labor conflict. The concept of a moving frontier of labor scarcity is the central idea that makes sense out of the regional patterns of strike activity and labor organization. Differences in the supply of railroad labor between one region and another are absolutely central for understanding the incidence of strikes, the evolving forms of labor organization, and the changing social structure of the railroad labor force. This economic fact cannot be understood without its political dimension. The railroad labor market was not simply a product of anonymous economic forces: it was a "project" of those in a position to effect changes in the supply of labor. Railroad managers and workers were not passive witnesses to the movement of wages, the migrations of workers, and the inexorable natural increase in the population. Each group actively intervened to protect its interests and to exert some control over the labor supply.

The third aspect of this study that deserves attention at the outset is its focus on the communities in which railroad labor conflict occurred. Although railroad operations were located in a variety of community settings, nineteenth-century railroad towns had certain attributes in common. They were division headquarters that serviced railroad operations over a portion of the line within a larger system. They possessed repair facilities and switching yards and often served as major collection or transfer points for freight. Most importantly, for our purpose, they were the home for a full complement of railroad men needed to operate trains and repair equipment within the division. These communities and the peculiarities of their development and class structure defined the social context within which railroad workers lived and worked. Like so many smaller industrial communities in the nineteenth century, railroad towns did not lack high aspirations. But the ambition of community boosters was tempered by factors beyond their control—the location and position of their communities within the developing systems of cities, the rates charged by railroads to carry their products, and the growth rhythms and division of labor in the national economy. The class polarization and conflict that characterized the era of the Great Upheaval was not absent from smaller communities.[3] Community ambition frequently collided with the imperatives of class conflict, leaving divided communities in the wake. The dynamics of class relations, the structure of opportunity, and the extent of community support for striking workers varied from one community to another, but the variations followed predictable patterns. In one sense, the story of each railroad town is unique, but, as with most local history, the essential attributes of the local story are embedded in larger social processes. This study attempts to unravel those social processes—the patterns of mobility, social organization, and class formation—and to place the histories of railroad towns and their worker communities within a wider social context.

The first chapter presents the problem of railroad labor conflict and systematically describes the configuration of strikes between

1881 and 1894, which must be explained. Chapter 2 discusses the evolving forms of labor organization that were a product of this industrial conflict. Railroad workers experimented with different organizations under different circumstances. More than anything else, their organizational experimentation was guided by their desire to impose some order on a chaotic and deteriorating labor market that undermined their wages and the rules that governed their work.

The next three chapters discuss, in turn, three important ways in which strike activity among railroad workers varied—by region, between communities, and among railroad men themselves. The concept of a moving frontier of labor scarcity is introduced in chapter 3 to explain geographical differences. It is argued that control of the labor supply was at the core of the cluster of issues that precipitated railroad strikes. A typology of railroad towns is developed in chapter 4 to explain differences in class relations and community economic growth among towns that served as railroad division headquarters. Those differences bore directly on the extent of community support for strikers and on the cross-class solidarity generated during railroad strikes. In chapter 5 the social structure of the railroad labor force is analyzed, and the concept of a *labor-force life cycle* is introduced to explain the relationship between geographical and occupational mobility and the effects of mobility on the solidarity among workers in different communities.

Declining labor scarcity, sharpening class differences in railroad towns, and diminishing opportunities for mobility in railroad work all reinforced each other. These developments drove railroad workers, on the one hand, to create broader, class-based forms of organization and, on the other hand, increased the vulnerability of those organizations to defeat and disruption as labor conflict intensified.

Chapter 6 discusses the evolution of management strategies to contain that conflict, to impose new forms of work discipline on the labor force, and to eliminate industrial unionism among railroad workers. To a large extent, railroad managers were reacting to conflicts with labor that were a by-product of the industry's competitive expansion and the cost-cutting imperatives that competition imposed. Only gradually did some managers begin to think systematically about labor matters. Rationalization of the railroad labor process ultimately came through the intervention of the federal government and the consolidation of the industry. But it was the persistence and growth of railroad labor conflict during the last three decades of the nineteenth century that fueled the search for a systematic corporate labor policy.

The work of historians, like that of railroad workers in the nineteenth century, has a certain boomer quality. Research and writing carry us all over the map in search of valuable evidence, sage advice, and remunerative employment to sustain the ongoing work. This piece of work is no exception. Begun as a dissertation in 1975, it took me to public libraries and local historical societies in numerous small railroad towns, to research libraries and state historical societies for somewhat longer sojourns, and to university libraries with important collections on labor and railroad history. During the course of this itinerant research, numerous railroad men, librarians, archivists, fellow historians, and friends provided invaluable guidance and moral support. I can directly thank only a small portion of those whose assistance and friendship were essential to this work. All are remembered and appreciated.

Valuable allies in any major piece of research are the librarians and archivists whose knowledge of the collections in their care and whose insight into the questions that researchers pose unlock evidence that would otherwise remain buried. I am especially grateful for the assistance I received from the staff of the Minnesota Historical Society, the Iowa Department of History and Archives, the Denver Public Library, the Chicago Public Library, the New York Public Library, the Industrial and Labor Relations Collection at the Cornell University Library, the University of Wisconsin Memorial Library, the State Historical Society of Iowa, the University of Iowa Memorial Library, the Carnegie Library in Pittsburgh, the Western Reserve Historical Society, the Cincinnati Historical Society, the Chicago Historical Society, the Library of Congress, the Montana Historical Society, the Union Pacific Historical Collection, the Burlington Northern Collection, and the public libraries in Burlington, Ottumwa and Creston, Iowa, Hornell, New York, and Brainerd, Willmar and Fergus Falls, Minnesota.

Special words of appreciation are due the staff of the Newberry Library in Chicago and the State Historical Society of Wisconsin. I spent an invaluable three months as a Newberry fellow at a critical point in the conceptual development of this project. The richness of the Burlington and Western Americana collections at the Newberry are, I hope, demonstrated in some small way by this work. Of equal importance was the invigorating intellectual atmosphere and the opportunity to exchange ideas with Newberry staff and with other visiting scholars. At the State Historical Society of Wisconsin I had the benefit of knowing the staff not only as a visiting researcher but as a co-worker. Their assistance and encouragement and their dedicated stewardship of an unsurpassed collection of nineteenth-century labor materials made this work proceed more smoothly than it might have.

I was generously assisted in my research and in the revision of the final manuscript by an Andrew W. Mellon Fellowship from the University of Pittsburgh, a Newberry Library Fellowship, and an Old Gold Summer Stipend and a grant from the Graduate College of the University of Iowa.

At every stage of my work on this project—from the preliminary research on Hornellsville railroad men through the dissertation to the completion of this manuscript—I have benefited enormously from the insightful guidance and persistent encouragement of David Montgomery. His stimulating seminars deepened my understanding of the history of the American working class. And his patience in plowing through primitive, early versions of these chapters contributed in no small way to the completion of this work. He has been an extraordinary teacher. My intellectual debt to him is great. Sam Hays regularly challenged me to adopt a comparative approach to the study of working-class life; through his seminar and from his service on my dissertation committee, I have gained a greater appreciation of systematic social analysis. Other members of the committee—David Houston, Richard Oestreicher, and Julius Rubin—offered helpful criticisms and suggestions for revision. The advice and encouragement of my friend and colleague Steve Sapolsky have been invaluable.

Walter Licht, Carl Graves, Alfred D. Chandler, Jr., William Tuttle, Daniel Rodgers, Barbara Tucker, Alan Dawley, and Jonathan Garlock read earlier versions of parts of this work and generously shared their views. Milton Cantor, Bruce Laurie, and Daniel Walkowitz read the entire manuscript and offered encouragement and helpful suggestions for revision. Herb Gutman, whose untimely death has left us without an essential friend and guide, read the manuscript in an early form and shared his enthusiasm for it. My colleagues at the University of Iowa—Ellis Hawley, Linda Kerber, Malcolm Rohrbough, and Jeff Cox—contributed useful ideas for the improvement of the manuscript, as did John Schacht, fellow labor historian and reference librarian at the University of Iowa. The value of all of this guidance has been great. The remaining deficiencies of this book are my responsibility alone.

The final typing and some very helpful editorial advice were provided by Gundega Korsts and Richard Claus. Dick Wentworth and Liz Dulany of the University of Illinois Press were steady guides through all phases of the preparation of the manuscript.

The final thanks are due my family. They have shared most intimately this historical journey in all of its phases. Jim and Mary Mullin offered encouragement and support at numerous points. Marjorie W. Stromquist gave moral support and valuable editorial advice. Her probing questions and tireless attention to the clarity with which ideas are expressed contributed immeasurably. Howard Stromquist did not live to see the completion of this work, but his integrity and love deeply influenced it. Chris, Matt, and Elizabeth, whose coming into the world made the life of this historian richer, were tolerant beyond their years of a father who was unfathomably preoccupied on occasion. This book is dedicated to them and to Ann Mullin Stromquist. She made this work possible through the critical judgment she brought to the text in its various stages of maturity, through her determination to make things work in a two-career household, and, above all, through her extraordinary gift of love.

A Generation of Boomers

Introduction:

The Political Economy of Railroad Labor Conflict

Railroad labor conflict of unprecedented proportions erupted across the United States during the last three decades of the nineteenth century. That conflict coincided with the most intense and unstable period of railroad construction. By the early 1890s the national rail network had brought service to all corners of the continent. As consumers of investment capital, as parties to the disposal of the public domain, as corporations consistently dependent on the courts to rationalize their operations and discipline their employees, the railroads were cast as major characters on the political stage of "Gilded Age" America. While this volume can only peripherally address the issue of the railroads' direct involvement in the political process, it is centrally concerned with explicating the patterns of railroad labor conflict as a by-product of the political economy of the industry.

Railroads, even more clearly than other large corporations in nineteenth-century America, were private entities whose very existence was dependent on the political environment within which they operated. If this was true for their financing, for their acquisition and sales of public lands, and for their manipulation of rates, it was equally true for their attempts to recruit, organize, and discipline a labor force. The courts and politicians at all levels of government were supporting actors in these matters. But beyond the direct intervention that public agencies consistently carried out in railroad labor relations, the labor process itself was an arena within which workers and railroad managers contested for control. At stake, above all else, was the capacity to control the supply of railroad labor. Neither side was prepared to sit by while natural market forces made adjustments to rapid expansion and the settlement that followed in its wake.

To understand the pattern and character of railroad labor conflict in this period, then, we must locate it within the geographical ex-

4

pansion of the industry; we must examine the role that railroad expansion played in the volatile economy of late nineteenth-century America; and we must consider the social and political consequences of that role for the settlement of the country. Just as the railroads pioneered new forms of corporate organization and managerial technique, so did they create, as a by-product of their conflicts with labor, a new framework for labor-management cooperation that was quintessentially political in nature.

Railroads and the Transformation of American Society

American society was profoundly redefined after the Civil War. Competition between a social system based on free labor and one based on slavery had defined the primary axis of social tension in the years leading up to the war, but as the war years receded, new tensions became manifest—tensions embedded within the free labor system itself and within expanding corporate capitalism.[1]

The existence of a class-stratified society was not news to shoemakers in Lynn, Massachusetts, or to factory operatives in Lowell. Well before the outbreak of the Civil War, seamstresses in New York City and handloom weavers on the outskirts of Philadelphia harbored few illusions about rising to independent entrepreneurship. The artisans and urban laborers who organized city centrals in Boston, New York, and Philadelphia in 1835 and the iron molders, puddlers, and tailors who organized effective trade unions during the early 1850s were already probing the limits of a free labor ideology that promised workers independence and control over the products of their labor. But it was in many respects a new class, a class of "hirelings for life," that assumed leadership of the labor movement in the immediate aftermath of the Civil War. That class confronted an expanding industrial system that imposed new forms of work discipline, new technologies, and new methods of wage determination on labor. Its innovations were not restricted to the old industrial centers of the Northeast. On the contrary, in the rapidly industrializing territories to the west, the shape of the new industrial system was also amply visible to contemporary observers.[2]

The geographical extension of American society westward, with the colonization and incorporation of new territories, revealed the new axis of social tension. As successive regions passed from frontier to settled society, the institutional impress of the economic forces driving expansion was deeply felt. Although the social distance between the frontier and its urbanizing hinterland remained great, the pressures of economic expansion shortened the time required for the transition from one to the other. Conflict between classes was not limited to the congested and Europeanized East.

American railroads lay at the very heart of the expanding economy. They offered a model for large-scale corporate organization, and they offered a market for durable goods, which promoted the application of that model in other economic sectors. They created the connecting sinews of a national market for American manufactured goods and an international market for the agricultural surplus of the West. They provided the logic and the means for establishing networks of urban settlement that implanted the nuclei of a class-stratified society in advance of agricultural settlement. And they shaped the instruments of capital formation and the "promotional" state in ways that produced a massive infusion of public resources into private enterprise with only minimal exercise of public control.[3]

The American economy at the end of the Civil War was poised for a period of significant growth. Although the war itself had brought with it inflation and only modest growth in output, other factors promised a surge in economic growth. The resumption of significant immigration together with a buoyant demand for consumer goods fueled the recovery of the civilian economy. Wartime conditions had created a favorable political climate for legislation that made possible expanded western settlement. Construction of a "Pacific railroad," hamstrung in a sectionally divided prewar legislature, was already underway. The Homestead Act of 1862 offered would-be settlers the promise of free land in the West. Support was readily available for additional grants of public land to finance construction of railroads in the West.[4]

Even as it grew, the American economy was hampered by forms of business organization and manufacturing technologies that had been the basis for an earlier period of growth. As late as 1870, the average American manufacturing firm employed fewer than ten workers. Traditional skills dominated production in important industries such as iron, glass, coal mining, metal fabrication, and construction. Only a few sectors of manufacturing had achieved the economies of scale that would be more generally characteristic within a few years. Massachusetts textile mills discovered the advantages of using relatively unskilled workers in highly mechanized factory production well before the Civil War, but those lessons had been applied in few other industries by the end of the 1860s.

Inadequate transportation, which limited the effective market that many producers could hope to reach, delayed the wide application of such methods. Balkanized, regional markets could still be served adequately by producers who had neither the means nor the incentive to invest in manufacturing processes that promised lower unit costs in return for increased volume of production. Except for maufacturing centers that enjoyed extraordinary locational advantages or a "home market" of considerable size, the incentives for growth were marginal.[5]

Two changes dramatically and qualitatively altered the postwar economic environment. First, the railroad network expanded both within areas of existing settlement and on the pioneer periphery. Second, the American population grew rapidly and relocated in massive numbers both westward and cityward.

Geographic expansion was the most important attribute of the railroad industry in the nineteenth century. Impressive as the growth of the railroad network had been before the Civil War, it had, in fact, barely crossed the Mississippi in the West, and it had offered only the most minimal service in the South, linking areas of concentrated cotton production with coastal shipping points. Even in the East, the trunk lines and their feeders left large areas of settlement unserved.

The period from 1865 through 1900 witnessed a frenetic pace of railroad construction that produced a truly national railroad network. The growth in track mileage alone conveys something of the changes accomplished (table 1).[6]

Railroad expansion was concentrated in three phases between the end of the Civil War and the turn of the century. Each burst of construction created a powerful demand for labor, not only to build the roads but to operate them. The first phase, between 1867 and 1872, saw the first transcontinental system completed, the construction of others begun, and the railroad network in the Midwest filled in. The second phase, which covered the years 1878 through 1883, saw the largest increase in new railroad mileage. Transcontinentals were pushed toward completion; competitive routes that intersected the transcontinentals were fought over. Julius Grodinsky noted that this vast expansion produced a railroad network that by 1883 was overbuilt.[7]

The final phase of expansion occurred from 1886 through 1892. Lines were extended beyond their established territories in competition with neighboring railroads. Multiple lines mushroomed to connect important routes such as St. Paul-Chicago. And the trans-

Table 1. Increases in Railroad Track Mileage, 1838–1909

	Miles of Main Track	Net Increase	Miles of Other Track	Net Increase
1838	2,633	—	132	—
1848	6,279	3,646	936	804
1858	27,621	21,342	4,598	3,662
1869	46,844	22,223	9,369	4,771
1879	86,566	39,722	18,200	8,831
1889	161,276	74,710	40,812	22,612
1899	190,046	28,770	64,418	23,606
1909	238,116	48,070	108,916	44,498

Source: Albert Fishlow, "Productivity and Technological Change in the Railroad Sector, 1840–1910," Conference on Reasearch in Income and Wealth, Studies in Income and Wealth, vol. 30, Output, Employment and Productivity in the United States after 1800 (New York: 1966), 596.

continental system in the Northwest was finished with the completion of the Great Northern. Grodinsky points out that even as early as 1887 "few location monopolies were left in western territories." Continued overbuilding and rate wars led inexorably to the consolidation of the railroads into large systems, a trend that was spurred on by the numerous bankruptcies of the 1893–97 depression.[8]

The expansion of the railroad network was related to the peculiar cycles of growth and contraction in the American economy and to the seasonal rhythms of a transportation system dependent on agriculture. During periods of expansion the costs of construction stretched public and private sources of capital to the limits. Overextension of railroad finance in 1873, 1883, and 1893 provided one catalyst for financial panics whose effects could not be isolated from the rest of the economy.

Periods of expansion also generated extraordinary demand for labor that translated into premium wages, generous work rules, and opportunities for very rapid promotion. However, changing economic conditions and the railroads' success in recruiting new workers from areas of labor surplus produced periodic and precipitous deterioration in the terms of employment.

Each wave of expansion created labor scarcity, which reproduced the standards of employment that had proved transitory in other regions during periods of growth. Workers who were stalled on the promotional ladder entertained the hope for rapid promotion in newly settled areas. Not only did they find that such opportunities were short-lived, but seasonal fluctuations also disrupted their expectations of steady employment. Between the peak of harvest traffic and another, more modest surge in the spring, many railroads made significant cuts in the service they offered and the numbers of employees they required. Even in periods of relative prosperity when overall employment grew each year, seasonal cutbacks caused months of underemployment. Both railroad managers and railroad workers kept a weather eye on the state of the railroad labor market. No better barometer of the costs of and returns to railroad labor existed.

American population growth and its westward migration were also major factors in the changing American economy of the late nineteenth century and in the shifting labor market conditions that confronted railroad corporations and their workers. Several causes lay behind these population shifts. The promise of free land offered by the wartime Homestead Act represented at least the partial fulfillment of a long-standing demand by workingmen. Together with the land patents given to Union army veterans, the Homestead Act drew settlers into the territories immediately beyond the Mississippi Valley.

Land grants of unprecedented scale were given to the railroads between 1865 and 1871 to finance construction.[9] Adding the function of land agent to their more basic functions as transportation systems, the western railroads marshaled formidable resources in the promotion of settlement. As the transcontinentals pushed into unsettled territory, at first in Iowa, Nebraska, and Minnesota and somewhat later in the Dakota territory and Kansas, modest urban settlements were left in their wake to service railroad operations and to funnel what agricultural surpluses the new territories generated.

Immigration from overseas, which had been bottled up during the war, leapt forward in response to a renewed demand for labor. Large numbers of German, Irish, and Scandinavian immigrants moved directly through the densely settled East, conveyed by rail in immigrant cars, to the new urban jumping-off points in the upper Midwest. Those cities—Chicago, Milwaukee, Saint Louis, Saint Paul—and other lesser towns in the Mississippi Valley held onto a substantial proportion of these newcomers to perform labor essential to the manufacturing and transportation that supported the frontline of settlement. Although each crescendo of immigration was followed by a decline, as the word of contraction in the American economy spread from immigrants to their countrymen in Europe, the successive waves of immigration produced a large increase in the foreign-born population of the Midwest and West.[10]

The transition from frontier to settled territory, which so fascinated Frederick Jackson Turner, was affected by the railroad and by the rapid shifts in population that it made possible. Not only was the period of time required for that transition shortened in successive regions, the very nature of the settlement process was altered. Turner argued that a witness standing at the Cumberland Gap in the late eighteenth century and at the South Pass in the Rockies nearly one hundred years later would have observed essentially the same sequence of settlers: the trapper, the miner, the herder, the agriculturalist, and the townsman.[11] In fact, as that troubled and perceptive critic of American society in the mid-1880s, the Reverend Josiah Strong, observed, the pattern of settlement had changed.

> In the Middle States the farms were first taken, then the towns sprung up to supply their wants, and at length the railway connected it with the world; but in the West the order is reversed—first the railroad, then the town, then the farms. Settlement is, consequently, much more rapid, and the city stamps the country, instead of the country's stamping the city. It is the cities and towns which will frame state constitutions, make laws, create public opinion, establish social standards and morals in the West. The character of the West will, therefore, be substantially determined some time before the land is all occupied.[12]

Between the years 1870 and 1890 the proportion of the population living west of the Mississippi River rose from 18 percent to 27 percent even as the density of settlement in the East increased.[13] A significant proportion of the settlers, both immigrants and internal migrants, sought the opportunities offered in the cities that followed the ribbons of steel rail through the West. These urban pioneers, many of whom found work constructing or operating railroads, created communities in which their equality of condition was inextricably bound up with their common status as dependents of distant corporations. The stark contrast between their pioneering aspirations of independence and their vulnerability to the decisions made by large corporations was fertile breeding ground for an anti-monopoly culture that celebrated their shared status as "producers." Railroad workers, who formed the core of the labor force in many of these new towns, successfully located their class interests within a broader producers' consciousness that sought to assert community rights in the face of "aggrandizing monopoly."

Economic Performance

The American economy after 1865 not only grew at a respectable rate of 1.5 percent per annum, but it underwent important structural changes.[14] Those changes were at least in part a by-product of the economy's cyclical pattern of growth. Periods of rapidly increasing productivity and heavy investment were followed by periods of violent contraction. A secular pattern of falling prices between the early 1870s and late 1890s was accompanied by a series of serious depressions: 1873–78, 1883–85, and 1893–97. Each depression created conditions that invited business reorganization and consolidation, the curtailment and redirection of investment, the liquidation of less-competitive firms, the reduction of labor costs, and the elimination of trade unions. The succession of depressions and the structural changes that they enabled were part of a long-term pattern of change in what has been called the "social structure of accumulation."[15] From an economy of relatively small-scale, technologically backward, family or privately owned firms at the end of the Civil War, American society by the end of the century came to be dominated in its key industrial sectors by corporate giants, which were the product of consolidation and restriction of competition.

Railroads in the late nineteenth century embody the structural changes that coursed through the economy as a whole. As a "leading sector," they bear some measure of direct responsibility for the cyclical pattern of the economy's growth.[16]

The railroads grew faster than the manufacturing sector in total output and employment. Their productivity increased at an annual rate of 2 percent between 1870 and 1910, significantly above the rate for the economy as a whole. The largest share of increased railroad productivity is attributable to the physical extension of the railroad system—the building and operating of new lines. A significantly smaller factor derived from the intensification of traffic on existing lines.[17] Productivity surged during periods of construction and contracted during the depressions that saw a curtailment of railroad building. Between 1868 and 1873 output grew by 115 percent, but during the subsequent five years of depression, by only 33 percent. By the 1890s, however, as the transcontinental system neared completion, important changes in technology and in the organization of the industry contributed to significant gains in traffic density. Standardization of track gauges and equipment, improvements in railroad car construction, the adoption of standard time zones, and uniform accounting procedures led to a smoother interchange of traffic and a more integrated railroad network. These improvements laid the foundation for increasing traffic density and sustained gains in productivity even as new construction fell off.[18]

Railroad construction required an enormous infusion of capital, dwarfing the requirements of both canal construction and the largest manufacturing firms. Between 1815 and 1860 canal construction absorbed $188 million. Even in 1859 railroad construction had far surpassed this level, with a total investment of $1,100 million and most of that in just the previous decade. The major East-West trunk lines of the 1850s—the Erie, the Baltimore & Ohio, the Pennsylvania, and the New York Central—were capitalized at between $17 million and $35 million. By comparison, only a handful of the largest textile firms and metalworking factories had reached a total capitalization of $1 million.[19] Gross investment in railroad track and equipment during the decade of the 1850s was $927 million. Although it declined slightly during the next decade, due largely to the effects of the Civil War, railroad investment during the 1870s reached more than $2 billion and doubled again during the 1880s. By 1900 total investment in America's railroads stood between $9.1 billion and $15.9 billion, depending on how much watered stock is included in the figure.[20]

Investment capital came from a variety of sources, whose relative importance varied from one period to another. Grants of public lands were an essential element in railroad financing during the period of construction from 1868 to 1873. Foreign investment, which in aggregate totaled almost $3 billion, was most important during the last phase of construction, from 1886 through 1893. Local and state subsidies, private investment funds, and retained earnings were also significant sources of investment capital. Real capital investment, however, lagged behind capitalization on paper. *Poor's Manual* in 1884 estimated actual investment at about 50 percent of the book value. The rest derived from paying contractors in discounted securities for overpriced services. Bondholders were also placated with discounted stock in return for deferred interest payments. Both the fixed costs and the assets on which dividends were due grew inexorably, contributing to the financial instability of many roads during leaner economic times. The ability of roads to reduce operating costs and to refinance their debts under court-ordered reorganization during the depressions of the late nineteenth century enabled them to carry the burden of excessive capitalization.[21]

Railroad Rates

The other crucial ingredient in the financial equation of the railroads was the rates charged for carrying freight and passengers. Just as prices in the economy generally fell during this period, so did railroad tariffs. Ton-mile rates fell from just over 2 cents per mile to 75 cents between 1870 and 1910; passenger-mile rates fell from 2.8 cents to 1.9 cents. Impressive as these price declines were, they affected shippers and travelers unevenly. Great discrepancies existed between rates charged on long and short hauls, between competitive and noncompetitive points, and for different types of products. The complaints of farmers and wholesalers in smaller towns served by a single road grew loud during the early 1870s and again in the 1880s, resulting in waves of state and, ultimately, federal legislation that attempted to eliminate the worst of the railroad rate abuses.[22]

As vital as low rates may have been to developing communities seeking to expand the markets for their products, the declining rates exaggerated the financial troubles of the railroads. They were a by-product of the competitive overbuilding that the roads themselves engaged in, and the falling rates persuaded groups of railroads to undertake a series of concerted efforts to contain competition and maintain fares. Before 1874 the primary form of cooperation was informal alliances between connecting and competing roads that set general rates and, in some cases, went so far as to divide traffic or revenue between competitive points. The depression of the 1870s led to the collapse of most alliances and rate agreements. Roads fought each other for larger shares of the declining traffic. Beginning in 1874 and lasting until nearly the end of the decade, a series of more-formal regional associations were formed to maintain rates. Failing to get national legislation that would have added specific sanctions to their authority, these associations collapsed in the face of competitive, transcontinental system building. In the 1880s system building of a defensive nature occupied those lines whose territorial claims Jay Gould challenged.[23] Charles E. Perkins of the Chicago, Burlington & Quincy had seen earlier than many the opportunities that the depression offered the stronger roads. He wrote to his mentor, John Murray Forbes, of the importance of acquiring roads with access to Kansas City and Saint Joseph. "If we do take them now, when they are bankrupt, and before others awake to the value of that region, we control that country and can extend the roads at our leisure.[24]

The system building of the 1880s and the addition of still more competitive lines in the burst of new construction from 1886 through 1893 led to another round of demoralized rates, a wider circle of bankruptcy, and finally the consolidation of 85 percent of the nation's railroad mileage into seven large systems. This was the bankers' final resolution of the railroad rate problem.

Linkages: Backward and Forward

That the effects of railroad expansion would be felt throughout the American economy was assured by its backward and forward linkages. Unlike the expenditures for canal construction, which were largely for unskilled construction labor and locally available building materials, railroads required large quantities of iron and steel for tracks, coal for fuel, and sophisticated capital equipment for operations. The effects of these outlays, which grew with each decade, reverberated through key sectors of the economy, producing changes in output and technology. Only after the Civil War, as improved steel demonstrated its durability over iron and as American manufacturers specializing in rail production improved their competitive position over British manufacturers, did domestic railroad demand have a substantial effect on American steel manufacturing. The development of large, integrated Bessemer steel mills serving the railroad market came in the 1870s and 1880s. Between 1867 and 1880 more than 80 percent of the total Bessemer steel output went into rails for the domestic market. After 1880 steel production gradually diversified into other products; railroads remained an important but not exclusive market for American steel products.[25]

Railroads had important but less-dominant linkages to the machinery industry. The railroad share of the market rose above 10 percent in 1869, only to decline thereafter; if repair facilities are included, that share was 20 percent. Although coal was rather slow to displace wood as the primary fuel in railroad operations, by 1880 railroads were consuming 20 percent of the country's coal production; this proportion was maintained as output grew until 1910.[26]

In spite of the large levels of initial investment in roadbed and capital equipment that the railroads required, labor was a factor of increasing importance in railroad output. The railroad labor force grew at an annual rate of 5 percent between 1870 and 1910, a rate of increase well ahead of the 3.25 percent annual increase in manufacturing. Railroad employment rose from 9 percent to 20 percent of all manufacturing during these same years. More significant is the fact that within the railroad industry, after the decades of most-extensive railroad building—the 1870s and 1880s—the ratio of capital to labor showed a steady decline. The intensification of traffic absorbed larger quantities of labor relative to capital.[27]

Faced with falling rates and burdened by a bloated debt and rising fixed costs, the railroads turned to cuts in operating costs as one way of restoring solvency. Draconian measures of cost reduction, often under the watchful eye of the federal courts, were integral to the pattern of railroad capital investment and overbuilding.

The "buy now, pay later" philosophy of railroad growth brought periodic catharsis and reorganization to the industry. Roads were built and capital stock multiplied in good times, as between 1867 and 1872. When the construction was in sparsely settled territory or represented watered capitalization rather than actual investment, the ratio of the earning power of the roads to the fixed costs on a growing debt decreased, investor confidence waned, and railroads went bankrupt. Railroads were not ordinary firms whose failure could lead to liquidation. The enormous levels of capital investment they represented and the communities whose fortunes rested on their continued operation demanded court-supervised reorganization that would salvage the investment by imposing cost-reduction measures and refinancing of debts. This process, most often occurring during a depression, led to wage reductions, revisions of work rules, and the elimination of trade unions as impediments to further rationalization of the labor process. Lower operating costs produced improvements in earnings. Existing railroad mileage remained in operation. The roads remained overcapitalized, paying dividends on watered and legitimate stock alike. But renewed traffic that came with a return to prosperity and the continued migration of settlers into new territory bought time for another round of competitive overbuilding before the next collapse.[28] Depression was absolutely integral to the process of railroad growth in the nineteenth century.

The capacity of the railroads to carry out depression-induced rationalization depended on their ability to attract a sufficient supply of labor at reduced wages and on their ability to limit or break the power of organized workers who sought to defend the standards of their wages and working conditions. Depression levels of unemployment clearly enhanced the capacity of employers to impose such changes. Long-term improvements in the labor supply from migration and specific management practices governing the recruitment and promotion of workers also helped to improve the position of management.

Corporate Control

Looking back at the late nineteenth century in his autobiography, Henry Adams asserted, in a poignant phrase, that his generation had been "mortgaged" to the railroads. He wrote that

> society dropped every thought of dealing with anything more
> than the single fraction called a railroad system. This
> relatively small part of its task was still so big as to need the
> energies of a generation, for it required all the new machinery
> to be created—capital, banks, mines, furnaces, shops, power-
> house, technical knowledge, mechanical population, together
> with a steady remodelling of social and political habits, ideas
> and institutions to fit the new scale and suit the new
> conditions. The generation between 1865 and 1895 was
> already mortgaged to the railways, and no one knew it better
> than the generation itself.[29]

His older brother, Charles Francis Adams, Jr., whose career was more directly entwined with railroad development, found that the language of nineteenth-century America was inadequate to describe the new reality of corporate domination. In his exposé of the financial scandals that lay at the heart of the Erie Railroad's growth, Adams wrote: "(Corporate dominance) is a new power, for which our language contains no name. We know what aristocracy, autocracy, democracy are; but we have no word to express government by moneyed corporation."[30]

A mere accounting of the economic effects of railroad growth vastly understates the impact of the railroads on American life. Railroad development was deeply imbedded in the political process. Corporate leaders used the strategic benefits of railroad service to win lucrative land grants, to amass personal fortunes from the sale of town sites, and to win government financing of corporate growth in an era that celebrated the laissez-faire ideal. Faced with local constituencies aroused by the corrupt practices of railroads and their officers, the roads further intervened in the political process to prevent or limit state regulation of railroad rates. Unable to rationalize the consequences of their own competitive excesses, they threw themselves on the mercy of the federal courts. And when faced with outright rebellion among their employees, whose cause was viewed with some sympathy by hard-pressed farmers and small merchants, the roads turned again to the federal courts for injunctive relief and to the executive branch for the assistance of federal troops.

The strategic and political role of the railroads in the Civil War established an important foundation for their subsequent influence. In excellent financial condition at the end of the war, railroad corporations had also firmly established their military and political connections through planning for logistical support of the war effort. Most importantly, railroad leaders had secured two key pieces of legislation, the Homestead Act and the Pacific Railroad Act, which had been blocked by southern votes in Congress before the war. With the instruments for western colonization available, the railroads moved quickly to push forward the settlement of the West.

Settlement Patterns

Before the Civil War, established communities in the East and much of the Old Northwest promoted railroads to expand their commercial and industrial opportunities. After the Civil War, the railroads promoted the establishment of communities in the West as a strategy of economic colonization to secure the traffic necessary to support an extensive railroad network. The earlier pattern of growth was uneven and reflected the mercantile aspirations of particular cities. Market areas were expanded by compounding established markets. The railroads that served these markets were the product of alliances between local and regional entrepreneurial elites. The result was a patchwork of short lines, which continued to impose diseconomies on long-distance travel and marketing even as the geographical reach of the railroads expanded. Investors in each of the eastern metropolises sponsored trunk lines—the Erie, the New York Central, the Pennsylvania, and the Baltimore & Ohio—to funnel traffic into a few major routes that offered more predictable service.[31]

The colonization of western territories where railroad expansion preceded significant settlement followed a different pattern.[32] Beyond the perimeter of pre-Civil War settlement, the railroads confronted new conditions. There were no established markets, no self-promoting interests to accommodate. Without existing short lines to consolidate and with little local capital to be mobilized, the railroads inevitably turned to other sources of capital. They had outgrown their parochial loyalties to particular eastern metropolises. Each strove to maximize the circulation of traffic within its own network.

Freed from their own dependence on coalitions of local promoters, the western roads were in a position to foster a reverse dependence. In many ways the railroads directed the settlement process west of the Mississippi. Because they held and sold vast tracts of federal land, the railroads were in a position to promote emigration, to locate and plat communities, and to endow certain areas with opportunities for economic development, while denying opportunities to others.

The role of the railroads in the settlement process engendered fierce opposition. They were attacked for inhibiting settlement by speculating on an artificial scarcity of saleable land. By holding large tracts of federally granted land off the market, they hoped to reap the profit from rising land values as settlement increased. By delaying the taking of patents on land grants, they avoided paying taxes on unsold land, thus shifting the tax burden for social-overhead investment onto the shoulders of other land owners.[33]

In selecting town sites, the railroads and their officials possessed prior information that enabled them to make timely investments in town sites and to realize enormous profits. They not only encouraged but directly participated in town site speculation. The economies of early shipping points and division headquarters were inevitably dependent on the railroads. Grain and sawmill operators, wholesale and retail merchants, and small manufacturers aspiring to reach a wider market were all vulnerable to railroad pressures. They constituted an elite, cultivated by local railroad agents, from whom railroads expected allegiance. Highly visible investment in a local library or a donation of land for a church was meant to cement local loyalty.

↳ ¿ local support?

Railroad Politics

Expanding railroad systems fostered the political, as well as economic, integration of newly settled areas. In their quest for land grants and state and local aid and in their effort to mobilize political support that would prevent the regulation of railroad rates or the taxation of railroad lands, railroad officers and lobbyists perpetually prowled the halls of Congress and state legislatures. The influence of railroad corporations extended, according to William Larrabee, "from the township assessor's office to the national capital, from the publisher of the small cross-roads paper to the editorial staff of the metropolitan daily." Larrabee, a reform governor of Iowa in the late 1880s, outlined the "non-partisan" character of railroad politics in a collection of essays published in the 1890s. The railroads "carefully canvassed" the records of potential candidates before the primaries; the most acceptable among the candidates of each party were selected as "the railroad candidates." During the campaign, the roads marshaled financial and editorial support and threw armies of campaign workers into the fray on behalf of railroad candidates.[34]

Elected officials and community leaders were showered with free passes and other courtesies to ensure their support of railroad interests. Until the passage of the Interstate Commerce Act of 1887, the free pass system provided a flexible means of reminding officeholders of the gratitude due the roads. In cases where the expected support was not forthcoming, passes were denied or their use restricted.[35]

In the most dramatic case of railroad intervention in the political process, Thomas P. Scott and other railroad leaders operated effectively behind the scenes to assist in breaking the deadlock in the political crisis of 1876–77, guaranteeing the election of Rutherford B. Hayes to the presidency and the political reintegration of the southern redeemer governments. In the process southerners won promises of substantial federal aid for internal improvements and federal support for a southern transcontinental railroad line.[36]

The railroads secured federal assistance in two other areas that were crucial to their expansion: court-supervised reorganization of bankrupt roads, and the use of federal government authority to limit or prevent railroad strikes. During the depression of 1873–78, as already noted, a wave of bankruptcies swept through the railroad industry, sending 89 out of 364 railroad corporations into court-ordered receivership. With the insistence and the protection of the federal courts, bankrupt railroads were reorganized: operating costs were cut, deferred investment and technological improvements were undertaken, and dividends were withheld. The courts, inexperienced in operating railroads, became responsive to the notion that the managers of a road were its most appropriate receivers.

With the precedent-setting Wabash case of 1885, this pattern of appointing receivers became the norm. The courts ensured that managers were freed from the constraints imposed by discontented stockholders and employees whose interests suffered most directly in such court-ordered rationalization.[37]

In seeking to prevent strikes, railroad companies appealed to the government for at least two forms of assistance. First, federal courts were asked with increasing frequency to enjoin certain types of strikes or strike-related activity. Although intially they limited their jurisdiction to bankrupt roads directly under the courts' supervision, federal judges extended their injunctive authority in the Southwest strikes of 1886 and the Burlington strike of 1888 to cover any roads engaged in interstate commerce. During the crisis of 1893–94 federal court bans on secondary boycotts were broadened by several judges to effectively enjoin railroad strikes per se.[38]

Second, railroads looked to federal troops for ultimate protection. After the 1877 strikes, railroads effectively lobbied for the construction of armories and the relocation of federal troops to "large cities and great population centers." Thus the proximity of Fort Sheridan, built on land donated by wealthy citizens of Chicago, made the timely intervention of federal troops possible during the Pullman boycott.[39]

The political connections of railroad managers are best symbolized in the person of Richard Olney. Olney was a prominent railroad attorney and director when he was offered the position of attorney general in Grover Cleveland's second administration. Charles Perkins, president of the Chicago, Burlington & Quincy and a longtime colleague of Olney's, urged him to accept the appointment in the interests of the railroads he had served as counsel. When Perkins learned that Olney had accepted the cabinet post, he wrote a congratulatory note. "In a certain sense of course the C. B. & Q. loses by your appointment," Perkins wrote, "but in a larger sense it, in common with every property interest, gains—I consider every share of my Stock worth more today than yesterday."[40]

In retrospect, Olney's appointment was fortunate indeed for the railroads. As attorney general, he formulated the strategy that led to massive federal intervention in the Pullman boycott and broke the back of the American Railway Union (ARU). He personally argued the case against Eugene Debs and the ARU in federal court, and he designed the essential components of the Erdman Act, which helped to establish a framework for labor-management cooperation that lasted well into the twentieth century. The origins of that framework lay not only in the political process by which the rail-roads sought to limit competition, enhance profitability, and reduce the risks of undesirable regulation, but also in the volatile and persistent strike activity of railroad workers. The changing character of railroad labor relations in the late nineteenth century and the more general processes of class formation are dramatically revealed in the pattern of railroad strike activity.

1

An Audacious Era: The Pattern of Railroad Strikes

You will acknowledge that the chances are ninety-nine against one in favor of the company should a strike take place, and in spite of all these things the strike seems to be the only thing the men can think of. No generalship will amount to anything with them, no diplomacy, no skill in meeting a difficult question. They will now take the bit in their teeth and go the whole length. . . .[1]
—Terence V. Powderly, letter to E. J. Lee,
Master Workman, District Assembly 246
(New York Central employees), August 6, 1891

. . . They might as well try to stop Niagara with a feather as to crush the spirit of organization in this country. It cannot be done. It may not come up in the form of the American Railway Union, but this spirit of resistance to wrong is there, it is growing stronger constantly, and it finds its outlet in labor disturbances, in strikes of various kinds. Even if the men know in advance that they are going to meet with defeat they are so impressed with a sense of wrong under which they are suffering that they strike and take the penalty. You ask what I would do, or what my ideas are about what should be done to avert strikes. To avert railroad strikes I would propose this: "That Government ownership of railroads is decidedly better for the people than railroad ownership of Government."[2]
—Eugene V. Debs, testimony before the U.S. Strike
Commission, 1894

Early on the morning of July 20, 1877, Barney Donahue and other members of the strike committee gathered on the fringes of the Erie Railroad switching yards in Hornellsville, New York. They talked over strategy for preventing the movement of trains in and out of town. Just a few days before, most of them had been officially discharged from employment for taking their grievances directly to H. J. Jewett, the road's court-appointed receiver in New York City.

In spite of this rather ominous and unprecedented step, which the Erie's vice-president argued was necessary to assert "the right of the company to operate its own property,"[3] the men were confident of their prospects in the strike. For one thing, they were not striking alone. Word had arrived of the strike on the Baltimore & Ohio at Martinsburg, West Virginia, a strike which was spreading eastward towards Baltimore. There were rumblings in Pittsburgh and Reading and other railroad centers in the East. More importantly, these men were seasoned strikers. There was no reason to believe that the tactics they had used so successfully for the past eight years—during strikes in 1869, 1870, 1871, 1873, and 1874—would not again bring victory.[4]

The first step in a successful strike, the men knew from experience, was to remove and hide the coupling pins. This was quickly accomplished, as it had been in 1874 when the newspapers reported that the men had "declined to work and the *usual* strategic movement of removing coupling pins was resorted to."[5] As each successive freight train arrived in town, "it was seized and uncoupled, the coupling irons were secretly and expeditiously disposed of, their brakemen joining the crowd."[6] Operating in large groups, railroad workers in this manner stopped all movement of trains through the community, and, because Hornellsville was the major switching point between the eastern and western divisions, all traffic on the Erie came to a virtual standstill.

As company officials struggled to make up trains and recruit engineers and firemen to take them out, the strikers gathered in crowds to heckle, cajole, harass, and persuade those who assisted the company. If a train was made up, strikers kept ahead of the cautiously moving engine as it left town, removing rails and leaving obstacles in the track, repeatedly forcing the train to stop and repair the damage, with each stop providing opportunities for the strikers to create further obstacles.

Trains leaving for the West had to climb a steep grade just outside the city limits. In 1870, 1874, and again in 1877 railroad workers, their families, and their supporters carried buckets of soft soap to the steepest part of the grade and soaped the rails. There they waited in a large crowd. When the train reached the soaped rails and lost speed with its wheels slipping, men mounted the train in large numbers and forcibly set the brakes, removed the coupling pins, and sent the cars careening back into the railroad yard.[7]

As in previous strikes, the strike committee imposed its own order on the town. They visited each saloon and requested that liquor not be sold during the course of the strike. Passengers who were stranded in town for the duration of the strike and who did not have the means to pay their expenses were taken to Simmons House, where their room and board was paid by the strikers. An out-of-town reporter observed that the committee conducted itself with a seriousness "reminiscent of Quakers."[8] While such behavior made tactical sense, for some strikers the self-discipline so evident in the strike had deeper roots. Several key leaders were also officers in the Saint Ann's Catholic Total Abstinence Society. When the sheriff was called during the strike to disperse strikers who were blockading the track at a nearby station, he found them engaged in a temperance meeting on the station platform, and he promptly disbanded his posse.[9] Barney Donahue himself, while sequestered in the county jail for several months after the strike, organized a "cold water" society among his fellow inmates.

Although the arrival of the state militia in 1877 was greeted with jocular confidence—one reporter noted that the strikers "effected to treat the matter as a joke and loudly ridiculed the idea of their movement being suppressed by a few soldiers with empty guns"— events took a more ominous turn.[10] With the occupation of the switching yards by fifteen hundred troops, the strikers were forced to operate from camps in the surrounding hills. The arrest of key leaders and their removal to New York City disrupted organization. The issuance of warrants for the arrest of one hundred additional strikers forced even more clandestine operations on them. And for the first time during the decade of conflict, significant numbers of leading citizens applied pressures for an end to the strike and a return to work on the company's terms.[11]

By the end of the week, community leaders, offering immunity from arrest for one evening, persuaded the strikers to attend a meeting to consider a compromise for ending the strike. Only the night before, a large crowd of men and boys had paraded through town holding aloft a huge transparency depicting Capital clutching Labor by the throat.[12] The meeting was well attended and boisterous. In spite of highly vocal opposition to the terms of the compromise offered by the company, the leading citizens, who were urging moderation and promising financial support for those strikers who would be discharged, won a majority of the badly divided and demoralized strikers and their community supporters.[13] The next day, reporters noted "a spirit of sulkiness" as the men went about their duties making up trains. "They obeyed the orders of the trainmaster, but they could hardly have done so with poorer grace."[14]

24

The railroad strikes that swept across the country in July 1877 were the clarion call of a new class. On the one hand, they foreshadowed nearly two decades of deepening labor conflict on the railroads, and on the other hand, they were the baptismal rite of a broader, urban working class not bound by differences of trade or skill. Building on patterns of industrial action like those in Hornellsville and igniting the widespread discontent of workingmen entering their fourth year of depression, the strikes (or riots as many comtemporary observers called them) inaugurated a new era of bitter class conflict. Although the symptoms of social crisis were by no means confined to the railroad sector, major national strikes of railroad workers continued to punctuate the crisis at regular intervals—in 1885 and 1886, in 1888, and most decisively with the Pullman boycott in 1894.

The generation living through the last decades of the nineteenth century was acutely aware of this rising tide of industrial discontent. "Somewhere," the journalist J. A. Dacus wrote in the aftermath of the 1877 strikes, "there must be something radically defective either in the system or in the manner of its control."[15] As strikes proliferated, business leaders, public officials, the federal courts, and military officers gradually assembled institutional machinery designed to contain and defuse industrial conflict. Railroad companies experimented with welfare schemes, court injunctions were sought, labor recruitment was streamlined, armories were built in strategic locations, state militias were reorganized, and units of the army were relocated. In spite of these efforts to contain industrial conflict, strikes spread.

Railroad workers were certainly not alone in the ranks of striking workers. Miners, construction workers, cigar makers, iron puddlers, steelworkers, and glass blowers were frequent strikers as well. But in most years between 1877 and 1894 a higher percentage of railroad workers were on strike than was the case for industrial workers as a whole. (See appendix A, figure A1.) Their strikes tended to be less localized, more disruptive to other economic activity, and more visible to a larger public than strikes in other industries. The interruptions in commerce and manufacturing that frequently accompanied railroad strikes made them particularly serious and brought to bear extraordinary pressures for their resolution.

Studies of railroad strikes during this period have tended to emphasize the episodic nature of industrial conflict. We have excellent profiles of the 1877 strikes, the strikes against Jay Gould's

Southwestern roads, the Burlington strike, and the Pullman boycott, but we have no study of the evolving patterns of strike activity that would link and help to make sense of the individual episodes.[16] Although the major strikes highlight wider developments in the world of railroad labor, those developments are not obvious when the strikes are taken out of their historical context and described individually. Without a systematic analysis of the underlying patterns of conflict, it is difficult to relate longer-term, secular changes in the nature of railroad work, the composition of the labor market, the social structure of railroad towns, the evolution of trade unionism, and the texture of industrial relations.

[Strikes offer useful observation points for studying changes in the relations of workers and managers. They are tremors of varying intensity that reflect shifts in the social geology of class relations. Although they are only one form of industrial conflict (others being collective bargaining, sabotage, absenteeism, slowdowns, and boycotts), they are generally measurable, visible, and comparable in form. They are usually better documented than other forms of worker protest. When examined over a reasonable period of time, they reveal changing patterns of behavior.[17] Most studies that have examined strike data for the United States have been concerned with the long-term relationship between strikes and industrialization, the effects of economic cycles, and the institutionalization of collective bargaining.[18]

This study looks at strike data in one industry between the years 1881 and 1894—a period for which superb data exist.[19] By limiting the analysis to a particular industrial sector, it is possible to see the effects not only of generalized economic factors such as the business cycle but of factors specific to the industry—its location, its labor market, the rate of technological change, and the level of trade unionism. We can see more clearly the role of particular trades, the evolution of strike demands, and the results achieved.

Strikes and Strikers

An analysis of strike patterns for a specific group of workers must begin with basic data on how often they struck and the numbers of workers involved. Between 1881 and 1894 the U.S. labor commissioner recorded statistical information on 668 railroad strikes. A strike might involve as few as a dozen skilled workers employed by a single road in one city, or it might involve thousands of employees in a half-dozen states employed by a railroad and its subsidiary companies.

The frequency of railroad strikes changed during the period 1881–94. Before 1885 they were relatively rare, and in no year were there more that 32. In 1885 and 1886 the number of railroad strikes increased sharply and the number remained relatively high for the rest of the period. There were never fewer than 40 strikes in a year after 1885, and frequently there were more than 60 (figure 1). While certain years stand out for their exceptionally high rate of strike activity (1886, 1890, 1894), more noteworthy are the two distinct periods of strike activity: 1881–84, when there were relatively few strikes, and 1885–94, when strikes were substantially more frequent.

Although the number of strikes increased during the period, the number of men on strike did not increase at a comparable rate. In fact, during most of the period of increased activity (1887–92) the number of men on strike remained relatively low. This meant a decline in the average size of strikes from an involvement of 300 to 400 men in the early years of less-frequent strikes (1881–84) to an average of 100 to 150 men in the period of increased strike activity. Only in 1894 did the average size of strikes increase, and then the change was unprecedented—with strikes averaging 800 men.

Strike activity among railroad workers varied significantly between occupational groups. Not all trades contributed equally to the crescendo of industrial conflict. For the purpose of examining the frequency of strikes among different occupational groups, we have selected seven job classifications: unskilled (laborers, freight handlers); skilled running trades (engineers, conductors); unskilled running trades (firemen, brakemen); skilled shopmen; unskilled shopmen; switchmen; and other trades (a wide distribution of skills and trades). For the entire period of 1881–94, the frequency with which each occupational group struck is given in table 2.

Especially noteworthy in these fiqures are those for unskilled railroad workers and switchmen. Not only did the men in these occupational groups have the greatest number of strikes with which they were specifically identified, they were prime movers in general strikes as well. Strikes of the unskilled, including unskilled shopmen and running trades, account for more than 52 percent of all strikes. With switchmen they account for 75 percent of the railroad strikes between 1881 and 1894.

Strikes of railroad freight handlers are prominent during the

Table 2   Railroad Strikes, by Occupational Group, 1881–94

	Number of Strikes	Percent of Total	Percent of Railroad Labor Force
Unskilled	201	30	30
Skilled—running	48	7	7
Unskilled—running	65	10	13
Skilled—shopmen	79	12	9
Unskilled shopmen	56	8	11
Switchmen	147	22	5
Other	72	11	25
TOTAL	668	100	100

period 1881–84. Congregating in large urban centers and early infected with the youthful, aggressive spirit of the Knights of Labor, the freight handlers were well situated to spread a strike citywide in a short time. The strike of New York and Jersey City freight handlers in 1882 is typical. On June 12, freight handlers for the New York Central and Hudson River Railroad walked off the loading platforms and out of the freight houses, quickly formed a procession, and marched from the freight depot of one railroad to the next, calling out other handlers.[20] The demand that surfaced was for a wage increase of three cents an hour more than the seventeen cents which they had been getting "for years." Men from the New Jersey Central and the Erie in Jersey City joined the next day, and in succeeding days the men attempted to spread the strike to other trades by similar methods.[21]

Daily meetings brought the information of what came to be called the "Freighthandlers' Protective Association," whose function was to manage the strike. An officer of the Knights of Labor was reported to have said that the Knights were deeply involved in "counseling and directing" the strikers. Many handlers were said to have joined the Knights of Labor, and most were expected to do so by the end of the strike.[22] In spite of assistance from the Knights and brief sympathy strikes by switchmen and freight brakemen, and in spite of the early high comedy of inexperienced workers trying to move the accumulating mountains of freight, the strike dragged on. The railroads began to move significant quantities of freight as the

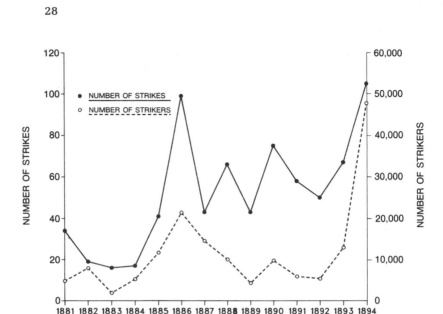

Figure 1.   Number of railroad strikes and strikers, 1881–94

Source: U.S. Labor Commissioner, *Third Annual Report* and *Tenth Annual Report* (Washington, D.C.: 1887, 1895).

inexperienced Italians who were brought in to replace the strikers began to cope with their task. Finally, with no prospect of their demands being met, the freight handlers called off the strike on August 12. Few places remained for them to return to, though some hoped to be at work again by fall. The strike had been large—over thirty-two hundred freight handlers. It had been long, lasting more than sixty days. Unlike many strikes of the unskilled during this phase, it did not succeed. Buffalo freight handlers struck in 1881, 1883, and 1884 for wage increases, and, though their numbers were smaller, their strikes met with some success in two of the three years.[23]

All trades contributed in some measure to the increase in the strike activity of the later period, 1885–94, but certain trades contributed disproportionately. Railroad laborers, switchmen, brakemen, and firemen struck much more often after 1885. They were joined in the early 1890s by skilled railroad shopmen. In 1894 general strikes of railroad workers became the dominant form of action taken by these occupational groups.

During the period 1881–94 there were distinctive phases of railroad strike activity. In the early years, 1881–84 (and probably dating back to 1879), strikes were relatively infrequent. Those strikes that did occur were large, and other data suggest that they were rather long and enjoyed a high rate of success, as railroad strikes went. (see appendix A, figure A2.) Between 1885 and 1892 railroad strikes were much more frequent, though smaller. Certain trades, especially switchmen and the unskilled, struck more often than others. The strikes also became shorter, on the average, and striking workers succeeded less frequently. The pattern changed in 1893–94 as railroad strikes became longer and larger and the rate of success fell precipitously. General strikes, rather than strikes by particular trades, predominated.

Regions

Railroad expansion within different regions inevitably affected the character of industrial relations. A look at the major strikes of the era (1877, 1885–86, 1888, and 1894) suggests a westward drift of strike activity. Adjustments in the labor market occurred behind the frontier of railroad expansion. Increased settlement, the attraction of high wages, accelerated promotion, and corporate policies designed to augment the supply of labor led rapidly to changing conditions for railroad labor. Disputes over wage levels, working conditions, and recognition of unions erupted in one region after another.

The sectional distribution of railroad strike activity confirms the broad outlines of this analysis.* While all sections showed low levels of strike activity during the early phase, 1881–84, midwestern states contributed disproportionately to the increasing frequency of railroad strikes from 1885 to 1894 (figure 2). The number of strikes in the West increased noticeably in 1885–86 and in 1888; they showed a sustained increase from 1890 to 1894 as well. The importance of the West is understated somewhat because of its relatively small proportion of the total railroad labor force (table 3).

*In this work the term section will be used when referring to the four segments of the territorial United States known as the East, Midwest, South, and West. Region will be used to refer to the ten groupings of states specified in the Annual Reports of the Interstate Commerce Commission (see map, appendix B). The sections include regions as follows: East—regions I–III; Midwest—region VI; South—regions IV–V; West—regions VII–X.

Table 3.   Sectional Distribution of the Railroad Labor Force

	1880 (percent)	1890 (percent)
East	8	7
South	10	13
Midwest	73	61
West	9	19

If we compare the percentage of railroad workers on strike by section, the importance of the West is restored. A high percentage (approximately 10 percent) of western railroad workers struck in 1885–86 and in 1894. By comparison the percentage of midwestern railroad workers is lower for those years, though still higher than in the East and South. With the exception of a couple of years, the frequency of strikes and the percentage of railroad workers on strike was consistently lower in the East and South. In the period 1892–94, when strikes were increasing in number and size in the Midwest and West, they were declining in the East and showing no significant change in the South. The increases were greatest in the states of the upper Midwest, the southern Great Plains, and in the northern Mountain states—precisely those regions where, during the 1880s and 1890s, there were significant changes in population density, economic development, and the railroad labor market.

Strike Issues and Success

The most important question that must be asked about any group of strikes is why they occurred. The specific issues articulated in a strike may only imperfectly reflect the more basic issues embedded in the changing relations between an employer and his employees. What had the appearance of a simple wage strike was often a strike over wage-related work rules. Strikes commonly involved multiple issues, especially when different trades walked out together. Having initiated a strike, workers frequently added demands either for bargaining purposes or to maximize the utility of their sacrifice. For all of their complexity, strike issues nevertheless are one of the most important codes for deciphering changes in strike behavior.

The analysis of strike issues necessitates some attempt to group and classify strikes. A number of competing classification systems

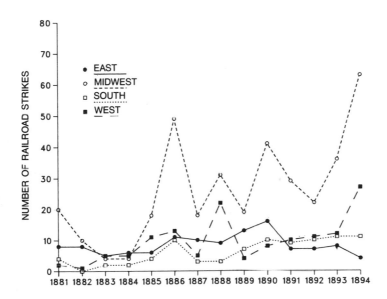

Figure 2. Number of railroad strikes by section, 1881–94

Source: U.S. Labor Commissioner, *Third Annual Report* and *Tenth Annual Report* (Washington D.C.: 1887, 1895).

have been suggested by scholars interested in strike behavior and its causes.[24] On the most basic level a distinction between wage-related strikes and strikes over noneconomic issues is warranted.

Causes of Strikes

The interplay between wage and non-wage issues and the expansion of economic strikes into contests over control of the labor supply is revealed in a number of struggles that erupted in the 1880s. Strikes earlier in the decade were often purely wage related but later in the decade they more frequently involved noneconomic issues. Chicago switchmen engaged in a series of strikes that graphically illustrates this transition.

Early in May 1881 switchmen struck seven Chicago railroads and demanded a wage increase. Several roads granted the full increase, and the others conceded partial increases. The Lake Shore & Michigan Southern, in an action that seared the memories of Chicago switchmen, granted a partial wage increase but then refused to allow ninety-two of the strikers to return to work. Unable to compel the road to rehire the men, the switchmen quietly organized during the next five years. By April 1886 the Switchmen's Mutual Aid Association claimed to have organized all but fifty switchmen in the city; those fifty had all scabbed on the Lake Shore in the 1881 strike and were barred from membership.[25] In mid-April the organization undertook a strike for the explicit purpose of compelling the discharge of these nonunion men. The Baltimore & Ohio transferred them to "other work" after the strike was only two days old.[26] The Lake Shore, however, resisted fiercely. The strike dragged on for months but was finally called off without succeeding after 181 days.

The switchmen's strike of 1886 raised the issue of who should have authority over the discharge of employees, but the origins of the conflict lay in an earlier wage dispute. The switchmen sought to guarantee the existence of their organization by winning the right to exclude objectionable employees (nonunion, scabs) from employment. This demand foreshadowed many strikes later in the decade over similar issues, some of which sought to extend that authority even further.

More well known is the series of strikes in 1885 and 1886 on Jay Gould's Southwestern system. These strikes followed a similar pattern. The three primary strikes—against the Missouri Pacific, the Wabash, and the Missouri, Kansas & Texas in March 1885; against the Wabash, June through August 1885; and against the Texas & Pacific and Missouri Pacific, March through May 1886—were long strikes. They involved many unskilled as well as skilled workers, they started over a wage-reduction dispute, and until the final strike (the Great Southwestern strike) they were remarkably successssful—so much so that these strikes are credited with being largely responsible for the explosive growth of the Knights of Labor in 1886.[27]

By the final strike of the series, in March 1886, a noneconomic issue had displaced wages at the center of the controversy. The Knights of Labor claimed that General Manager Hoxie was not living up to agreements on rules reached in the previous strikes. When he directly challenged their authority by firing a leader of the Knights on the Texas & Pacific, they struck. Missouri Pacific Knights struck in sympathy, but on neither road were they joined by the skilled running trades, whose brotherhoods refused to sanction strikes. The strikes were lost.

As these examples suggest, many strikes did not have wages as a central issue. Workers fought to protect the organizations they had built or to change the rules under which they worked. The actions of an arbitrary supervisor or the discharge of an employee without cause might precipitate a strike. These contests did not directly raise questions about the wages workers were paid, but they did raise questions about who should allocate, control, and discipline labor.

Wage Strikes

Wage strikes were those strikes that directly involved the demand for a wage increase or the resistance to a wage reduction. Analyses of strike data have generally classified worker-initiated strikes for wage increases as offensive strikes and strikes over employer-initiated wage reductions as defensive strikes. Both offensive and defensive wage strikes follow the business cycle rather closely— workers demand wage increases during periods of expansion, and employers exact wage reductions when the economy is contracting. Strikes over noneconomic issues, however, do not appear to follow a pattern that corresponds to swings in the business cycle.[28]

During the period 1881–94 approximately 66 percent of all railroad strikes were directly wage related. The other 34 percent were concerned with noneconomic issues. Of the wage strikes, 76 percent were offensive (for wage increases), and 24 percent were defensive (to resist a wage cut). Offensive and defensive wage strikes moved rather consistently in opposite directions, as would be expected (figure 3). These strikes appear to have been directly related to the business cycle. In fact, they anticipated slightly the movement of the business cycle. As economic conditions worsened, offensive wage strikes declined and strikes against wage cuts rose (1882–84). During a period of relative prosperity (1886–92), strikes for wage increases were high relative to strikes against wage cuts. Although offensive wage strikes declined between 1892 and 1894, defensive wage strikes did not increase significantly. This supports the contention of some railroad labor leaders that railroad employers generally refrained from cutting wages during the depression of the 1890s and resorted instead to reductions in levels of employment as a means of cutting costs.[29]

Noneconomic strikes followed a very different pattern. For the period as a whole, they occurred with increasing frequency, surpassing both offensive and defensive wage strikes in 1892–94. The increase in noneconomic strikes does not appear to have had any direct relationship to movements in the business cycle or to wage strikes. What pauses there were in their ascent do not correlate with noteworthy changes in the general business climate. The increasing frequency of noneconomic strikes suggests that railroad

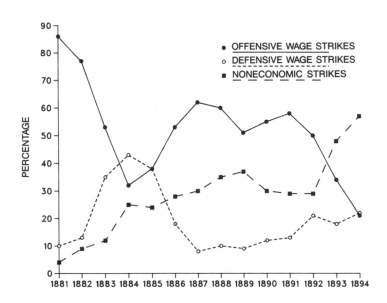

Figure 3. Distribution of causes of railroad strikes, 1881–94 (three-year moving average)

Source: U.S. Labor Commissioner, *Third Annual Report* and *Tenth Annual Report* (Washington, D.C.: 1887, 1895).

workers, by choice or necessity, were turning their attention to work rules, to their right to representation, and to broader concerns about the governance of the industry.

It is interesting to note that railroad workers' rate of success in winning different types of strikes followed distinctive patterns. The success rate in offensive wage strikes followed closely the frequency pattern of offensive strikes. Workers struck for higher wages when their chances of winning were greater and they refrained from striking when their chances were less. (See appendix A, figure A3.) In defensive wage strikes, employers cut wages so that workers were forced into such strikes during depressions, when the chance of success was lowest. (See appendix A, figure A4.)

Noneconomic Strikes

If it is possible to classify wage strikes as offensive or defensive, may there not also be some utility in similarly distinguishing among noneconomic strikes? Workers initiated strikes for the discharge of a supervisor or for union recognition; they were compelled to strike against employers who discharged employees or who violated agreements over work rules. The issues were, of course, complex. Offensive strikes could be undertaken to reclaim lost ground, and defensive strikes might result when employers sought to roll back significant gains made by workers. David Montgomery has suggested that strikes over noneconomic issues, or what he calls "control struggles," were often attempts to protect older patterns of authority under new industrial conditions, where workers were forced to innovate new control demands. These strikes looked like demands for new authority, but they occurred in response to management's attempts to undermine prerogatives that workers customarily regarded as their own.[30] In spite of the obvious difficulties that the distinction between offensive and defensive noneconomic strikes has on a theoretical level, it does appear to have some utility when railroad strikes are analyzed. The offensive and defensive noneconomic issues that precipitated railroad strikes may be broadly distinguished as follows:

Offensive	*Defensive*
Sympathy strikes	Against the discharge of an employee
For the discharge of an employee	Against reduction in the force
For increase in the force	In anticipation of lockout
For union recognition	Against violation of agreement
For change from monthly to mileage rate	Against acceptance of firm's terms
For semimonthly pay	Against apprentice doing journeyman's work
For the adoption of new rules	Against discrimination
	Against work outside trade
	Against change from day to piecework
	Against reduction in switch engines
	Against doubleheader freights
	Against employment of nonunion men
	Against employment of foreign labor

The relationship between the incidence of noneconomic strikes as a whole and the rate at which workers succeeded in winning them does not follow a consistent pattern. (See appendix A, figure A5.) Here the distinction between offensive and defensive noneconomic strikes is essential. Offensive strikes over noneconomic issues outnumbered defensive strikes in every year during the period 1881–94 with the exception of 1886 and 1890 (figure 4). The higher incidence of offensive noneconomic strikes is particularly noteworthy during two periods, 1886–89 and 1891–94. During the period 1886–89, offensive noneconomic strikes outnumbered defensive ones forty to twenty-five. In this period, the relationship between incidence and success for noneconomic strikes resembles the pattern for offensive wage strikes; railroad workers struck over noneconomic issues when their chances of success were greatest. There was, indeed, a rising assertiveness during those years, encouraged in part by the comparatively expansive economy.

During the second period, from 1891–94, a different pattern emerged. Offensive noneconomic strikes rose further, outnumbering defensive noneconomic strikes eighty to twenty-two. Even more noteworthy is the fact that this sharp rise in the incidence of offensive strikes took place in the face of a sharp decline in the rate of success for noneconomic strikes. Railroad workers pushed to the fore the issues of control and authority over work practices, even as their success plummeted. These were audacious demands that were the product of a sense of impending crisis among railroad workers—a crisis that required decisive action.

The strike experience of railroad workers between 1886 and 1893 was a mixture of success and failure. Noteworthy victories emboldened workers even in the face of determined employers whose positions were backed by a sympathetic judiciary. The demoralizing defeat of engineers, firemen, and switchmen on the Chicago, Burlington & Quincy in 1888 and the shattering of Knights of Labor District Assembly 224 on Franklin Gowen's Reading Railroad the previous year did not prevent switchmen and members of the running trades, almost one thousand strong, from walking off the job on the Illinois Central in June 1890 and tying up traffic as far south as Cairo, Illinois. They demanded the discharge of E. G. Russell, superintendent of the northern lines, and the reinstatement of two trainmasters whom Russell had discharged. The strike was similar to the major confrontations of 1892–94 in size and in its multi-trade composition. It was without official union sanction. But what merits closest attention is the demands and the way in which

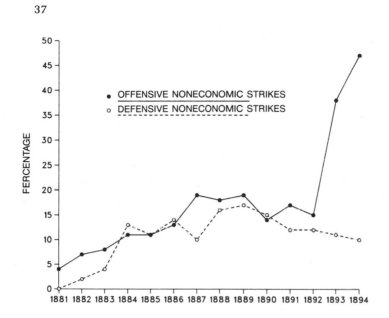

Figure 4. Percentage of offensive and defensive noneconomic strikes, 1881–94 (three-year moving average)

Source: U.S. Labor Commissioner, *Third Annual Report* and *Tenth Annual Report* (Washington, D.C.: 1887, 1895).

the charges against Superintendent Russell were phrased. The language of the charges reflects the presumption of workers' right to a voice in some management decisions. The "charges" against E. G. Russell were as follows:

1. General obnoxiousness
2. Unreasonable decisions
3. Conduct unbecoming an official
4. Criticizing action of superior officers
5. Making places for outsiders
6. Interfering with fixed arrangements of various department heads.[31]

These were employees discussing the managerial practices of a high railroad official! The strike ended in compromise after four days. Russell was retained, but his authority to handle grievances was restricted. The discharged trainmasters were offered positions should they choose to "reapply." None of the strikers were discharged.

It may be argued that the aggressive spirit of the times pushed railroad men into ill-timed struggles in which their chances of success were slim. However, there was enough success to feed railroad workers' hopes. The *Irish World and Industrial Liberator* carried a regular column of news from railroad workers, "along the railroads," and in 1890 it printed in one item after another remarkable examples of railroad workers' power. In March 1890 switchmen in the Chicago yard of the Chicago & Northwestern struck for the removal of their yardmaster; he was discharged. They struck again the same day to have two other employees discharged; that likewise was acceded to.[32] In April, Rock Island Railroad switchmen won a brief strike for similar demands.[33] In June, Union Pacific conductors, brakemen, and baggagemen won agreement to their demands for "more crews, less mileage, and additional pay."[34] In June 1890, at the first meeting of the Supreme Council of the United Orders of Railway Employees (a national federation of all major brotherhoods, except the engineers), President Frank P. Sargent of the firemen reported that the Supreme Council had won concessions for workers in four threatened strikes—on the Erie, among yardmen in Pittsburgh, for conductors on the Queen & Crescent, and for engineers and firemen on the Ohio & Mississippi.[35]

Sympathy Strikes

Remarkably, even as the effects of the depression were felt in 1893 and 1894, railroad men did not curtail their aggressive strike activity over noneconomic issues. The broad-based sympathy strikes of the Pullman boycott crystallized a growing sentiment among railroad workers that they faced a crisis of a new magnitude. These were not strikes over incremental control issues: they were contests over the fundamental relationship between labor and capital—or, as Fred Hall put it in his study of sympathy strikes, "Is labor or capital to rule?"[36]

Sympathy strikes were an increasingly important segment of offensive, noneconomic strikes among railroad workers. They were the highest manifestation of the mutualistic ethic captured in the slogan of the Knights of Labor, "An injury to one is the concern of all." Railroad workers had galvanized themselves and the working class generally with a series of large sympathy strikes between the years 1884 and 1888. The proportion of railroad strikers involved in sympathy strikes during those years is remarkable: 1885, 11 percent; 1886, 27 percent; 1887, 45 percent; and 1888, 35 percent. There were scattered sympathetic actions from 1890 to 1893, but they were small and generally strikes of skilled workers. Although the number of railroad strikers involved in the Pullman boycott has to be viewed as exceptional—85 percent of all railroad strikers in 1894 were engaged in sympathy strikes—the general movement of strike indicators made the boycott less exceptional than appearances might indicate. The sympathy strike had taken deep root in the industrial experience of railroad men. The fact that it was used less frequently between 1888 and 1893 was due largely to the formidable legal web which had been spun around its use and to the timidity of the brotherhoods. When an organization emerged that appeared to be strong enough and to possess the political will to defy the sanctions threatened against sympathetic action, the most dramatic sympathy strike in the history of organized labor was undertaken.

Between the strikes of the early 1880s and those of the early 1890s, a quantitative and a qualitative change in the noneconomic strikes of railroad workers occurred. The defense of traditional standards of pay and working conditions and the effort to impose some control over the supply of labor through restricting entry to the trades gave way to a broader and more assertive insistence on control. Believing that thoroughness of organization and the ability to universally tie up railroad traffic would make it possible for railroad workers to insist on and win the rights that bargaining through craft organizations had failed to achieve, unions extended their notion of control beyond the day-to-day, incremental contests over issues such as the discharge of supervisors, changes in the method of pay, or the adoption of new work rules. The open-ended control consciousness that many railroad workers achieved was a logical extension of their own industrial experience. Such views were reinforced by a politically mobilized, producers movement that was demanding public ownership of the railroads. For Eugene Debs, as for many other railroad workers, government ownership of the railroads was a logical next step from their efforts to achieve control through universal organization. "I believe," he told the U.S. Strike Commission, "that if the people owned and operated the railroads in the interest of the people instead of for private gain and profit, that the service would be greatly improved, the condition of the men infinitely better, and another strike would never come. I do not believe it is possible to avert railroad strikes any other way."[37]

In summary, the evidence on strike issues suggests that railroad strikers after 1885 were increasingly on the offensive. They raised demands for higher wages and for the resolution of noneconomic issues that involved the redefinition of their collective authority in the productive process. The power that was asserted primarily through the wage struggles of the 1880s came to be the issue itself as noneconomic struggles pushed to the front in the 1890s. In spite of a sharp decline in their ability to protect and enlarge their power, railroad workers in still larger numbers participated in sympathetic actions that boldly asserted their rights.[38]

Unions and Power

Unions played a complex role in this period of intensifying industrial conflict. They were at different times agents of craft exclusiveness and industrial solidarity, instruments of practical discipline and soaring idealism, and institutions offering benevolent security and challenging the very structure of authority in private industry. The period saw the efforts of unions to regulate strike activity through the official sanctioning of strikes, and it witnessed numerous spontaneous actions without benefit of union sanction, let alone their active support.

The general increase in union-sanctioned strikes during this period has been noted by others. Approximately 50 percent of all strikes had union support in 1881. That proportion rose to nearly 75 percent in 1891 and fell to just above 60 percent in 1894. The proportion of union-sanctioned *railroad* strikes followed a more uneven course but was consistently lower than for industry as a whole.

The aggregate data on union support for strikes have led historians and labor economists to believe that increasing union involvement in strikes produced greater effectiveness, selectivity, and restraint among striking workers, whether as a product of workers' own "calculation and organization" or as the result of the institutional discipline imposed by trade unions. However, if the data on railroad strikes are indicative of patterns of strike activity in other industries, a very different interpretation may be warranted.

The railroads were an industry in which different forms of trade union behavior were manifested in competing organizations—the brotherhoods on the one hand, and the industrial unions of railroad men, the Knights of Labor and the American Railway Union on the other.

The spread of union-sanctioned strikes on the railroads must be interpreted in the context of the competing types of organization. The proportion of union-sanctioned railroad strikes rose from a low of 18 percent in 1881 to a high of 53 percent in 1894 (figure 5). The two most pronounced bulges in the number of union-sanctioned strikes are attributable to the industrial unionism of railroad men. Between 1884 and 1886 the role of the Knights of Labor among shopmen is clearly evident. In two of those years, 1884 and 1886, 35 percent and 62 percent of all union-sanctioned strikes were strikes of shopmen and were authorized by the Knights of Labor. The second major bulge occurs from 1890 to 1894. It is particularly significant that most of the increase in union-sanctioned strikes in this period occurred *before* the American Railway Union was organized and in a position to sanction strikes. From 1891 to 1893, the distribution of union-sanctioned strikes is spread rather widely over all trades. It must be concluded that the brotherhoods and other railroad unions were forced to sanction increasing numbers of strikes. The ARU should, therefore, be seen as the product of a rising level of militancy *within* the brotherhoods and as the final form of that militancy. The pressures that created the ARU came from within organized railroad labor, not from without.

Between the bulges in union-sanctioned strikes came an equally

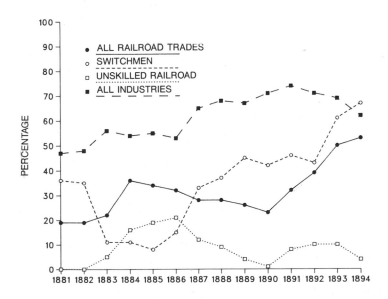

Figure 5.   Percentage of union-sanctioned railroad strikes by occupation, 1881–94

Source: U.S. Labor Commissioner, *Third Annual Report* and *Tenth Annual Report* (Washington, D.C.: 1887, 1895).

significant low point from 1886 to 1890. Only switchmen had more union-sanctioned strikes during that period. With the decline of the Knights of Labor influence and with a reluctance on the part of the brotherhoods to approve strikes, a larger proportion of railroad strikes were conducted without the benefit of union sanction. The Switchmen's Mutual Aid Association carried the torch of railroad labor militancy through these years and engaged in the exemplary actions (the 1888 Burlington sympathy strike), which broke new ground for a railroad labor federation.

The fact that union-sanctioned strikes increased despite a sharply declining rate of success was a further indication that the early 1890s were extraordinary times. Setting aside their existing craft organizations, militant railroad workers fashioned new organizations to confront control issues that were perceived to be the key to improving their condition.

Displaced Workers and Strike Effectiveness

One measure of how effectively railroad workers disrupted normal business through strike activity is the number of workers thrown out of work as a result of strikes. We have data only for the years 1887–94. In order to arrive at a standard for comparing one year with another, we have calculated the strikers as a percentage of the number of workers thrown out of employment. A low percentage indicates that the strikers enjoyed substantial strategic power: a relatively small number of strikers made it necessary for a much larger number of workers to stop work.

The data show that the strategic power of railroad workers increased during these years. In 1887 the number of railroad strikers was 89 percent of the number of employees thrown out of work. In 1893 railroad strikers made up only 41 percent. It is interesting to note that when these data are compared with similar data for workers in all industries, striking railroad workers were consistently able to throw larger numbers of their fellow employees out of work.[39] In spite of this strategic power, their success rate was consistently lower than that for workers in all industries, and it declined further during the very years when their strategic power appeared to have been growing.

The final evidence of the disruptive character of industrial relations on the railroads is the rate at which railroad workers who struck unsuccessfully were displaced or blacklisted. For strikes during the period 1881–94 the records of the labor commissioner

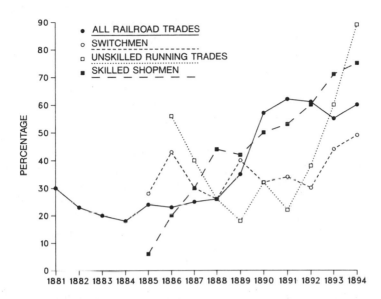

Figure 6. New workers hired at end of lost strikes as a percentage of strikers, 1881–94 (three-year moving average)

Source: U.S. Labor Commissioner, *Third Annual Report* and *Tenth Annual Report* (Washington, D.C.: 1887, 1894).

give a figure for the number of "new workers hired at the end of the strike." Many strikes saw no new workers hired, but, for a large number of strikes that were lost, many workers were hired during and after the strike, and by obvious implication a roughly comparable number were displaced.* Whether these workers were permanently blacklisted on the particular road or on the other roads cannot be determined with any certainty except for a few strikes. But it is safe to assume that these workers left because of strike participation and for at least some brief period became part of the floating unemployed railroad labor force. As the basis for comparison, we have shown the number of new workers at the end of the strike as a percentage of the number of employees who struck (figure 6).

In a period when the proportion of railroad strikes that succeed-

*The data do not permit us to distinguish workers fired and blacklisted from those who left voluntarily during the course of a strike and were replaced. Whatever the case may be, those *displaced* workers added to the generally growing labor surplus.

ed rose barely above 50 percent in only two years (1884 and 1885), 38 percent of the men who participated in unsuccessful strikes lost their jobs. There was a general upward movement in the number of displaced workers among all railroad trades from a low of 18 percent in 1884 to a high of 60 percent in 1894. Certain trades contributed disproportionately to the number of workers displaced during strike activity. The proportion of skilled shopmen rose from 6 percent to 75 percent between 1885 and 1894, and the proportion of switchmen rose from 27 percent to 50 percent. The likelihood of brakemen and firemen being displaced for strike activity rose between 1891 and 1894. These casualties of industrial conflict grew more numerous as the period being examined progressed. They swelled the ranks of the unemployed.

These statistics suggest important dimensions of railroad workers' strike activity in the late nineteenth century. Even though most railroad strikes were conducted without benefit of union sanction, the periods of most intense strike activity were also the periods of greatest union support for strikes. That support, provided largely through new industrial organizations that promised greater solidarity, grew even as success rates plummeted. Even though railroad workers demonstrated greater strategic power to disrupt traffic, the losses mounted, and with the losses, the numbers of workers displaced for strike activity swelled.

Terence Powderly, grand master workman of the Knights of Labor, did not welcome strikes under any circumstances. He regularly warned against them and after 1886 found himself perpetually out of step with the young and militant recruits to the Knights of Labor. When District Assembly 246 on the New York Central called its members out on strike in August 1890 to resist the summary discharge of stalwart union members, Powderly, in dismay, wrote the district master workman over the "untimely" nature of the strike. He accurately characterized the aggressive spirit with which railroad workers entered strikes over noneconomic issues in this phase of strike activity, while missing the nature of the crisis that made it imperative for them to do so. "It is a pity," Powderly wrote, "that the labor movement cannot be allowed to move ahead for two years, the critical period, without having some such thing as this take place and shatter the hopes of the toilers." But, he concluded that "the patience of the workingmen will not hold out to remain organized quietly while doing their part to organize other parts so that they will be as one man when these years come."[40]

45

Summary

What we see in the statistical record of railroad workers' strikes in the period 1881–94 is an extraordinary rise in strike activity under extremely adverse conditions. The years 1885 and 1886 and the Gould strikes that highlighted those years are a dividing line between two distinctive periods. Before 1885 strikes were relatively infrequent; the strikes that did occur tended to be large and comparatively successful. No particular regions or occupational groups stand out as being chiefly responsible for the strikes. In 1885 a very different pattern emerged. Strikes were more frequent, though from 1887 to 1892 they were also smaller. The rate of success declined steadily and then after 1892 fell sharply. Strike activity moved westward and was particularly intense in the upper Midwest and in the northern Mountain and southern Great Plains states. Switchmen and unskilled workers accounted for a disproportionate number of strikes, though in 1893 and 1894 a broad cross-section of railroad trades joined the general strikes.

While strikes over wages followed fairly predictable patterns that were related to the business cycle, strikes over noneconomic issues did not. Noneconomic strikes had been a minor factor in the first phase of strike activity, but by the years 1893 and 1894 they outnumbered strikes over wages. More significant was the fact that offensive strikes over noneconomic issues outnumbered defensive strikes in the 1890s even as the rate of success declined. The declining rate of success was apparently not related to the strategic power of railroad strikers to disrupt service. The number of men thrown out of work during strikes grew between 1887 and 1894. The increase in industrial unionism between 1884 and 1886 and between 1890 and 1894 did not appear to have deterred strikes but rather facilitated them. The casualties that resulted from those strikes—the large number of workers who lost their jobs—only seemed to fuel the intensity of the confrontation which was building after 1885.

The dimensions of the conflict are missed if the focus is entirely on the episodic, big strikes. The strikes after 1885 evidenced a different sort of behavior, based less on short-term calculations of advantage and more on a sense that fundamental issues governing the work lives of railroad workers were being decided. The frequency of contests involving noneconomic issues of control over work relations, the growing number of sympathy strikes, and the fact that strike losses did not diminish the appetite of railroad workers for striking indicate the nature and intensity of the conflict which had built up.

Railroad workers, particularly those in the rapidly changing western and midwestern sections, were caught in a web of rationalization that played havoc with the standards and expectations they had for their work. The centralization of railroad management eliminated the bane of arbitrary local officials but substituted general rules and personnel procedures that eroded railroad workers' customary autonomy. The promotion of land settlement by the railroads, the inducement of high wages, and deliberate attempts by railroad managers to flood the market with newly recruited railroad labor swelled the labor supply even in recently settled areas to the point where wage rates softened and managers felt it was safe to rewrite work rules. Railroad workers found that their skill and experience, which had been their ticket to employment, were not honored as railroads promoted their own men from within. Security lay in loyalty to the railroad corporation, not to the organization of one's trade. And the foundation of those organizations was threatened even further by the substitution of company-sponsored insurance, pensions, and reading rooms for the collective amenities that workingmen had provided for each other.

The generation of railroad workers that entered employment in the expansionary post-Civil War period had established certain expectations of what the return for their labor should be. As reasonably well-paid workers in an expanding, highly visible, and demanding industry, they enjoyed a measure of collective pride. Through organizations of their own they maintained standards of skill and collectively insured themselves against the personal misfortunes of their trade. As they experienced the erosion of their earnings and the customary rules governing their work, they struck first to defend their wages and work rules, then to defend their organizations, and finally to defend their pride. In the course of those struggles, many of which were lost, some railroad workers began to define a new agenda. They did not simply seek the reinstatement of old traditions by which different groups of railroad workers had bartered with local officials. Rather, they sought new measures by which general organizations representing all trades (coequals of large corporations) could exert some control over the railroad labor supply, wage determination, employment security, and even the operation of the railroads in the general public interest. By 1894 the idea that a final struggle between the assembled legions of labor and capital could lead to fundamental reorganization of the relations of production was widespread. Many railroad workers had come to believe that control over work relations could only be achieved through a broader public control of the railroads that might be a consequence of such a struggle.

2

Brotherhoods, "Strikers' Unions," and
the Strategy of Class Organization

There is no one brotherhood of any class that can say in time of
trouble with their employers they are independent of the others, for
that has been proved to the contrary too often. There are too many
men in all departments who are competent to fill the places of the
others, if it was not for the sense of honor in them.

—Switchmen's Journal, July 1886

But suppose the effort could succeed and the Brotherhood be
destroyed, what then? Out of its ashes will arise a federation of
labor, less conservative and forbearing, and in time there will
come a conflict the results of which we shudder to even
contemplate.

—Engineer's Journal, May 1888

During the last three decades of the nineteenth century, railroad
workers experimented with a variety of organizational forms to assert their rights and to contend with the changing conditions of
work in the industry. Faced with dangerous working conditions,
arbitrary and increasingly remote management, declining wages in
areas of labor surplus, and the growing interchangeability of skills,
railroad workers were forced to examine repeatedly the adequacy
of their protective organizations. Each episode of expansion and increase in the demand for labor renewed faith in the brotherhood
model of organization. When labor was scarce and workers could
bargain from a position of strength, the brotherhoods offered a reasonable basis for defining and protecting job territories. However,
economic adversity and a growing labor surplus persuaded many
workers, skilled and unskilled alike, to seek the protection of
broader organizations. Wage reductions, the undermining of established work rules, and the loss of strikes that accompanied
increases in the supply of labor forced even members of the broth-

erhoods to search for ways to augment the strength of their craft organizations.

Throughout the period railroad men returned persistently to the notion of an organization that would encompass in some way the various trades employed by the railroads. Efforts to create an industrial organization of railroad workers came in four identifiable phases, each embodying certain lessons learned from previous experiences.

Between 1874 and 1877, under the pressure of successive wage cuts, railroad workers on the eastern trunk lines transformed organizations of railroad brakemen into temporary industrial unions in an effort to resist further cuts. These unions, which disappeared in the aftermath of the 1877 strike, were organized on individual systems but appear to have had some contact with each other.

Second, during the depression of 1884–85, western shopmen and men in other trades joined the Knights of Labor in droves. District assemblies, which were "systemic" in character, engineered a series of successful strikes on the Gould system, the Wabash, and the Union Pacific.

Third, the Chicago, Burlington & Quincy (C. B. & Q.) strike in 1888 was marked by sympathy actions of engineers and firemen from other roads and of switchmen on the C. B. & Q. itself in support of the striking firemen and engineers. Their actions sparked debate over federation, and their defeat prompted a serious effort to federate the running trades, which lasted from 1889 to 1891. Jurisdictional conflicts tore the federation apart before it was complete.

Finally, in 1893 veterans of the federation attempts joined forces with surviving enclaves of the Knights of Labor to form the American Railway Union (ARU), the most ambitious and comprehensive industrial union yet undertaken. Depression conditions and the cumulative aspirations of railroad men for an organization attuned to their needs brought thousands of recruits, but in spite of this interest, the ARU did not survive the conflict that so many had predicted would sooner or later come to railroad labor and capital.

A tension between alternative strategies underlay the organizational efforts of railroad workers in this period. The proponents of one strategy continued to insist on the prerogatives of skill as the basis for organization; their model was the Brotherhood of Locomotive Engineers. The other strategy reflected the changes in the industry and the demand for an organization that could contest for control on a basis broader than the privileges and scarcity of skill.

Only infrequently and reluctantly did the brotherhoods become involved in outright conflict with railroad companies. Rooted in their original objectives of providing insurance and guaranteeing the position of skilled men, they preferred a conciliatory posture. As brokers for skilled labor, they cultivated an image of reliability. Although they found themselves in occasional serious conflicts with the railroad companies, these were always seen as aberrations. The Brotherhood of Locomotive Engineers specifically eschewed alliances with other labor organizations and on occasion helped to break their strikes.

In contrast to the brotherhoods, a more volatile and cooperative organizational style surfaced with particular vitality during many railroad strikes. It was rooted in the perception that the privileges of craft were fast dissolving. It flashed in the sympathetic actions of one trade in support of another, or during a general strike. It was embodied in the various industrial organizations—the Brakemen's Brotherhood, the Knights of Labor, and the American Railway Union. It was wholly protective in character and ecumenical in spirit. It encouraged workingmen to believe that if they were organized solidly enough they could relegate the strike to the ash can of history, not out of timidity or good manners, but out of the sheer power of organization.

Early Industrial Organization

The depression of the 1870s took its toll on the railroad men's organizations as it did on trade unions in other industries. The Machinists' and Blacksmiths Union (M. & B. U.), an early member of the Industrial Congress, lost two-thirds of its members as a result of the Great Railroad Strike of 1877. Countless machinists trod a path parallel to Terence Powderly in moving from an M. & B. U. lodge to an assembly of the Knights of Labor.[1] Among the running trades, only the engineers retained a viable craft union. The Brotherhood of Locomotive Engineers (B. of L. E.) survived its ordeals of 1877 on the Boston & Maine, the Philadelphia & Reading, and in the Great Strike itself by reducing both its membership and its aspirations. While affirming the Grand Principles of the Order— "Sobriety, Truth, Justice, & Morality"—the B. of L. E. disavowed "all entangling alliances with other classes of labor." Peter M. Arthur placed the onus for the organization's difficulties on members who had "violated their obligations" by participating in the 1877 strike. The Expulsions column of the *Brotherhood of Locomotive Engineers Journal* was filled with their names through the early months of 1878. Seeking to protect the organization against the "prejudice" created by the "hasty, ill-advised, unwarranted actions" of some brotherhood members, Arthur castigated the strikers for having "disgraced themselves, their families, and the society of which they were members. It is mortifying," he continued, "to think that we had such characters in our midst, and I hope we are forever rid of them."[2]

The Brotherhood of Locomotive Firemen (B. of L. F.), first organized in 1874 for strictly benevolent purposes, had an even narrower escape from the events of 1877. This brotherhood reaffirmed its opposition to strikes through the pen of Secretary-Treasurer Eugene V. Debs, recalled the charters of striking lodges, and quietly began to rebuild. Not until 1885 did the brotherhood adopt "protective measures" that legitimated strikes by its members.[3]

Brakemen's Brotherhood

While the brotherhoods were scrambling to survive the rigors of the depression and the industrial turmoil it unleashed, railroad workers both inside and outside these craft organizations were experimenting with new, more broadly based formations of railroad men. The strikes of 1873–74 saw joint actions of railroad workers in a number of trades in the East and Midwest.[4] The most interesting and elusive organization of the running trades during the 1870s was the Brakemen's Brotherhood, which began on the Erie Railroad.[5]

The Brakemen's Brotherhood was organized formally in Hornellsville, New York, in 1873. There is evidence, however, of an earlier union of brakemen dating from the summer of 1869.[6] The "1st Annual Convention" of the Brakemen's Brotherhood was held in Hornellsville in January 1875 with representatives of three lodges attending: Hornellsville; Port Jervis, New York; and a third lodge, not identified. In certain respects it seemed to have been formed in the image of the Brotherhood of Locomotive Engineers. It provided the services of a benevolent society, possessed its own meeting hall, and met in secrecy on a weekly basis to conduct its business. But in significant ways it diverged from the organizational style adopted by the engineers. Brakemen did not hesitate to join with other trades in strikes. In fact, they were the central figures in all major work stoppages of the 1870s (and there were a great number in Hornellsville). Once organized in 1873, their brotherhood provided an organizational umbrella for industrial action. More important, it seems clear that the Brakemen's Brotherhood assumed rather early the form of a nascent industrial union of railroad workers.

W. L. Collins, a prominent conductor, served as first president and chief organizer of the Brakemen's Brotherhood. In January 1876, Collins was singled out by members of the brotherhood for valuable service in a light-hearted surprise ceremony. A local policeman made a mock arrest as Collins stepped off his train. At the Brakemen's Hall, charges consisting of three parts were read: "did aid and assist in organizing the Brakemen's Brotherhood" and "did travel through the West and Southern states as far as Florida during the Fall of 1875 and at different times and in many places represent the organization known as the Brakemen's Brotherhood." As a "sentence," a "magnificent tea set" was presented to him with the appreciation of the members and their wives who were present.[7]

A newspaper interview with a "veteran engineer" in 1878, after the Great Railroad Strike, revealed additional details about the breadth of this organization of "brakemen." "Its members are not all brakemen, as the name of the union would imply. There are many locomotive engineers among the members. . . ." In addition, he said it numbered among its members "thousands of trackmen and workmen in the shops."[8] Its extreme secrecy left many observers puzzled as to the precise size of the organization, but in the aftermath of the strike of 1877 its influence was seen to be extensive indeed. The "Veteran Engineer" further noted that the Brakemen's Brotherhood was strongest in the West, with members on virtually every railroad in Ohio, Indiana, and Illinois.[9] From a single lodge of roughly 150 men, the Brakemen's Brotherhood grew in a short space of time into an extensive industrial union. As late as 1881, a *New York Times* reporter discovered "meetings of members of the Trainmen's Union" in communities all along the Erie. "A prominent officer of this organization, whose membership includes nearly every department of railroad service and whose influence extends to every state and territory in the Union, says the association was never in a better condition than at present to begin a strike."[10]

The crucial point is that, at least on the Erie, the *industrial* character of the Brakemen's Brotherhood had been shaped by the intertrade cooperation in strikes that occurred during the depression of the 1870s. While the particular issue that precipitated the strikes varied from one to another, the strategy and style of organization showed continuity.

Several characteristics of the strikes are apparent. Brakemen played central roles in nearly every one. Other trades showed an increasing tendency to act with the brakemen, initially in supportive roles and later adding demands of their own. The later strikes featured a broad range of demands, and though they reflected the interests of particular trades, all strikers stood behind all of the demands. A case in point is the strike of 1874, in which the company initially conceded every issue except a wage increase for trackmen, which it promised later in the spring. The firemen, brakemen, and switchmen broke off negotiations and insisted that "now was the accepted time."[11] The company conceded the trackmen's wage increase as well.

More well-known and short-lived than the Brakemen's Brotherhood was the Trainmen's Union. Its story comes exclusively from the testimony of Robert Ammon before the Pennsylvania State Assembly Committee, which was appointed to investigate the 1877 railroad strikes.[12] According to Ammon, the Trainmen's Union was organized on June 2, 1877 by men from the "three grand trunk lines" to resist proposed cuts in wages. A general strike of men in the running trades on the trunk lines was set for June 27, but the plans were disrupted at the last minute by internal dissension and suspected company chicanery. Although the Trainmen's Union did not formally call the strikes in July 1877, clearly it was in a position to link spontaneous outbursts in different centers. The problem is that to date we have only Robert Ammon's testimony as evidence of its role.

Data on the Brakemen's Brotherhood from the Erie indicate that an industrial organization older and more extensive than the Trainmen's Union did exist. The evidence suggests that it evolved directly out of the strikes on the Erie and that as early as 1875 it spread to other roads. It may well be the precursor of the organization described by Ammon.[13]

The central point is that during the depression of the 1870s railroad workers in the East and Midwest were groping toward new organizational formations. Confronted with successive wage cuts and numerous other grievances that affected all employees, they found new bases for common cause. The brotherhoods of engineers and firemen were ill-suited to this particular challenge. Their leaders regarded the less skilled with suspicion and some contempt. The engineers were reeling from defeats on the Boston & Maine and the Reading, which they feared would destroy them. The firemen had not even adopted the provisions of a protective organization, and their principal objective was to perfect their benevolent machinery. The Brakemen's Brotherhood and the Trainmen's Union were experimental; they evolved out of the immediate needs of railroad men for an organization that could defend their common interests. For all practical purposes, these unions were destroyed in the wreckage of 1877, although they may have survived in very secretive forms for some time thereafter. More important, it is likely that many railroad men who joined the fledgling industrial unions and participated in the 1877 strikes later moved directly into the Knights of Labor.

The collapse of the Great Strike, the end of the depression in 1879, and the upsurge in western railroad expansion induced a massive migration of railroad workers. They carried with them into new western communities vivid memories of 1877 and in many cases direct experience with industrial organization.

Railroad shopmen had led the way into the Knights of Labor before the Great Strike when the organization was still identified publicly as "* * * * *" and was undergoing rapid growth in the coal regions of eastern and western Pennsylvania. Terence Powderly, who earlier in the decade had attempted to push the Machinists' and Blacksmiths' Union toward opening its ranks to other railroad shopmen, organized a Local Assembly of railroad machinists in Scranton. By 1878, reports of the Knights were appearing in the national press with some regularity. No doubt the numbers reported were exaggerated, but the phenomenon of heightened industrial consciousness was certainly not. In July 1878 the *New York Times* referred to the report of a Philadelphia meeting of local "clans": "The report shows an increase of 800,000 members since July 1877, the most numerous class being former members of different railroad organizations which have disbanded since the strike." The Knights of Labor and the Brakemen's Brotherhood provided a model for industrial organization, which westward-migrating railroad workers packed away with their belongings. Many years later, Powderly recalled that "the great strike of 1877 in Pennsylvania made victims of hundreds of Knights of Labor, who left the state and went in all directions."[14]

Brotherhoods and Strikers' Unions

With the return of prosperity in 1879, the railroad industry began an unprecedented period of growth, and the brotherhoods struggled to recover from the disorganizing effects of the wage cuts and the strikes. Over the next ten years railroad mileage grew by nearly 100,000 miles, the largest increase of any decade. Most of the expansion during the decade occurred between 1879 and 1884, and it placed an enormous strain on the manpower pool.[15] The "push" effects of the depression and the post-strike recrimination combined with the "pull" effects of an intense labor market demand to set into motion a substantial westward migration of railroad men.

Such labor market and economic conditions created a propitious environment for the brotherhoods. The Brotherhood of Locomotive Engineers was in the best position to take advantage of the situation. Although it had lost ground on the Reading and on the Boston & Maine, in the afterglow of the 1877 strike it appeared a relatively reasonable partner to many eastern railroad managers, particularly after it purged from its ranks that element which had openly participated in the conflagration. In the early 1880s the Brotherhood of Locomotive Engineers signed a series of agreements with both eastern and western roads that established favorable wage rates and work rules for engineers. In his report to the 1882 convention, Peter M. Arthur noted "a growing disposition" on the part of railway officers to look to the brotherhood for engineers. "Let it be our constant aim to foster and encourage that disposition by furnishing them with good, reliable, trustworthy men."[16]

The Brotherhood of Locomotive Firemen, a much more youthful and vulnerable organization in 1877, did not bounce back as quickly. It too excoriated its members for participating in the strike and in retaliation withdrew the charters of entire lodges. By June 1881 editor Eugene V. Debs could report that the brotherhood was getting back into favor with railroad officials after the "disaster of 1877" and was actively reorganizing on eastern roads.[17] In spite of inevitable tensions that arose from the fact that the short-term interests of firemen were bound to suffer as engineers sought to protect their standards by limiting entrance to the trade, firemen modeled their brotherhood and its fraternal and social trappings directly on that of the engineers.

The pomp and ceremony of brotherhood conventions and grand balls exceeded the standards of even the most aristocratic of their working class brethren. They prided themselves on the patronage bestowed by company officials. As Arthur noted in 1881, "Many [officials] evince a willingness to aid us when called upon to honor us with their presence at our social gatherings, there addressing words of encouragement and cheer to members."[18]

Not all brotherhood men found virtue in such social fare, but at the height of the brotherhood's prestige Frank J. Smith, a veteran of seventeen years in the cab, sounded like a voice in the wilderness as he mocked these functions. "We, here, are not convention goers. We have never tasted the sweets that are so daintily provided to tickle the palates of our representatives. We have not had the delusive eloquence of admiring statesmen vibrating in our ears at grand openings, neither do we think that such distinction is needed to keep our friends at our sides."[19]

By 1886 a new brotherhood of railroad brakemen had organized along lines similar to the engineers and firemen. The Order of Railway Conductors had preceded them and forsworn protective measures of any sort. In short, what might be termed a brotherhood style of organization, born and nurtured under conditions of labor scarcity, flourished during the early and middle 1880s. Chastened by the depression experiences, the brotherhoods turned away from industrial conflict. Convinced of the indispensability of skilled railroad labor, they successfully pioneered agreements that provided eminently attractive wages and work rules on a number of roads. But proponents of this organizational model went further and turned their backs on protective measures and alliances with other segments of organized railroad labor.

During the early 1880s the leadership of the Brotherhood of Locomotive Engineers was called into a number of wage disputes on western roads. In each case, they resolved the dispute without a strike and signed agreements stipulating favorable rules governing the payment of engineers. It was hardly surprising that they became even more convinced of their own indispensability and believed they were capable of acting alone to protect their interests. Peter M. Arthur was certain that even a restoration of the 1877 wage reduction was inevitable if such a careful policy were pursued. "Let us strive," he argued, "to improve every opportunity offered to maintain the peaceful and friendly relations now existing with our employers, relying on our merit to secure the restoration of the reduction made in 1877."[20]

One consequence of this separate course which the engineers charted and the firemen followed after the 1877 strike was a gulf between them and other segments of railroad labor. When the shopmen on the Gould system struck in 1885 and in 1886, they called for the support of the engineers. The brotherhood not only turned a deaf ear but, according to Terence Powderly, actively worked to undermine the strike. "What mystifies me most," Powderly wrote to Arthur after the strike, "is that they [the strikers] positively assert that previous to a visit from you the engineers were in sympathy with them in their struggle."[21] Arthur replied that he had simply advised the engineers to do their jobs as if no struggle existed.

Such attitudes deeply embittered other railroad men toward the brotherhood engineers. In March 1886 the *St. Louis Post-Dispatch* reported shopmen on the Missouri Pacific road as saying, "The engineers need never strike again. They have acted a mean and despicable part through this whole trouble and the switchmen, brakemen, firemen, and shopmen have no further use for them or their brotherhood."[22] Similar experiences during the Reading strike of 1887 and bitter memories that went back to 1877 only widened the gulf separating the Brotherhood of Locomotive Engineers from other railroad men.

When in 1888 the engineers faced their own Waterloo, some would look back at this record of arrogance and aloofness with regret. S. E. Hoge, head of the grievance committee on the Chicago, Burlington & Quincy during the 1888 strike, circularized other members of the B. of L. E. divisions on that road with his view of why the strike was failing.

> Men flocked to Chicago by the hundreds that would not listen
> to persuasive language, and money was no temptation to them
> to return home. It was revenge they wanted and revenge they
> would have. They were expelled members of the B. of L. E.
> and B. of L. F., the opposing Knights of Labor, the O. R. C.,
> and in fact, all organized labor arrayed themselves against us.
> They had waited for the opportunity to down the B. of L. E.
> and P. M. Arthur. . . . Instead of us lending them a helping
> hand in time of trouble, either financially or morally, we have
> stood by the companies being ready and willing to go out the
> moment the companies got SCAB LABOR to fill their places.
> The brakemen have had strikes, and we have gone out with
> one brakeman on the train, and that a scab. You have held the
> train with your engines; you have worked with scab
> switchmen and learned them the yard.[23]

Even before the Chicago, Burlington & Quincy strike, the Brotherhood of Locomotive Engineers faced changing conditions that foretold troubles for engineers. In the more-settled regions of the upper Midwest and the Great Plains, railroad corporations had adopted policies aimed at increasing the supply of skilled men. More and more roads adopted rules providing for the promotion of engineers from within. This device, generated in part by the scarcity of engineers in the early 1880s, placed in the hands of the companies standards for judging the skills of prospective engineers. Engineers could be made as the needs of the companies dictated. There was a continual threat that companies would flood the market with engineers as demand rose and fell with seasonal and economic cycles. As companies promoted exclusively from within, employment opportunities for tramping engineers dried up, and they were required to begin anew at the bottom of the promotional ladder. Under such circumstances the B. of L. E. traveling card meant very little. It was neither a ticket to employment nor a generally recognized standard for measuring skill. Faced with this threat, the brotherhood tried to negotiate agreements whereby companies would hire one engineer from the outside for each man promoted from within.

A further threat was embodied in the classification of engineers, a policy adopted by a great many companies in the 1880s. Under this system newly promoted engineers were paid at a lower rate during their first and second years. The companies compared it to an apprenticeship and noted that the Brotherhood of Locomotive Engineers itself did not admit engineers to membership until they had worked for a year at the trade. Although Arthur himself was not particularly annoyed by the system of classification, it was a sore point with most engineers. They saw it as a reduction of wages in another form and claimed that many companies kept an inordinately large number of men in the lower-wage classifications by recycling them before their third year. This practice tended to exacerbate the oversupply of engineers and undermine the strength of the brotherhood.

Inevitably, the problems created by promotion from within and by classification deepened existing tensions between engineers and firemen. Although the days when engineers ruled directly on the promotion of firemen had passed, firemen were still under the direct supervision of engineers, and the influence of engineers over their fortunes was still great. Firemen looked at these new policies with mixed feelings. In the short run, they benefited from promotion from within, because excluding experienced engineers meant more-rapid advancement for them. But in the long run, as engineers-to-be, they would suffer from the oversupply of men in the trade. Leaders of the Brotherhood of Locomotive Firemen consistently urged firemen to oppose these measures.

During the early 1880s, as the Brotherhood of Locomotive Firemen grew into a stronger organization with an eminent journal and a viable insurance program, many firemen chose to maintain membership in the brotherhood even after they became engineers, and the Brotherhood of Locomotive Engineer's policy of delayed admission only encouraged this practice. As a result, the firemen's brotherhood loomed as a potential dual union and rival to the engineer's rather than merely "a breeding ground" as brotherhood engineers preferred to call it.

In 1885, the Brotherhood of Locomotive Engineers amended its constitution to prohibit its members from holding membership in other labor organizations. Henceforth, engineers who wanted to become members would be required to withdraw from the Brotherhood of Locomotive Firemen or the Knights of Labor. The firemen were outraged. Not only was it an attack on a substantial segment of the B. of L. F.'s membership (some estimates put the number of dual memberships as high as five thousand), but it undermined the fraternal spirit that seemed to be growing between the brotherhoods. It relegated the leaders of the firemen's brotherhood to a junior status. Mutual denunciations appeared in the respective journals for some months.[24]

The Chicago, Burlington & Quincy strike, initiated by the Brotherhood of Locomotive Engineers, drew support from firemen in spite of the hard feelings generated in 1885. Firemen argued that the trades were so closely and organically linked that they must act together. Leaders of the firemen later claimed that their support was lent in part because of an understanding that in return the obnoxious section of the B. of L. E. constitution which forbade joint membership would be stricken. Faced with internal conflict over this issue as well as a strike that dragged on for months with little hope of victory, Peter M. Arthur proposed placing the disposition of the strike in the hands of a special committee of engineers, chaired by the leading member of his opposition. This was an adroit political move as far as the internal problems of the B. of L. E. went, but it totally bypassed (either by design or by oversight) the firemen and switchmen who had fought so faithfully with the engineers. And in the end the engineers did not eliminate the despised provision from their constitution.[25]

The B. of L. F. reacted angrily when the engineers unilaterally negotiated an end to the Chicago, Burlington & Quincy strike and when they refused to support the federation plans of the other brotherhoods. With Debs's editorial encouragement, the columns of the *Firemen's Magazine* were opened up to vehement denunciations of the B. of L. E. and of Arthur. The proposal by Debs that the name of the brotherhood be changed from "firemen" to "enginemen" was debated at great length in the magazine. As Debs argued, this would reflect the reality that many engineers chose to remain in the B. of L. F. rather than join the B. of L. E. and drop their association with the firemen. Clearly, they felt, dual unionism should be pursued if the engineers were to violate so flagrantly the good will of the firemen.[26]

Conditions that favored the development of the brotherhood model of organization earlier in the decade and gave enormous prestige to the Brotherhood of Locomotive Engineers had changed by the end of the decade. The booming western railroad development of the early 1880s appeared fragile, indeed, as early as the downturn of 1884. A number of roads initiated reflexive wage cuts only to find that expansive prosperity had bred confidence among their workers. In May 1884, the Union Pacific Railroad announced a 10 percent wage reduction. The largely unorganized shopmen struck and called for assistance from a Denver leader of the Knights of Labor, and within three days wages were restored to the old rates.[27] In August a 15 percent reduction in Kansas drew a similar show of strength. Selig Perlman, speaking of the successful Gould strike of 1885, noted the pattern accurately: "They struck first and joined the Knights of Labor afterwards."[28]

"Strikers' unions" were industrial organizations forged by workingmen in the heat of battle to accomplish immediate objectives. They ignored the usual lines of division between the trades and adopted whichever organizational trappings were available and consistent with their industrial sentiments. In the 1870s it was the Brakemen's Brotherhood and the Trainmen's Union. In the 1880s they turned most often to the Knights of Labor, and in 1893–94 they swelled the ranks of the American Railway Union. Such industrial formations were usually ephemeral, although new evidence demonstrates the remarkably stable role of the Knights of Labor on the Union Pacific. Each succeeding generation of industrial unions built on the experience of previous efforts, and after 1888 organizational direction was guided by an explicit debate among railroad men over which form of industrial organization was most appropriate to their purposes.

Undergirding these industrial formations were the dual memberships in labor organizations held by many railroad men and their willingness to engage in sympathetic strike actions, brotherhood discipline notwithstanding. Countless regional "union" meetings brought men together across skill lines and familiarity bred of local joint-grievance committees buttressed industrial sentiment.

During the 1888 strike, rank-and-file engineers and firemen of the Chicago, Burlington & Quincy, along with their fellow workers who went out on sympathy strikes, formed what were explicitly called "Strikers' Unions" in several railroad centers. Early in the strike the *Chicago Interocean* reported the formation of a temporary organization that took in all strikers, whether brotherhood members or not. "This combination of heterogeneous forces is for fighting purposes only, and on the conclusion of the strike it will be resolved into its original elements." Although the organization was temporary in nature, the newspaper observed that the men "assume all the dignity of a high legislative body. . . . The president of this 'Strikers' Union' holds tri-daily conferences with these gentlemen at the Grand Pacific Hotel."[29]

The gentlemen at the Grand Pacific Hotel—the national officers of the brotherhoods—were not altogether pleased with the frequent meetings of this new deliberative body or with the representatives from it who interjected themselves into the decision-making process. When asked about these meetings, Frank P. Sargent, head of the B. of L. F., retorted, "Meetings? No. What do we want of meetings? Our men are all at home for once in their lives, chopping wood, tending to the babies and getting acquainted with their wives. That is, that's where they ought to be anyway. Oh, some of them may get together at the lodge rooms and sing songs and enjoy themselves but there is nothing to meet about; they are out—that is all."[30]

Such gatherings of strikers dispensed with the pomp of brotherhood ceremony. Men discovered common interests and formed alliances that crossed skill and trade lines. In addition to being a protective coalition for pursuing immediate strike objectives, the strikers' unions were a cultural alternative to the brotherhoods. A reporter for the *Galesburg Tribune* observed that the only "happy" people in town during the strike were the company officials and the strikers themselves. "[The strikers] congregate in the largest public hall here and when in session sing songs, listen to violin playing and engage in a regular frolic."[31]

The Knights of Labor

During the crisis of the mid-1880s western railroad men readily turned to the Knights of Labor when their organizational needs could not be accommodated within the framework of the brotherhoods. The Knights were decentralized. Their organizational flexi-

bility could meet whatever unusual circumstances industrial workers faced in near-frontier conditions. New railroad towns in the
Midwest and West were ideal settings for the Knights of Labor to
flourish. The social solidarity of such communities, where class
lines were not rigidly defined and where the influence of the workingmen was great, readily found expression through the fraternal
and political aspects of the Knights' organization. As a protective
organization, the Knights could mobilize broad community support
behind the grievances of railroad workers. District assemblies were
an ideal vehicle for carrying grievances beyond the local level to
the seat of economic power on a railroad system. The Knights were
expansive and aggressive in the West. Most important of all, the
principle of "an injury to one is the concern of all" provided a
stunning insight for railroad men in the mid-1880s who confronted
the consequences of corporate policies designed to increase the
supply of labor and undermine standards of skilled labor. Martin
Irons, leader of District Assembly 101 during the 1886 Gould strike,
looked back to that moment, only two years before the strike,
"when that beautiful watchword of Knighthood, 'an injury to one
is the concern of all,' resounded through my life." Converted by his
shopmates in Sedalia, Missouri, to this new gospel of a "broad and
comprehensive union" that promised to "give to the creator of
wealth a just share of the wealth he creates," Irons was convinced
that he had "reached a field on which I was ready to spend the
remaining energies of my life."[32]

The Knights' organization virtually disappeared on the southwestern system in the aftermath of the strike on the Gould lines,
which took place in March and April of 1886, but the Knights of
Labor continued to provide an organizational framework that
linked men across trade lines on particular systems where conditions pointed toward "war."

Not all railroad workers in the Knights of Labor were organized
in districts that represented workers on an entire system, but many
were. At one time there were district assemblies on the Union
Pacific, the Denver & Rio Grande, the Wabash, the Missouri Pacific,
the Texas & Pacific, the Hannibal & St. Joseph, the Reading, the
Pennsylvania, and the New York Central. With the exception of
District Assembly 82 on the Union Pacific, most district assemblies
suffered serious defeat in their strikes and were "nipped in the
bud" within a couple of years.[33] They were a species of "strikers'
unions" that formed under unfavorable conditions, and their
members were soon swept away in the migratory streams that so
often flowed from such defeats.

Frank P. Sargent, Grand Master Fireman, Brotherhood of Locomotive Fireman. Drawing from *Harper's Weekly*.

P. M. Arthur, Grand Chief Engineer, Brotherhood of Locomotive Engineers. Drawing from George McNeill, *The Labor Movement of Today* (1886).

Martin Irons, Chairman of Executive Committee, District Assembly 101, Knights of Labor. Drawing from *Harper's Weekly*. Courtesy of R. G. Gardner, Kansas City.

Eugene V. Debs, Secretary-Treasurer, Brotherhood of Locomotive Firemen, and President, American Railway Union. Drawing from *Harper's Weekly*.

Blessed are the horny hands of toil—Protection, Sobriety, Charity, and Industry, Brotherhood of Locomotive Firemen, Lodge No. 397 Banner, 1895. Photograph courtesy of New York State School of Industrial and Labor Relations, Cornell University.

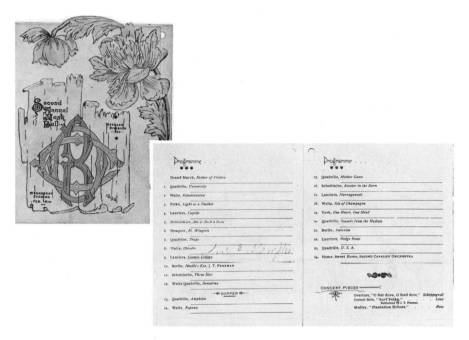

Programme for Mask Ball, Order of Railway Conductors, Needles, California, February 1894. Photograph courtesy of University of Iowa, Special Collections.

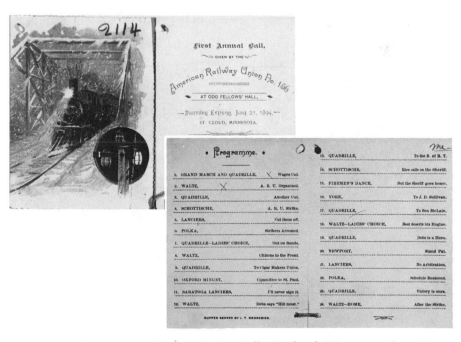

Programme for American Railway Union Ball, St. Cloud, Minnesota, June 21, 1894. Photograph courtesy of the Minnesota Historical Society.

1877 railroad strike, Hornellsville, New York: Soaping the rails. Drawing from *New York Graphic*. Courtesy of the American Social History Project.

Crowd and strikers, Corning, New York. July 1877. Drawing from *Frank Leslie's Illustrated Weekly*. Courtesy of the State Historical Society of Wisconsin.

Terence Powderly, Grand Master Workman of the Knights of Labor, and Martin Irons, Chairman of the Executive Committee, District Assembly 101, symbolized the divided leadership of the Great Southwestern strike, March-April 1886. A Thomas Nast drawing from *Harper's Weekly*. Courtesy of University of Iowa, Special Collections.

TAKE THE GREAT AMERICAN
SCAB ROUTE
C. B.  & Q.
PREPARE TO MEET THY GOD.
Close Connections with the Hereafter
THROUGH TICKETS <u>TO</u> POINTS ON THE STYX.

N. B-Death Claims Promptly Settled.

PAUL MORTON, G. P. A. M. L.

FROM THE WYMORE DEMOCRAT.
General Prevaricator and Monumental Liar.

The strike is not off, nor will it be until the C. B. & Q. recognizes the fact that it must pay as good wages as its competitors, and then sign a treaty with its old engineers and firemen, who had worked, and been so successful in bringing it up to its former standing and standard of excellence.

The public realize the fact that a railroad like the C. B. & Q. cannot be run with threshing machine engineers and vagrants and drunkards in the places of their old reliable engineers and firemen; and the working men and their friends, or the business public of good judgment will not patronize a road which is at present a menace to life and property, and a road which seeks to crush out an organization which has done more to make traveling a safety than all the companies on this continent combined, by placing competent and sober men on the engines, and an organization which practices industry, sobriety, truth, justice, and morality.

COMMITTEE.

ST. JOSEPH, JUNE 8, 1888.

Strikers' broadside, Chicago, Burlington, & Quincy strike, 1888. Photograph courtesy of Chicago Historical Society.

Chicago, March 19th, 1888

H. B. Stone, Esq.

Gen'l. Manager C.B. & Q.R.R.

City

Dear Sir:--

Following you will please find report of operative 'F. M.'

Friday, March 16th, 1888

To-day in Creston

Operative was in company with the striking Engineers and fireman most of the day. The strikers are in good spirits to-day on account of the Union Pacific Engineers and firemen going out and say they have won the fight now. Some of the strikers have been making a great deal of talk about tying up all the Roads in the country.

They keep away from the Company's property or do not interfere with the new men now at work. At present there is no sign of trouble.

Thursday, March 15th, 1888

Operative mingled around the town in company with the strikers. The pay car arrived here to-day and the strikers were all paid off. A great many of the strikers were intoxicated, but were all quiet. The only man who was boisterous was Engineer Fox, he was very boisterous and wanted to kill all the scabs and stop the roads. He was taken away by some of the other strikers and kept still. The strikers are taking no steps to molest the Company's property

"We Never Sleep," report of Pinkerton undercover operative, Creston, Iowa, March 1888. Photograph courtesy of the Newberry Library.

Troop encampment near the lake shore, Chicago, July 1894. Drawing from *Harper's Weekly*. Courtesy of Chicago Historical Society.

Conflagration in the railyards, Pullman boycott, Chicago, 1894. Drawing from *Harper's Weekly*.

The Pullman strike on the Northern Pacific Railroad, Billings, Montana, July 1894. Photograph courtesy of Montana Historical Society, Helena.

Vol. XXXVIII.—No. 1901.
Copyright, 1894, by Harper & Brothers.
All Rights Reserved.

NEW YORK, SATURDAY, JULY 21, 1894.

TEN CENTS A COPY.
FOUR DOLLARS A YEAR.

THE VANGUARD OF ANARCHY.

"The Vanguard of Anarchy"—The American Railway Union and its populist allies. Drawing from *Harper's Weekly*. Photograph courtesy of State Historical Society of Wisconsin.

Organization of the Knights of Labor remained incomplete on many systems where local assemblies of railroad workers fended for themselves or formed temporary alliances. In some cases, where their relatively weak position did not permit them to challenge the roads, they survived longer. In other cases they came and went in a comparatively short time, a product of temporary enthusiasm or of a premature effort to federate trades that were already organized.

The Knights: Organization and Membership

A historical reassessment of the Knights of Labor is underway. Clearly the organization was broader and more durable and enjoyed greater strength among skilled workers than has previously been assumed. But without numerous local studies, it will be difficult to fully understand the critical role the Knights played in the development of the nineteenth-century labor movement. Data for the Union Pacific and the Chicago, Burlington & Quincy make it easier to identify more clearly than before the role that railroad workers played in the upsurge of Knights' organizing during the 1880s and the role that the Knights in turn played in nurturing still broader forms of industrial organization among railroad workers. In the process the data also provide some insight into the composition of Knights membership among railroad workers.

Structurally, the Knights of Labor was organized at the local level in one of two forms—the *trade* assembly and the *mixed* assembly. Trade assemblies generally were comprised of workers in a specific craft or industry. The mixed assembly provided an organizational home for workers from a variety of crafts or industries. From data available in the Knights of Labor Data Bank, we can readily identify trade assemblies of railroad workers. While these data also permit us to specify the locations of mixed assemblies, we are unable to determine without additional local sources whether they embraced railroad workers.[34]

The data on railroad trade assemblies, however, suggest some important characteristics of the Knights. First, there was indeed a notable surge in the organization of railroad men within the Knights of Labor during the 1885–86 period. Second, at the 1886 peak, railroad trade assemblies comprised 5 percent of all local *trade* assemblies within the Knights.[35] Beyond the comparatively solid information about trade assemblies lies the marshy terrain of mixed assemblies as they were defined by the Knights. In how many of the mixed assemblies were railroad workers the dominant industrial group?

At this time the only systematic data are those from the Union Pacific Railroad and District Assembly 82. The columns of the *Union Pacific Employees Magazine* identify thirty-six local assemblies that were at one time attached to District Assembly 82. Of those thirty-six assemblies—all composed of employees of the Union Pacific Railroad—only ten were identified as railroad trade assemblies. Twenty-four of the assemblies were "mixed," with no particular trade identification. Small as this sample is, it seems to indicate that the number of railroad trade assemblies significantly understates the number of local assemblies whose members were predominantly railroad workers. In fact, on the Union Pacific there were nearly two and one-half times more mixed assemblies of railroad workers than trade assemblies. If the relationship of trade assemblies to mixed assemblies on the Union Pacific has any wider statistical significance, it suggests that the organization of railroad workers was a greater factor in the 1886 bulge in Knights of Labor membership than the figure of 5 percent suggests. Under such rapidly changing conditions, the mixed assembly was an obvious and appropriate instrument.

The question remains: Which railroad workers found their way into the ranks of the Knights of Labor? The scattered evidence generally points to the shop trades as the base of greatest support on most roads. There is, however, considerable evidence that men in the running trades, laborers, freight handlers, and others joined in most of the major strikes organized by district assemblies. Dual membership—in the Knights and a brotherhood—was common and reflected the competition of alternative organizational strategies. During an 1885 speaking tour, Richard Trevellick wrote to Powderly saying that of the ninety-seven men proposed for membership in a local assembly in Saint Thomas, Ontario, twenty-seven were members of the Brotherhood of Locomotive Engineers.[36] D. G. Johnson, a locomotive engineer living in Armondale, Kansas, wrote to Powderly in 1885 to request an organizer's commission. He noted that he had been a member of the Brotherhood of Locomotive Engineers since 1864 (its second year of existence) and of the Knights of Labor since 1877.[37] In 1887 a correspondent to the *Union Pacific Employees Magazine* from Ellis, Kansas, said that membership was growing so fast there was no hall to accommodate it. "Our membership consists of all the shopmen as well as engineers, firemen, conductors, brakemen and sectionmen."[38]

It is probable, however, that the bedrock support for the Knights still came from shopmen. Charles Williams, the recording secretary of Local Assembly 3703 on the Missouri, Kansas & Texas Railroad, wrote to Powderly in 1885 asking for a special dispensation to bend the Knight's rules in order to receive applications and initiate members on the same night. Clearly referring to the predicament of trainmen and enginemen, he observed that, there are men who "cannot be here at stated intervals and whom it is necessary to gather into the order. They are men with whom we are well acquainted and who are in a position to render us substantial aid in cases of emergency."[39] Their schedules made regular attendance uncertain, but they were in a position to stop trains in the event of an "emergency." Many were recruited into the Knights, held dual memberships, and aided in emergencies. But during this period most did not abandon their identities as brotherhood men.

Systematic data regarding the membership of railroad men in the Knights are limited, indeed, but do point toward a membership on some roads of predominantly unskilled shopmen and laborers. In the summer of 1885, just a few months after the successful strike of railroad men on the Wabash and the Missouri, Kansas & Texas, the general officers of the Chicago, Burlington & Quincy began a quiet investigation of the strength of the Knights of Labor on their road. The evidence gathered by most division superintendents was of a general nature. Several admitted their ignorance. But a few of the reports stand out as useful assessments of the Knights. In Creston, Iowa, Division Superintendent C. W. Eckerson estimated that 35 percent of the men "in and around the shops" belonged to the Knights. T. E. Calvert recorded the following numbers of Knights on the Burlington & Missouri-Nebraska in towns that had shops and roundhouses: Plattsmouth, 40; Lincoln, 35; Hastings, 22; and McCook, 18. He volunteered that he had "ordered superintendents and others having members, to watch them and get rid of them as fast as possible, for other reasons if they can."[40]

The most comprehensive report in this series came from the master mechanic of the Chicago, Burlington & Quincy shops in Galesburg, Illinois. Through a number of informants R. W. Colville put together a detailed accounting (table 4). He estimated that between the two assemblies of the Knights of Labor in Galesburg, there were approximately 400 members. About 150 were railroad men working in the locomotive and car shops. He claimed to have the names of 130. Nearly one-half of that number were unskilled men working around the shops, "such as Helpers, Wipers, Sweepers." He estimated no more than 25 to 30 skilled mechanics belonged and very few of them were older men. "Quite a number of our young men barely out of their apprenticeship have been decoyed into it, as well as some of our apprentices."[41]

Table 4.   Knights of Labor Members in Galesburg, Illinois, Locomotive and Car Shops, 1885

Shop	Number of Employees	Number of K. of L. Members	Percent
Machine	98	32	32.7
Boiler	35	8	22.9
Blacksmith	36	5	13.9
Copper	8	3	37.5
Car	137	36	26.3
Paint	33	25	75.8
Round house	97	35	36.1
Store house	29	2	6.9
Total	473	146	30.9
Engineers	100	1	1.0
Firemen	100	2	2.0
Total	673	149	22.2

Source: Engineers' Grievance Committee Papers, 1885–86 (33 1880 3.1), Burlington Archives.

He added that he had been told that there were not a great many local trainmen in the order. Believing that the "Wabash troubles" stirred up by the Knights would soon quiet down and end in their defeat, he hoped to resume his "missionary" work among the members in his shops. "If I am not badly mistaken, a large majority of them would prefer leaving the order to leaving the company's employ." When Charles Perkins, president of the Burlington, assembled all of the evidence from his subordinate officials, he recommended against "wholesale" discharge, fearing a general strike. He seconded the views of G. W. Holdredge, a railroad official from Nebraska, who had written, "I do not hope to keep the K. of L. off our line entirely, but I do hope to keep them down so that some other fellow will make the fight which must be made with them."[42] Jay Gould seized that opportunity less than a year later.

District Assembly 82: A Model of Strength

The stability of District Assembly 82 on the Union Pacific Railroad stands in bold relief against the instability of the Knights' organization on most railroad systems. While the Knights on most roads made it possible for a temporary amalgamation of trades to engage in action for redress of their grievances, the Knights on the Union Pacific created a durable, practical, and successful industrial union, which caused the Union Pacific to be generally recognized as the best-organized road in the country. T. E. Calvert, an official of the Burlington, told a company investigator "The Union Pacific is more under the control of its employees than any other road. They have a strike on the average of about once a month, and many of the subordinate officials are little better than the men on such occasions. . . . The U.P. pays better wages than other companies."[43]

The Knights' success on the Union Pacific, especially between 1886 and 1888, is all the more remarkable because this was a period when the prestige of the brotherhoods was still high. In fact, it appears to have been through dual membership that the Knights maintained their leadership on the Union Pacific. A "plea for federation" sent to Powderly by District Assembly 82 in 1885 pointed out that most of the employees on the Union Pacific Railroad system were loyal members of the Knights of Labor, "and none more faithful and earnest than the members of the Brotherhoods of Locomotive Engineers and Firemen . . . [they] owe equal fealty and allegiance to their respective orders."[44] Samuel Callaway, an officer of the Union Pacific Railroad during the 1880s, recalled in testimony years later that "they had 25,000 of our men in the Knights of Labor. . . . I had more or less trouble with them."[45]

In the famous 1894 wage-reduction case between the Union Pacific and its employees, Judge Henry Clay Caldwell, federal circuit judge in Nebraska, asked Edward Dickinson, general manager of the Union Pacific, whether the company had ever before in the previous twenty years unilaterally changed rules and regulations affecting employees.

Dickinson: No sir, it has always been the other way; the men have always invited the company—or notified the company that they were going to make changes.
Caldwell: That they were going to invite a conference for that purpose?
Dickinson: Yes, sir, we have sat with them there seven weeks at a time.
Caldwell: And the changes that were made were made in conference?

Dickinson: Yes sir.

Caldwell: And after a full conference?

Dickinson: Yes sir.

Caldwell: Now, did they subdue you or overawe you every time, or was it a matter of a conference, and did you act as reasonable intelligent men and independent men on such occasions?

Dickinson: Well, I don't know as we were overawed or subdued exactly, but we were given to understand that they would insist upon the rules they submitted, and without saying so directly intimation was thrown out that they would carry their point some way or other.[46]

In later years the leaders of District Assembly 82, surveying the carnage among railroad labor organizations on other roads, would speak of the "accident" of the 1884 wage cut as the factor which differentiated their experience from that of other railroad men. The across-the-board wage cut in May 1884 generated a spontaneous strike across trade lines. It prodded the strikers, flushed with victory after three short days, to enlist the assistance of the Knights of Labor in developing a permanent organization. Earlier organizations of shopmen on the Union Pacific—the Machinists and Blacksmiths Union, as well as craft organizations of boilermakers and of moulders—had lapsed before 1884.[47] There was a vacuum of organization among shopmen, and even the brotherhoods could not match the protection that broad organization under the Knights seemed to offer in the 1884 strike.

Other factors besides the "accident" of the 1884 wage cut contributed to the Knights' success on the Union Pacific. Charles Francis Adams, Jr., assumed the presidency of the Union Pacific less than two months after the 1884 strike. Preoccupied with congressional relations, improving the railroad's image, and battling the efforts of Gould to encroach on his territory, Adams was inclined to be conciliatory toward his employees.[48] The *Union Pacific Employees Magazine* welcomed his comments on the railroad issues of the day in their columns, while reserving wholehearted support for his policies.[49] His tenure as president lasted until late 1890 and spanned the period of solid Knights of Labor organization on his line. He showed no evidence of actively trying to undermine the Knights.

More important than Adam's moderation was the solid leadership that guided the fortunes of District Assembly 82. Thomas Neasham was the district's first master workman; he remained in office from 1884 through 1891. Raised in the English collieries, he had also served as an apprentice boilermaker and an active participant in English trade unions and cooperatives. Although he had been in the United States only six years when the 1884 strike broke out on the Union Pacific, he was, according to the *Union Pacific Employees Magazine*, "pushed to the front because of his experience."[50] He was succeeded in the leadership of the district by J. N. Corbin, another able organizer, who had edited the magazine since its inception in 1886. The magazine itself was an exemplary labor journal whose correspondence columns were regularly filled with letters from many divisions. No other railroad district assembly in the Knights of Labor is known to have had its own journal.

Most of the Knights' assemblies on the Union Pacific were organized in the period between 1884 and 1886 and remained in existence until 1894. In early 1886, agitation for what was loosely termed "federation" began in the columns of the *Union Pacific Employees Magazine* and, through federation, the assemblies recognized the dual allegiance of many railroad men. Engineers and firemen on the Union Pacific became the core of the "radical" factions in their respective brotherhoods. Such factions surfaced during the Burlington strike and challenged the national brotherhood leadership to accept federation with other railroad men.

There is evidence that by the early 1890s some skilled railroad shopmen were withdrawing from the local assemblies of District Assembly 82 to join the new "associations" of machinists, boilermakers, and blacksmiths. Although at first District Assembly 82 applauded these organizations as complementary, it came to see them as a threat to the solidarity it had achieved.

Notwithstanding these problems with "class" organization in its ranks, District Assembly 82 was highly visible as a model of intertrade solidarity throughout the period. In February 1888, when engineers and firemen struck the Chicago, Burlington & Quincy Railroad, the Union Pacific men were the most consistent supporters of the boycott of C. B. & Q. cars. Their renewed advocacy of federation, backed by their own sympathetic actions, endowed them with considerable moral authority

Federation in Theory and Practice

The strike of engineers, firemen, and switchmen on the Burlington in 1888 was a critical turning point in the evolution of industrial organization among railroad men. Occurring at a time when brotherhood prestige remained high, it undermined confidence in the brotherhoods and in the case they made for the autonomous trade organizations. Opposition movements in the brotherhoods of both engineers and firemen surfaced with renewed vigor in the western states. The federation of railroad employees, promoted through the sympathetic actions of enginemen on a score of western roads, became the "great lesson" of the strike. "This strike has done more to bring labor closer together than all the orations that have been delivered," wrote an enthusiastic railroad man from South Butte, Montana, to the *Union Pacific Employees Magazine*. The editor noted that "the strikers and their supporters and friends...have met daily and heard reports and discussed the situation. This naturally brought the principles that are involved in the labor question out. . . . Education will outlast victory."[51]

Out of the early days of the strike and the imposition of the boycott on C. B. & Q. cars, an alternative strike leadership developed parallel to that provided by the brotherhood officials. Peter M. Arthur and the national leadership of the two brotherhoods, including Frank P. Sargent and Eugene V. Debs, were in and out of the center of operations in Chicago. The Chicago, Burlington & Quincy grievance committee, representing enginemen on all divisions of the road, directed day-to-day operations from the Grand Pacific Hotel in Chicago. But representatives of grievance committees on "foreign" roads to the west also came and went. They maintained liaison with the C. B. & Q. men and with the committees that directed the boycott of Burlington cars in Omaha, Minneapolis, Kansas City, and other western centers.[52]

In his history of the strike, C. H. Salmons, a Chicago, Burlington, & Quincy engineer and grievance man, recalled that "there came. . . a faction who organized themselves into an advisory board, something not warranted by the laws of the engineers and evidently not desired by the grand officers . . . this board held meetings and adopted plans for their own guidance, exercised influence over the grand officers, meeting with them and doing diverse things."[53] As the strike entered its third month, the gulf between the western grievance men and the brotherhood leadership widened. Switchmen whose sympathy strike had all but collapsed and who felt abandoned and ignored by the brotherhood leadership added their sentiments to those of the radical faction of engineers and firemen.

Hoge and Murphy, leaders of the C. B. & Q. grievance committee, found themselves caught in the middle, between the brotherhood officials that sought an early end to the strike through compromise and the western militants that sought to extend the boycott and sympathy strike into a more general struggle. Arthur and Sargent consistently refused to attend meetings where anyone except the Chicago, Burlington, & Quincy grievance committee was present. However, the demand for a more militant strategy continued to surface at mass meetings in Chicago and in western division towns. A Pinkerton operative ensconced in a room adjacent to the headquarters in the Grand Pacific Hotel recorded the appeal by one delegation of railroad men to Arthur and Sargent for their appearance at a general meeting. When informed that they would meet only with committee members, the men reportedly "used very abusive language against Arthur."[54]

Debs, who ventured out to speak to a meeting at 14th and Blue Island, was interrupted by shouts and catcalls when he argued against the renewal of the boycott. The Pinkerton eavesdropper reported that an engineer who had attended one of the switchmen's daily meetings told the leaders that he had "a thousand questions put to him and did not know what to say." He warned Hoge that if he went to one of those meetings "he would have his hair pulled."[55] The brotherhoods conducted an advisory referendum in each division of striking Burlington enginemen. The returns from the voting, intercepted by Pinkerton agents at the hotel desk and recorded, showed virtually unanimous support in the western divisions for continuing the strike.

Frustration with the conduct of the strike, among the more militant western railroad men, led directly to plans for a July general meeting of western railroad workers in Saint Joseph, Missouri. "Radicals" in the brotherhoods fanned out to spread word of the proposed meeting. Its purpose was twofold: to consider methods for winning the C. B. & Q. strike (renewal of the boycott) and to formulate longer-range plans for the federation of railroad employees. An estimated one thousand engineers, firemen, switchmen, brakemen, and other railroad men attended the three-day meeting, which saw the leadership of the brotherhoods castigated and resolutions for federation and a continuation of the strike adopted. Debs was present but did not play a major role. Arthur and Sargent did not attend.[56]

In a distinctly separate move from this unofficial agitation for federation, some brotherhood officials pushed for concrete steps toward the federation of existing organizations. Although the differences between those advocating various forms of federation were not clearly articulated in the summer of 1888, they would be clarified during the coming year. In June 1888 the *Switchmen's Journal* threw out a challenge, asking if the first organization to hold its convention in the coming months would be "wise enough, broad-guaged enough, brave enough to take the initiative toward the federation of all railroad employees?"[57] Debs, writing in the *Locomotive Firemen's Magazine* two months later, assured the switchmen that federation would be pursued at his organization's September convention.[58]

The firemen and switchmen adopted Articles of Federation in their successive conventions. The brakemen supported them in principle but deferred action on technical grounds. A bitter fight erupted in the engineers' October convention, reflecting the divisions that had been sharpened during the Chicago, Burlington & Quincy strike. A prominent eastern engineer who was also a Pinkerton agent reported in detail the maneuverings that led to the election of A. R. Cavner, a western radical, to the position of first grand assistant chief. Arthur managed masterfully to place the disposition of the C. B. & Q. strike, by that time universally recognized as lost, in the hands of a committee headed by Cavner. Federation resolutions were watered down to a vaguely worded statement for "cooperation" with the firemen alone. Western proponents of federation left discouraged. At the end of the convention season, federation had stalled at the doorstep of the engineers. The next move was not clear.[59]

Members of the Knights of Labor on western roads had actively supported the striking Chicago, Burlington & Quincy men. The strike was perceived as an occasion to demonstrate the value of federation. On the Union Pacific, District Assembly 82 supported the boycott and promoted federation throughout the course of the strike, pointedly noting that some railroad men had been talking federation for several years. From their experience with strikes during the previous four years, the Knights believed that "federation in spirit" was already perfected, and Thomas Neasham reported in August 1888 that practical federation was "booming" all along the line of the Union Pacific.[60]

The arrangement proposed by the firemen in September 1888 and seconded by the switchmen and brakemen was a federation of *systems*. The resolution read: "Upon each system of railroads, within the confines of North America, there shall be organized a Board of Federation to consist of three members from each organization represented." It specifically included the Knights of Labor among the logical prospective members of such systems' federations.[61]

The Rise and Fall of the Supreme Council

With the engineers officially uncommitted, the three brotherhoods decided to move ahead with the implementation of federation plans. A meeting was called for June 1889 in Chicago. Each organization was represented by a grand officer. S. E. Wilkinson, president of the Brotherhood of Railroad Trainmen, John A. Hall, grand organizer for the Switchmen's Mutual Aid Association, and Eugene V. Debs, secretary of the Brotherhood of Locomotive Firemen, were delegated to draw up a specific plan for federation of the organizations. Initial reports did not make it clear how fundamentally the plan diverged from the one originally proposed by the firemen the previous year. It became apparent within a few months that the plan of organization adopted for the "Supreme Council of the United Orders of Railway Employees" diverged in critical ways from the original federation proposal. It was a federation of national organizations, not a federation of classes, a distinction pointed out by the *Union Pacific Employees Magazine*. And it did not include the Knights of Labor as a constituent organization.

The distinction was critical. The Knights consistently argued for federation that began at the bottom and embraced all trades. Authority would be decentralized. They advocated federation in order to expand organization and directly challenge centralized railroad corporations by organizing their workers from the bottom to top. The brotherhood leaders, who after the Chicago, Burlington & Quincy strike came around to the notion of federation, were committed to federation from the top, the formal affiliation of the national organizations and the collective maintenance of their centralized authority. They pursued a strategy of federation as a means of defending and protecting their existing organizations. Their proposed structure left open the door for the Brotherhood of Locomotive Engineers to affiliate formally while fully protecting its separate organizational identity.

Under the modified plan offered by the brotherhood officials, a dispute with an employer that could not be resolved from within an organization was to be referred to the Supreme Council—the grand officers of the member organizations. A strike became legal only if sanctioned by unanimous vote of the council. Even a member of the Brotherhood of Locomotive Firemen questioned this centralization of authority, when he wrote to the *Firemen's Magazine*, "Should it have the right to prohibit organizations from taking action on their own responsibility after being refused aid by the Council?"[62]

The Knights of Labor on the Union Pacific did not immediately reject the plan proposed for the Supreme Council, though they were not invited to be a party to its deliberations. Organizational activity on the Union Pacific was proceeding at a different level. The June *Union Pacific Employees Magazine* had expressed some impatience with the progress toward federation: "The way to federate is for those who can federate to federate and let others await their own pleasure." Evidence quickly developed over the summer that federation was moving ahead rapidly "on at least one road." Correspondents wrote of local federation efforts that were consummated. From Dalles, Oregon, a Knight wrote, "The Brotherhood of Firemen and Locomotive Engineers have confederated with the K. of L. here. . . ." Brakemen, firemen, engineers, and Knights of Labor at Pocatello elected a "Division Federated Board" and consecrated their action with a banquet. This federation from below was in marked contrast to the centralizing action of the "Supreme."[63]

Five months after the formation of the Supreme Council, the *Union Pacific Employees Magazine* issued the first volley in what was to become an acrimonious war of words between the Knights of Labor and the members of the council. "We said nothing," J. N. Corbin wrote, "for several months after it was offered to the anxiously waiting rank and file, as the federation they had been hoping for." Only when it was clear from the decisions made by the leaders of the Supreme Council "that they intended to prevent any federal relations on systems or steps to be taken that would create unity," did the Knights speak out.[64] He noted that the council bore no relation to the original plan proposed by the firemen and excluded from participation such federated systems as those on the Union Pacific. The crucial point, Corbin argued, was that if federation was to work, it had to be formed at the bottom first, "bringing together men working for the same corporation who rarely see, to say nothing of being acquainted with, each other." The plan must then follow logically from a well-organized base: "federation locally, federation of a division, federation of a system and federation of systems."[65]

The Knights on the Union Pacific saw the Supreme Council as an effort by the officers of the brotherhoods, shaken by the defeat on the Burlington, to contain and gain control of the federation movement. "Nine grand officers of three organizations of railroad employees met in Chicago last June supposedly to prepare a plan of federation for railroad employees' organizations, but succeeded only in federating themselves."[66] The Knights asserted that the power to call strikes should rest with system federation committees when called into disputes by local federation committees. The federation's foundation, according to Corbin, "must rest among those on the engines, trains, tracks and in the yard, roundhouse, shops and offices."[67] The Knights were not unmindful of the implications such a federation scheme would have for the position of the grand officers, when they acknowledged that one of their duties would be removed, that of traveling around and adjusting grievances. With measured sarcasm, the Knights noted that this change would leave the officers "more time to devote to that higher and more important duty, the study of the conditions of the day."[68]

The Brotherhood of Locomotive Firemen and the Switchmen's Mutual Aid Association countered almost immediately, by acknowledging that a national federation with a centralized authority had been formed but claiming that it reflected the lessons learned in the C. B. & Q. strike. The switchmen's grand organizer, John Hall, wrote, "We had local federation to perfection on the 'Q,' and several thousand men dropped their jobs there, which never could have happened had there been a national federation of those three organizations, with the necessary discipline to maintain it."[69] In the minds of the Supreme Council members the continuing allegiance of the engineers to a higher authority in their own brotherhood vitiated the usefulness of any local federation. Debs lashed out at the Knights' charges with particular vindictiveness in the columns of the *Firemen's Magazine*.

The Supreme Council's first year was remarkably successful. Interventions in three strikes brought success and seemed to confirm that the united orders had discovered the appropriate instrument for extending their influence. The second year, 1890–91, brought difficulties and ultimately disaster. The Supreme Council's expression of sympathy for striking Knights of Labor on the New York Central had no effect. And in the spring of 1891, jurisdictional conflict erupted between the Brotherhood of Railroad Trainmen and the Switchmen's Mutual Aid Association of the Chicago & Northwestern. When members of the trainmen's organization, by prior arrangement, took the places of the switchmen, who were locked out, the Brotherhood of Railroad Trainmen was summarily dismissed from the council. With this act, the Supreme Council of the United Orders of Railway Employees effectively died.[70]

Even as the Supreme Council wended its way toward disaster, the Knights, on the one hand, and Debs and some of his brotherhood colleagues, on the other, moved closer together. From the beginning, the men on the Union Pacific looked beyond local and systems federation to a higher objective. In April 1890 a correspondent from Council Bluffs took the opportunity to castigate "Aunty Debs," but in doing so he tellingly predicted the future drift of events. "At this state of the play we feel secure in saying that the first trouble to arise in the shape of a strike will wipe out the supreme and cement the whole into one body worthy of being called grand."[71] A new general organization, whose dim outline appeared in the statements of Knights, had to be a "federation of classes, which is feasible, instead of a federation of organizations which has proved to be utterly impracticable."[72] Clearly, the American Railway Union was beginning to take shape in the minds of many.

A crucial "union meeting" took place in Denver in July 1890, well before disaster struck the Supreme Council. It was attended by both Debs and the rebel Denver lodges of the Brotherhood of Locomotive Firemen. G. W. Howard of the conductors (a future leading figure in the ARU) and Frank Sweeney of the switchmen were there, as was Corbin of District Assembly 82 and representatives of the Brotherhood of Locomotive Engineers, the Brotherhood of Railroad Trainmen, the Brotherhood of Conductors, and the Knights of Labor "from throughout the west." Bringing together both sides of the federation controversy, the meeting saw "various proposed details of practical federation . . . thrashed out with profit to all."[73] Early in the next year, Debs announced his intention to resign from his position with the Brotherhood of Locomotive Firemen. G. W. Howard was, according to Samuel Gompers's recollection, actively seeking support for a general union of railroad men.[74]

The debate and experimentation that characterized the period from 1889 to 1892 reached a climax in the fall of 1892. In August switchmen in Buffalo lost a bitter strike, which again demonstrated the shortcomings of existing "federal" relations. Leaders of the respective brotherhoods backed away from calling a sympathy strike that might have salvaged the switchmen's cause. Eugene Debs, whose dissatisfaction with the brotherhoods had grown particularly acute after the breakup of the Supreme Council in the summer of 1891, carried through with his stated intention to resign as grand secretary of the Brotherhood of Locomotive Firemen but remained editor of the *Firemen's Magazine*.

The views of the disaffected brotherhood men had moved away

from national federation toward general unionism in the space of a short time. During the fall of 1892, L. W. Rogers, former editor of the *Trainmen's Journal* and ally of Debs on the Supreme Council, advocated a form of general unionism that drew explicitly upon the Knights of Labor. Noting that systems federations had been a logical transition to general unionism, he acknowledged the contribution of the Knights of Labor when he wrote, "The times demand an organization of railway employees that holds within its ranks every man on the road from the tie tamper to the engineer, conductor and dispatcher. Unless the whole working force of the corporation can be controlled at one time and united in common defense of their rights, no more grievances need be presented. We all understand that 'an injury to one is the concern of all,' and organized labor has reached the point where that principle must become the simple and single platform."[75]

Similarly, the Knights of Labor on the Union Pacific explicitly looked beyond "systems federations" to general unionism. They continued to insist, however, that general organization must be rooted in the "spirit formed by everyday associations," which "build up a common sympathy that would be more likely to prove formidable under many circumstances."[76]

With "common sympathy" and industrial sentiment on the rise within the membership of the brotherhoods as well as outside, Frank Sargent and the other brotherhood chiefs moved with dispatch to fill the interorganizational void. The collapse of the Supreme Council left them without a federation alternative. In December 1892, national leaders of the conductors, firemen, switchmen, trainmen, and telegraphers drew up the "Cedar Rapids Plan" of "system federation." As late as the September convention, Sargent had argued for national federation and against a system-based organization. In fact, the Cedar Rapids Plan which was adopted, although providing for federated boards of the respective brotherhoods as the first step in the grievance machinery on various systems, bore considerable resemblance to the Supreme Council in several important respects. The inauguration of strikes required "the consent of the chief executives of the organizations represented" in the federation.[77] Just after the turn of the century, a Department of Labor analysis of the various federation schemes that had been proposed described this 1892 plan as "a conservative idea in the minds of those who wanted to see the brotherhoods federated in that the stronger ones could exercise more control over the newer and weaker ones and possibly prevent some disastrous or ill-advised strikes."[78] The shadow and shock of the Burlington strike still hung over the brotherhoods.

Existing interpretations of the federation movement in the late nineteenth century see a direct line leading from the formation of the Supreme Council by the brotherhood officials to the founding of the American Railway Union. In Donald McMurry's words, "the continuity of purpose and leadership in these two developments suggests that the second grew out of the first."[79]

But the continuities of the period are somewhat different. In the aftermath of the Burlington strike, brotherhood officials moved cautiously in the direction of federation through the organization of the Supreme Council. Their concern was to prevent the recurrence of strikes such as the Burlington. The Cedar Rapids Plan, although termed a system federation scheme, embodied the same intent for centralized authority to prevent strikes. Therein lies one continuity.

Western railroad men promoted federation not to prevent strikes but to make them successful. They wanted to ensure that future "Burlington" strikes would be pursued to the full limits of sympathetic action. Knights on the Union Pacific argued for and practiced federation from the bottom up. They insisted on vesting the right to declare strikes in the federated board of each system. They perceived the centralized federation of grand officers created by the Supreme Council as a direct threat. As disaffection within the brotherhoods mounted after the jurisdictional fight of switchmen and brakemen on the Chicago & Northwestern and after the loss of the Buffalo switchmen's strike, they turned toward the notion of a general union of railroad men. The Knights continued to insist on strong local and system organizations and eventually saw their sentiments embodied in the American Railway Union. Therein lies the second continuity.

The "missing presence" in previous interpretations of the federation movement has been the decentralized, rank-and-file, general unionism espoused and practiced by the Knights of Labor. The American Railway Union had far more in common with the railroad unionism promoted by the Knights of Labor than with that promoted by brotherhood officials through the Supreme Council. Granted that a number of key individuals—former brotherhood officials E. V. Debs, George Howard, and L. W. Rogers—were associated with both the Supreme Council and the ARU, but they were converted from belief in one form of organization to faith in another during this vital period of debate and experimentation. These leaders were led away from the brotherhoods and their conservative goals by forward-looking members of their own organizations and by the advanced positions staked out by the Knights of Labor.

Undergirding these sentiments were the practical lessons railroad men were drawing from their own strike experience. If defeats such as that on the Burlington pushed leaders of the brotherhoods toward caution and forbearance, they pushed many rank-and-file railroad workers who were faced with job competition and declining wages toward broader organization and more militant action. As strikes proliferated and the legions of blacklisted workers grew, western railroad workers, in particular, renewed their efforts to form a union of all railroad workers capable of prosecuting the struggle to its ultimate conclusion.

The American Railway Union

Less than two months after the brotherhood officials drew up the Cedar Rapids Plan, Debs, Howard, Rogers, and a handful of other former brotherhood men met in Chicago to launch the American Railway Union. The step was immediately greeted with enthusiasm by the editors of the *Union Pacific Employees Magazine*. "We are pleased to learn that such a step has been taken," they wrote. Continued expressions of support came from the Knights on the Union Pacific during the next few months, although they indicated some concern that there be greater emphasis on local organization and educational work. In the absence of a plan for local organization, they feared the ARU membership card might simply mean that "each signified his willingness to throw his individual force on the side of a *general* resistance in support of a demand when so decided as necessary by the organization."[80]

During the spring of 1893, the organizers of the American Railway Union drafted a Declaration of Principles that reflected the development of their thinking on the new organization. It offered a rambling critique of the existing organizations and a catalog of their failings. The central thesis, however, was simply that "Protection is the cardinal principle of the present organizations; but they do not protect."[81] The preamble to the ARU Constitution adopted in June 1893 provided a clearer notion of how the direction of the new organization might differ from past attempts at federation. "There will be one supreme law for the order with provisions for all classes, one roof to shelter all, each separate and yet all united when unity of action is required." And then in language reminiscent of the Knights' critique of the Supreme Council, the preamble declared: "In this is seen the federation of classes which is feasible, instead of the federation of organizations which has proved to be utterly impracticable."[82]

The Declaration of Principles noted that the vast majority of railroad workers were excluded from the brotherhoods because: (1) most were not eligible to join; (2) they could not bear the financial burden of the dues; or (3) they simply declined to join. Other defects of the brotherhoods that contributed to their ineffectiveness were enumerated. They promoted antagonisms and jealousies among themselves. They burdened their membership with costly conventions, autocratic leaders, and secrecy that promoted distrust. Petty grievances and complex machinery for resolving them poisoned relations with employers, and the authority to call strikes was vested in a single person at the head of the organization. "The extraordinary fact cannot be overlooked, that while present organizations are provided with expensive striking and boycotting machinery . . . they have with scarcely an exception been overwhelmed with defeat."[83]

The organizers of the American Railway Union noted that the failed policies of the brotherhoods had "filled the land with scabs who swarm in the highways and byways awaiting anxiously, eagerly, the opportunity to gratify their revenge by taking positions vacated by strikers."[84] While they proposed to exclude from membership all railroad employees of a supervisory rank above foremen, they opened membership to unemployed and former railroad workers. In his speech to the first annual convention of the American Railway Union more than a year later, Debs made a particular point of stressing the ARU's mission to win back even railroad men who, against their better natures, had been persuaded to scab. "What can the American Railway Union do to redeem such men from the ranks of nonunion workingmen?" he asked, and he went on to suggest that the union "extend to such men an opportunity to make good their professions of fealty to organized labor."[85] By opening its ranks wide, the American Railway Union expressed the conviction of many railroad men that the supply of labor could no longer be effectively regulated by the traditional methods of the brotherhoods.

The inclusiveness of the new organization and its particular concern for the idle and surplus railroad men that "filled the land" is evidenced in a lengthy critique of the seniority system. This critique demonstrated how fundamentally the perspective of the union would depart from the brotherhoods in the matter of regulating the supply of workers. The increasing body of idle railroad workers, "is the legitimate fruit of promotion on a seniority basis." The system works its pernicious effects on experienced railroad men. "When dismissal comes, oft-times for trivial offense, the victim finds the doors of his calling everywhere barred against him. He is compelled to go to the very bottom and serve again his entire apprenticeship." Ultimately, the ability of labor to organize effectively is undermined by the presence of a surplus of experienced men "whose necessities make them available to corporations in recruiting their services in times of trouble." The ARU argued for an open door to unemployed and formerly organized men and for the rights of unemployed, experienced men to a fair share of employment opportunities.[86]

Initially, the ARU expressed an undiluted interest in organizing all railroad workers including the would-be sources of scab labor. In the first constitution adopted when the organization was formed in June 1893, "all classes of railway employees" (excluding officials of the corporations) were declared eligible providing they were of "good character."[87] However, at the first convention a year later in June 1894, a full day was consumed in debate over new constitutional provisions that made only employees "born of white parents" eligible for membership. (All of the railroad brotherhoods had provisions that effectively excluded blacks.) Debs argued vehemently against the imposition of a racial barrier in the ARU, but when the measure came to a vote, it passed 112 to 100.[88]

An analysis of the distribution of the votes by regions indicates that support for the racial bar was widely scattered. A substantial western vote from locals in Wyoming, Utah, Montana, and Oregon (among some of the earliest ARU locals organized) combined with a large vote of Illinois and Indiana locals and what locals there were in the Southwest and South to exclude nonwhites. The substantial western vote suggests that the sentiment for exclusion was directed at Chinese and Japanese section hands as well as at blacks. The convention did go on record as expressing its "sympathy and support" of efforts to organize black railroaders in separate unions, a small step beyond the position of the brotherhoods that advocated exclusion of blacks from the industry.[89]

ARU Philosophy: The Power of Organization

From the outset the American Railway Union placed the authority to mediate labor disputes or call strikes in the hands of local and system boards of mediation. In this aspect of its organization, as in the provision for locals of mixed trades, the ARU drew heavily on the model of the Knights of Labor. National directors of officers of the organization might be called on for their advice and counsel, but the decisions were made at the local level. Delegates at the first annual convention had to telegraph their respective locals for the results of votes authorizing the boycott against Pullman cars in 1894.[90]

In the initial Declaration of Principles and in numerous subsequent statements, leaders of the American Railway Union professed such faith in the power of organization that they foresaw an end to strikes as a means of settling labor disputes. "Organized upon correct principles," they declared, "governed by just laws and animated by unselfish purposes, the necessity for strikes and boycotts among railway employees will disappear."[91] A year later, speaking before the assembled convention of delegates from more than four hundred locals and painfully aware of the possibility of an impending boycott of Pullman cars, Debs again professed faith in the power of organization to create industrial peace. "Let the proposition go forth from this convention to all railway employes to meet upon common ground and there unite forces for the protection of all. Such an army would be impregnable. No corporation would assail it. The reign of justice would be inaugurated. The strike would be remanded to the relic chamber of the past. An era of peace and good will would dawn."[92]

The events of the Pullman boycott had a profound impact on the way that leaders and members of the American Railway Union perceived the nature of the labor problem and the avenues for its resolution. From the conviction expressed in the Declaration of Principles in early 1893 that thorough and efficient organization would lead to more harmonious relations with employers to the belief that only the abolition of the "wages system" would better the condition of the workingman was a long march, indeed. And yet threading through the evolving views of ARU leaders is the consistently held faith that thorough organization was the instrument for producing significant change in the relations of labor and capital. In his testimony before the Strike Commission, Debs argued against applying expedients to a problem. "Let it do its worst, and out of that will come a better condition." Thorough organization would permit labor to "stop the whole machinery." "And," he added, "it would stop on the very spot by abolishing the wage system . . . that is what I desire."[93]

Between his resignation as grand secretary of the Brotherhood of Locomotive Firemen in September 1892 and the aftershocks of the Pullman boycott in 1894, Debs embraced industrial unionism and deepened his critique of the existing relations between labor and capital. Always sensitive to the ideological drift of those he sought to lead, he drew on his own experience with the militant factions of the brotherhoods and on the actions of the Knights of Labor and other railroad men who stood outside the brotherhoods.[94] From an early reluctance to consider broader social control of the railroads as a solution to the problems facing railroad labor, Debs and the other leaders of the ARU moved very rapidly to embrace government ownership of the railroads and other public utilities.

The issue of government ownership of the railroads was widely debated during the early 1890s in the trade union press and in popular periodicals. Terence V. Powderly, writing in *The Arena* magazine in 1892, argued that the attempt to publicly regulate railroads in the absence of public ownership was doomed. "Ownership must precede control, and the question must be solved in a very short time, or those who own the railroads will own the government."[95] Economist Richard T. Ely asserted in another widely read article that private ownership of "natural monopolies" such as the railroads led to waste, corruption of public life, and poor service.[96] In the months before the June 1894 convention of the ARU, the *Railway Times* carried regular articles advocating public ownership.

At the convention, Debs spoke out for these principles, noting that "we are becoming familiar with the subject, and the more it is discussed the more practical and patriotic the scheme appears." And in words echoing Powderly's, he asserted that "the time is approaching when the government will be required to *own* the railroads, to prevent the railroads from *owning* the government."[97] Convention delegates resolved to support the Peoples' Party in pursuit of government ownership and greater social control of the economy. The Pullman boycott and the use of federal authority to suppress it made political action even more imperative. R. M. Goodwin, an ARU director, suggested that the logic of government ownership led inevitably to "the cooperative commonwealth" as an alternative to the wages system. When the strike commissioners asked him to define more precisely what he meant, Goodwin replied that "the government or the people" should own all the labor-saving machinery and all the products of labor. This would include "the nationalization of railroads and coal mines, and if it is fair to nationalize railroads and coal mines, it is proper that they should nationalize all industries."[98]

What Debs, Goodwin, Howard and the other initial organizers of the American Railway Union set in motion with the Declaration of Principles in early 1893 caught fire among railroad workers as no previous industrial organization had done. After the June 1893 meeting in Chicago, attended by fifty men, at which the organization was officially launched, organizers fanned out across the country.

The West: Cradle of ARU Strength

Initially, the ARU's greatest success was among western railroad men and particularly among the less skilled and the previously unorganized. Debs noted the high proportion of trackmen. A correspondent from Ogden indicated that "many here who have not before seen the need of organization do now. . . ."[99] By November 15, 1893, 96 lodges had been organized, and by the end of the year a number of western roads were solid—the Union Pacific, the Denver & Rio Grande, and the Rio Grande & Western. Twenty-two locals had been formed on the Northern Pacific alone, and 40 on the Southern Pacific.[100] Debs and Howard paid "glowing tributes to the K. of L." during a successful organizing trip to Shoshone.[101]

With the Switchmen's Mutual Aid Association virtually destroyed as a result of jurisdictional fights with the brakemen and the embezzlement of funds by an officer, whole lodges of switchmen went over to the ARU. Likewise, the fledging organizations of railway carmen and the International Association of Machinists found their ranks rapidly depleted.[102] Dual membership was also common as brotherhood men and Knights joined the growing movement.

Apparently, the Knights did not see dual membership with the new organization as a problem. A correspondent from Council Bluffs wrote the *Union Pacific Employees Magazine* that most Knights were inclined to "forward the interest of the new organization." Another from Portland noted that the ARU was growing "wonderfully" at all points on the Pacific Division of the Union Pacific. The new organization took on the "detail work of a trade organization" and left the Knights to extend their activity in "the broader field of social reform."[103]

With 125 locals on January 1, 1894, the American Railway Union was decidedly an organization of western and southwestern railroad men. Only a smattering of locals had been formed in the "Old Northwest." Not a single local was to be found in New England, the Middle Atlantic states, or the old South (figure 7).

Six months later on the eve of its first convention, the American

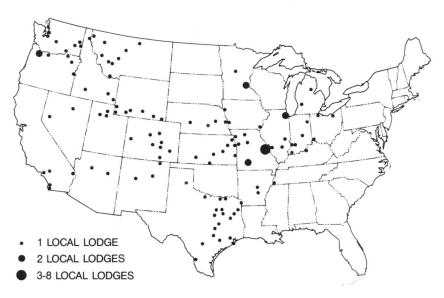

Figure 7. American Railway Union locals, January 1, 1894

Source: Railway Times, January 1, 1894.

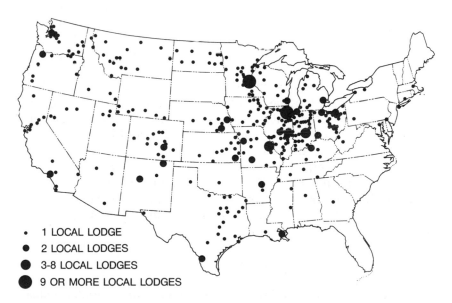

Figure 8. American Railway Union locals, July 2, 1894

Source: Railway Times, July 2, 1894.

Railway Union had 453 locals.[104] Their distribution among the regions of the country showed some differences (figure 8). The organization was substantially strengthened in the Old Northwest, even stronger in the Far East, but remained anemic in the East and the South.[105] This organizational pattern is consistent with the regional shifts in labor market conditions and the location of railroad worker militancy in those areas experiencing the transition from labor scarcity to surplus.

Debs's confidence in the American Railway Union, even as the Pullman boycott faced imminent defeat, was rooted in his faith in the western railroad men who pioneered federation from the bottom and who had been the first to join the ARU. He believed that the fight could be won in the West because of superior organization. "There is brawn and energy in the West. Men there are loyal, fraternal and true. When they believe they are right, they all go out and stay out until the fight is over."[106] Indeed, toward the end of the Pullman boycott, federal troops were not withdrawn from the strike areas of Colorado, New Mexico, and Montana until late August and September, long after strike activity had ceased in other parts of the country.

When ARU members struck in railroad division towns in the Far West, they enjoyed the kind of community support that railroad workers in similar communities in other regions had found before. The mayors of Havre, Great Falls, Butte, and Helena, Montana, gave outspoken support to the Great Northern strikers in April 1894. Citizens' meetings in Great Falls on two occasions during the strike drew large crowds, including prominent businessmen. The president of the Montana Central Railroad saw the meetings as "representative of the sentiment of the businessmen," who are "entirely dependent on the railroad men, and I cannot blame the businessmen for taking the side of the strikers. It is their bread and butter."[107] The sympathy of citizens in such communities was also extended to contingents of Coxey's Army moving through Montana at the same time as the strike. These unemployed workers were welcomed by local citizens, fed, housed, and encouraged in their mission.[108]

The Northern Pacific and the ARU

While the logic of industrial organization became particularly clear to many railroad men after the Burlington strike and the failure of federation experiments, for many western railroad workers the depression of 1893 provided their first direct lesson in industrial organization. Men on these western roads, particularly their mountain divisions, saw the first real challenge to the wages and work rules they had won when labor was scarce. The Northern Pacific was a case in point, and the organization of its workers during the 1893–94 crisis offers a perspective on the sources of ARU strength in the West.

The Northern Pacific Railroad had been blessed with relatively tranquil labor relations over the course of its nearly fifteen years as a transcontinental line. General Manager W. S. Mellen was well liked by his men and had negotiated and signed agreements with the various trade organizations, which reflected their strength and the scarcity of skilled labor in the Northwest. Apparently railroad men on the Northern Pacific had felt little need for organization beyond the brotherhoods and a loosely knit federation for the periodic negotiation of agreements. Mellen's death in the summer of 1893 coincided with deepening signs of depression. Within a matter of weeks the Northern Pacific was plunged into receivership. The receivers (major stockholders and powers on the previous board of directors) appointed J. W. Kendrick as general manager of the road.[109]

Signs of the changing tenor of labor-management relations were manifested almost immediately in the response of Kendrick and general managers on other major western roads to the deepening depression. Kendrick returned from a meeting of the General Managers' Association in Chicago soon after taking over as general manager on the Northern Pacific and reported to Receiver T. F. Oakes that "various means for reducing the expenses of operating railroads were discussed." He said there was a general consensus "that the existing provisions in the present schedules must be greatly modified so as to afford greater latitude to the railroad companies in the management of their affairs; and that the rates of pay must of necessity be reduced."[110] Kendrick's plan, as he outlined it to Oakes, was to call a meeting of the western transcontinental lines to coordinate the cancellation of existing agreements and the implementation of a wage reduction. Initial reactions from the general managers of the Union Pacific and the Great Northern were supportive, but no specific agreement was forthcoming. Kendrick stressed in another letter to Oakes that "the mere question of a horizontal reduction in wages" was not the main point but rather the opportunity it afforded to rewrite the entire schedule governing wages, work rules, and grievance procedures. The position of the company with respect to receivership and "its power to invoke the protection of the forces of the U.S. government for its property; all afford an opportunity that certainly should not be neglected."[111]

Although the roads operating in the Northwest did not move with the dispatch or coordination that Kendrick might have wished, each in its own time announced a cancellation of wage schedules. As Kendrick prepared to receive the committees of men who objected to the unilateral imposition of new schedules, he sifted through intelligence gleaned from agents and company officials along the line. Kendrick expressed some relief to Edward Dickinson of the Union Pacific that "committees are coming to us from the different orders, and we, apparently, shall not be subjected to the embarrassment of being called upon to receive the federated committee of all the men."[112] The negotiations in late December conducted by brotherhood representatives resolved none of the issues, and when the schedules took effect in early January, the likelihood of a strike arose. The company secured an injunction preventing the strike and later had it broadened to prevent railroad men from consulting with the heads of their respective brotherhoods. Although the brotherhood chiefs, Arthur and Sargent, were able to get the injunction modified, their inability to secure a reversal on key points of the new schedules left the sting in place.[113]

Numerous ARU locals had been organized on the Northern Pacific during the previous fall. But the brotherhoods remained the visible spokesmen until their tacit acceptance of the new schedules in early February 1894. Between February and April, many Northern Pacific men carried their anger and their hopes into the American Railway Union. When the strike of the ARU against the Great Northern broke out in April, the men on the Northern Pacific came close to taking sympathetic action. Only the caution of the Northern Pacific regarding transportation of scabs and the resistance of the regional ARU leadership to a second strike prevented the men from going out.[114] Peter Arthur was questioned by a Minneapolis newspaper reporter about the Northern Pacific situation, and he reflected on the events of the previous months: "We advised the men to accept the schedules until better times came, but the men did not like the schedules nor did they approve the action of their committee in accepting them. They saw fit to express their dissatisfaction under the auspices of the American Railway Union."[115]

Kendrick recognized that with the ARU victory over the Great Northern, the Northern Pacific was put in an increasingly vulnerable position. He reflected in a letter to T. F. Oakes that it would be necessary to "quietly and gradually, if possible, effect certain read-justments . . . in order that there may be no ground for a formal demand by the new organization. . . . The danger lies in a demand being made by the Union, before we are prepared to move intelligently in the matter."[116] Kendrick noted that he expected the most trouble from employees west of Billings, Montana, and from shop-men on the entire system.

Contrary to his expectation, no formal demand for restoration of the old schedule was made immediately. In fact, Kendrick received assurances late in May from Debs and George Howard that there was no danger of an ARU strike on the Northern Pacific.[117] By this time the strike of Pullman shop employees was moving to center stage.

Pullman Boycott on the Northern Pacific

When the annual convention of the American Railway Union declared a boycott of Pullman cars, men on the Northern Pacific were among the first to respond. Promptly on June 26, switchmen in the Northern Pacific yards in Saint Paul refused to handle trains with Pullmans attached. They were discharged. Division by division a strike ensued with the demand for reinstatement of the switchmen. By June 28, General Manager Kendrick telegraphed Oakes that service was thoroughly interrupted. Passenger trains were stranded at a number of stations in Montana, and though the action was not confined to any one class of employees, "nearly all the employees in the lower branches of service are out." While a committee from the eastern divisions stressed that the strike was only a sympathetic action with the Pullman workers, strikers on the Montana Division demanded the complete restoration of pay and former schedules. The trouble predicted by Kendrick in the spring began somewhat later but was far more widespread than expected. Kendrick noted the common misfortune shared by all roads centered in the Twin Cities. He appealed for support from the General Managers' Association in Chicago. A month later, looking back over the developments, he would see the strike as not unwelcome: "The relations between labor and management had to be adjusted and a more opportune time could not have been selected.[118]

Between June 28 and July 13, 1894, the Northern Pacific, like virtually all railroads in the West and Midwest, was thoroughly tied up. For more than a week the general manager had no contact with several of the western divisions. Bridges were burned and some track destroyed, preventing the movement of federal troops to key locations. The strike enjoyed its most thorough support among railroad men and whole communities in Montana. Kendrick declared it impossible to find reliable marshalls to protect company property in that state. West of Glendive, on the Montana Division, Kendrick observed that "the engineers seem to be as firm as ever." On the eastern divisions the solidarity of the strikers was less complete. On July 9, a committee of engineers and conductors on the Minnesota Division declared their willingness to return to service. They asked for the privilege of returning in a body, but this suggestion was sharply denied by management. If the men desired to return, they were told, they must do so as individuals and abandon the protective cloak of the American Railway Union.[119]

Agents for the Northern Pacific had been dispatched as early as June 29 to recruit new workers in the East. Their instructions were explicit. They were to avoid the "coal roads" where unionism was endemic and were to concentrate on roads in the Middle Atlantic and New England states. The extra lists of various eastern roads were expected to be the best source. Such men as could be secured were to be sent in small groups by various routes to Saint Paul.[120] By July 12, the fruits of this recruitment were felt between Saint Paul and the Missouri River, and General Superintendent Kimberly had successfully filled positions west of Ellensburg, Washington, through local recruitment. Kendrick telegraphed each of the division superintendents regarding his re-employment policy: "I consider that this road is without a working force and must at some future time organize a new one. Our former employes have no claim upon us and should be treated as individuals. No man who has been taking any part in the present agitation or is a member of the A.R.U. should be employed. Labor agitators and mischief makers should also be avoided. Let us clean house thoroughly now that we have the opportunity."[121] He proposed, in his words, to "exterminate" the ARU on the Northern Pacific.

Between July 13 and July 26, a massive deployment of federal troops and marshals along the route made it possible for Kendrick to resume most traffic and proceed with his program for "improving our work force." Only isolated pockets of resistance in Montana remained at the end of the month.

J. W. Kendrick's decision to seize this opportunity to remake his labor force was not an idle threat. Methodically, a list of men "not to be re-employed at close of strike" was compiled. Identified by name, division, and occupation, their numbers reached 1,944.[122]

Predictably, the greatest number of men were in the western divisions, although a substantial number of shopmen in Brainerd, Minnesota, and switchmen in Saint Paul were also denied future employment. The proportion of relatively skilled men in the running trades was significantly higher in the western divisions. Judging by the discharges, the strike was weaker in Minnesota and North Dakota.

A comparison of the distribution of trades among the strikers and among the railroad labor force in general (1890) sheds interesting light on the character of the American Railway Union (table 5).[123] These data show that men in the running trades (particularly firemen and brakemen) were represented in disproportionately large numbers. Such a view contradicts the widely held impression that

Table 5. Distribution of Trades in the Railroad Labor Force, 1890, and the American Railway Union, Northern Pacific, 1894.

	Railroad Labor Force, 1890 (percent)	ARU N.P., 1894 (percent)
Engineers	4.5	5.8
Firemen	4.6	14.4
Conductors	3.1	4.1
Trainmen	8.2	12.0
Running trades total	20.4	36.3
Shopmen	19.6	34.0
Switchmen	5.0	6.3
Section foremen	3.6	3.3
Section laborers	21.0	3.0
Sectionmen total	24.6	6.3
All other trades	30.4	17.1

Source: U.S. Department of the Interior, "Railway Labor" (Washington: 1893), from *Eleventh Census of the United States* (1890); "Classified Statement by Division of Number of Men Not Re-Employed at Close of Strike," General Manager's Correspondence Files, Box 2266, Northern Pacific Archives.

the strength of the ARU lay among unskilled shopmen and laborers. The Northern Pacific data confirm that shopmen were heavily represented (out of proportion of their numbers in the labor force generally), but we are unable to distinguish between skilled and unskilled. Section men, on the other hand, formed a much smaller proportion of the ARU strikers than has been commonly assumed or than their proportion of the labor force would suggest. Ironically, section foremen were more numerous than laborers among the strikers.

Such an occupational profile also suggests that the inroads into the running trades made by the ARU may have been deeper than those of the Knights of Labor during the previous decade. The impact of the Burlington strike on engineers was one factor, along with the worsening position of these trades in the labor market. Data on participation of railroad men from the Atchison, Topeka & Santa Fe in the Pullman boycott indicate that a cross-section of trades struck: for the road as a whole, more brakemen and firemen than engineers and conductors, and a somewhat larger proportion of skilled than unskilled shopmen. [124]

The distribution of Northern Pacific strikers in various trades was not evenly spread through the divisions of the road. Shopmen were a larger element among strikers on the five eastern divisions, whereas men in the running trades were dominant among strikers on the four western divisions (table 6). It appears from these limited data that the makeup of the ARU varied significantly from one region to another. Regional differences also existed in the timing with which ARU locals were organized (figures 7 and 8).

Several factors contributed to regional differences within the American Railway Union. First, regional labor market differences persisted even in the 1890s and affected trades in various ways. Western men in the running trades on the Northern Pacific bore the brunt of wage reductions and the elimination of special rules on that road in 1893. This surely contributed to their more extensive participation in the 1894 strike. Second, the rebellion among brotherhood members against their conservative leaders was, as noted earlier, centered in the West. A constituency for industrial unionism had been prepared by the debates over federation. Third, the earlier strength of the Knights of Labor among shopmen of the Midwest and Southwest and the subsequent collapse of district assemblies throughout those regions had also prepared the ground for industrial unionism. Railroad shopmen remained largely unorganized in areas where the Knights had previously been strong un-

Table 6.   Regional Distribution of Northern Pacific Strikers, 1894

	Eastern Divisions (percent)	Western Divisions (percent)
Engineers	4.7	6.3
Fireman	13.0	15.0
Conductors	.5	6.2
Brakemen	9.3	13.5
Running trades total	27.5	41.0
Shopmen	29.4	12.4
Roundhousemen	10.0	17.8
Shopmen total	39.4	30.2
All other trades	33.1	28.8

Source: "Classified Statement, by Divisions, of Number of Men Not Re-Employed at Close of Strike," General Manager's Correspondence Files, Box 2266, Northern Pacific Archives.

til new inroads were made by the American Railway Union. Finally, the composition of the American Railway Union on any road was shaped by the particular history of attempts to organize the road. A case in point is the Chicago, Burlington & Quincy.

In most areas, the Chicago, Burlington & Quincy remained unorganized after the defeat of the engineers, firemen, and switchmen in 1888. Only a flicker of activity was evidenced on the C. B. & Q. as the Pullman boycott spread feverishly across the country. Secret locals of the ARU had apparently been organized in Burlington and Creston, Iowa, in June 1894. The *Burlington Hawkeye,* quoting someone "in a position to know," reported that there were 500 ARU members on the Burlington system in Iowa.[125] As other Chicago roads struggled desperately to move traffic in the early days of July, General Superintendent J. D. Besler smugly asserted that "the last big Burlington strike was enough to last the men awhile. . . . If all the roads were as strong as the Burlington this fight would not have been started. There is no union organization to speak of on our road, and the men get along better without one."[126]

At the end of July, with the Pullman boycott virtually over, except in Montana, the Burlington payroll ledgers bear witness to the unfailing vigilance of that railroad's management in the face of admittedly feeble attempts at organization by the ARU. The payrolls for the Galesburg, Burlington, and Creston divisions list 276 men fired, under columns headed "Time Given."[127] The exceptionally large number of men fired (when compared with other months in 1894 and with July in other years) was strike related. This list provides a limited look at those assumed by management to be members of the American Railway Union or their sympathizers. (No other divisions list a significant number of "time givens.") Who were ARU men on the Burlington under the exceptional conditions that had been created by the history of labor-management relations on that road?

The men discharged by the Burlington at the end of July 1894 were overwhelmingly shopmen—71 percent in Galesburg, 100 percent in Burlington, and 97 percent in Creston. The mix of skilled, semi-skilled, and unskilled shows considerable variation from one division to another, but this probably is due in part to the nature of the particular shop, the kinds of repairs done, and the skills required. Of those shopmen fired on the Burlington Division, a majority (52 percent) had been in the community for at least seven years and had direct knowledge of the Great Burlington strike of 1888.[128] The persistence of these shopmen links them with the period in which the Knights of Labor exercised considerable influence over shopmen on the Chicago, Burlington & Quincy and other midwestern roads.

With all of their limitations the data confirm the general character suggested for the ARU in the Midwest. The greatest response to the ARU was probably among unorganized segments of the railroad labor force and particularly among shopmen whose previous organizing efforts lay within the Knights of Labor.

Participation in the Pullman boycott was clearly broader, even in the Midwest, than this formulation would suggest. Members of the running trades on the Burlington had compelling reasons for abstention. But it seems fair to suggest that in the Midwest, at least, widespread participation in the ARU, coming as it did just prior to the Pullman boycott, reflects the heady atmosphere of change generated by the spring victories on the Great Northern and the Union Pacific, the expectation that the ultimate conflict with management had arrived, and the solid organizational base for industrial unionism that had been laid farther west.

Although the appeal of industrial unionism had grown enormously since the days of the great strikes of 1877, the depth of such organization varied. The American Railway Union embodied this unevenness. In many western railroad centers, particularly on the Union Pacific, the continuity between the Knights' assemblies of railroad men and the American Railway Union was direct. Other parts of the West experienced rank-and-file insurgency within the brotherhoods, which was not tied directly to a previous Knights organization but prepared the ground for a more general organization of railroad men. Until the onset of the depression in 1893, parts of the Northwest remained comparatively isolated from influences that drove railroad men toward more general organization. Between 1893 and 1894, they moved very quickly through federated committees of trades and into the American Railway Union.

The Knights of Labor had most extensively organized railroad workers—particularly shopmen—in the Midwest between 1884 and 1886. Large numbers of assemblies were formed in Minnesota, Iowa, Illinois, and Missouri, but they did not survive the major strikes of the middle 1880s. The brotherhoods remained a factor in midwestern railroad centers, but lodges were torn by internal dissension after the Burlington strike. Cautious and divided from the experiences of the 1880s, many midwestern railroad men did not jump into the American Railway Union until its appeal became almost irresistible.

Eastern men were the most demoralized segment of the railroad work force. As the supply of labor grew during the 1880s, wage levels were driven down by comparison with wages in the West. Bitter strikes on the Reading and the New York Central and among Buffalo switchmen left discouragement in their wake. The most conservative factions within the brotherhoods hailed from the established eastern railroad centers. Having struck bargains of various sorts with management guaranteeing their survival, these brotherhood stalwarts found Peter Arthur's arguments against "entangling alliances" particularly compelling. The ARU made virtually no inroads among eastern men. It was among eastern railroad men that agents for western roads effectively recruited scab labor.

Even after the collapse of the Pullman boycott, which was more protracted in the West than elsewhere, the ARU remained will organized in many parts of the West. The *Railway Times* reported on a highly successful tour by Debs in the Northwest during the spring of 1895. It announced that fourteen organizers were at work in his wake, with old ARU locals reviving and new ones being organized. In October, thirty-six locals were said to be in good working order on the Great Northern Railroad.[129]

The Dissolution of the ARU

By 1897, however, Debs and the other leaders of the ARU de-
spaired of reviving the organization. Their own "short course" in
the Woodstock Jail had convinced most of them that the "cooperative commonwealth" was the only real solution to labor's woes.
They assembled remnants of the American Railway Union in Chicago on July 15, 1897, and with about two dozen delegates present
voted to dissolve the organization and found in its place the Social
Democracy of America. Supporters of the new organization were
initially divided between those who favored a scheme to set up
cooperative colonies of unemployed and blacklisted workers in a
western state and those who favored political action.[130]
    Apparently not all western railroad workers agreed with this ac-
tion by the leaders of the ARU. Some workers saw possibilities for
continued organization of western railroad men along industrial
lines. William J. Pinkerton, a switchman and former western
member of the ARU bitterly denounced Debs in a 1911 polemic, for
having "swept from under our feet . . . our economic organization
and forced us back, to use your own language, 'into the scab craft
organizations.' There was no reason for the American Railway Union passing out of existence on account of losing a strike—we lost
one—we won one—other organizations have lost many strikes and
have won some strikes and have materially benefited the conditions of the workers." He pointed out that the ARU had quickly
recovered in many western railroad centers, where the sentiment
for industrial unionism remained strong, and he challenged Debs
to prove that a legitimate referendum had been conducted on the
change to a political organization. "You turned them over to a political party and they were given no voice in the transfer."[131]
    The question of Debs's responsibility for failing to sustain indus-
trial organization among western railroad men aside (and that issue
cannot be settled here), it is clear that some industrial sentiment
survived the collapse of the American Railway Union and was
manifested in the United Brotherhood of Railway Employes. Organized in 1901 in Roseburg, Oregon, by men from the Southern
Pacific, the United Brotherhood established locals in both British
Columbia and the continental United States. After unsuccessfully
petitioning to join the American Federation of Labor (AFL), it formally joined the American Labor Union, predecessor to the Industrial Workers of the World (IWW).[132] The official organ of the United Brotherhood, the *Railway Employes' Journal*, listed fifty-six

lodges active in 1903. Forty-seven of these or 84 percent were in the Far West or in Texas, with nineteen in California alone.[133] Together with other western, syndicalist organizations, the surviving locals of the United Brotherhood of Railway Employees joined the IWW in 1905, closing a chapter of industrial organization among railroad men in the West.

Summary

For a period of nearly twenty years a succession of industrial organizations of railroad workers had vied with the brotherhoods to represent the interests and articulate the needs of railroad workers. While the brotherhoods attempted to maintain themselves as providers of skilled labor by restricting entry and sharply defining their respective trades, the realities of a growing surplus of railroad men whose skills were interchangeable was forcing many men to search for a broader form of organization that would provide protection of a different sort.

Because the crisis of a labor surplus and the attack on wages and work rules that accompanied it was most acutely felt in different regions at different times, it is not surprising that the center of organizational innovation should have shifted with each decade. In the 1870s, eastern railroad workers felt the brunt of wage reductions and transformed the Brakemen's Brotherhood and the Trainmen's Union into vehicles for industrial action that cut across trade lines. During the middle of the 1880s, midwestern railroad workers flocked into the Knights of Labor to maintain wages and working conditions through the sheer power of organization, when the prerogatives of skill could neither arrest the dilution of skilled labor in railroad shops, nor maintain the privileges won when labor was scarce. Their success on the Union Pacific was notable. Finally, in 1893, western railroad workers led the way into the broadest industrial union yet formed, the American Railway Union. The ARU specifically asserted its intention to organize so thoroughly that railroad workers of all classes could insist on just wages and working conditions, even without the use of the strike. It sought to organize current and former railroad workers in the hope of eliminating the reserve of scabs that railroad companies had used so effectively to break previous strikes.

Each phase of industrial organization drew on the social experience of railroad workers in railroad division towns. The new communities of the Midwest and West that were created to service the expanding railroad network as division headquarters were an ideal environment for the breeding of industrial consciousness. In these worker communities, railroad men exercised enormous influence. They enjoyed broad-based community support. Their participation in the social, fraternal, and political life of the communities reinforced the strength of their protective organizations. Joint committees of trades and local federations were a natural and inevitable by-product of the social solidarity developed in such towns.

The brotherhoods thrived on the railroad expansion of the late nineteenth century only to discover that the fruits of labor scarcity were delicate indeed. Although the period from 1879 through 1884 produced numerous precedent-setting contracts that appeared to guarantee the privileged position of skilled railroad workers, the brotherhoods soon encountered a corporate offensive that attacked the position of skilled men by creating a labor surplus. Classification, promotion from within, and the maintenance of excessively large extra lists threatened to flood the market with skilled men. Jurisdictional warfare between the brotherhoods reflected the disintegration of clear lines separating one trade from another. The strike of engineers and firemen on the Burlington made manifest the inability of the brotherhoods to protect their members through traditional means. Within the brotherhoods themselves, a serious debate surfaced over the necessity for broader organization. Experiments with federation at the local and national levels and debates over how railroad men should cope with the new reality of a surplus of men in every calling prepared the ground for a massive exodus of workers out of the brotherhoods and into the American Railway Union.

As Terence Powderly had prophesied, as Eugene Debs and other leaders of the ARU feared, the major confrontation with the railroads that so many had anticipated as bringing a final resolution of the crisis facing railroad labor came *before* railroad workers had achieved the thorough organization that would have been required for them to succeed. In the crisis, thousands of workers left or were expelled from the brotherhoods, leaving those organizations in a shambles. But the collapse of the American Railway Union some distance short of the cooperative commonwealth left railroad workers without a protective shelter.

Nurtured back to life by their leaders and remaining members, the brotherhoods found themselves the unexpected beneficiaries of the audacious aspirations of railroad industrial unionism. After the Pullman boycott and the inevitable recrimination that followed in its wake, railroad corporations were prepared to accept, and in fact sought, "responsible" partners among the old and conservative brotherhoods of railroad labor as insurance against another episode of industrial unionism. At least to the organized men in the running trades, the railroads were prepared to grant a measure of security that only a few years before had seemed so elusive.

Patterns of organization and strike activity among railroad workers in the last three decades of the nineteenth century intersected to produce an industrial and social crisis of major proportions. However, even as the numbers of strikes grew and the breadth of organization expanded, participation was uneven. Some regions, some division towns, and some groups of railroad workers were more consistently to be found in the ranks of the strikers and among the most organized than were others. To understand these patterns of participation is to explain more precisely what fueled and limited organization among railroad men in this "era of great upheaval." It is to this task of explanation that the following chapters are devoted.

3

Wages, Work Rules, and the Supply of Labor

Mr. O'Dell (Locomotive Engineer): We feel that the system dictates a policy that ruins our future prospects. We feel that the capitalists are doing this in order to flood the market with labor.

Mr. Potter (General Manager, C. B. & Q. Railroad): I don't think we ever thought of such a thing. You should all expect that as the country grows older there will be more engineers. It is a branch of the service that is bound to enlarge. . . . It would make me uneasy too, if I were in your place, but I do not see how you are going to stop the natural growth in this direction.

Mr. Porter (Locomotive Engineer): Mr. Stone told us that supply and demand regulate the price, but the feelings of the Engineers of this system and a good many other ones is that the classification is for the purpose of making so many engineers that the supply will always be beyond the demand. . . .[1]

> —Wage negotiations, Chicago, Burlington & Quincy Railroad and Grievance Committee of the Brotherhood of Locomotive Engineers, March 20, 1886.

Beneath the turbulent episodes of railroad labor conflict in late-nineteenth-century America lay a pattern whose meaning is closely linked to the expanding frontier of settlement, the movement of population, and dramatic changes in the labor market. Within a relatively short span of years after the Civil War, successive regions underwent the transition from a frontier of scattered outposts of railroad workers and occasional enclaves of miners to a settled agricultural society with a developing network of diversified cities. That transition brought with it changes in the supply of labor and in the terms of industrial employment. While those changes reflected in part the "natural growth" to which T. J. Potter referred, the supply of labor also grew as a result of specific measures taken by railroad corporations to reduce labor costs and enhance their flexibility in defining the terms of employment. They produced, in turn, a widening circle of conflict.

As the railroad network expanded, the supply of experienced workers required to maintain and operate it was continually stretched thin. Railroad managers faced conflicting pressures as they attempted to meet this problem of a shortage of labor; two routes appeared open to them. They could raise wages and in other ways make employment attractive in those areas where labor was required, or they could introduce labor-saving technology to reduce the need for additional workers. Both solutions posed problems.

Railroad labor was most in demand in areas of recent settlement. While the railroad labor force did expand and contract as the volume of business grew or declined, railroads had to maintain a basic level of service even in territories that were generating relatively little business, and providing that service required a full complement of railroad trades. Roadbeds had to be maintained; repair facilities had to be available; and a certain frequency of passenger and freight service was required to sustain what business there was and to attract additional business. In areas of new settlement, then, the labor requirements of the railroads were large relative to their income. At the same time they were forced to pay higher wages than usual to attract workers into what was often a relatively harsh environment without the usual amenities of civilized life and where the cost of living was higher than in more settled areas.[2] Only the advantages of locational monopolies and the chance to charge higher rates offset their higher costs. As competition grew, so did the pressure to reduce rates.[3] The initial advantages of location were often fleeting, for railroad workers as well as for corporations. With increased competition, railroad managers came to perceive the wages and privileges accorded to scarce railroad labor as a burden. They sought to assist the natural growth of the labor supply through initiatives that would lead to reduced operating costs.

The second route by which railroad managers could solve the problem of a labor shortage was through the introduction of labor-saving technology. Technological innovation during this period of rapid railroad expansion held relatively little promise for reducing the labor required to operate railroads. The two most dramatic innovations—the automatic coupler and the air brake—were not adopted widely until the 1890s.[4] The arguments for their use were based almost entirely on the possible savings in human lives, not on their economic benefits. Among their most vociferous promoters were the Brotherhood of Railroad Trainmen and the Switchmen's Mutual Aid Association, trade unions that represented the employees in greatest danger of being displaced.[5] As will be noted later in in some detail, there is evidence that the adoption of air brakes on western railroads earlier and more widely than in the East led to reduced numbers of brakemen in the West. However, the evidence shows that these innovations brought little, if any, overall savings in operating costs, a fact that helps to explain their slow diffusion.[6]

Other innovations—steel rails substituted for iron, more powerful locomotives, and freight cars with greater carrying capacity—bore more directly on savings in operating costs. If railroads could operate longer trains and carry heavier loads, they could increase their productivity, and there were clearly some improvements in this area. However, the diffusion of even these innovations was gradual, extending over the forty years between 1870 and 1910.[7] Since it was dependent on the pace of innovation in the steel industry, much of the improvement in locomotive traction and freight car design occurred after the period of most rapid expansion in the railroad network and, therefore, did not ease the labor requirements of western railroads significantly. The larger locomotives, when introduced, required two firemen, instead of one, to fuel them, and longer, heavier trains needed pusher engines or doubleheaders to get them over steep grades. At least until 1890 the dramatic improvements in railroad productivity were due largely to geographic expansion rather than to technological improvements or intensification of traffic.[8]

Skilled shopmen in western railroad shops probably felt the effects of technological change more directly than any other segment of railroad labor. The consignment of locomotive and car construction to specialized manufacturers, standardized construction, and the use of interchangeable parts led to the elimination of some workers and the substitution of less-skilled apprentices and specialists for others. Although these changes eased the demand for skilled railroad shopmen in some crafts, their effects were not felt until the late 1880s.[9]

Neither the inducement of high wages to attract experienced railroad workers nor the adoption of available technology to reduce the demand for additional labor solved the labor-supply problem for western railroads. During and immediately after the rapid expansion of the 1880s, railroad managers turned to other solutions.

They attacked the problem of labor scarcity through a series of initiatives that included active and systematic recruitment, rapid promotion or the "making" of skilled workers, redefinition of work rules to permit a fuller utilization of existing labor, adoption of personnel policies that discouraged turnover, and the introduction of disciplinary procedures that created a larger pool of available labor. To the extent that these initiatives eased the labor shortage, they also triggered a deterioration of working conditions and a reduction of wages. These wage reductions did not usually mean across-the-board cuts in wage rates (the "horrors" fo 1877 were all too vivid). They more often took the form of revisions of work rules, which affected the total earnings of individual employees, but in varying degrees.[10]

Railroad labor organized to meet the challenge of these attacks on its earnings and also to tackle the more basic problem posed by the efforts of railroad managers to manipulate the labor supply. On the one hand, workers sought to regulate the supply of labor through the traditional means of restricting entry to skilled positions and protecting their job territories through work rules; the brotherhoods sought to maintain their position as suppliers of skilled workers. On the other hand, as the supply of labor grew and as skills were redefined to make railroad workers more interchangeable, they asserted through general organization their claim to a broader control of working conditions and wages.

One railroad manger recalled for the Industrial Commission the boldness of workers' assertions during this period: "They were just as unreasonable and arbitrary as they could be. You could not do anything with them. They would even object to rules that regulated the running of trains. We have had them come in and say 'We will not have these rules; we must have some others.' "[11] It is not surprising that workers represented by the brotherhoods and the Knights of Labor celebrated Judge Henry Clay Caldwell's assertion, in the 1894 Union Pacific wage case, that a fair and adequate compensation of railroad labor had the first claim on railroad earnings. The judgement, coming as it did in the midst of a deepening economic and social crisis, confirmed for railroad men the value of broad-based organization. In restoring the old schedule of wages and work rules, Judge Caldwell ratified the organizational lessons of the previous years. The management of the Union Pacific correctly asserted that the old schedule had been negotiated under the duress of a labor shortage and was now maintained under the perennial threat of a general strike.[12]

104

The Structure of Railroad Employment

The division of labor on the railroads reflected the complexity of railroad operations. The diversity of trades, forms of supervision, and modes of payment under a single corporate structure varied more than in other industries. Among the shop crafts alone, numerous specialized trades were needed to construct and maintain locomotives and rolling stock. Workers as varied as boilermakers and coppersmiths, carpenters, and machinists, painters and woodcarvers worked in a single shop facility.[13] Within a given occupation, such as engineer, there were numerous gradations based on the type of engine, the nature of the run, and the regularity of service.[14] Some railroad employees working for a single company were strung out over hundreds of miles and operated with only the most distant and occasional supervision. Others worked in closely supervised, factory-like settings, doing routinized jobs.

Most railroads operated with two intersecting (and sometimes competing) organizational structures.[15] Railroad operations were divided into geographical units, called divisions. Each division represented a complete unit of operation: local and through freight was received and delivered; passenger trains were operated from one end of the division to the other; track and roadbed were maintained and replaced; locomotives and cars were repaired and rebuilt. Each division encompassed two hundred to four hundred miles of track. The division headquarters with its repair shops was usually centrally located so that engine and train crews could be sent out in either direction; a minimum day's run for any operating employee was conventionally defined as one hundred miles. A division commonly included branch-line as well as mainline runs of varying lengths.

A second, systemwide organizational structure was based on functional departments. The usual departments were: locomotive and transportation—encompassing engine crews (engineers and firemen) and shopmen; train and yard service, including train crews (brakemen and conductors) and switchmen; station service—including various agents, clerks, telegraph operators, and baggagemen; and finally, road service—including section men and track laborers.[16]

Each department had both local and systemwide officers. At the division level, a road foreman supervised the engine crews, while shop foremen supervised the shopmen; the foremen, in turn, were supervised by a master mechanic. A division superintendent was in charge of all departments at the division level. Systemwide, the locomotive and transportation department was headed by the superintendent of motive power, who was in turn under the general superintendent.

It has been argued that responsibility gradually shifted from local to department officers as management became more systematic and rules were enforced more uniformly.[17] Employees frequently complained of arbitrary treatment by local officials, and they often preferred to bring their grievances directly to general officers.[18] Other employees pointed out that local officials operated within a system, designed and sanctioned by general officers, that made them accountable for the profitable performance of their divisions.[19] The arbitrariness of some local officials was compensated for by the generosity and fraternal feeling that many master mechanics showed their men.[20] Standardization of rules and systemwide bargaining cut both ways for railroad employees. While the restriction of local officials' authority eliminated some abuses, it also permitted the systematic manipulation of wage rates and work rules in ways that violated customary work practices and earning levels.

Railroad employment required some unique skills gained only through experience in railroad work. The work of locomotive engineers reflected this uniqueness most clearly. Their craft had its origins in the mechanical trades that built, repaired, and operated steam engines. The men who ran locomotives during the first decades of railroad operations commonly spent a substantial amount of time in the shops working on them. As the length of runs grew and the machinery became more specialized, engineers defined their work more narrowly in terms of the movement of trains. In fact, as the *Engineer's Journal* pointed out in a defense against the charge that engineers were all sons of "farmers," what was essential for an engineer to know could only be learned "on the footboard" itself. "What railroad officials require of their engineers is not that they know how to build or repair their locomotives, but how to run them successfully, and indicate the repairs necessary to be made by the shopmen."[21]

Other railroad work, though requiring less-practical training, was no less unique to railroading. Switchmen, whose deftness and nimbleness had a direct relationship to their longevity, had to make up trains in yards that contained a maze of tracks and switches. Before the diffusion of the Westinghouse air brake, brakemen had to ride for long periods precariously perched atop freight cars and, on a signal from the engineer, be prepared to move rapidly from car to car applying the hand brakes.

In the shops and on section crews, skills common to other industries were used. In railroad repair shops, metalworkers such as machinists, boilermakers, and blacksmiths were often required to apply their basic knowledge to new situations or under circumstances that found them without the precise parts or tools needed. Outlying shops or roundhouses faced a broad range of engine and car repairs that taxed the ingenuity of skilled men. Section bosses and their crews were responsible for the maintenance of a certain portion of track on a division. Even a section hand performed labor that required care and precision which came only with experience or very close supervision. A former section hand and switchman paid tribute to the necessarily "infallible" section boss, whose roadbed the engineer has followed "with the confident trust of a child." Although regarded as "ignorant and dense," the section boss had to know "the proper elevation to give a curve of certain degrees; he must understand the scientific principle of easements, or runoffs, the gradual reduction of the elevation of a curve, which causes a car to regain equilibrium after rounding it."[22]

The railroad labor force was highly differentiated by place of work, skill, extent of supervision, and opportunities for promotion. These differences were reflected in pay scales that ranged fivefold—from $.80 per day for section hands on poorer-paying roads in the South to $4.50 per day for passenger engineers on better-paying roads in the West.[23] Actual earnings, of course, varied more widely, conditioned as they were by factors such as overtime, seasonality, and run assignments.

The "running trades"—engineers, firemen, conductors, and brakemen—were the most visible and strategically placed trades in railroad operations. They occupy a prominent place in this discussion because their position in the railroad labor market fluctuated dramatically as the scarcity of experienced men in the running trades gave way to a surplus and the privileges of scarcity, which they had enjoyed, came under attack. The tensions between craft and industrial consciousness were most visible among their members and their actions were critical to the success or failure of any railroad strike.

Labor Aristocrats: Engineers and Conductors

Locomotive engineers enjoyed enormous prestige both inside and outside of railroad circles. They were the highest-paid railroad workers and the differential between their pay and that of railroad laborers was well in excess of the 100 percent standard that E. J.

Engine and train crew, Chicago, Burlington & Quincy Railroad, 1889, Galesburg, l. to r., call boy, fireman, engineer, conductor, and two brakemen. Photograph courtesy of State Historical Society of Wisconsin.

Division headquarters men, Wisconsin Central Railroad, Stevens Point, Wisconsin, ca. 1890. Photograph courtesy of State Historical Society of Wisconsin.

Chicago, Burlington & Quincy engine house, Galesburg, Illinois, 1869. Photograph courtesy of Burlington Northern Railroad.

Green Bay & Western Railroad shop, Green Bay, Wisconsin, 1879-80. Photograph courtesy of State Historical Society of Wisconsin.

Omaha shops, Union Pacific Railroad, car cleaning and inspecting crews, 1875. Photograph courtesy of Union Pacific Historical Collection.

Engine house and repair crew, Creston, Iowa, 1886. Photograph courtesy of Bernard Corbin, Red Oak, Iowa.

Bridge crew, LaCrosse division, Chicago, Burlington and Quincy Railroad, ca. 1888. Photograph courtesy of Burlington Northern Railroad.

Section crew, Minneapolis & St. Louis Railroad, ca. 1900. Photograph courtesy of Minnesota Historical Society.

General Regulations.

In all cases of doubt take the side of safety. These Rules are all deemed important and a strict observance of each and all of them is absolutely required

Standard Time. 1. The chronometer in the office of the Train Dispatcher, Cedar Rapids, gives the standard time, which will be telegraphed to all Stations at 8 o'clock each morning. Conductors and Engineers are required to daily compare and regulate their watches with standard time.

Leaving Terminal Stations. 2. Conductors must call at Train Dispatcher's Office before leaving Cedar Rapids, and at other Terminal Stations, and ascertain if there are any orders for them. They will examine the Bulletin Boards and Train Registers carefully before starting their trains, note any special orders, and any information concerning the condition of track, bridges and roadway.

Conductors Responsible. 3. Each Conductor will have the general direction and government of his train, from the time of receiving passengers and freight to its arrival at its destination. He will be held responsible for its safety, and for the proper conduct of all men employed on his train. Train men are required to yield prompt obedience to his orders, except when such orders conflict with these rules, or involve risk or hazard, when all employed on the train will be held alike responsible.

Duties of Passenger Conductors. 4. Conductors of passenger trains must see before starting from a Terminal Station, that their cars are clean and in good order; that a bell-cord is attached from the signal bell of the engine to the rear end of the last car in the train, and not detached until the train has stopped at its destination; and that they have signal flags, lanterns, torpedoes, spare links, pins, &c., and must be at the Terminal Station thirty minutes before the time for their trains to leave.

Keep Order. 5. Conductors must prevent PASSENGERS ENDANGERING THEMSELVES, by imprudent exposure. In the event of any PASSENGER being DRUNK or DISORDERLY, to the annoyance of others, he must use all gentle means to stop the nuisance, failing in which, he must, for the safety and convenience of all, exercise his authority, and keep him in a separate place, until he arrives at the next Station, where the passenger may be left.

Report Absentees. 6. It is the duty of the Conductor to report the names of all Station Agents, who are absent from their offices, or who do not keep the same open at the time of the passing of Passenger Trains

Duties of Freight Conductors. 7. Freight Conductors must be on hand a sufficient time before starting from Terminal Stations, to check their trains, examine and receipt for sealed cars, see that their trains are properly coupled, the necessary signals out, and everything in order to start promptly on time.

Conductors Responsible. 8. Each Conductor of a Freight train will be held PERSONALLY RESPONSIBLE for the faithful performance of the duty of the Brakemen on his train. He will require the doors of the Freight cars to be ALWAYS closed, and will in all cases see that the Brakemen are at their posts. He will also see that the Brakemen do not slide the wheels.

Way-Bills. 9. Conductors of Freight Trains will not in any case receive into their train, cars containing freight, unless each car is accompanied by a separate way-bill, OR UNLESS SPECIALLY AUTHORIZED.

Switching. 10. Conductors of Freight trains will do such SWITCHING as may be reasonably required by the Station Agent, who must furnish a switching list. They will leave cars where in the judgment of agent they can be conveniently loaded or unloaded. Running Switches will not be made except for urgent reasons; in such cases the rear end of train must first be stopped, and brakes and switches tried and known to be in perfect order. Be very careful.

Tools 11. Conductors of Freight Trains MUST know that their trains are provided with Chains, Switch Ropes Wrecking Frogs, Extra Brasses, &c. Loaded cars must not be set out on account of defective or broken draw-bars or brasses.

Cars Short of Destination. 12. Conductors must notify the Train Dispatcher by telegraph of any cars that may have been left short of their destination giving full particulars of cause. This report must be made in al cases, before leaving the car or cars unless telegraph communica tion cannot be had. When cars are left short of their destination way-bills must be left with the Agent where car is set out, but in case no Agent at that Station, then to be left with the next nearest

Cars not to be Left on Main Track. 13. Cars must never be allowed to stand on the main track unless by special authority from the Train Dispatcher, and when so left the brakes must be firmly set and the wheels securely blocked.

Stations, Crossings and City Limits. 14. On approaching stations, bridges, switches, and passing railroad crossings, the greatest care must be taken. Within city limits the train must not be run at a rate of speed to exceed eight miles per hour, and must be kept under such control as to be easily stopped should any streets be obstructed by teams or otherwise. Particular attention must be given that public crossings are not blocked, to the inconvenience of the public.

On Sidings. 15. Conductors of trains, when occupying or using side tracks, must personally know that their trains and cars clear the main track, for any passing train or trains, and when ready to leave, THAT SWITCHES ARE SET RIGHT FOR THE MAIN TRACK and locked. Cars left on side tracks must have their wheels well blocked and brakes set.

R. R. Crossings 16. All trains must come to a full stop at the distance of FOUR HUNDRED FEET from all crossings at grade of other railroads, and will not proceed until the Engineer has blown two short blasts with whistle, and the Conductor is satisfied that the track is clear. Brakemen on passenger trains are required to stand at the brake wheels on approaching R. R crossings ready to apply the brakes in case the air brake fails to work. Engineers are required to try the air brakes a sufficient distance from R. R. crossings to ascertain if in working order, and if not in order must signal brakemen to apply brakes. It is the duty of Conductors to see that these rules are strictly observed.

Following Trains 17. When one train follows another, great care must be taken to avoid rear collisions. The following train must proceed with great caution, and keep at least one mile in the rear, and between Latty and B & N. W. Junction, not less than two miles in the rear with train under full control.

Speed of Trains. 18. THE SPEED OF PASSENGER TRAINS MUST NEVER EXCEED THIRTY-FIVE MILES PER HOUR. FREIGHT TRAINS MUST NOT BE RUN FASTER THAN FIFTEEN MILES PER HOUR. CONSTRUCTION TRAINS EIGHTEEN MILES PER HOUR. ALL TRAINS MUST BE RUN VERY CAREFULLY OVER TRACK, BRIDGES, CULVERTS, ETC., NOT IN GOOD CONDITION, AND AT A LOW RATE OF SPEED. Conductors and Engineers will be held strictly responsible for any violation of this order.

Report of Trains. 19. Conductors of all freight trains, before leaving any Telegraph Station, must furnish the Telegraph Operator, on the blanks printed for that purpose, a report of the number of loads and empties in his train, together with the arriving and leaving time of the train. Operators will telegraph this report to Train Dispatcher's office.

Leaving Stations 20. No trains WILL UNDER ANY CIRCUMSTANCES leave a Station before the time specified in the Time Table, unless specially authorized to do so.

Time Used. 21. It is important that the time allowed in the Table (except so much as may be required at stations to perform the work in a prompt and expeditious manner) should be consumed in running regularly and evenly over the road. Conductors are required to give this their especial attention.

Stoppage on Main Track. 22. In cases of accident or stoppage on the main track, from any cause, Conductors must immediately station men with torpedoes and red signals at least six hundred yards or seven hundred paces distant in both directions, and if on a down grade 1 000 yards distant on the up-grade end. Two torpedoes must invariably be used at night time, or in day time when view is obstructed, in addition to the regular day and night danger signals, and when flagmen are recalled one torpedo will be left on rail.

Report of accidents. 23. All accidents, including breakage, getting off the track uncoupling of trains, &c., or failure in any way of the engines, must be reported by the Conductor to the SUPERINTENDENT by Telegraph, and as soon as practicable a written report must be made to him as per instructions for guidance of Conductors and other train men in case of accidents. Delays to passenger trains of ten minutes or more, and to freight trains of twenty minutes or more, will be reported to the Superintendent, giving cause of delay.

Engineers use of air and Steam Brakes. 24. Engineers when applying air brakes must not use the full pressure of the air, except in case of emergency. For ordinary stops, the air must be applied slowly, and at a sufficient distance from the stopping place to enable them to stop without discomfort to passengers, sliding the wheels, or injury to the machinery of the train. Engineers will use their steam brake only in switching at stations, or in case of emergency.

Engineers. 25. Engineers of wild trains will, in every instance, when approaching curves or like dangerous localities, sound the whistle, that section men may be properly warned.

Engineers will run as nearly as practicable upon Time-Card and with regularity, and will be equally responsible with Conductors for keeping off the time of other trains.

Drinking. 26 Drunkenness, or drinking intoxicating liquors while on duty, is strictly prohibited, under penalty of dismissal.

Signals.

Red Signals Carried on Engines. 27. Two (2) *red flags* by day, or two (2) *red lights* by night, carried upon the front of an engine, indicates that another train or engine is following, *which has precisely the same Time Card rights as the engine bearing the signal, and* NO MORE. Double signals are used as a measure of safety only; if from any cause but one signal is displayed it will give the same rights as two.

Other Flag and Lantern Signals. 28. A white flag by day, or a white light by night, borne on the front of an engine shows the train to be wild. Conductors of all wild trains must see that their engine carries a white signal.

29. A red flag by day, or a red light by night, waved upon the track, signifies that a train must come to a full stop. So of all violent signals.

30. A red flag by day, or a red light by night, placed *between the rails* signifies that the *track is impassable* and when seen trains must come to a full stop and cause be ascertained.

31. A stationary red flag by day, or red light by night, at the *side* of the track, signifies that the track is not in good order, and must be run over with great care.

32. In running at night a head light must be carried on each engine, and kept in good order, and *always lighted*, and *two red lights* must be carried on the *rear* of each freight train, and two red lights on the *rear* of each passenger train.

Signals with Engine Gong. 33. One stroke of the Engine Gong signifies STOP; two strokes, GO AHEAD; three strokes BACK UP.

Signals with Whistle. 34. 1. One short sound, Apply brakes. 2. Two short sounds, Let off brakes. 3. Three short sound, Back up. 4. Four short sounds, Recall flagmen. 5. One long and two short sounds, Highway crossings. 6. One long sound, R. R. crossing or station. 7. Five or more sounds. Stop the train. 8. Two short sounds followed by one short sound—observe signals carried by engine—which will be answered in the same manner, if signals are noticed.

35. Engineers must sound the whistle when within one-half mile of Station, also when approaching bridges undergoing repairs.

Signals with Lantern. 36. Raised and Lowered vertically, to go ahead. Swung across the track, to stop. Swung in a circle, to back up.

37. The engine bell must be rung 80 rods before crossing a public highway, and be kept ringing until the crossing is passed. Likewise, when moving about stations, and when passing or meeting trains on sidings.

Call attention to Signals. 38. Conductors and Engineers of every train carrying signals for another train must be particular to call the attention of Conductors and Engineers of trains they meet or pass, also other employes concerned, to the signal carried. Signals must in all cases be carried on the front of an engine, in full view of the Engineer and Fireman.

Signal Board at Cedar Rapids. 39. When the Signal Board at south end of double track, Cedar Rapids, is in a horizontal position, trains of the B., C. R. & N. R'y have the right to pass. When in a vertical position, C. & N. W. R'y trains have the right to track. The position of signal board will be indicated at night by *two* red lights.

Rules and regulations for employees. Burlington, Cedar Rapids & Northern Railroad, to take effect December 9, 1883. Photograph courtesy of University of Iowa, Special Collections.

Railroad freight brakeman setting the hand brake. Engraving from
Scribner's Monthly, November 1888.

Hobsbawm uses as one means of identifying "labor aristocrats." [24] Those engineers who acquired regular freight or passenger runs generally enjoyed high and stable earnings, but recently promoted engineers with relatively little seniority saw their earnings fluctuate wildly with the level of business and their assignment to irregular runs.

Engineers enjoyed considerable independence in their work. In the early decades of railroading, they hired their own "cubs" (firemen), though this privilege was gradually lost. [25] They festered under the conductor's technical authority to manage the train, although the latter had no real voice in how the engine was run. From the time an engineer received his orders until he delivered his engine to the roundhouse at the end of the run, he was his own boss. Locomotive engineers held widely differing views of the proper relations between themselves, other employees, and higher officials. A significant number of engineers saw the interests of engineers and the railroads they served as identical. These views were faithfully represented by the national leadership of the Brotherhood of Locomotive Engineers.

The Brotherhood of Locomotive Engineers, initially dubbed the Brotherhood of the Footboard, was formed on the Michigan Central in 1863. Craft exclusiveness was the hallmark of the organization from the outset. Faithfulness to that principle, it was argued, and to the "Grand and Comprehensive Principles of the Order"— "Sobriety, Truth, Justice, and Morality"—would lead to an amelioration of the conflict between labor and capital. As Charles Wilson, the organization's first grand chief engineer, put it, the objective of the brotherhood was "to win the good graces of the employers through elevating the character of its members and thus raising their efficiency as workmen. The employer would be so well pleased with their work that he would of his own free will provide better recognition of labor and higher pay." [26]

Wilson's successor as grand chief was Peter M. Arthur, who though initially classed as an insurgent quickly adopted his predecessor's more conservative views. Arthur, who commonly lectured at brotherhood conventions on the mutual interest of labor and capital, wrote in 1886, "Much has been said and more written concerning the antagonism between capital and labor. To my mind there is no such thing. I will venture to say that most men of thrifty and industrious habits are capitalists. When we consider that capital is only invested wealth, I hope there is not one among you, my hearers, but can count himself a capitalist, be your pile ever so small. The workingman of today may be the capitalist five or ten years from now."[27]

The brotherhood fostered an image of respectability and officially forswore alliances with other labor organizations. This stance and the convoluted pomp and ceremony of brotherhood conventions and balls brought much criticism from engineers within the order and even more from railroad men in other occupations. Such opposition notwithstanding, the brotherhood style of organization had wide influence, not only among locomotive engineers, but also among railroad men in other less-well-remunerated callings. A yearning after the kind of respectability enjoyed by engineers was reflected in the imitative balls and convention proceedings of the brotherhoods of other operating trades.

The period was one of flux, and engineers were not immune to change. As the scarcity of engineers diminished, their status was called into question and their earnings were subjected to serious downward pressure. Calling himself "Patsy Poke the Fire," a locomotive fireman wrote to the *Firemen's Magazine* during the Burlington strike of 1888 that "it has been shown to a certainty that the refusal of the engineers and firemen to continue in the company's service does not tie up the road."[28] The Burlington, Iowa, *Saturday Evening Post* exulted with some measure of exaggeration: "It is probably true that if every locomotive engineer in the United States now running a train were to be incapacitated tomorrow from further service on the rail, the trains could be moved again in less than a week with a capable force enlisted from the ranks of this great army of the reserve."[29]

Conductors did not have earnings comparable to those of locomotive engineers. However, their trade had certain characteristics that gave it eligibility for membership in the fraternity of elite railroad trades. Conductors were the officers technically in charge of the trains they worked, with more general authority than engineers. They supervised from two to four brakemen. Their responsibility for overseeing freight and passengers brought them into contact with agents of the company at many points. Generally, they did no manual labor, but supervised that of others. The privileged position of conductors within the train service was touched relatively little by technological change. If anything, as the size of trains grew, their responsibilities increased, and their identification with management became more firmly established. The Order of Railway Conductors (ORC), founded in 1868, was until 1891 infamous in the circles of organized railroad workers for its identification with the interests of management. Under the hot-house conditions of the early 1890s, a segment of the ORC member-ship left the organization to form a new union, the Brotherhood of Railroad Conductors, which was more closely identified with mili-tant segments of other railroad trades.[30]

The Less Skilled: Firemen, Brakemen, and Switchmen

Fireman and brakeman were entry positions in the running trades. The work entailed arduous and frequently dangerous labor as a price for the promise of future promotion. Firemen were most com-monly recruited from unskilled workers in railroad shops who pos-sessed qualities that caught the eye of a master mechanic. Engine wipers frequently were tapped when regular firemen did not ap-pear for a scheduled run. They were generally young, had acquired some knowledge of the engines, and, most importantly, were avail-able. Eugene Debs's experience was typical. While painting stripes on cars in a Terre Haute railroad shop one night in 1871, Debs found himself summarily drafted by an angry yard engineer whose fireman was too drunk to work.[31] Firemen, like engineers, moved through a series of promotions from irregular to regular service and from less-favorable to more-favorable runs.[32] For firemen who as-pired to positions on the other side of the cab, the length of time they had to wait for promotion was of critical importance.

Brakemen were most often green hands to railroad work. Before the late 1890s, when air brakes became common on freight traffic, their primary responsibility was to set the hand brakes when sig-naled to do so by the engineer. It was exceedingly dangerous work, made even more so by exposure to the elements. Brakemen also performed incidental services as flagmen, baggagemen, clerks, and switchmen when needed out on the road. They were responsible to the conductor, and to the extent that they sought promotion, brake-men aspired to become conductors. But for every freight conductor, there could be as many as four brakemen. Because of their more limited prospects for promotion and the risks inherent in their trade, turnover among brakemen was much higher than in any of the other running trades.[33]

Fireman and brakemen organized brotherhoods modeled on the experience of the engineers. The Brotherhood of Locomotive Fire-men was founded in 1873, weathered the 1877 railroad strikes, and only developed the protective features of a trade union after 1885. Although the firemen's relations with the Brotherhood of Locomotive Engineers were strained on occasion, they did not deviate fundamentally from the organizational model offered by the engineers. The Brotherhood of Railroad Brakemen was established in 1883 and bore no direct lineage to the industrial unions—the Brakemen's Brotherhood or Trainmen's Union—that preceded it in the 1870s. The brakemen renamed their organization the Brotherhood of Railroad Trainmen in 1886 and, thereafter, claimed some jurisdiction over switchmen and flagmen. This dual unionism produced sharp jurisdictional conflict with the Switchmen's Mutual Aid Association in the early 1890s and effectively destroyed the first serious attempt to federate the operating trades. Like the firemen, the brakemen who organized their brotherhood in the 1880s looked to the engineers for their model.

Switchmen deserve particular attention in this review of railroad trades because of their strategic importance in railroad operations and their prominence in the labor conflicts of the late nineteenth century. They occupied a peculiar niche in the world of railroad employment. Their work of making up trains from a collection of cars connected them directly not only to men in the operating trades but to workers in allied industries—meat packing, grain milling, freight handling—whose products were shipped by rail. Though immobile by comparison with enginemen and trainmen whose work ranged over hundreds of miles, switchmen, at least in larger metropolitan centers, moved routinely from one rail yard to another with the interchange of cars. In regular contact with men on other railroads, they were a natural bridge between workers employed on different roads. They were the quintessential sympathy strikers whose actions could quickly disrupt traffic over a wide territory.

Switchmen worked by the day or hour, rather than by the mile or piece, and though their hours might be long (often twelve or more), they were fairly predictable by comparision with the hours of men in the running trades. Switchmen were not forced to live away from home part of the time. Unlike the running trades, they were directly supervised in their work by a foreman (only slightly removed from the ground switchman) and by a yardmaster and his assistants. Supervisors had direct authority over the pace, the distribution of work, and the length of the work day. Switchmen enjoyed relatively little opportunity for significant occupational or income advancement.[34] Foremen earned only $5 to $10 more per month than ordinary switchmen; wages of $65 for switchmen and

$70 or $75 for foremen were standard during the 1880s. Positions of yardmaster were relatively few and were frequently filled from the ranks of white-collar workers. It was not routine for switchmen to be recruited onto the occupational ladder for the running trades, though some did move into brakemen's positions when the demand for labor was great. The wages of switchmen were in general slightly lower than those of brakemen, although there were important exceptions.[35] Because payment by the hour and overtime pay were won by switchmen much later than by the running trades, switchmen's pay did not enjoy the same kind of seasonal bulge (although the work intensified), and, consequently, annual earnings fell further below those of brakemen.[36]

Switchmen must in most respects be classified as relatively unskilled workers. According to Joel Seidman, men were regularly put on as extras with as little as three days training in signals, safety, and working rules.[37] By all accounts, their work was the most dangerous in railroading, involving ceaseless, deft movement in and out between railroad cars which were usually in motion.[38] Switchmen were generally regarded in the nineteenth century as the most transient of railroad men.[39] Yet in spite of apparently high turnover and a relatively low level of skill, which created a large potential supply of labor in cities, switchmen were among the most thoroughly organized railroad men in many centers.

It can be argued that the position of switchmen in the railroad labor market was not all that different from more skilled members of the running trades—their high turnover and easy entry to the trade notwithstanding. While engineers were scarce in some regions during much of the period we are examining and struggled to maintain wages and work rules that preserved their scarcity, switchmen secured their position through thoroughness of organization and militant action. Strikes by switchmen over noneconomic, "control" issues increased in the late 1880s and early 1890s. Their demands for control over the hiring and discharging of supervisors and fellow switchmen represent an attempt to further secure their working world from the arbitrary and unilateral actions of management. They also debated less over work rules than their skilled brothers in the running trades and sought instead direct authority over the selection and tenure of those who managed them. Their control, though achieved by another route, was no less effective in some railroad centers than that of skilled workers, nor was their sense of self-respect and pride in their work any less.[40]

Railroad Shopmen

Shopmen, like switchmen, worked in a specific location and generally by the day or hour, although piece-rate systems for skilled shopmen were beginning to be found in the 1890s. They were supervised directly, but the extent of the traditional autonomy enjoyed by machinists and other skilled craftsmen varied greatly from one shop to another. Within railroad shops there was a wide range of crafts and a complex hierarchy of skill. Traditionally, occupational advancement had been almost exclusively from apprentice to journeyman. However, as the number of helpers, handymen, and specialists increased in relation to the number of journeymen and since movement from one class to another was not precisely regulated, occupational advancement became less predictable. What is clear is that many shopmen were frozen below journeyman status and that opportunities for earnings above those of journeymen were very limited. In 1892 a journeyman machinist's wages were closer to a railroad brakeman's or fireman's than to a locomotive engineer's. While railroad shop machinists averaged $2.41 a day, brakemen averaged $1.98, firemen, $2.13, and engineers, $3.85. Carpenters in railroad shops averaged $2.16, and all other shopmen (including skilled men such as boilermakers and blacksmiths as well as the unskilled) averaged $1.81.[41]

Railroad shopmen worked in a factory-like situation. Their numbers included a variety of craftsmen in both metals and wood, along with their apprentices, helpers, and laborers. Because of the repair nature of much of their work, craftsmen continually confronted problems that could not be handled by standard processes. Their skills had to be "all-around" in one sense. Many problems had to be met in an ad-hoc way to get rolling stock back on the track in the shortest possible time. There was a hierarchy of repair shops from the most outlying roundhouses, through larger shops at division headquarters towns, to the main company shops where not only repair but new construction was undertaken.

Skilled railroad shopmen were aware of the low wages they earned in comparison with men in the running trades, and they struck frequently to resist further reductions. However, in the face of the dilution of their skills at the hands of cost-cutting railroad management, their more pressing concern was maintaining some control over the supply of skilled labor and, most importantly, the integrity of their crafts.

P. J. Conlon, a vice-president of the International Association of

Machinists in the twentieth century, put it quite simply in a retrospective look at the machinists' trade, "The wage of a machinist is controlled by the idle market. If there are hundreds of idle machinists applying for positions daily, the tendency of the wage is downward. If the demand for machinists cannot be supplied, extra monetary consideration is the inducement that will secure men."[42] The problem of a growing surplus of machinists and other skilled railroad shopmen had two aspects. On the one hand, certain technological changes and managerial practices were reducing the numbers of skilled men required for many railroad shop tasks. On the other hand, the comparatively high wages in the West were a reflection of a relative scarcity of skilled labor and an inducement toward greater mobility, which ultimately lowered those wage rates. This was, of course, characteristic of the entire railroad labor market. The militant resistance of western shopmen to the wage reductions of 1885–86 and 1893–94 was an attempt to protect relatively high wages in the face of a growing labor surplus.

Changing Composition of the Railroad Labor Force

The distribution of trades within the railroad labor force was wide.[43] In 1890 locomotive engineers comprised only 4.5 percent of the work force nationally. The relatively anonymous trackmen were more than four times as numerous, being 21 percent of the work force. But when clustered in three obvious occupational groups—running trades, shopmen, and maintanance of way—each group comprised roughly equal shares—20 percent to 25 percent of the labor force. By comparison, management and white-collar employees—officers, clerks, agents, operators, and dispatchers— were between 9 percent and 10 percent of the total (table 7).

The railroad labor market was comprised of a complex structure of old trades and new, of finely subdivided hierarchies of skill and large pools of immobile and unskilled labor, and of well-worn promotional paths and exceptional opportunities for advancement. Above all, the size of the labor force and the mobility of workers within it were governed by the extraordinary expansion and contraction of the demand for labor. Two aspects of the distribution of trades within the labor force bear closer scrutiny. First, an industry that expanded geographically at an uneven rate created substantial sectional differentials in the growth and distribution of the labor force. Second, the mix of skilled and unskilled workers, particularly in the railroad shops, changed over time and at different rates

Table 7.   Railroad Labor Force, 1890

Title	Number	Percent
General officers	5,160	.7
General office clerks	22,239	3.0
Station agents	25,665	3.4
Telegraph operators and dispatch	18,968	2.5
Other stationmen	66,431	8.9
Engineers	33,354	4.5
Fireman	34,634	4.6
Conductors	23,513	3.1
Trainmen	61,734	8.2
Machinists	27,601	3.7
Carpenters	37,936	5.1
Other shopmen	80,733	10.8
Section foremen	27,129	3.6
Other trackmen	157,036	21.0
Switchmen	37,669	5.0
Empl.—floating equipt.	6,199	.8
All other employees	83,300	11.1
Total	749,301	100

Source: U.S. Department of the Interior, ("Railway Labor" Washington: 1893), from Eleventh Census of the United States (1890), vol. 4.

from one section to another because of differences in the application of technological changes.

Between 1880 and 1905 the railroad labor force increased by 230 percent. The rate of growth varied substantially from one section to another. In the East, the number of men employed on the railroads grew by 157 percent, from 244,359 to 620,822 men. In the West, railroad employment grew more than sevenfold during the same period, from 38,668 to 323,202 workers. In the South, railroad employment grew more slowly but still above the national average.[44] These differences in the growth of the railroad labor force suggest differences in the demand for labor that had a powerful effect on the migration, the expectations, and the organization of railroad workers.

Not only did the labor force grow, but the mix of railroad trades changed from one decade to another and from one section of the country to another. Railroad enginemen—engineers and firemen—were relatively immune to the effects of technological change. Changes in locomotive design and traction did not create opportunities for the substitution of less-skilled for more-skilled workers. The ratio of firemen to engineers remained virtually constant throughout this period, regardless of section. The same cannot be claimed for trainmen or shopmen.

Changes in coupling and braking technology that were gradually introduced led to the elimination of one or more brakemen per train. The rate of displacement, however, varied significantly from a 25 percent reduction in the East to a 48 percent reduction in the West. Air brakes were used earlier and more widely in the West. Only in the twentieth century was technological parity between regions achieved.[45]

Skilled railroad shopmen, and particularly machinists, did not enjoy the insulation from the effects of technological change that enginemen experienced. The standardization of locomotive and car construction, the increasing use of templates and interchangeable parts, the routinization of repair and maintenance, and its consignment to specialized shops meant that increasing numbers of workers specializing in a single operation or the use of a particular machine could be substituted for the all-around machinist or other skilled worker. Indeed, the ratio of machinists to "other shopmen" fell by over 47 percent between 1880 and 1905. Again, the sectional figures are even more dramatic than the national figures would suggest. In the West the ratio of machinists to other shopmen declined by 84 percent, while in the East, the decline was a mere 3 percent. The displacement of machinists from railroad shops during the late nineteenth century was to a large extent a western phenomenon, on newer roads with newer technology.

A dynamic if fitfully growing railroad industry in the late nineteenth century offered eastern and western railroad workers very different and essentially transitory opportunities. Rapid growth led to extraordinary labor market demand in the West that, in turn, precipitated changes in technology, work rules, and modes of payment as railroad managers tried to reduce labor costs.

The Determination of Wages

The income that railroad workers earned for the labor they performed was governed first by the basic rate of their wages. That rate varied widely depending on their trade, the region in which they worked, and the unit of work upon which that rate was based. Their income was also affected by the regularity of employment—a function of the season, the state of business, and their seniority. Finally, a number of other factors affected their net income. These were gradually defined in a series of wage-related work rules and included overtime, apprenticeship, delayed time, deadheading, special service, extra mileage rates, and "arbitrary" allowances.

We have already noted the wide variation in wage rates among different trades and among regions for the same trade. Most railroad work outside of the running trades was performed for a specific daily rate. The length of the day was defined. For these trades, there was generally no attempt to define a unit of work in terms other than the work-time elapsed.[46]

Because the work of men in the running trades varied so widely both in intensity and in the number of hours worked, the basis for their pay showed wide variation and was a constant point of contention with management. When we picture the movement of trains over a road, we usually think of carefully framed train schedules and the remarkable ability of engine and train crews to perform their tasks within the predictable parameters of those schedules. In fact, only a relatively small proportion of most railroad freight traffic followed regular schedules. "Irregular service," as it was called, came to be the rule rather than the exception for freight traffic in the late nineteenth century, and the ratio of freight to passenger crews was at least three to one, and on some roads even higher.[47] Freight trains were made up on demand. When sufficient freight had accumulated, crews were called (commonly on the basis of "first in, first out") and the train dispatched under special orders.

Until the early 1880s, and even later on newer roads, regular freight service was more common. Engine crews operated their own engines regularly and exclusively and also did a great deal of the routine maintenance on their engines.[48] As might be expected, wages were paid on the basis of a standard day's work—a run (or series of short runs) and the attendant engine maintanance was conveniently defined as a day.[49] Some roads even guaranteed their engineers a certain number of days' work in a month. With increased traffic, the pressure to keep engines in constant service grew. The volume of freight, combined with its irregularity, fractured schedules. Although some regular freights were usually maintained, irregulars became the rule. As engines were "pooled," engine crews fought to have some of their roundhouse work eliminated and demanded that they be called on a "first in, first out" basis, so as to equitably distribute the work among the available crews. Since their irregular work was no longer predictable or easily measured in terms of days, a struggle that lasted nearly two decades erupted over how to measure and compensate the work performed.

Many factors affected both the intensity of the work and the number of hours worked by engine and train crews. Payment computed simply on the basis of days worked did not allow for variations in the difficulty of the work, and it was not common to pay overtime for work of excessive length before the 1880s. Both workers and managers were interested in another system of payment that would reflect their interests more accurately. The men sought compensation for extra work as freight grew in volume and faster engines made longer runs possible; they favored payment according to a fixed rate per mile. Managers wanted flexibility and a system of payment that did not itemize the work performed; they preferred payment according to the trip.

Trip Rates, Mileage Rates, and "Arbitraries"

In the early 1880s, a system of payment known as "trip rates" emerged, although its practice, particularly on western roads where it met determined resistance, was not long-lived.[50] Under the trip system, which was a form of piece-rate payment, every run was assigned a specific and unique rate. In theory, the rates were designed to reflect peculiarities of each run, such as length, difficulty, number of stops, and special labor required. By 1889, only fourteen out of sixty roads in the West still maintained trip rates. Some eastern and southern roads, however, such as the Pennsylvania and the Louisville and Nashville, maintained trip rates well into the twentieth century.[51]

In his negotiations with the engineers' grievance committee in 1886, T. J. Potter, general manager of the Chicago, Burlington & Quincy (C. B. & Q.) Railroad, offered "to take up every run there is on the system . . . and adjust it to what we think is right." "But," he asserted, "when it comes to fixing wages, it is clear that they cannot be the same all over even these roads which the C. B. & Q. does own, because the circumstances and conditions which fix prices in Chicago, for instance, may be very different from those affecting prices 1100 miles away in Denver." And he added, "Wages may be higher in Colorado than in Illinois."[52] Under such a trip system, wage rates could vary from one run to the next within the same division, and they could vary sustantially between divisions according to the state of the railroad labor market as reflected in prevailing wage rates. Such variations on the Pennsylvania were enormous, because the company bargained separately with local committees and distributed favors in the form of higher trip rates among the "natural leaders" so as to retard the spread of union-ism.[53]

Men in the running trades had two primary objections to the trip system of payment. The first was that it "fails to itemize the details of the service," as William Z. Ripley noted. "That is precisely the advantage to the employer of the plan for branch-line work where little division of labor obtains and where all sorts of incidentals creep into the day's work."[54] As engineers saw the labor for which they were compensated defined more and more specifically in terms of the trip, they came to redefine "engineers' work" to exclude that labor for which they were not compensated. Engineers and firemen, in negotiations with the management of the Northern Pacific Railroad in December 1893, sought to eliminate a provision of the proposed schedule of wages that would have required engineers to do work other than that falling within an "engineer's duty."

> Mr. Vetter (Engineer): We object to this rule as under its application an engineer may be required to do work that is not considered engineers' duty. They might tell an engineer to wipe his engine or clean his fire or file his brasses or do machinist's work. . . .
> Mr. Kendrick (General Manager): What determines what an engineer's duty is?
> Mr. Vetter: I don't know; general practice, I suppose. An engineer gets paid by the mile for running an engine. He does not get paid for keeping her in repair.
> Mr. Hickey (Superintendent of Motive Power): . . . But if your time should belong to the company you should be willing to do anything reasonable you should be asked to do.[55]

The second objection that engine and trainmen had to the trip system was that it encouraged individual bargaining. As Ripley noted, "By covering up, in one lump sum, all the possibilities of incidental service . . . it thus renders it possible to bid one man against another to the utter breakdown of standardization"[56] This was a primary issue in the Great Burlington Strike of 1888 in which engineers sought to get one standard mileage rate for all freight service whether branch-line or mainline and regardless of division.[57]

The mileage system of payment was relatively simple. Men were compensated for the miles run at a specific rate per mile. A minimum rate based on the standard 100 miles was demanded and written into most schedules beginning in the mid-1880s. The mileage rate became a scaffolding on which was hung a variety of payment plans designed to compensate for exceptional types of work. Freight and passenger rates were differentiated, the former being paid at a higher rate to compensate for slower movement over an equivalent distance.[58]

All runs did not arbitrarily stop at 100 miles, nor was it always possible to complete even a 100-mile run within a reasonable length of time because of accidents, delays, and road conditions. Some type of overtime to cover both miles and time was sought by men in the running trades. By 1885 a system of dual compensation was beginning to find its way into the wage schedules.[59] Initially, any miles over the basic 100 were to be compensated at the same rate per mile (in some cases a higher or lower rate per mile was specified). This did not provide for time delays that extended the working hours beyond the conventional ten. The Missouri Pacific schedule of 1885 was the first to introduce overtime based on hours of work. It provided that on freight runs of under 100 miles but extending beyond twelve hours, workers would be compensated at the overtime rate of thirty-five cents an hour. On runs of more than 100 miles that extended beyond twelve hours, workers were to be paid on the same overtime basis for all hours above ten.[60]

Finally, an innovation in the schedule of engineers on the Minneapolis, St. Paul & Manitoba Railroad in 1885 laid the basis for a system of combined miles and overtime hours, which was to become common in the twentieth century. Under this clause, overtime was figured on a "speed" basis. That is, the length of a run was divided by a standard speed (usually 10 mph, or 100 miles in ten hours) to figure the number of hours a given run should consume before overtime would commence. If the run was 130 miles, overtime would begin after thirteen hours (but the men would be compensated for the 30 miles above 100 at the usual mileage rate).[61] These rules spread slowly, though as Ripley points out, they were generally accepted more rapidly west of the Mississippi, "either because conditions were worse or because the demand for labor was greater."[62]

On the scaffolding of mileage pay rates were added a variety of what were called "arbitraries," which were rules negotiated into wage schedules and designed to provide specific compensation for specific extra duties or hardships. While the speed basis of overtime had the effect of converting the mileage pay system to a quasi time-basis of compensation, the introduction of arbitraries created what appeared to be a new "trip" basis of pay. One of the most common arbitraries was the payment of "extra mileage" on certain runs. According to the men, these "fictitious miles (defining a run of 100 actual miles as having 130 miles for wage purposes), represented legitimate compensation for increased labor required on mountainous runs and reimbursement of higher living costs in remote regions (a cost of living clause). To management, the case for "extra mileage" rested solely on its need to attract labor where it was scarce. Once the supply of labor was adequate, this "arbitrary" was dispensable.[63]

The determination of wages was a constant point of contention between railroad workers and their employers. Whereas workers sought to standardize wage rates, win extra compensation for special conditions, and earn overtime for work beyond the standard day, the railroad corporations sought to individualize pay, lump all compensation under an undifferentiated trip payment, and maintain flexibility in job classifications and the prerogative to assign work.

The Supply of Labor

Conflicts over wage determination were symptoms of underlying shifts in the market for railroad labor. Earnings were a function not only of the mode of compensation but of the rates of payment as well. Those wage rates were above all conditioned by the supply of workers available. During the late nineteenth centry, the supply of railroad workers varied significantly from one section to another. Writing in the early twentieth century, economist W. Z. Ripley suggested that many work rules and labor practices were first adopted in the nineteenth century under conditions of labor scarcity in the West and then spread "like the measles" from road to road. Recognition of unions and collective agreements followed naturally under such conditions; however, roads that enjoyed a more favorable supply of labor were in a position to resist collective bargaining and pay lower wages. As Ripley noted,

> Remotely located properties with hardships incident to desert or mountainous operation, with harsh living conditions, were compelled not only to pay high rates in order to procure labor, but also to concede the principle of organization, and thereafter to negotiate schedules under a severe handicap. Other roads with more condensed traffic, convenient places of residence for the men, and minuter division of labor, enabling employment of hostlers for engines, switching crews, terminal attendants, and the like were able to procure their labor without conceding so much in the way either of collective bargaining or of rates or rules thereunder.[64]

The substantial regional differences in wages paid to railroad men during the late nineteenth century are mentioned in numerous contemporary sources. For example, during the great Burlington strike of 1888, the Iowa *Burlington Hawkeye* noted the ease with which the C. B. & Q. recruited new engineers and firemen. And once hired the new men seemed immune to the appeals of the strikers because of the higher wages they earned. "The eastern men fairly open their eyes at the wages they are able to make on the Burlington as compared with the lines they left. They are sending on for relatives and friends who are still working on the roads they left."[65]

Even labor of less-exalted skill was in short supply in many regions, especially during the construction of new roads. Contractors for railroad construction competed with each other for laborers and in so doing drove up wages. As Chief Engineer Roswell Mason on the Illinois Central noted in 1853, "Men are scarce. Contractors are bidding against each other and south of the 6th Division contractors are paying all prices from $1 to $1.25 per day. . . . It is a constant struggle to get men, and they are constantly changing from one place to another.[66] Seasonal shortages persisted, due, in part, to the demand for agricultural labor. A correspondent ot the *Union Pacific Employees Magazine* from Laramie, Wyoming, observed in September 1886 that "laborers have been in good demand the past month as many were wanted to go out on the ranches haying. Many of the ranch hands are now through and men become more plentiful"[67]

Interregional migration was a decisive factor in the shifting currents of the late-nineteenth-century railroad labor market. The redistribution of population from East to West appeared most notably in the decade of the 1870s in the states just west of the Mississippi and in the 1880s in the "West 'proper.' "[68] The net loss of native population was heavier in the Northeast and the eastern portions of the north central region than in the southern states. Between 1870 and 1890 the proportion of the population that lived west of the Mississippi grew from 18 percent to 27 percent. During the 1890s westward migration slowed dramatically. The western share of the total population increased by a scant 1 percent. The twentieth century saw little further increase.[69] It is clear that by the 1890s an exceptional period of demographic change, lasting roughly two decades, was completed.

As might be expected, regional shifts in per capita income followed closely on the heels of the westward migration. Between 1880 and 1900 the wide differences in regional incomes narrowed significantly. The largest factor contributing to this convergence of per capita incomes was a sharp decline in the relative position of states in the West, Far West, and upper Middle West. The convergence of incomes is directly attributable to regional shifts in the supply of labor.[70]

The period of the 1870s through the 1890s saw a transition in the market for railroad labor in one region after another, from relative scarcity to relative surplus, characterized by downward pressure on wage levels and the revision of wage-related work rules. That transition, well underway in the East by the depression of the 1870s, was particularly pronounced in the territory west of the Mississippi thereafter. It parallels the general patterns of growth in the labor supply and convergence of personal incomes. By the early twentieth century, data on railroad workers' wages show a general decline from the levels of the 1890s and little regional variation. This convergence strongly suggests a more plentiful supply of railroad labor. Data from the Interstate Commerce Commission in 1908 confirm diminished regional variation in the wages of railroad workers and suggest a largely stabilized railroad labor market.[71]

As railroads expanded westward into relatively unsettled territory, they left behind large population centers and immediately available sources of labor. Once opened up, each road required a full range of railroad trades. The settlement process itself created considerable demand for railroad traffic in both passengers and freight. But the lure of agriculture also created formidable competition to railroads for a relatively limited labor supply.

It was under these conditions that western railroad employees were offered, or won, wage rates that were high relative to those of railroad employees in other parts of the country. They also gained extra mileage rates, overtime, other "arbitraries," and a measure of recognition for their unions, which few eastern railroad men enjoyed. Such advantages, however, were far from stable.

The Railroad Labor Market: Sources of Supply

Several factors tended to increase the supply of railroad men: a natural increase in the population, a relative contraction of agricultural opportunity as land prices rose and better lands were sold, higher earnings and favorable conditions of railroad employment, the push of lower wages and unemployment in the East, and, to some extent, deliberate management strategies to increase the labor supply.

Violent cycles of railroad expansion and contraction led to alternating labor shortage and glut from one season to the next. When traffic volume rose, especially in the fall, and available labor surplus was exhausted, normal paths of occupational advancement were bypassed. Men were hastily promoted, often with inadequate experience, into more skilled positions. As traffic fell off these men were either "bumped" back or put on the "extra board." There was a net increase in skilled men with each phase of the cycle. A railroad worker from Cheyenne, writing to the *Union Pacific Employees Magazine* under the pen name "Critic," suggested that these spasms of contraction and expansion in the labor force had deleterious effects on the level of skill in the railroad work force and the overall operations of the road. "We have stumbled into one of our periodical attacks of economy," he wrote, where experienced men, many of them with families "are sent adrift to seek work hundreds and perhaps thousands of miles away . . . the uncertainty of the situation tends to discourage men of real mechanical skill, who as a rule settle down and build up the place where they work and reside."[72]

Many western railroad companies established recruitment offices or engaged the services of employment agencies in the East to assist them in meeting their supply problems.[73] The brotherhoods through their journals, "union meetings," and annual conventions were important sources of information on conditions of employment and availability of work in various parts of the country. This improved information tended to increase the distance of migration at some skill levels and the effective market area for certain classes of employees.

The high demand for railroad labor in the West and the generally high levels of mobility among railroad workers combined with the interrelatedness of many occupations to create unusually high levels of occupational interchangeability among many classes of railroad employment.[74] Most hostlers and firemen could run an engine over the road if necessary. Brakemen and switchmen performed closely allied work and were, under certain conditions, interchangeable. Brakemen were only a step away from conductors, and many were capable, on short notice, of moving into their shoes. Nearly all skilled men had worked at lower grades and were capable of doing so again. These circumstances tended to create more flexible supply conditions. There were frequent sharply drawn battles over work rules that defined a job and the person capable of performing it. The railroads sought flexibility in order to use their available labor to best advantage. Workers sought to protect their earnings by restricting the number of men who could do certain jobs.

The ways in which railroads disciplined their labor force had a significant impact on the supply of labor. It was common for men in the running trades to be suspended for a variety of offenses, from running through switches to being responsible for major or minor accidents.[75] Suspensions varied in length from one division to another depending on the temperament and practice of the local master mechanic. But they inevitably required adjustments in the labor force to fill such vacancies. Strike activity and the increasing use of the blacklist during this period provide a measure of "involuntary" turnover that amounted to 38 percent of the men involved in unsuccessful strikes.[76] It was commonly charged that one strike's blacklisted workers became the next strike's scabs. True or not, the Brotherhood of Locomotive Engineers decided in the 1880s to stop publishing the names of those men expelled from the brotherhood in the hope of eliminating another source of scabs. Disciplinary suspensions and firings swelled the supply of labor as new workers were promoted or hired to fill the vacancies.

Another means by which employers could affect the supply of labor was to "promote from within" as opposed to hiring skilled men from outside. Complaints against this practice poured into the brotherhood journals from the mid-1880s onward.[77] General Manager Clarke of the Illinois Central was frustrated in his attempts to cut engineers' wages to the extent he wanted to in 1877; he saw promotion from within as the key. "It would be a good thing," he argued, "if all the railroads of note in Illinois would make about twenty-five engineers per year, so as to produce a surplus of this grade of employees."[78] Pressured by the brotherhoods, many railroads finally agreed to a formula for regulating promotion and the hiring of skilled workers; for engineers it was most commonly a 1:1 or 2:1 ratio. By the time such rules were adopted, much of the damage had already been done. The supply of skilled railroad men had been increased.

One consequence of an increased number of railroad workers was that the rate of turnover among railroad men declined noticeably as competition for job opportunities increased. This tendency was somewhat offset at the lower levels of the job ladder as promotion slowed down and some frustrated younger men migrated in search of other opportunities. Another consequence was that as regional differentials in the supply of labor diminished, wages became more standardized from one region to the next.

Although technological change offered relatively few opportunities for reducing the railroads' requirements for skilled labor in the running trades, the opportunities were more abundant in the railroad shops. The mix of skilled and unskilled shopmen underwent a notable change during the 1880s, particularly in the West. The introduction of new technologies and innovations in personnel management contributed directly to the relative decline in the numbers of skilled men in railroad shops.

During the 1880s railroad managers debated the merits of having railroad cars and locomotives built in "contract" shops rather than by the roads themselves. The superintendent of a railroad shop noted in the *Railway Gazette* the economies in labor that might be expected under the contract system. "Working continually on the same operations enables a mechanic to do much more work than when he is continually changing operations."[79] A few years earlier, a correspondent to the *Engineers Journal* had criticized the outmoded practices of the Cleveland, Columbus, Cincinnati, and Indianapolis Railroad (C. C. C. & I.) shops in Cleveland where eight-wheel engines were individually built with no standardization of parts. Western shops, it was noted, were building the same type of engine for 13 percent less through the use of templates. The C. C. C. & I. "engines were not interchangeable, and the men were of the universal class—working on this job today and that tomorrow."[80] Standardization in western shops led to the introduction of

126

specialists—workers who were proficient on one machine or in one operation but who did not have the all-around skill of journeymen machinists. The declining position of skilled machinists is vividly illustrated in the payroll records for the West Burlington shops of the Chicago, Burlington and Quincy Railroad. As these shops grew in size and importance within the C. B. & Q. system, the ratio of skilled machinists to helpers and apprentices declined from .82 in 1894 to .62 in 1900.[81]

Some railroads attacked the apprentice system directly by increasing the numbers of apprentices and shortening the time for apprenticeship. P. J. Conlon recalled his own experience in western railroad shops:

> The worst feature, however, was the fact that young apprentice boys and helpers were representing themselves as machinists in such numbers that all confidence in the craft was being lost and master mechanics and proprietors said to themselves we will make our own men. This they started to do with an energy that almost took away the breath of the machinists of that day. I witnessed in one western shop in 1890 the spectacle of sixteen apprenticeboys to one journeyman. By actual count there was ninety-six apprentice boys and six machinists in this one shop. Of course this naturally contracted the market for a machinist to sell his labor.[82]

By the opening years of the twentieth century, the place of the specialist in the industry was well established, so well, in fact, that the International Association of Machinists (IAM) in a defensive move broadened its membership criteria to include "any man working in a machine shop and engaged in any manner with the making or repairing of machinery."[83] Although restriction of the number of apprentices in machine shops was again agreed to by most employers, control of the trade by journeymen machinists had already been undermined through the entry into the shops of large numbers of semiskilled machine operators and specialists.

Beginning in the mid-1880s, as these changes began to be felt, many shopmen, like switchmen, sought the security of broader organization and abandoned the exclusive commitment to the restriction of numbers as a strategy for protection. Somewhat later and less completely, men in the running trades also abandoned restrictive organization for federation and ultimately industrial unionism.

127

The Shifting Frontier of Labor Scarcity

While the general outlines of the transition from labor scarcity to labor surplus are clear, and indicators of the change can be indentified on various roads at different times, it is difficult to pinpoint within regions the precise timing of the transition. When engineers and firemen struck the Chicago, Burlington & Quincy in 1888, they discovered that the supply of engineers available to replace them was greater than they had estimated. This was due partly to the fact that their actions activated a variety of supply-increasing mechanisms—migration, promotion, occupational interchangeability, and the willingness of men blacklisted from other strikes to take their positions. It was not until 1893–94 that roads such as the Union Pacific and Northern Pacific, serving some of the same territory, felt in a position to risk a walkout as they attempted to reduce wage differentials between themselves and other roads. Perhaps they had misread the actual supply conditions, or perhaps they had hesitated to act for a variety of other reasons, but by the time of the Pullman boycott of 1894, they proved that they could readily replace nearly every man who struck, even while many other roads were doing the same thing.

It is clear from the available wage data, inadequate though they are, that between 1880 and 1900 substantial sectional differences in the wages of railroad workers existed.* Those differences tended to be reduced during this twenty-year period, particularly during the 1890s, with western regions registering reductions in wage rates and eastern regions showing modest increases.

For the period 1880 through 1889, wage data for engineers from a cross section of state bureaus of labor statistics demonstrate the existence of sectional differences in the average daily wage (figure 9).[84] The wages of eastern engineers were lower and showed greater volatility, particularly during the depression of 1884–85, than those of western and midwestern engineers. The limited nature of the data for the 1880s makes it difficult to draw other conclusions. Sectional differences in switchmen's wages in 1889 parallel those found for engineers during the 1880s.[85] The average daily wage of switchmen in the East was $1.49. In the West, switchmen's wages averaged $2.02 per day.

The final and most complete wage data for the nineteenth centu-

---

*For a discussion of the sources of ninteenth-century railroad wage data, see appendix C.

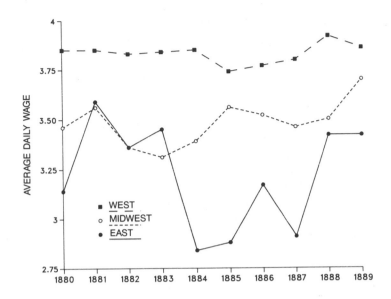

Figure 9.   Sectional differences in engineers' wages, 1880–89

Source: U.S. Department of Labor, Bureau of Labor Statistics, *History of Wages in the United States from Colonial Times to 1928*, Bulletin No. 604 (Washington: 1934), 430–35.

ry were collected by the Interstate Commerce Commission for the period 1892–1900. These data reveal that sectional differences in the wages of engineers and switchmen continued during the 1890s (appendix C, figures C1, C2). However, the wage rates of western engineers and switchmen were generally lower at the end of the decade than they had been at the beginning. Equally important is the fact that the volatility of western wage rates was significantly greater than that of eastern and midwestern rates. This represented a turnaround from the previous decade.

Another way to examine the volatility of wage rates is to compare the difference between the highest and lowest wage rates for different sections during each decade (table 8). Highly volatile wage rates and wide disparities between the highest and lowest paid workers suggest periods of adjustment in the labor market. During the 1880s, those adjustments appear to have been most profound in the East, and to a somewhat lesser extent in the Midwest. During the 1890s, the western railroad labor market was, in its turn, undergoing major adjustment. Although western wages were more volatile during the 1890s, the differential between highest

Table 8.   Differences between Highest and Lowest Wage Rates for
Engineers by Section, 1880–1900

	East	Midwest	West
1880–89	$.75	$.39	$.13
1890–1900	.14	.13	.28

Source: U.S. Department of Labor, Bureau of Labor Statistics, *History of Wages in
the United States from Colonial Times to 1928*, Bulletin no. 604 (Washington:
1934); U.S. Commissioner of Labor, "Railroad Labor," *Fifth Annual Report, 1889*
(Washington: 1889); U.S. Industrial Commission, *Report of the Industrial
Commission on Transportation*, vol. 4 (Washington: 1900).

and lowest wage was smaller than for eastern and midwestern engineers in the 1880s. At least two factors contributed to the smaller
western differential. First, railroad corporations were much less inclined to cut basic wage rates during the depression of the 1890s
than they had been during the previous decades. Second, changes
in wage-related work rules were often substituted for cuts in basic
wage rates and had a profound effect on the earnings of railroad
workers, although they are not reflected in wage rate data.

If we are limited in our ability to measure and compare specific
labor market conditions by inadequate wage data, by the apparent
wide variations between different localities within the same region,
and by the perceptions of both workers and employers whose actions continually altered supply conditions and interfered with
their own assessments, we may nevertheless make some general
statements about shifts in the supply of railroad labor. Based on the
wage data, it does appear that eastern and western railroads were
faced with very different conditions. The relative downward trend
in western wage levels over the entire period, but especially in the
1890s, would indicate gradually changing conditions in the West.
It was in the states west of the Mississippi that Ripley found major
trend-setting contract provisions. It was also in the West that the
fiercest battles over these work rules and wage rates were fought.
Eastern railroads pioneered the new systems of employee discipline and company-sponsored relief and pensions that gradually
spread westward into territory newly "pacified" in the aftermath of
major strikes.

The wages paid to railroad workers were a source of contention
in the late nineteenth century. Managers sought to keep methods
for determining wages as flexible as possible. They preferred

modes of payment that encouraged individual bargaining and trip rates that did not itemize and specifically remunerate additional "incidental" labor. Under the pressure of an inadequate labor supply, managers were forced to pay higher wages and accept mileage rates and other special payments. They made every effort to increase the supply of men available, and in time, but not without major disputes with their workers, they reduced wages to national standards and reincorporated a modified trip system of payment.

Railroad workers, particularly those in the running trades, made every effort to define specifically their job territories, maintain standards of skill, and, as much as possible, restrict entry and limit the supply of men. In the West, they took advantage of the scarcity of their numbers to gain recognition and contract language that provided for payment according to the miles run and additional arbitrary allowances. They fought to protect these privileges, even as their skills became more easily replaceable.

Promotion, Seniority, and the Distribution of Work

If wages and work rules in some measure reflect the state of the railroad labor market, the issues of promotion and seniority were perceived by both workers and managers as crucial instruments for restricting or increasing the supply of labor. The rules governing promotion and seniority determined how workers would move up or down the occupational ladders and who would have first claim on job opportunities. Not surprisingly, the positions taken by workers and managers on these issues reflected their divergent interests in the labor market. The regulation of promotion and the application of seniority principles also on occasion created conflict between workingmen who occupied different positions in the occupational hierarchy.

Standard paths of occupational succession were established fairly early on the railroads and were maintained with remarkable consistency. Engineers were at the top of one occupational ladder. Their climb began in the railroad shop. In the early years, engineers were recruited and promoted from among machinists, but later, almost universally, enginemen began their climb as engine wipers.[86] Wipers were promoted to firemen; firemen, to hostlers (who ran engines in the yards and shops); finally, hostlers, to engineers. For firemen and engineers, there were numerous intermediate stages of promotion delineated by special kinds of work (on switch engines, work trains, and snowplow service) or types of runs (local or through freight and passenger). Similarly, conductors were recruited from among brakemen. Switchmen and other station hands occupied no such position on a promotional ladder. There were, of course, local exceptions to these particular promotional paths. E. C. Scudder, official company historian of the Burlington strike, noted that on the Western Iowa Division of the Chicago, Burlington, & Quincy at Creston, the master mechanic worked in brakemen rather than wipers as firemen and engineers. In so doing, he was convinced that a better class of engineers was created, a class that included fewer of the "foreign element" that predominated in the shops.[87]

Two crucial questions were involved in the promotion of men from one occupational grade to the next. The first question concerned the basis for determining the order of men to be promoted. The second question involved the factors that determined how fast a man might move from one level to the next.

The railroads generally preferred to promote according to what they considered to be "merit." As George Chalender, an officer of the Burlington, explained to Joel West, master mechanic at Burlington, Iowa, in 1877, "The company reserves to itself entire discretion as to promotion. Merit will have the preference over seniority in all cases."[88] The earliest seniority clause recorded was adopted by the Erie Railroad in 1870. It stipulated that promotion to preferred engines, trains, and runs should be governed by length of service.[89] Though similar clauses were widely adopted in the following two decades, they were often qualified in some manner, giving ultimate discretion in promotion to management. Promotion according to seniority provided railroad employees with some measure of security against arbitrary discharge and an equal opportunity for advancement in earnings. The other side of promotion according to "merit" from the point of view of railroad workers was favoritism. Letters appeared regularly in the brotherhood journals complaining that, as one brakeman from Missoula, Montana, wrote, "Only those that have personal friends stand in for promotion. Many of the old men have left there and more will leave this spring."[90] Indeed, nepotism in railroad hiring was fairly widespread at the higher occupational levels as officials moving from one road to another brought with them trusted subordinates who displaced regular employees on the promotional ladder.[91]

The length of time normally required to advance from one occupational level to another was a function of the supply of labor and the rate of railroad expansion. J. E. Phelan, a locomotive engineer from Brainerd, Minnesota, described early conditions on the Northern Pacific. He wrote, "While the Northern Pacific Road was building, there was an urgent and constant demand for engineers. It was a good field for firemen of experience. It was profitable employment for engineers to go firing, for being on the ground and at hand, promotion was certain in a short time. . . . Cases were noted by firemen on the Minnesota Division where firemen on the western division did not have to go much beyond one year's experience to promotion."[92] A brakeman from Nickerson, Kansas, was bemused in 1887 that another man would have "broke" for nine years in order to get "his train," that is, be promoted to conductor. "I would like to see the road I would brake nine years on for the best train in the county."[93] Even as these western railroad men wrote, the length of time required for promotion on eastern roads was increasing. A fireman from Hamilton, Ontario, noted in 1886 that some men on his division had been "shoveling" for more than ten years.[94] By the twentieth century, such relatively short promotional periods would be almost unimaginable. A study in 1917 showed that older trainmen on eastern roads "have been in service 22 years without promotion." Firemen on the Southern Pacific *averaged* eleven and one-quarter years, and many firemen on New England roads had been on locomotives since 1902 or earlier without being examined for positions as locomotive engineers.[95]

Seniority—The Interests of Labor and Management

The application of seniority to the contraction of job opportunities was as important as its application to promotion. Railroads were subject to severe seasonal and cyclical declines in business. The ups and downs in railroad traffic affected earnings in a number of ways. Except in relatively stable passenger traffic, work was rarely distributed evenly throughout the year. "A man may double the road today and he may not go over the road at all tomorrow. In one busy month he may show excessively high earnings. In another dull month he may show no earnings at all," was the way Grand Chief Clark of the Brotherhood of Locomotive Firemen characterized the pattern.[96] J. E. Phelan described the impact of the depression of 1884-85 on engineers of the Northern Pacific, where a scarcity of men was suddenly turned into a surplus by the "prostrated" business conditions. "Engineers quietly worked and for months the pay received by many engineers on freight did not figure in amount favorable to that drawn by passenger firemen."[97] Even in relatively good times there was a fear, especially among men with families, of the "starvation period" that attended promotion. A man might move from passenger fireman with a regular run to engineer on the "extra board" taking only an occasional freight. His actual earnings frequently fell as a result of such a promotion.

Just as the men had sought seniority as a fair basis for regulating access to higher earnings, they also looked to it as a basis for distributing meager earnings in hard times. The distinction between regular and irregular service is crucial. Even during severe business declines, regular passenger service and a large proportion of regular freight traffic was maintained. Men operating these runs, generally the older men, did not suffer an appreciable decline in earnings. Men in irregular service, operating on a pool basis whereby runs were taken in rotation, were the first to notice a decline in business. The length of time between calls grew. When, in addition, work was distributed to men on the extra board, the decline in earnings could be catastrophic. A demand incorporated into many early settlements was a limitation of the extra board. Article 10 in the Gould Settlement of March 24 1885, read: "The company agrees not to assign any more extra engineers than are necessary to move the traffic with promptness and certainty. . . . Engineers who feel aggrieved by the assignment of extras may appeal."[98] Men cut from irregular service or from the extra board were "bumped" back or "took to the woods." On some, but not all, roads engineers had the privilege of bumping switch engineers and they, in turn, bumped hostlers, then firemen, and so on down the occupational ladder.[99] Under the strict application of the seniority principle, once a man moved up the occupational ladder, even if only onto the extra board for firemen, his seniority in that rank began, and even if he were bumped back into the roundhouse, that seniority would govern when he was recalled.

Railroad workers and managers were not always in conflict over how the principle of seniority should be applied, nor were railroad workers always in agreement among themselves. As railroads pushed into new territory where labor was relatively scarce, both management and labor were interested in rapid labor mobility. Promotion came quickly; there was ample opportunity for skilled men to be hired from the outside. Seniority was generally accepted and practiced, but it was relatively unimportant when men saw themselves advancing rapidly.

As the supply of labor increased, the brotherhoods became more and more concerned with limiting it. Engineers sought to eliminate the capriciousness used in determining their access to preferred runs and to put a floor under their earnings by limiting the extra board. At the same time, they sought to slow down the making of engineers by requiring railroad companies to hire a certain proportion of engineers from the floating population. Firemen found themselves in a position of divided interests. As prospective engineers, they were interested in protecting the earning power of engineers, which meant limiting the supply. On the other hand, they sought to maintain their own access to a fair proportion of the engineers' jobs that opened up through regular promotion.

Railroad corporations had no interest in limiting the supply of railroad men. In fact, under the pressure of declining freight rates, they sought to augment the supply in every way possible. During this phase, companies sought flexibility in the manipulation of wage rates and work rules, and serious conflict developed over the regulation of the labor supply.

Finally, as the supply of railroad men saturated a regional labor market, workers accepted the constraints of an "internal labor market," whereby promotion was essentially from within, seniority ity rules were applied strictly and within fairly narrow geographical areas, and any serious attempt to protect the access of unemployed fellow tradesmen to jobs was abandoned by the brotherhoods. Railroad companies under more favorable labor supply conditions were persuaded to abandon efforts to increase the supply any further; in fact, the reduction of regional wage differentials in itself tended to slow down the movement of labor. As the labor supply increased, voluntary turnover rates declined. The brotherhoods and the companies reached a consensus with regard to the implementation of the seniority principle.[100] It is the more contentious middle phase in the efforts of labor and management to regulate the supply of labor that interests us here. That phase falls most directly within the period of intense industrial conflict in the West between the mid-1880s and the mid-1890s.

Conflict over Promotion

Three issues, involving promotion and the distribution of work, were the greatest sources of conflict during this period. The first was the classification of engineers and conductors according to length of service. The second was the issue of whether skilled men should be promoted from within or hired from the outside. The third concerned the size of the extra board, which directly affected the distribution of work and the earnings of members of the running trades.

No issue relating to promotion stirred the ire of men in the running trades more than classification. This system, inaugurated in the early 1870s on some roads but prevalent in the 1880s, required men who were newly promoted to work for a period of time at reduced wages before being promoted to "first class." The system was most widespread for engineers but was not uncommon for brakemen and conductors as well.[101] Engineers, for instance, might be paid $2.40 per trip the first year, $2.65 per trip the second, and the full rate of $2.90 per trip the third. Engineers argued that their "apprenticeship" (as companies preferred to label classification) had already been served as firemen. If they were required to do first-class work, they should not be paid second- and third-class wages; if they were not qualified to run a first-class engine, they should not be allowed to do so.[102] A lead editorial in the *Firemen's Magazine* argued that the real reason for classification was not "rewarding experience" as some managers claimed but economy and increasing the number of engineers. *"Classification* of engineers' wages is simply a *reduction* of wages under a new name," the editor wrote. "Competent engineers are dismissed upon the slightest pretext, simply because they draw first-class pay, and by that means idleness is multiplied until the land swarms with engineers looking for employment."[103] The *Brakemen's Journal* argued that the system was equivalent to offering a premium to subofficials who can "run things cheap" by finding a pretext for discharging old engineers and replacing them with new, cheaper ones.[104]

Classification was resisted by railroad employees almost from the day it was introduced. Engineers on the Pennsylvania Railroad sought its elimination when they included it in their strike demands in July 1877.[105] Engineers on the Burlington had begun what was to be a long and bitter agitation on the issue the year before. The Chicago, Burlington & Quincy had instituted the system in September 1876 and faced a petition of engineers and firemen that demanded its elimination in December 1876.[106] After some vacillation within management, it was upheld with increasing firmness.

Beginning in 1882 with the Missouri Pacific, a small number of roads, under intense pressure from the brotherhoods, began abolishing classification.[107] The New York Central followed; then the Northern Pacific complied in 1886, and between that year and the outbreak of the Burlington strike of 1888 a number of other roads fell into line including the Union Pacific, the Santa Fe, the Wisconsin Central, the Louisville & Nashville, and the Baltimore & Ohio.[108] By 1888 it was mandatory under Brotherhood of Locomotive Engineers law that no contract that included the classification provision should be agreed to; it was the central issue in the great Burlington strike. Gradually, throughout the 1890s, classification disappeared on one road after another.[109] As the supply of engineers increased in the West and wages became more standardized at reduced levels, the use of classification diminished and continued brotherhood opposition ushered it out.

There was not the same unanimous opposition to promotion from within. Nevertheless, it was perceived by many skilled men as another device for depressing their trade. In announcing the new wage schedule adopted by the Chicago, Burlington & Quincy on September 1, 1876, George Chalender not only dropped the classification bombshell but indicated a shift in the company's position on the hiring of engineers. Henceforth, he announced, the road would fill all vacancies among engineers from among "our best and oldest firemen" instead of hiring new engineers. This arrangement would make "a fireman sure of promotion if found competitive and worthy."[110]

Engineers on some roads in the 1880s succeeded in limiting the practice of promotion from within in order to guarantee positions for unemployed engineers. The Northern Pacific agreed to a provision in its 1886 contract which read, "The company should refrain from promoting firemen as long as they can procure experienced runners at the same wages."[111] Others agreed to hire one engineer for every fireman promoted. One of several points of tension between engineers and firemen, the issue erupted in the correspondence columns of the engineers' and firemen's journals in 1886 and, though quieted, it was never entirely resolved. J. E. Phelan, an engineer and prolific correspondent from Brainerd, Minnesota, contributed a brief and polemical history of how the schism on this issue had developed between engineers and firemen.

> Evidence of the breach did not show itself again to my mind until the master mechanics had resolved to hire no more engineers but to make their engineers. Then it commenced to loom up. Many firemen favored that policy. Competent engineers seeking employment were constantly met with the information that the policy of the companies was to make their engineers. Firemen were promoted to engineers' positions who had not worked on an engine long enough to

know how to fire. These assertions are taken from evidence. Firemen favored such a policy. On a certain road an attempt was made to have an agreement enforced with the company to pick future engineers from the ranks of the oldest firemen. Can engineers be blamed for resisting such encroachments?[112]

Promotion from within was inevitable; all engineers were at some point made on some road. The issue was what limitations, if any, should be placed on that process, so as to restrict the number of skilled men who were idle. Although fixed ratios were introduced into many schedules as a means of settling the issue, years later Victor S. Clark, in his report to the Eight-Hour Commission, observed that rules governing the ratio of hired to promoted men were "the most laxly observed provisions in those agreements, because the tendency is for the number of promoted men to exceed rather than to fall below the specified proportion."[113]

Finally, the distribution of work in the face of cutbacks was a point of contention between some companies and their men. It also created some divisiveness between junior and senior men in the same occupation. In general, it was in the interest of the railroads to retain as large an extra board as possible in order to have an adequate supply of labor for changed business conditions. The brotherhoods sought to limit the extra board so as to maintain earnings at some minimum level for those employed. The minimum was sometimes expressed in terms of miles to be run.[114] But as the supply of skilled men increased in a region, companies were less and less averse to "furloughing" or discharging extra men, knowing that additional men would be available. Among the shop crafts, there is some evidence that a division developed over whether cutbacks should be met by a reduction of hours (sharing the work) or by a reduction in the force. District Assembly 82, Knights of Labor (the Union Pacific Employees Association) argued for work sharing in the 1893 depression but was opposed by some skilled machinists in the new International Association of Machinists.[115] In arguing for a limitation of the size of the extra board and the application of seniority to reductions in the labor force, the brotherhoods sought to maintain the earnings of skilled railroad workers. In a labor market flooded with skilled men, such a policy seemed to some the only reasonable protection for their earnings and the standards of their trades. To others, the new conditions of a labor supply hopelessly swollen by management design required new and broader forms of control.

138

Regulating the Supply of Labor: A Question of Control

Both railroad management and labor saw the size and growth of the labor supply as a central concern in the late nineteenth century. It was the lever by which wages were raised or lowered. Railroad managers sought to maintain adequate supplies of labor in order to hold down wages and operating expenses. For labor to interfere was, in the words of *Railway Age*, to institute a "system of dictation, which would ultimately turn over the possession of [the railroad's] property into the hands of its employees."[116] The brotherhoods—preeminently the Brotherhood of Locomotive Engineers—sought to restrict the supply of skilled labor in order to maintain standards and protect their craft. In a sense, each party had an alternative program for regulating the supply of labor, although neither was articulated completely at one time.

Railroad managers sought to base wage payment on the trip (piece rate) rather than the mileage or the time elapsed. Their ideal was a different rate for each run; a different wage for each man. By logical extension, such a system would have led to individual bargaining and to a collapse of trade union organization. The head of the machinists' union in the 1890s calculated that piece rates tended to reduce the labor requirements of employers by one-fourth.[117]

Although most railroad companies accepted at least a limited form of seniority as the basis for promotion, they preferred, in Charles E. Perkins's words, "the only solid rock to anchor to, namely: that merit amd merit only shall be rewarded."[118] Promotion exclusively according to merit would have allowed railroad companies a freer hand in the creation and allocation of a skilled labor force.

The railroads consistently sought to promote from within their own corporate ranks to the extent that their requirements for labor could be met from that source. Such a system tended to induce loyalty and to increase the supply of skilled labor generally.

Railroad companies appropriated unto themselves, to the greatest extent possible, the right to determine the skill and reliability of prospective employees or those seeking promotion. They came to require a letter of reference or a detailed service record from other employers. They gradually instituted company-sponsored examinations.

Finally, they sought to define work rules in the most flexible way, which would permit them to allocate labor according to their needs without regard to restrictive rules of the brotherhoods. Such changes materially increased their supply of labor without adding more workers.

The brotherhoods took different views of each of these points. They promoted the principle of uniform pay systems and resisted the tendency toward individual pay. This principle was at stake in the Burlington strike in 1888. The *New York Times* stated it briefly: "It is simply that those who do the same work for the same length of time shall be paid the same wages, without regard to the varying degrees of skill, experience or fidelity."[119] Engineers and other operating men did not object to, and in fact fought for, pay differentials based on extra work. Larger engines, mountain runs, snowplow service, and overtime were all considered legitimate bases for differences in pay, which, if itemized, did not violate the fundamental principle of pay equality and did not open the door to individual bargaining.

The brotherhoods fought for the application of strict seniority, not only to promotion but to layoff. For companies to promote according to their own definitions of merit was viewed as opening the door to favoritism and to lower trade standards.

Although the brotherhoods accepted some promotion from within as inevitable, they sought to protect the access of fellow craftsmen "on the tramp" to some portion of the job opportunities. Such a policy was regarded as absolutely necessary to brake the growth of the supply of skilled labor.

The brotherhoods regarded themselves as the exclusive source and judge of skilled labor, and they prided themselves on their own standards of discipline. In the early 1880s, when their skills were in great demand, members of the brotherhoods expressed confidence that the railroad corporations were beginning to look to them to furnish "the reliable, trustworthy men" they required.[120] This recognition of the brotherhoods was uneven. It reflected their capacity to exercise effective control over the labor supply. The traveling card was seen by brotherhood men as an alternative to the letters of reference required by companies; it was, they argued, a more reliable test of qualification. As companies began to instutute examinations, many within the brotherhoods argued that they should examine their own members and thereby vouch for their competence. Such a program would also "elevate the intellectual culture of the brotherhood."[121]

Finally, the brotherhoods resisted company efforts to define more flexible work rules that would blur the distinctions among crafts and between skilled and unskilled, journeyman and apprentice.

They stood by what they understood to be "engineers' work." In the shops where technological change was eroding the control of skilled men over the production process, machinists fought to uphold the apprenticeship system which regulated entry to the trade and defined the skills of a machinist, even if much of the work formerly done by machinists was finding its way into the province of specialists.

Summary

The period we are examining saw important shifts in the supply of railroad labor, particularly in the West. As the impact of this growing labor supply was felt, the brotherhoods and other organized railroad workers resisted changes in wage rates and work rules that threatened to reduce their earnings, and they attacked those corporate initiatives that they felt were contributing to the oversupply of men. The effort of engineers to roll back classification and to introduce standard mileage rates of pay on the Burlington between 1886 an 1888 was a key turning point. Their loss in the strike of 1888 opened a far-reaching debate among railroad men of all grades over the future course of action. Writing at the height of the Burlington strike, a Union Pacific employee put the issue squarely before his fellow railroad workers: "Keep away from here! 'But where will I go?' cries the laborer; 'No work at home, no work abroad; others holding the natural opportunities.'. . .True, but you will never relieve those conditions by merely complaining and allowing these opportunities to run away or be taken away. They are fast disappearing and the only hope is to boldly attack these conditions that surround you everywhere."[122]

Broader organization and sympathetic action which had been pioneered by the Knights of Labor and the Switchmen's Mutual Aid Association gained support, especially in the West, after the defeat of the Burlington firemen and engineers. The objectives espoused by the advocates of broader organization differed from those of the brotherhoods. Implicitly, at least, they abandoned the attempts of the brotherhoods to protect crafts through restriction of entry and more precise delineation of job territories. First through federation and then through industrial organization, western railroad workers fought for a different kind of control, akin to that which switchmen had achieved in Chicago, where their thorough organization permitted them to protect a wage scale and to demand certain managerial prerogatives such as hiring and firing supervisors. Eventually, under the auspices of the American Railway Union, skilled and unskilled railroad workers alike demanded the highest form of control—outright public ownership of the railroads in the interest of workers and the general public.

The program of the brotherhoods survived the industrial struggles of the 1890s, but its success was based less on an ability to reassert the privileges of skill through the strength of organization, and more on their attractiveness to management as an alternative to more militant, industrial forms of organization. Members of the running trades used this new recognition to great advantage. They rejoined the brotherhoods in larger numbers than ever before and, within limits of the new government-regulated framework for labor-management cooperation, they improved their position in the industry.

If the cyclical rhythms of railroad expansion in the late nineteenth century made control of the labor supply the central issue between workers and their employers, it also defined the urban environments and the class milieu in which railroaders worked. Towns that serviced railroad operations differed in the extent of their prerailroad development, the diversity of their economies, and the structure of their class relations. Railroad workers, often numerically dominant within the labor force of these division towns, enjoyed varied success as they formed protective organizations, sought community support from fellow townsmen during their strikes, and attempted to locate their class opposition to the railroad corporation within the broader anti-monopoly ideology of their community brethren.

4

Town Development, Social Structure, and Industrial Conflict

Omaha Capitalist: Do you call that a survey for a new Railroad? Why it looks like a pumpkin vine.

Kansas Speculator: Well, you see, we had to twist it around a good deal, so as to take in all the points at which we could buy land cheap.

Omaha Capitalist: A road like that will never pay. It doesn't start anywhere or go anywhere.

Kansas Speculator: Oh! We can keep it running awhile on the profits of our town lots; that's easy enough.

Omaha Capitalist: But what will you do after all the lots are sold?

Kansas Speculator: Straighten it out.

—*Switchmen's Journal* (May 1887)

Aside from the principle involved, we deem it of vast interest to us and to every citizen of Creston and every town along the Q. line and every businessman, especially, that the boys win the present struggle. They are part of us; they are our best citizens. . . . Some have their all invested in a home, others have homes part paid for, and others have obligations contracted which if the strikers lose and were compelled to look elsewhere for employment, would be such a blow to the financial condition of our city that she would not recover for years to come.

—Creston, Iowa *Daily Advertiser*, March 4, 1888

Railroad expansion in late nineteenth-century America accelerated the settlement process and extended it continentwide. Within twenty-five years, from 1865 to 1890, a dense fabric of railroad lines was woven across the lands west of the Mississippi. This expansion created a profound demand for labor to construct, operate, and maintain these new roads. It opened new territories to settlement, provided a transportation mode for the massive relocation of population, and created truly national markets for manufactured goods. This growth, grafted onto existing commercial and transportation networks, also generated profound instability. Frontier conditions were transitory; the scarcity of labor and the plentifulness of land did not persist; and the benefits of an immediate national market for agricultural products were offset by the flood of cheap manufactured goods that stifled local industrial growth in many communities.

Railroads decisively altered the urban landscape of nineteenth-century America. For older market cities that had been sheltered from outside competition by a "tariff barrier" of isolation, commercial growth unlocked opportunities and unprecedented perils. Some towns limited to waterborne commerce saw their fortunes decline by comparison with "backcountry upstarts" that happened to be located on the new rail lines. Many towns competed frantically in the tribute they offered the iron horse and its corporate masters. Others that were heavily committed to servicing the wagon or canal trade turned their backs on the unsightly intruder. Not only did the railroads promise spectacular growth to some existing settlements, they also created "magic cities" (a common nickname for railroad towns) to service their operations. Blessed by the arrival of a substantial railroad labor force with its considerable payroll, a retinue of tradesmen, land speculators, and dealers in "liquid hardware," these towns exploded at regular intervals on the vacant prairie. The redirection of land settlement, townbuilding, and the flow of commerce and immigration along new rail lines restructured the pattern of urban growth.[1]

Railroad development stimulated two overlapping networks of urban economic activity. First, it extended an existing marketing network that had been built on prerailroad commercial activity, quickening the flow of goods and population and stimulating diversification in manufacturing. Second, it generated a service network of divisional operating and repair facilities.[2] The locational requirements of the marketing network were different from those of the service network. Some established marketing centers built on their initial advantages by acquiring railroad connections to a wider market and became regional centers for the wholesale trade, for manufacturing, and for processing agricultural products. Some also acquired the added economic stimulus that came with servicing railroad operations. Urban settlements in the service network were blessed with the direct economic stimulus of railroad-related spending and construction.

Beyond the existing market cities, the railroads, with a relentless logic, platted and brought into existence division towns at intervals of 200 to 300 miles to provide repair facilities and the changeover of train and engine crews. The economic growth and diversification of these towns beyond their divisional functions was initially incidental to their primary function. A few division towns happened to be located in areas where a substantial demand already existed for marketing agricultural or mineral resources. The diversion of that trade from water to railroad transportation meant rapid urban growth. A more common pattern was that new railroad division towns experienced an initial period of spectacular growth fueled by the construction and development of railroad operations, followed by a period of very slow growth or even stagnation as they fought to overcome the advantages of more established urban marketing centers and waited for their hinterlands to fill up. For many such railroad towns that aspired to grow beyond their service function, the perceived critical ingredient for future growth was the acquisition of a competing railroad line and the competitive rates that this would bring.

The combination of marketing and service functions varied from one railroad division town to another, as did the specific patterns of their growth. However, two basic types of communities stand out from the welter of towns within the railroad service network: market cities and railroad towns. Market cities were communities, generally settled before the entry of railroads, that enjoyed initial advantages based on favorable location within the prerailroad commercial networks. The river towns of the Ohio, Mississippi, and Missouri river valleys are good examples. The railroads extended the commercial domination of these towns, enabled them to diversify in manufacturing and processing, and sustained if not spurred their spectacular growth. Many of these towns also were deemed appropriate sites for the location of railroad shop and switching facilities. Most acquired in time multiple railroad connections to larger urban centers.

Railroad towns, in the way the term is used here, were communities whose very existence was predicated on the location of railroad shop and service facilities. Generally created through the direct or indirect agency of the railroads themselves, they enjoyed no initial commercial or industrial advantages. Their location was strictly determined by the logic of railroad construction. Their initially spectacular growth was commonly limited by the slower pace of agricultural settlement and the absence of a flourishing commerce that could provide the basis for diversification and growth. Lying within the commercial hinterlands of more developed cities and generally lacking competitive railroad connections, they found it difficult to grow beyond the direct services they provided to their patron railroad.

Both types of towns had a full complement of workers to repair and operate their railroads. Whether small or large, diversified or limited to railroad operations, each town had a force of railroad shopmen, enginemen, trainmen, and track repairmen. The size of the division town did not directly affect the size of the railroad labor force. Only in the case of switchmen and freight handlers did a community's nodality in a regional market and its interconnections with other roads significantly affect the number of men that would be required.

The position of railroad workers within the social structure of a railroad division town varied with the size and composition of its working class and with the extent of its commercial and industrial diversification. In larger market cities the proportion of railroad workers in the total labor force of the community might be as low as 1 percent. In outlying railroad towns, they comprised as much as 35 percent and effectively dominated the labor force.[3] Market cities commonly possessed a self-conscious and well-organized elite that promoted, with notable success, a series of transportation improvements and other measures to strengthen and diversify the local economy. Railroad towns had a smaller, more locally oriented elite whose aspirations were frustrated by their inadequate means and their inability to grow beyond the limits imposed by a single transportation route.

Patterns of Local Conflict

As conflict between railroad workers and their employers spread from one region to another, communities in the railroad service network found themselves in the middle, pulled in one direction by the roads that held out the promise of economic growth and in the other by some of their own citizen-strikers whose very livelihoods and protective organizations were in jeopardy. Numerous commentators on the strikes of railroad workers discerned differences in the community support workers enjoyed. For instance, during the engineers' strike of 1888 on the Chicago, Burlington & Quincy Railroad (C.B.& Q.), company officials cited the "disloyalty" of division towns from Creston, Iowa, west through Nebraska as being particularly nettlesome.[4] During the Pullman boycott, officials of the Northern Pacific identified the Missouri River as a rough dividing line between the communities that were in outright rebellion and those that manifested a more conciliatory attitude toward the road.[5] At the same time that citizens in Spokane, Washington, organized in strong support of the company, those in Sprague demonstrated "a very bitter attitude" toward the company.[6] A historian of the Great Northern strike of 1894 found Saint Cloud, Minnesota, to be a similar dividing line on that road.[7] Citizens in Kansas railroad towns responded in diverse ways to the railroad strikes of 1877 and 1878—from active support of strikers to adamant hostility.[8]

Even in communities where workers at one time enjoyed vigorous community support, conditions could change and support be withdrawn. An analysis of strikes on the Erie Railroad in Hornellsville, New York, demonstrates that the strike of 1877 was a turning point. Under increased pressure from the company and fearful for the economic future of the town, community leaders pressured the railroad workers to return to work. When the workers struck again in 1881, the community leaders directly opposed them.[9] Economic development could alter the class relations of local businessmen and railroad workers; changes in the racial and ethnic composition of the labor force could shatter the social solidarity that townsmen and workingmen formerly enjoyed.[10]

The importance of community support and its fragility is testified to by workers and by company officials throughout this period. During the strike on the Great Northern in the spring of 1894, American Railway Union Director W. P. C. Adams urgently telegraphed a stern warning to his men on the Northern Pacific, who were anxious to strike in sympathy. "Popular sentiment must be our weapon. It is the millstone of the scriptures; fall upon it and it will break you; fall under it, it will crush you. Jim is rolling down Hill with his stone; let him go. It is the silent force, irresistible in the affairs of men. Do not forget this, nor the people who set it in motion. The strikers of the Great Northern have a monopoly of its use now, but it is only loaned to us. Let us not lose it. It is a weapon we must win often before it is ours to keep."[11] Early in the Burlington strike, company officials felt that community attitudes were so important to the outcome of the strike that one railroad official carefully monitored and tabulated editorial comment in the region.[12] Public relations campaigns were mounted by both the Burlington and the Northern Pacific to plant favorable editorials in the local press.[13]

The question of how communities responded to industrial conflict in the late nineteenth century has received its most extensive treatment in the work of Herbert Gutman. In a series of case studies of industrial strikes in the 1870s, Gutman sketched a remarkable pattern of community support for working-class townsmen who struck against "outside" corporations. Citing the peculiarities of small-town life that permitted face-to-face relationships even during rapid industrialization, Gutman attributed the support to an "organic" sense of community and to a distrust of the new, impersonal forces of economic life embodied in the corporations. This support for workingmen in smaller industrial towns and cities he contrasted to the repression and isolation that workers faced in larger metropolises such as New York and Chicago.[14]

Gutman's analysis does not account for the differences in response *among* smaller industrial communities. That such differences existed is apparent from even a cursory examination of the descriptions of western railroad strikes. Of equal importance, his analysis does not explain why popular sentiment might change from support of striking workers to neutrality or opposition.[15]

Railroad towns, like other industrial communities, were changing entities whose class relations reflected their economic growth and whose elites imbibed deeply the elixir of community progress. In their pragmatic pursuit of progress, community leaders bristled under their competitive disadvantages, attributing their misfortunes to unfair rates and land engrossment of "monopolistic" railroads. Under such conditions the trials of striking railroad workers who owned homes and bought from local merchants seemed clearly allied with their own. However, in the face of the enormous power of the railroads to consign certain communities to oblivion and others to future dominance, business and professional leaders were often more than willing to accept the railroad's modest promises of future benefits and to turn their backs on the shattered remnants of worker organizations and community solidarity. These changes in the class relations of railroad division towns occurred as railroad workers experienced the effects of a growing labor surplus. This wider crisis deepened local antagonisms.

The scattered and sometimes conflicting evidence of differences in the ways communities responded to railroad strikes invites systematic analysis.[16] The first task is to identify more precisely the differences between towns in the railroad service network.

148

Location and Growth of Railroad Towns

Although railroad division towns shared many characteristics with urbanizing America, they were distinctive in the concentration of occupations and investment serving transportation. Because of the specific locational requirements of railroad service, their distribution initially did not fit within the traditional hierarchy of central places that was found in more evenly settled areas.[17] Because the network of railroad service functions was imposed on a preexisting, if incomplete, network of urban commerce and production, differences in size, economic activity, and growth of railroad division towns were wide indeed.

The pattern of prerailroad urbanization varied from the thickly settled, commercially oriented Ohio Valley to the far-flung outfitting towns of the upper Missouri River Valley. Indeed, except for areas with peculiar natural resource endowments, urban settlement correlated closely with the extent of commercially oriented agriculture and with access to water transportation. Railroads began in the East as a series of local connections between well-established commercial centers, overlapping existing transportation networks but providing the advantages of low cost, flexibility, and speed in the movement of goods and passengers.

In the Old Northwest, railroads quickly overtook what one historical geographer has called the "pioneer periphery." The existing urban settlements were in areas with much lower density of agricultural settlement than in the East, and river transportation was very unevenly complemented by canal and plank road development. The middle Ohio River Valley is a case in point.[18] Prior to railroad development, urban settlement was heavily weighted toward the river entrepôt of Cincinnati. Smaller agricultural settlements on the Miami River in Ohio and along the Whitewater Canal and River in southeastern Indiana funneled agricultural produce to Ohio River towns for processing and "export" to distant markets.

Railroad development had a number of consequences for urban growth in the region. The location of major trunk lines north of the Ohio Valley caused a general shift in population growth and trade flow away from towns on the Ohio River. Cincinnati alone was able to maintain its leadership because of the size and economic diversity it had attained. Geographer E. K. Muller has noted that interior "intermediate-size towns" (1,600 to 6,399 population) benefited directly from railroad development. Their size influenced the location of new rail lines, and the railroads accelerated town growth by providing access to wider markets as the collection and processing of agricultural products was dispersed to a larger number of centers. "Local trade centers" (400 to 1,599) experienced more selective and uneven growth as commerce and small manufacturing agglomerated in intermediate-size towns and the collection of farm products moved outward to more remote locales.[19]

As tho rail network approached and finally passed the frontier of settlement, thereby becoming the primary "engine" of new settlement, it acquired even more decisive power over urban growth. Competition among existing commercial centers became a less-important factor in locating rail lines than government land grants. Urban settlements had promoted railroads in the East. In the West, railroads promoted settlements.[20]

The pattern of prerailroad settlement was dimly visible beneath the lines of urban growth generated by railroad building. The initial advantages enjoyed by settlements built to serve the outfitting trade, riverboat commerce, and mining promoted their further growth. But they were joined by booming settlements whose growth could be attributed exclusively to the railroads.

Two factors in addition to the location of railroad division operations influenced the further growth of western urban places: first, the capacity of towns to dominate the wholesale business of their hintorlands; and second, the ability of budding cities to develop a diversified manufacturing base.

Wholesaling, Manufacturing, and Railroad Rates

Towns developed as wholesaling centers by providing the sophisticated urban goods that a commercially oriented, if thinly scattered, population required. These "unraveling points of trade," as they have been called by the geographer James E. Vance, were in a position to maintain their regional dominance even as the frontier advanced farther, providing they were able to make "quantity price adjustments" in order to forestall the emergence of a next generation of unraveling points.[21] The critical factor was of course railroad freight rates. Railroads were in a position to make or break the wholesale interests and the growth of cities they connected. As the economist W. Z. Ripley noted. "Railway traffic managers hold the welfare of entire communities, as it were, in the palms of their hands." It was theirs to decide whether consumers on the Pacific slope would be supplied by jobbers in their own cities, who break bulk and ship out to smaller towns, or whether they would be supplied by jobbing houses thousands of miles away, in Chicago or Saint Louis. "The rivalries of jobbers and middlemen are inevitably borne into the offices of traffic managers."[22]

Competition among rival railroads and among aspiring centers of wholesale trade were deeply intertwined. The success of one type of enterprise influenced the fortunes of the other.[23] Discriminatory and special rates for major shippers shifted a disproportionate share of the fixed costs for railroad operations onto local traffic. Such rates were a product of what Ripley called, "the overweening ambition of the great cities to monopolize the jobbing trade," and a consequence of the competition of railroads for traffic at some locations and the absence of competition at other locations. The demand for rate equity had some basis in the poor growth performance of many new and ambitious western towns that were dependent on a single road. It also derived, as Ripley noted, from the desire of such communities to compete for the wholesale trade of their hinterlands—trade that high freight rates denied to them.[24]

The second determinant of urban growth was the development of manufacturing. Small-scale processing and manufacturing were ubiquitous on the urban frontier. Even small settlements boasted a few artisans who produced shoes, wagons, cigars, clothing, hardware, and windows and sashes. Such a pattern of manufacturing reflected an economy that, in Sam B. Warner's words, "had not yet settled into the pattern whereby each specialty located in its best site, and from such a base or cluster of bases sold its products throughout the nation."[25]

Railroads made it possible for specialized manufacturing to break out of the local market orientation of artisanal production. Small manufacturers in some towns managed to extend their markets. In other towns they did not, and such places grew fitfully. The urban economist Wilbur Thompson has suggested that there exists an "urban size ratchet" in city growth "short of which growth is not inevitable and even the very existence of the place is not assured, but beyond which absolute contraction is highly unlikely, even though the growth rate may slacken, at times even to zero."[26] Very rapid growth in a single industry such as railroads may generate short-term, rapid urban growth. Thompson suggests that such growth is inherently destabilizing and that "transitional pauses" are inevitable, during which diversification occurs and complementary industries emerge or the city stagnates.[27] But as Allan Pred has demonstrated, an uneven distribution of large-scale manufacturing led to a still more uneven distribution of urban economic growth, as some cities were able to capitalize on the position of their manufactured products to win favorable freight rates. "Large-scale production brought ton-mile or freight-volume economies to a firm, enabled still greater extension of its market area, and continued the accretion of initial advantages."[28] Other communities and their aspiring manufacturers fell farther behind.

Chicago was clearly a city that successfully negotiated the hazardous shoals of rapid urban growth because of favorable location and early investment in transportation, but the country is littered with railroad towns that did not. In Chicago, Warner noted, "the transportation activity itself—tending the yards, repairing cars and locomotives, building all sorts of equipment from fishplates to Pullman cars—generated an enormous volume of employment." But what separated Chicago from other railroad-servicing communities was the fortuitous location that aggregated rail lines and transportation services. "By complementarity and the sheer expansion of urban business, these new rail sectors attracted industry."[29] Chicago's rapid rise to metropolitan status was a model of urban growth whose influence radiated outward much as did the rail lines themselves. Throughout the West, would-be promoters of railroad division towns looked at the spectacular growth of their own communities in the first decades of their existence, illuminated by Chicago, and confidently predicted that metropolitan status was just around the corner for their towns as well.

Railroad Town Site Development

Railroads not only had a substantial impact on the degree of urban growth experienced by existing communities, they also had a direct hand in the urbanization of relatively unsettled territories. The Illinois Central (I. C.) was the first company to build rail lines through comparatively unurbanized territory. It is certainly the road whose colonization history is best known, thanks to the work of Paul W. Gates. The Illinois Central selected its route in Illinois primarily on the basis of where the most government land was available. As the first beneficiary of federal land grants for financing railroad construction, the Illinois Central was in a position to control the dispersal of much of the land adjacent to its route. Land grant railroads received by act of Congress alternate sections of land within a strip of territory six to twenty-five miles wide through which they proposed to build. While a more populous route would have ensured an even more rapid development of traffic, the Illinois Central sought to limit the amount it spent to acquire rights of way and land for railroad facilities. Illinois legislators manifested some concern that if the road were permitted to lay out town-sites on land it acquired from the federal government, it might simply bypass well-established communities and create competing towns a short distance from existing ones, which would ultimately spell the latter's doom. The legislators pushed through an amendment to the railroad's charter forbidding it to establish towns on or near its rail line.[30]

The company planned to locate stations approximately every ten miles as shipping and receiving points for agricultural produce. The points were known to the directors of the company. According to Gates, four of its most influential directors and the engineer in charge of construction formed a private town-site company, dubbed the "Associates," through which government land was purchased adjacent to the stations. "The Associates in turn deeded to the railroad sufficient land for its depots and yards in the new towns. As soon as the station sites were announced and before construction was complete, there was a rush for locations at the incipient towns."[31]

An almost identical pattern of town-site development along the Burlington & Missouri River Railroad (B. & M.) in both Iowa and Nebraska has been recounted by Richard C. Overton. Major directors and stockholders of the Chicago, Burlington & Quincy Railroad (the former's parent road) formed a series of town-site companies, the most well-known of which was the Eastern Land Association, formed by J. W. Brooks, J. M. Forbes, J. W. Ames, C. E. Perkins, and others. They bought up prospective town lands, especially those west of Lincoln.[32]

If many disapproved of these transactions, others who happened to be well situated hailed them as guaranteeing the future prominence of their communities. The town-site companies commonly donated land for churches and educational facilities and actively promoted development of flour mills, lumber mills, and stockyards. Such donations brought a return to the town investors through enhanced land values.[33] Railroad town-site promotion led to substantial urban growth. Gates found that in 1850, there had been only ten towns in the vicinity of the Illinois Central route, but by 1860 there were forty-seven and by 1870, eighty-one. The urban population (not including Chicago) rose from 12,000 to 172,000.[34]

Town-site promotion such as that practiced by the "Associates" along the Illinois Central and by the Eastern Land Association on the Burlington & Missouri in Nebraska planted numerous rapidly growing towns in comparatively undeveloped territory. Their growth reflected the dominant influence of the railroad and the limited extent of other industrial and commercial opportunities.

An examination of western railroad-town development suggests some diversity of experience within these basic patterns of development (figure 10).[35] North Platte, Nebraska, for instance, was founded in November 1866 as a division town and winter terminus of the Union Pacific. A western traveler described the process of settlement that accompanied the construction of the Union Pacific west of Omaha.

> It was the custom of the builders of that road to establish at various intervals according to the character of the locations, certain halting places for all trains . . . . which were designated as termini. Instantly, upon such location being made known, the city on wheels would move forward at the word of command. Sometimes large fortunes were made by those in authority, whose peculiar privilege it was to determine and lay out the site of a road terminus and subdivide it into building lots. . . .
>
> Hotels for travelers would spring into existence in a day; a bank and an opera house would rise simultaneously side by side; stores and outfitting establishments of every variety would line the main streets with their quaint signs and emblems of trade. Mechanics and artisans would pour in from other parts of the road and with them would come the lawyer and the doctor, both great healing mediums with peculiar methods. The morning's dawn would be greeted with the daily newpaper, the first to herald the name and wondrous fame of the new town and winter terminus.[36]

When westward construction was resumed in 1867, about 150 persons remained behind in North Platte to carry out the basic tasks required by a new division. The city consisted of a new roundhouse, machine shops, and a few frame houses. Many of the workers slept on bunks or benches in the shops. A peace treaty with neighboring Indian tribes was negotiated in the machine shops on September 24, 1868. That same year the shops provided the first meeting hall for Free Masons in North Platte.[37] By 1884, North Platte claimed nearly 3,000 inhabitants. The Union Pacific shops employed 350, and the railroad payroll averaged about $30,500 per month. Sixty percent of the railroad men owned property.

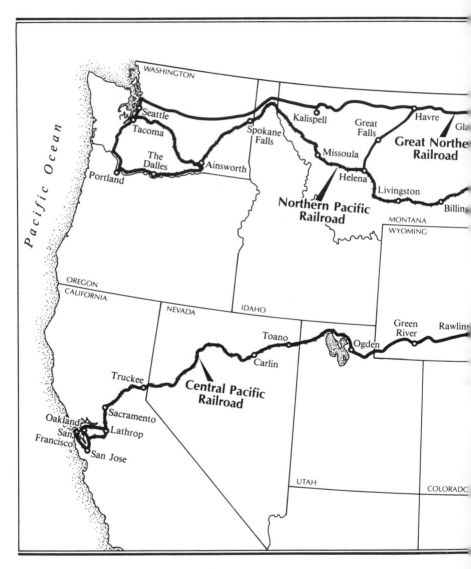

Figure 10. Map of major transcontinental railroad r

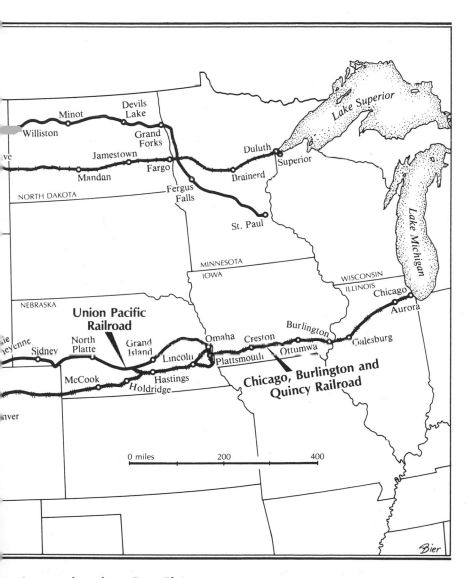

Midwest and northern Great Plains

Numbers of them gradually moved into other trades and businesses and occupied prominent niches in the local economy.[38]

Cheyenne had similar origins but grew much more rapidly. Settled in 1867 by the Union Pacific, it too experienced the ephemeral growth of a winter terminus. A "history" of Cheyenne, written ten months after the community was settled, described the feverish progress of land prices, a phenomenon common to many new railroad towns. "Town lots, 66 x 132 feet, that were sold by the Union Pacific Railroad company for $150, only one-third *cash* required, within thirty days after sold for $1000 cash, and in from two to three months following, the same lots were in demand at from $2000 for $2500."[39] Cheyenne's growth, however, was buttressed quickly by the construction of major railroad shop facilities for the eastern half of the road, by the rapid development of extensive stockraising in her hinterland, by her importance as a distributing point for supplies to military outposts, and by her designation in 1869 as the territorial capital.[40] Even so Cheyenne only gradually outdistanced smaller railroad centers like North Platte. Her population in 1880 was 3,456 and in 1890, 11,690. By 1888 the community boasted the acquisition of a small, diversified manufacturing base and four additional rail lines. A community historian writing in 1888 noted the presence of "an elegant club house" with a membership of 100 "well-to-do gentlemen" who made it a practice to show "properly accredited" visitors the "usual courtesies." Cheyenne's prosperous stock growers, who formed a frontier leisured class, were the backbone of the new Lawn Tennis Club.[41] Economic diversification and more rapid growth apparently generated a discernible infrastructure of class institutions.

Pocatello, Idaho, bloomed rather late as a division town on the Union Pacific. In 1887 the railroad purchased two thousand acres of land from the Fort Hall Indian Reservation and offered homesites to its would-be shopmen and operating employees. The town grew rapidly, displacing Idaho Falls and later Shoshone in the network of division towns servicing the Union Pacific. Between 16 percent and 20 percent of the population worked directly for the railroad; most of the rest depended on the trade that its payroll generated. Railroad workers played key roles in the major social and cultural organizations of the town.[42]

Visitors to Mandan, Dakota territory, in the early 1880s were struck by the rather ostentatious physical presence of this railroad town of about a 1,000 souls. Its depot was in the Queen Anne style,

"Skyscraper" dormitory car, used for transporting construction crew to the railhead, Chicago, Minneapolis & Manitoba Railroad, western Dakota territory 1887. Photograph courtesy of Burlington Northern Railroad.

Old Beartown, Bear River, Wyoming, on the Union Pacific, 1869. Photograph courtesy of University of Iowa, Special Collections.

Two hundred Scandinavians sought for construction work on the Cascade Division of the Northern Pacific Railroad at $2.00 per day. Photograph courtesy of Minnesota Historical Society.

"Go west, young man!" Chicago, Rock Island & Pacific Railroad. Photograph courtesy of Chicago Historical Society.

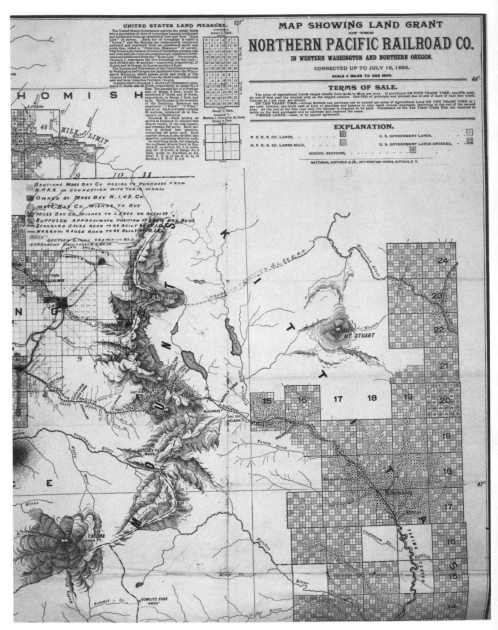

Sectional land map showing the lands of the Northern Pacific Railroad, available for sale in western Washington, ca. 1885. Photograph courtesy of Minnesota Historical Society.

HOW THE PUBLIC DOMAIN HAS BEEN SQUANDERED

Map showing the **139,403,026** acres of the people's land—equal **to**

871,268 FARMS OF 160 ACRES EACH

Worth at $2 an acre, $278,806,052,

GIVEN BY

Republican Congresses to Railroad Corporations

This is more land than is contained in New York, New Jersey,
Pennsylvania, Ohio, and Indiana.

We believe that the public lands ought, as far as possible, to be kept as homesteads for actual
settlers; that all unearned lands heretofore improvidently granted to railroad corporations by the
action of the Republican party should be restored to the public domain; and that no more grants of
land shall be made to corporations, or be allowed to fall into the ownership of alien absentees.

DEMOCRATIC PLATFORM. 1884.

"How the public domain has been squandered." Democratic Party broadside for the
presidential election of 1884. Photograph courtesy of Chicago Historical Society.

Glendive, Montana, platted a few months before by the Yellowstone Land and Colonization Company 1881. Photograph courtesy of Haynes Foundation Collection, Montana Historical Society.

A Burlington and Missouri River Railroad freight leaving Burlington, Iowa, ca. 1869. Photograph courtesy of State Historical Society of Iowa.

Twenty-five steam whistles sound off in Creston, Iowa, to announce the adoption of standard time, 12:00 noon, November 18, 1883. Photograph courtesy of State Historical Society of Iowa.

RAILROAD OFFICIALS

J. W. Kendrick, General Manager, Northern Pacific Railroad, during the labor crisis, 1893-94. Photograph courtesy of Minnesota Historical Society.

Charles Francis Adams, Jr., President, Union Pacific Railroad, 1884-90. Photograph courtesy of Union Pacific Railroad.

Charles E. Perkins, President, Chicago, Burlington & Quincy Railroad during the Great Burlington strike of 1888. Photograph courtesy of State Historical Society of Iowa.

Jay Gould, President of the Southwest Lines during the strikes of 1885-86. Photograph courtesy of the State Historical Society of Iowa.

and it possessed a fine hotel, clearly the best they had seen since they left the "Nicolett" in Minneapolis. Enjoying the favor of the railroad and anticipating a bright future, the two-year-old town already possessed a commodious public hall, a lyceum course, and "the inevitable brace of rival newspapers." The swarming crowds of people on its store-lined main street made passage difficult for the travelers.[43]

Other divisional towns like Helena, Missoula, and Butte, Montana, had been laid out as mining settlements well before they were reached by the railhead of the Northern Pacific and Great Northern.[44] Railroad connections and the location of divisional headquarters nevertheless accelerated growth. In 1880 the population of Helena was 3,624. The Northern Pacific arrived in 1883 with shops and a roundhouse, and by 1890 Helena's population had grown to 13,834. She became, in addition to a major mining and railroad center, the state capital of Montana. Local businessmen had organized a Board of Trade in November 1877, but as early as January 1866, just two years after the town site had first been entered for mining purposes, "businessmen were in the habit of holding meetings for the protection of their interest."[45]

By contrast Glendive, Montana, developed much in the manner of the railroad-planned towns in other areas. One of Glendive's historians has described her siting.

> In anticipation of the arrival of the grade, a lively village, half of it saloons and most of the rest 'dance halls' had sprung up on the Mesa south of Glendive creek. But the railroad instead of crossing this prairie, made a curve and came out on the flat where the town presently lies. Here the Yellowstone Land and Colonization Company, formed by Major Merrill, Henry Douglas, J. W. Raymond, J. W. Kendrick and others (N. P. officers and directors), using Sioux scrip, had platted the town. The village on the mesa was soon deserted in favor of the planned site.[46]

The town's first merchants were closely associated with the Northern Pacific, supplying goods to construction crews and the troops guarding them. Within a short time, two of them had opened a large general retail store, a bank, lumberyard, ferry service, and a cattle company. The town acquired between 1,200 and 1,500 persons in its first year. Three hundred men were employed in its machine shops. Glendive's early "boosters" advertised for men "with a few hundred dollars" but discouraged clerks, cashiers, and bartenders, of which "the town already has enough."[47]

In the tangle of individual community histories, it is possible to identify some common patterns of growth and to distinguish "market cities" and "railroad towns" in the railroad service network. What separated one type of town from another was not the appetite of their citizens for metropolitan status—that was almost universal. Instead, it was their ability to realize their urban ambitions. That ability was based first and foremost on the initial advantages of some towns and on their capacity to utilize access to multiple transportation routes to expand markets and diversify their manufacturing. Lacking such advantages, other towns nevertheless found their expectations raised by their fortuitous selection as railroad division headquarters, only to discover the limits to growth which dependence on a single road and the payroll of its employees imposed. Economic growth and diversification, or its absence, shaped the social environment and structured the relationships between classes. These attributes help to explain the differences in the way communities responded to the conflicts that erupted between railroad corporations and their employees.

The Iowa Setting

The state of Iowa offers a remarkable setting in which to examine more closely the effects of railroad development on urban growth and the social structure of communities. Its comparatively uniform topography and its agricultural specialization have attracted historical geographers looking for an "ideal" setting for the identification of central place hierarchies.[48] The history of railroad expansion in the state is strikingly symmetrical. Within a period of four years (1854–1857) three trunk lines radiating from Chicago reached Iowa's eastern border on the Mississippi—the Chicago, Rock Island & Pacific at Davenport in 1854, the Chicago, Burlington & Quincy at Burlington in 1856, and the Chicago & Northwestern at Clinton in 1857. Each of these roads connected with Iowa-initiated roads, and though construction was interrupted by the depression of 1857 and by the Civil War, all three reached Council Bluffs, their Missouri River terminus, between 1867 and 1869. By that time they had been joined by a fourth line, from Dubuque to Sioux City (the Dubuque & Pacific Railroad). All of these roads received substantial financial assistance from local communities in the eastern part of

the state and, most critically, federal land grants totaling more than
4.5 million acres, under legislation enacted in May 1856. According to Governor William Larrabee, these swaths of railroad land represented nearly one-eighth of Iowa's total land area. [49]

The Iowa trunk lines created and maintained one of the first and most persistent "pools," stabilizing rates and regulating the flow of freight over their lines to and from the Union Pacific in Nebraska. Iowa shippers and farmers were likewise pioneer agitators against exorbitant and discriminatory freight rates. Under legislation passed in 1874, Iowa railroad commissioners regulated freight rates on a strictly mileage basis, crystallizing an era of warfare between the railroad corporations and what they perceived to be "the granger element" in Iowa politics. After a lapse of nearly ten years, and supported by different political interests, Iowa legislators in 1888 again sought to impose some order on the rates through a revitalized board of railroad commissioners. [50]

Iowa's extensive and parallel railroad development created a network of division towns that serviced railroad operations. The presence of older commercial towns on the Mississippi and Missouri rivers, which antedated but promoted railroad development, and newer settlements in the interior of the state which were created to service trunk-line operations, offers an opportunity to test the utility of our typology as a basis for differentiating the responses of communities to industrial conflict. [51]

For the purpose of identifying Iowa towns that had significant divisional functions within the railroad network, we have selected all towns that had more than 100 railroad employees in 1895. The designation of 100 or more railroad employees as the criterion for a town having significant divisional functions is to some extent arbitrary. A division headquarters required the residence of both operating and shop employees. While the size of the required labor force varied a good deal, from towns having only a small roundhouse and light branch traffic to those having major repair shops and heavy mainline traffic, some minimum number of railroad workers is a prerequisite for a town's designation as the headquarters of an operating division. We are interested in those towns in which substantial numbers of railroad workers resided and whose divisional functions within the railroad network were more major. A town with 100 or more railroad men in a predominantly agricultural state would seem to meet both the test of a sufficiently large work force to perform divisional functions and to reflect a significant level of industrial concentration (figure 11). Twenty-four towns meet that criterion, with numbers of railroad workers ranging from 100 to 685. (Thirty-five towns had 9 to 50 railroaders, and twelve had from 51 to 99.) These twenty-four towns had 93.6 percent of all railroad employees in the state, while the remaining forty-seven towns had only 6.4 percent of the state's railroad employees.

The growth patterns described previously suggest that one attribute separating market cities from railroad towns was size. If we use size as a working basis for classification, Iowa towns with railroad service functions can provisionally but very clearly be divided between market cities and railroad towns. (table 9).[52]

Within every region a few cities grew beyond the size and functional limits of a market city. Although they may have continued to function as railroad division headquarters, their exceptional growth led to the diminished importance of the railroad service function. While they shared many characteristics with market cities, the dimensions of their growth and the extent of their diversification ultimately set them apart. Des Moines is such a city in Iowa.

Not surprisingly the larger towns in the railroad network general-

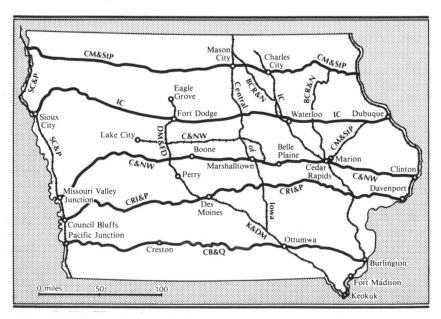

Figure 11. Map showing the location of major Iowa railroad towns, ca. 1879/80.

Table 9. Classification of Selected Iowa Urban Places

Regional City (50,000–200,000)	Market City (10,000–50,000)	Railroad Town (under 10,000)
Des Moines	Burlington	Belle Plaine
	Cedar Rapids	Boone
	Clinton	Charles City
	Council Bluffs	Creston
	Davenport	Fort Dodge
	(Des Moines)	Lake City
	Dubuque	Marion
	Fort Madison	Mason City
	Keokuk	Missouri Valley
	Marshalltown	Perry
	Ottumwa	Eagle Grove
	Sioux City	
	Waterloo	

Source: Secretary of State, Census of Iowa for the Year 1895 (Des Moines: 1896).

ly had experienced some settlement prior to the railroad. The larger of the market cities were all prerailroad river entrepôts on the Mississippi or Missouri Rivers. With few exceptions the cities that were settled by the railroad remained the smaller towns in 1895, located generally in the western interior of the state.

Although the larger river cities grew noticeably with the acquisition of rail lines, the railroad labor force declined as a proportion of the total labor force as the towns grew further. By 1895 railroad men were as few as .6 percent of the labor force in Davenport and as much as 10.2 percent in neighboring Clinton. By contrast, in smaller, interior towns rail employees were a much higher proportion of the working population. In very small towns such as Lake City nearly 16 percent of those gainfully employed worked on the railroad, and in Creston fully 35 percent of all employed people were railroad men.

Market cities and railroad towns differed not only in the proportion of railroad workers in the local labor force, but also in their growth patterns and economic diversification. Market cities in Iowa were generally settled before 1860 and before they had acquired railroad service. From the Mississippi River westward in the eastern half of the state, rail lines were built during the 1850s. Council Bluffs and Sioux City did not acquire rail lines until the end of the 1860s. The railroad towns in the interior of the state were settled in the late 1860s and early 1870s, during the same years in which they acquired railroad lines. If we compare the growth rates of market cities and railroad towns at intervals from the time their populations were first recorded in the Iowa state census, significant differences are apparent (figure 12). Population data for Iowa cities are first available for 1850. With the exception of the Missouri River towns, population data for the first five-year period of all division towns being analyzed reflect at least the anticipatory growth effects of railroad expansion.

When Iowa market cities first appeared in the state census, they were on the average 40 percent larger than railroad towns. During the first decade for which population data are available, the growth of market cities was significantly greater than for railroad towns. The initial impact of railroad development is reflected in the population growth of market cities during this first decade. For most railroad towns, their initial size as first recorded in the census reflects the presence of railroad operations. It is during the

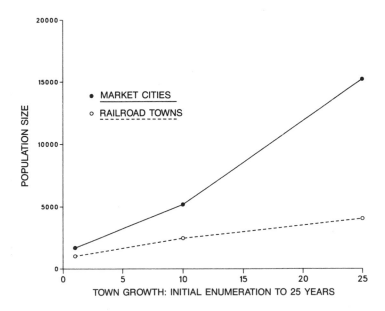

Figure 12.   Average size of selected Iowa urban places, 1850–1900

Note: Because Des Moines' growth did not exceed that of "market cities" during its first twenty-five years, it has been put in that class for the purposes of this figure.

Source: Secretary of State, Census of Iowa for the Year 1895 (Des Moines:1896).

second and third decades of growth that the character of market cities fully blossomed. Building on their initial advantages, they enjoyed more sustained economic growth than the railroad towns. The average initial size of railroad towns was 60 percent of the more established market cities. After twenty-five years of growth the average size of railroad towns had fallen to 27 percent of that of the market cities. While railroad towns grew an average of 297 percent during their first twenty-five years, market cities grew by 800 percent. Servicing railroad operations was still an important economic function for market cities, but during this period of growth they also acquired major manufacturing and wholesaling enterprises.

Manufacturing and wholesaling activity were overrepresented in market cities as compared with railroad towns. Manufacturing was conducted on a larger scale in market cities—firms were on the average three times larger and nine times more numerous. The contrast in terms of wholesale marketing was even greater. Fully two-thirds of the railroad towns had no wholesalers at all, whereas market cities averaged fifteen. The three railroad towns with some wholesale business had fewer than three firms each.[53]

Only with respect to railroad employment itself did railroad towns outstrip market cities. Together, market cities and railroad towns possessed 93.6 percent of all railroad employment in the state. Although railroad towns had only 15.8 percent of all employed persons in the two types of cities, their share of railroad employment was nearly double that figure, 35 percent.

The impact of railroads on urban development in Iowa produced a configuration of cities that is explicable in part by distinguishing the growth performance and social structure of market cities from that of railroad towns. Market cities were urban settlements that had enjoyed some notable economic development prior to the entrance of the railroad. Their growth was enhanced, and their dominance over a significant area of wholesale trade was secured by the railroad. By contrast, railroad towns were smaller, newer settlements that generally originated with railroad expansion itself. Their growth though initially spectacular was subsequently more sluggish. Their share of the state's manufacturing and wholesale trade was disproportionately low, though their share of railroad employment by comparison to market cities was disproportionately high. An analysis of two representative communities will provide a detailed comparison of the formation of their social structure and their response to industrial conflict.

164

Railroad Development and Urban Growth in Southern Iowa

Between 1855 and 1869 southern Iowa acquired a major trunk line with direct connections to Chicago and thence to the East. This brought the promise of a place in the transcontinental system pioneered by the Union Pacific and the Central Pacific. Urban growth followed close on the heels of the Burlington & Missouri River Railroad's construction, which connected the intrepid Mississippi River entrepôt of Burlington with an impatient and ambitious Council Bluffs on the Missouri. In so doing, it vitalized the growth of numerous agricultural villages in the eastern part of the state that were fortunate enough to be located on the new road, and it planted settlements in the central and western parts of the state whose ambitions, if not their growth, quickly caught up with the older towns on the state's borders.

Two towns are particularly noteworthy. In addition to the different functions they performed in the commercial and manufacturing network of southern Iowa, each was an important service center for railroad operations. Burlington maintained a large complex of machine shops and roundhouses, whose importance within the Chicago, Burlington & Quincy system grew over time.[54] More than three hundred men in the running trades alone made their homes in the city.[55] The city's switching yards offered interconnections with four other roads.[55] Creston, approximately two hundred miles farther west, was also a major divisional headquarters with large machine shops and a sixty-stall roundhouse. More than three hundred railroad men operated trains east and west from that point.

Burlington and Creston provided similar railroad services. They differed enormously, however, in the ways they developed and in their size, economic diversity, and class structure. One was a market city; the other a railroad town. Although each was an important center of strike activity in 1877 and 1888, their responses to industrial conflict were widely divergent.

Burlington

In 1850, with just less than two decades of development under its belt, Burlington had a population of over four thousand. Its "flint hills" and river frontage were already thickly settled. A generation of cabin stores that supplied the needs of settlers and river travelers had already given way to a panoply of small retailers, who specialized in dry goods, groceries, hardware, and drugs. Even by 1840, Burlington exported significant quantities of pork, grain, and cattle. Small-scale manufacturing started early. In 1833, R. S. Adams began producing shoes and boots (fifty years later his grandson employed one hundred men who turned out four hundred pairs a day); the manufacture of carriages and buggies began in 1844; and by 1850 two "seven by nine" foundries were doing an annual business of about $10,000.[56]

Also by 1850 a small but cohesive group of merchants and lawyers had begun a campaign to improve the poor transportation that was an obstacle to Burlington's further development. Twelve miles of rapids on the Mississippi just north of Keokuk at the southeastern tip of Iowa made river navigation impossible during low water. Estimates of Burlington's losses in business due to the rapids varied from $50,000 to $160,000 annually. Her leading citizens organized and reorganized between 1845 and 1855 in pursuit of the latest internal improvements.[57] Men from Burlington initiated regional conventions at which river dredging, plank roads, and finally railroads were discussed and where political support and financial commitments were sought from a broad constituency of Iowa and Illinois residents. "Plank fever" did produce a road that traversed the thirty-five miles inland to Mount Pleasant, but even as it was completed in 1851, stronger interests coalesced around the prospects for railroad development.[58]

In 1852 the Burlington & Missouri River Railroad was incorporated by forty-six Burlington promoters. More significantly, as early as April 1851, Burlington voters overwhelmingly approved a loan of $75,000 to secure a branch of the Peoria & Oquawka Railroad. This promised a connection to the Chicago market, which would permanently eliminate the problem of the Keokuk rapids. Because of the enthusiasm of the Burlington promoters and the financial commitment from the city and from numerous private stock subscribers, Burlington ultimately beat out Oquawka, Illinois, for the position of western terminus. Simultaneously, promoters in Galesburg, Illinois, fought to be included by forging an alliance of separate railroad lines that connected the Chicago and Aurora Railroad with Mendota, Galesburg, and (via the Peoria & Oquawka) Burlington. Local promoters won financial backing for these linkages from the Michigan Central Railroad, which was searching for a western outlet, and from the citizens of Aurora, Galesburg, and Burlington. Each town ultimately became the headquarters of an operating division of the Chicago, Burlington & Quincy Railroad.[59]

Burlington's ambition to build a road linking the Mississippi and Missouri rivers was actively pursued between 1852 and 1855. After a desperate fight in the state legislature, a charter for still another parallel road across Iowa was finally secured. (Two lines had been designated to receive land grants, but four finally did so.) Burlington's coterie of tireless promoters, frustrated by Congress's slowness to act on the federal land grant, turned once again to the hustings for financial support. A "railroad convention" in Fairfield, Iowa, in 1853 saw representatives of six counties along the projected route to the Des Moines River resolve for the road's construction and for legislative authority that would allow counties to subscribe stock. Michigan Central and Chicago, Burlington & Quincy officials, moving quickly to consolidate control over their western extension, acquired a controlling interest in the Burlington & Missouri and specified the conditions for the road's extension to the Des Moines River. The counties between Burlington and Ottumwa had to subscribe $450,000, with an additional $150,000 in individual subscriptions. In response to a direct appeal from James F. Joy of the Chicago, Burlington & Quincy, the city of Burlington contributed an additional $75,000 and a long-term lease to the riverfront land that was needed for shops and a depot.[60]

Even before the first C. B. & Q. train entered town Burlington's economy had taken a leap forward. Its population grew by 79 percent in the four years after 1850. "Nearly every branch of mercantile and mechanical enterprise has tripled or quadrupled," a local business directory boasted in 1856. "Some of our enterprising merchants have given up the retail business entirely and have turned their attention to the jobbing of Dry Goods, and their arrangements have been so perfected as to guarantee to western and country merchants that they will not only *save* but will make money by getting their supplies here."[61] Even during the first year of the railroad's operation, Burlington lumber dealers sold almost as much on a wholesale basis outside the city as they did within it. Of the 10 million feet of lumber brought into the city, 1.25 million was "sold into the country east of the river," 3.5 million in the country west of the river, and 5.25 million was consumed in the city itself. "Manufactories" multiplied rapidly. By 1856 there were three breweries, two plow manufacturers (one employing 20 hands), a planing mill, a sash factory (10 hands), and three iron foundries (140 hands).[62] The first private bank, owned by F. J. C. Peasley, was founded in 1851 and was intimately connected (through its offspring, the National State Bank) to the B. & M. Railroad.[63]

Although Burlington's place among the metropolises of the upper Midwest seemed assured, the city's relationship with the B. & M. and with the C. B. & Q. Railroad was occasionally frayed, as control of the road passed farther and farther from the hands of local citizens. On May 11, 1858, a letter from "Justice," which appeared in the Burlington Hawkeye, questioned the city's financial contribution to the construction of the road. "Why," he asked, "should the city donate accretions and city credit for the purpose of filling the pockets of a few individuals who make it a practice (warrior-like) of demanding tribute money every time they visit us, and threaten us, if we do not comply with their request, with total annihilation."[64]

The next year John G. Foote, former treasurer of the B. & M. Railroad, who had been displaced as corporate control shifted to Boston, expressed concern over the impact of absentee ownership on the community. In his account of this period, Richard C. Overton refers to an open letter to the Burlington Hawkeye, in which Foote insisted that the B. & M. be managed so as to "promote . . . . the interests of the State and of the City and not entirely the interests of a few nonresident stockholders and directors."[65] Foote was further concerned over the personal interest of the railroad directors in land adjacent to the road and the letting of construction contracts.

When Mayor Corse signed over conveyance of the land leased by the B. & M. Railroad in Decemeber 1866, it contained certain stipulations designed to assure a "continuing identity of interest between the city and the company." Specifically, it required that the B. & M. shops be located in perpetuity within the city limits and that the conveyed land be used for railroad purposes only.[66]

Differences between citizens of Burlington and the railroad erupted again in the early 1870s, shortly after the consolidation of the Burlington & Missouri with the Chicago, Burlington & Quincy. The Hawkeye pronounced the consolidation a benefit to Burlington, in spite of the anxiety of some that it might suffer in the freight rate-making process. C. E. Perkins, a Burlington resident of nearly fifteen years and a C. B. & Q. vice-president, wrote to his mentor, John Murray Forbes, a Boston director of the road. Perkins indicated "that consolidation did not please the Burlington people but he did not see how it could 'set the town back any.' "[67]

As a result of a successful suit by Burlington businessman Elisha Chamberlain and a number of other citizens, which restrained the city from levying a tax of .25 percent on real and personal property to pay the interest on bonds issued to the B. & M. in the 1850s, the

City Council and the County Board of Supervisors repudiated their bonded indebtedness to the railroad. The citizens claimed that the city "had no authority. . . to create an indebtedness for a private purpose.[68]

Controversy between Mississippi River towns and the Iowa pool railroads over freight rates reached fever pitch in the 1870s. But this conflict was resolved during the course of the decade, when numbers of individual wholesalers and jobbers in the river towns reached understandings with the roads over rates that would grant them control of their "natural" markets. Freight rate agitation and anti-railroad sentiment shifted westward in the next decade as new towns sought to carve out their own tributary areas in the face of discriminatory rates that favored eastern Iowa interests.[69]

A final point of irritation between the city of Burlington and the railroad involved the relocation of the C. B. & Q.'s shops to land annexed by the city in 1881 (thereby permitting the railroad to fulfill the terms of the lease conveyed in 1866). The road then proceeded to lay out a new town, West Burlington, outside the city on company-owned land to house the shop work force. The Chicago, Burlington & Quincy organized this new "company town" without the encumbrances of an established municipality, selling building lots to its employees on an installment plan and offering building sites to churches, businesses, and manufacturers.[70]

Such "abuse" at the hands of an outside corporation served to complicate the relationship between the city and its railroad, but Burlington's continued growth constantly buttressed recognition of the underlying common interests of the city's business leaders and their railroad benefactors. In 1891 local historian Clara Rouse noted that "Burlington never has a 'boom.' She marches quietly to success and is steadily advancing, reaching out a little further all the time, cautious, but growing richer and richer in her advantages. . . .[71] Local Burlington railroad officials, most notably Charles E. Perkins, maintained a close and proprietary relationship with the city, promoting its newspapers and political leaders for wider recognition, participating actively in its Board of Trade, and occasionally holding political offices. The National State Bank, Burlington's largest bank and a descendant of F. J. C. Peasley's private bank, gave up its president, J. C. Peasley, to serve with the Burlington as a financial officer and ultimately first vice-president. Both Peasley and Perkins continued to serve on the bank's board of directors through the 1880s.[72] The city's largest lumber dealers were closely related through stock ownership and interlocking directorates; the largest, the Burlington Lumber Company, did business almost exclusively with the railroad and its subsidiaries, providing bridge timber and "large dimension stuff."[73]

Burlington's wholesale dealers and manufacturers dominated the councils of the Board of Trade, comprising 64 percent of the membership. Retail merchants, though much more numerous in the population, made up only 10 percent of the membership of the Board of Trade. An informal survey conducted by the *Hawkeye* during the early days of the 1888 Burlington strike testifies to the interlocking interests between wholesalers, manufacturers, and the railroad. The survey indicates that wholesalers "doing business with the smaller towns along the Burlington system" had their business reduced by 50 to 75 percent. Manufacturers found their operations "greatly limited," though not as much as wholesalers because their markets were more widespread and they could thus to some extent use other routes. All were unanimous in their condemnation of the men on strike.[74]

Creston

Creston's development and its relationship to the railroad followed a different route. Its origins lay in the maneuverings of town-site promoters for a profit-maximizing location of the western Iowa division headquarters. An 1889 history of the town noted that "the site for the town was purchased by inside officials of the railroad company who organized themselves into a town company. Their individual names are never used, the property being managed by a trustee. About 250 acres were included in the town as first laid out."[75] Indeed, when the road reached Union County in the fall of 1868, Afton, the county seat, enjoyed a minor boom as the temporary terminus of the road. Some local investors, believing that the division headquarters would be located in the existing village of Cromwell in Union County, made substantial investments in land there, which resulted "unprofitably to them by reason of the changes in plans."[76]

Creston rose dramatically in the manner of new railroad towns from the soil of the unsettled prairie in central Union County. By early 1870 the town boasted "the largest engine house in the West," with attendant machine shops employing several hundred men. Only a few months before, the community had consisted of two frame houses, twelve cabins, and five tents.[77] In 1875 the visiting editor of the *Prairie Farmer* was impressed by the bustling air of this little prairie city. From fifty to eighty trains were made up daily, and the Burlington & Missouri employed 650 local men, with a payroll of nearly $40,000 per month. "Business in Creston," he noted, "is conducted nearer on a cash basis than any other point along the line in Iowa." Railroad men had built and occupied "some of the finest residences in the town."[78] The city directory in the next year pointed out that the railroad workmen "contribute largely to the support of its businesses and municipal interests."[79]

During its first decade Creston's population rose no less spectacularly than its railroad facilities. A population of 416 in 1870 had risen to 4,081 in 1880. That growth, however, was based largely on servicing railroad operations and employees. In 1876 approximately 33 percent of the labor force worked directly for the railroad, and by 1895, 35 percent of the labor force was employed by the C. B. & Q. Railroad. The 1880 U.S. Census of Manufactures lists only a handful of small firms in "blacksmithing, clothing and saddlery," averaging three employees apiece. Two building contractors employed ten workers apiece, making them the largest employers in town, outside of the C. B. & Q. Two flour mills employed seven and nine men, respectively. The town had no wholesale dealers.[80] Even in 1892, Creston had only a few small manufacturing firms—a sash factory, a cigar factory, a soap works, and a small foundry and machine shop.[81]

By the early 1880s, Creston's growth slowed considerably, and local community leaders were haunted by the possibility of stagnation. In a January 1885 editorial, the editor of the city's largest newspaper, the *Creston Daily Advertiser*, raised the question, "What Is Creston's Future?"

> Many times, within the past few years, in the *Advertiser's* "cranky" efforts to awake the citizens, businessmen and taxpayers of Creston to a realization of the necessities of our young city, have we stated that Creston was far ahead of herself; that every branch of business in the city was overdone, and that unless a new railroad, manufactories or some enterprise besides what she possessed were soon added, she must step down from the proud position she has occupied as the boss city of the slope, the metropolis of Southwestern Iowa, and degenerate into a small inland town with limited prospects for her future.[82]

As previously noted, Burlington's difficulties with the C. B. & Q. Railroad irked a portion of the city's population, but they did not fundamentally affect the prospects for the city's continued growth. The economic benefits of Burlington's relationship to the railroad were readily apparent. In contrast, leading citizens of Creston in the mid-1880s persistently identified the city's inability to sustain economic growth with the "iron grip of the mighty and avaricious Q. still on its throat." Without "railroad competition" cities like Creston saw themselves victimized by inherently discriminatory freight rate-making practices. As the *Advertiser* pointed out, manufactories, wholesale and jobbing firms "are what build up and make a place substantial" by adding to the producing and consuming population of a town. But plainly, "such institutions cannot exist where there is no railroad competition."[83]

Committees of leading businessmen, and indeed the newly instituted Board of Trade, organized, just as Burlington businessmen in the early 1850s, to secure a competing railroad line through the city. Like their Burlington counterparts, they sought to secure Creston's economic future through improved transportation. But unlike the Burlington experience, their campaign was infused with an explicit opposition to the "monopolistic" C. B. & Q., and unlike their Burlington counterparts, they were ultimately unsuccessful.[84]

Creston's Board of Trade, organized in 1886, was dominated by retail merchants, who comprised 60 percent of the membership and dominated the committees that sought competing railroad lines.[85] (Only one manufacturer and two aspiring wholesalers were members.) Storekeepers were tied directly to the interests of their customers, so that in towns like Creston, where railroad men dominated the labor force and generated a substantial amount of the town's income, the interests of railroad workers were likely to find support among the retail merchants they patronized.

Retail merchants in both Burlington and Creston found their interests directly affected by the railroad strike of 1888. Their problem, unlike that of wholesale merchants, was not the absence of transportation and the interruption of business, but rather "many of their best customers were among the striking men," and those men had significantly less disposable income to buy goods or to go toward "paying old bills."[86] What differentiated the two communities, among other things, was that in Burlington retail merchants had significantly less influence in the business councils of the city than had wholesalers and manufacturers, whereas in Creston they were community leaders and their views dominated in the Board of Trade and the press.

Speaking for Creston's leading merchants during the 1888 strike, the *Daily Advertiser* urged the support of "every citizen of Creston, . . . that the boys win the present struggle." It warned that because of the investments in homes and "obligations contracted," if the railroad men were to lose the strike and have to leave the community, it "would be such a blow to the financial condition of our city that she would not recover for years to come."[87] Such a position was consistent not only with the basis of Creston's economy as it existed in the 1880s but with the "anti-monopoly" framework within which Creston boosters fought to unlock the city's potential for economic growth. The initial advantages of older market cities that secured early railroad connections and more favorable treatment in the making of freight rates continued to operate in a manner that was perceived by the newer railroad boom towns as systematically inhibiting their own development.

Comparing Town Elites

During much of the first decade of Creston's existence, a small coalition of railroad officials and men with sizeable real estate interests dominated political and social life. Men like R. P. Smith and J. B. Harsh settled in Creston early and built considerable wealth on their "judicious investments" in land. In 1887 it was said of Harsh that "but few tracts of land within a radius of twenty miles of Creston . . . have not at one time or another passed through his hands."[88] Five of the fourteen men whose biographies appeared in the city directory of 1876 listed their primary occupation as real estate dealer.[89]

Less than ten years after the town's settlement, with the population of the community nearly doubled, a much more diverse pattern of economic and social influence was apparent. Of the ninety-six individuals whose subscription biographies are included in the 1887 county history, 65 percent had arrived within the previous ten years.[90] Nearly 20 percent had worked at one time for the Chicago, Burlington & Quincy, many of them in the shops and running trades. No railroad workers had been elected to public office during the first half of the 1870s, but by the early 1880s, railroad workers were regularly elected to local offices. The Knights of Labor was highly visible in local affairs, members being elected at various times to justice of the peace, the city council, and the state legislature. The town was among the stronger centers of support for Greenback and Union Labor politics in the state. Chicago, Burlington & Quincy estimated that 35 percent of Creston's shopmen belonged to the Knights of Labor.[91]

Burlington's business and political elite stands in sharp contrast to Creston's. Manufacturers and wholesalers dominated the city's affairs with considerable continuity throughout the railroad era of the nineteeth century. Wholesalers were prominent among the incorporators of the Board of Trade in 1872, and they were a dominant bloc on the board in 1881 (when they comprised 31 percent of the membership and 39 percent of the officers and members of standing committees).[92] In contrast to Creston's elite, where an overwhelming majority of the members were very recent arrivals even by "new town" standards, Burlington's upper crust were older and sank deep roots in the economic and social structure of the city. An examination of the subscription biographies of 252 Burlington residents that were included in a history of Des Moines County published in 1888 reveals that 68 percent had been in the community at least eighteen years, longer than Creston had even existed as a community.[93] Forty-three percent had been in the community for more than twenty-eight years. The greatest number who arrived in any decade (seventy-four) were either born in or entered the community during the decade of the 1850s, in the midst of the economic transformation wrought by the railroad. Their business careers reveal remarkable patterns of interaction in the formation of partnerships and the purchase and inheritance of businesses. An identical proportion of Burlington's and Creston's elite (20 percent) evidenced some background in railroad work. The noteworthy difference is that while 57 percent of the Creston men with railroad backgrounds were identifiable primarily as operating employees (running trades) or shopmen, only 25 percent of Burlington's railroad elite came from such working-class occupations. Upper-class Burlington, however, had a much larger proportion of men with railroad backgrounds who had been supervisors or officers. In Burlington, 33 percent of the men had been supervisors (shop foremen, roadmasters, and so forth), and 25 percent were officers (presidents, solicitors, superintendents); in Creston, the proportions were 10 percent and 5 percent.

Creston and Burlington were a study in contrasts as they entered the era of the "Great Upheaval" in the late 1870s. Burlington's elite, based in manufacturing and wholesaling, was comparatively stable and well organized. Its leadership of the community, secured in the agitation for "internal improvements," was not fundamentally challenged. In Creston, members of the business elite, many of whom were new to the community, rode uneasily at the head of a broad coalition of small merchants, railroad men, and dealers who serviced the agricultural trade. In Burlington, railroad workers were one segment of a heterogeneous labor force; in Creston, their numbers dominated. In Burlington, a diversified local economy had been built on the foundation of prerailroad economic growth; the railroads enabled the city to extend these initial advantages into regional dominance of wholesaling and jobbing and into the development of diversified manufacturing. Creston's economy was created and limited by the railroad. Local capital generated from land sales or from the railroad payroll, though substantial when compared with the cash flow of neighboring (and envious) farm villages, was not the stuff of which great manufacturing centers are built. Dependence on a single rail line, it was perceived, discouraged further economic development.

Differences in the economic structure and growth performance of a market city and a railroad town led to differences in the composition, turnover, and solidarity of local elites. The eruption of industrial conflict elicited divergent responses that were consistent with the structure of class relations in these communities.

Industrial Conflict and Community Response

Many factors shaped the way communities responded to industrial conflict. On one level, as Herbert Gutman suggested, personal relationships and loyalties within smaller communities were a more compelling basis for action than the impersonal influences of outside corporations. But on another level, as the foregoing analysis has suggested, even industrial cities like Burlington had experienced a level of economic development and market growth that created the basis for significant class differences and for the mobilization of public opinion by elites whose loyalties to their railroad benefactors were stronger than their sense of community with local railroad workers. The antimonopoly perspective of Creston's local boosters provided the basis for a more sympathetic response to the plight of railroad workers striking against the "avaricious Q." And that response was secured by the power that Creston's railroad workers wielded as the primary consumers of the goods that the town's leading businessmen retailed. But even in Creston, this community support was more transitory and the sense of community solidarity more fragile than might have been predicted.

An examination of how Burlington and Creston responded to the railroad strikes of 1877 and 1888 provides an opportunity to test for one market city and one railroad town the way in which differences in their development, their social structure, and the composition of their elites help to explain community responses to strikes. By implication, such comparisons could be undertaken for other sets of railroad towns and other types of industrial communities.

Wage cuts during the depression of the 1870s ushered in an era of tumultuous labor relations on the railroads. The Chicago, Burlington & Quincy Railroad was not immune. Between 1876 and 1888 men in the running trades and switchmen and shopmen agitated over wage rates and work rules. The road experienced major strikes in 1877 and in 1888. Even after the epochal "Great Strike" of engineers, firemen, and switchmen in 1888, isolated pockets of shopmen managed to assert their sympathy with the Pullman strikers in 1894. The purpose in this section is to compare the extent of community support in two very different division towns in Iowa.

Burlington and Creston in the 1877 Strike

The railroad strike of 1877 spread westward and reached Iowa on July 24, more than a week after it had begun in the East. All classes of employees on the Chicago, Burlington & Quincy had experienced recent wage cuts. Further, in September 1876, engineers found themselves with a new "apprenticeship" system imposed by the company that reduced the wages of first- and second-year engineers. "Classification," as the system was called, stirred resentment from the beginning and continued to be a source of unrest until the Great Strike of 1888.

Large meetings of railroad men were held in Creston, Ottumwa, and Burlington on July 23. The Creston men acted first, resolving to strike the next day and sending a committee east. The men in Burlington waited for results from the other divisions. They met again on the evening of July 24, admitted only railroad men, and heard speakers from Galesburg and Creston exhort them to join the work stoppage. They drew up a list of demands representing the sentiments of dozens of different trades and on July 25 joined the strike.[94]

Charles E. Perkins, still a vice-president of the C. B. & Q. and stationed in Burlington, immediately recognized his helplessness in the face of the strikers' numbers and the support they enjoyed from the state's "pastoral" government and populace. A lumber dealer from rural Afton had indicated in a telegram to Perkins on July 25 that "the railroad enemies here are confined to the 'granger element' with a few exceptions." Perkins already appreciated that public sympathy ran against the railroads and "rather to the rebels." His remedy, for which he argued vociferously within Chicago, Burlington & Quincy management circles, was a suspension of all traffic, and to "say to the mob and the public, 'until our property is protected by the constitutional authorities we will go out of business.' "[95] Within his realm of authority he stopped all passenger trains out of Burlington, hoping thereby to exert pressure on the community, and he was instrumental in activating the Burlington Board of Trade to use its good offices to end the strike. By the next day, July 26, Perkins telegraphed President Robert Harris that public opinion was "beginning to come around." The initial solidarity of the strikers was shattered on July 26 when conductors in Burlington voted to return to work, taking with them a significant number of brakemen.[96]

Most revealing about the quality of community support for the strikers in Burlington were the activities of the Board of Trade and results of two "citizens' meetings." The striking railroad men called a meeting at the Opera House on the evening of July 27 to "consult" with citizens. The well-attended meeting heard brief opening remarks by two attorneys, a minister, and the land commissioner of the railroad, which were cautious and noncommittal. They were followed by three engineers and a shopman who vigorously defended the strike. At this point, "adjournment was hastily procured" by the striker who chaired the meeting, amid much shouting and confusion. There was a call for a meeting the following night and a resolution urging "the appointment of a committee of businessmen to act with us in endeavoring to procure what we think we are entitled to."

The next afternoon, invited members of the Board of Trade met in their offices without consulting the railroad men and drafted a series of resolutions stating that: "On behalf of the businessmen of this city we deprecate and have no sympathy with strikers among employees in any calling . . . and recommend to the workingmen immediate resumption of work so that trade may be restored to its proper channels." They went on to offer their assistance in presenting the grievances of railroad employees to the company and in procuring assurances against the discharge of the strikers. They also appointed a Committee of Ten," who represented the wholesale interests of the city, with one railroad official and a minister added for good measure.

It was already apparent that the men on strike and many citizens viewed the second "citizens' meeting" from very different perspectives. In urging a large turnout for the meeting, the Burlington *Gazette* reported, "the workingmen have called the meeting. They claim their grievances are not understood by the citizens generally and they want to explain them." The paper also noted that the Committee of Ten from the Board of Trade proposed to meet with the Strikers' committee while the meeting was going on, to negotiate an end to the difficulties—not at all what the men on strike had in mind.[97]

George Price, a striking engineer, was chosen permanent chairman of the meeting. He called on Robert Donahue, a member of the Board of Trade's Committee of Ten and a wholesale dealer in iron and steel. Donahue argued to the large assemblage that the strike was unwarranted and ill-advised, declaring that labor and capital were not inherently antagonistic. His remarks were drowned in hisses and shouts. Chairman Price took the podium and "spoke excitedly" and with much anger. "I propose to counsel with men who are directly interested and not with outside parties. If they cannot discriminate between actual want and capital, the sooner the crash comes the better [loud applause]. . . . We don't want to advise with outside parties; we haven't asked anybody here to advise us." Other businessmen who were called upon refused to speak, citing "the ungentlemanly way Mr. Donahue had been treated." The meeting was temporarily patched together with a new chairman but finally broke up, with the underlying divisions in the community visible to all.

The next day, July 29, the *Burlington Gazette* declared the meeting "a pronounced failure" that had "rather the effect of widening the breach between the men and the company than of helping to close it." The *Gazette* also noted that those few businessmen who did speak up in sympathy with the striking railroad men "have been attacked in private . . . and attempts made to injure them in their business. . . ."[98]

The strikers' solidarity continued to dissolve as divisions widened in their own ranks. Shopmen voted in the late afternoon of July 29 to return to work. Perkins noted to President Harris that "public opinion here in Burlington has finally reached the point where it would not only give us moral but physical support if necessary."[99] The *Gazette* also took note of the changed mood in the community. There were more "harsh words and angry altercations" on the street. "The citizens are becoming irritated with the interruption of service." By the next day, the strike in Burlington was over.[100]

In Creston the strike began earlier and ended later. The strikers' meeting on July 23 was "quiet and orderly." Resolutions were passed outlining their demands, including a restoration of shopmen's pay to the level of 1873 and of engineers' and firemen's pay to the 1876 levels. A committee was appointed and instructed to meet with strikers in towns on the eastern divisions of the road and to present the demands to management. Crowds in excess of fifty were constantly on hand at the depot to stop incoming trains. A local official warned vice-president T. J. Potter that "it would probably be best not to excite them" by sending any further trains, and a roadmaster advised Perkins to send state troops, as "the law and order element is intimidated there." Perkins grew restive with Creston's intransigence on July 30 as the strike moved to a conclusion on the eastern end of the road. He telegraphed threateningly to a handful of Chicago, Burlington, & Quincy friends in the town that Creston might find itself "left out, if they wait a little longer." Warning that the town would experience greater harm than the railroad, he added sternly, "I mean just what I say." And later in the day he again telegraphed R. P. Smith, a land dealer, A. D. Temple, a banker, and William Scott, a grain dealer, to say that his patience was nearly exhausted and that "I shall be sorry to see many mechanics owning property in Creston give up their permanent occupations, and I suppose you will." Urging them once more to "make the men see the situation as it is," he warned that "the interest of the community is at stake in this matter." Even as Perkins noted to his Creston confidants that the men in Burlington were returning to work on the assurances offered to them, T. J. Potter warned him that a committee from Creston was proceeding to Burlington with the intention of getting the shopmen and engineers to go out again.

With the strike movement collapsing nationally, Creston strikers from all departments met on July 31 and resolved to end their strike in the same orderly fashion they had begun it and to return to work "in a body." A relieved R. P. Smith telegraphed Perkins that night, "Thank God, Creston breathes again." The strike in Creston ended the next day, August 1, with no visible lines of division among strikers or between the men and the community.[101]

Antimonopoly and Class Interests

Although the Chicago, Burlington & Quincy experienced no major labor unrest for the next eleven years, its workers, led particularly by engineers and firemen from western Iowa and from Nebraska, continued to push for equalization of pay and the abolition of classification.[102] Creston entered a period of stagnation and even lost population, while Burlington began another cycle of vigorous growth.

As the Mississippi River towns of Iowa consolidated their grip on the state's jobbing and wholesale trade, agitation for railroad regulation was renewed in the western section of the state. Assertions against the dire effects of railroad monopolies found a ready constituency among owners of small businesses in isolated towns served by a single road, among the "granger element" of western farmers who felt victimized by both railroad rates and land policies, and increasingly among railroad workers themselves, though their participation in this predominantly agrarian coalition was always more tenuous. As political support for a renewal of mandatory state regulation of railroad rates mounted in early 1888, a Knights of Labor assembly of railroad workers came out vigorously for state regulation, protesting the coercive methods of railroads in forcing employees to sign petitions opposing the legislation and objecting to the habitual threats by railroad corporations to withhold benefits to towns that failed to support the railroads on this issue.[103]

The economic and political solidarity that crossed class lines in communities like Creston and was buttressed by ties of small community life—proximity of residence, property ownership, and participation in social and fraternal organizations—found its most common manifestation during the mid-1880s in the Noble and Holy Order of the Knights of Labor. The Knights articulated an antimonopoly ideology around which a broad class of self-styled "producers" could rally.

Chicago, Burlington, & Quincy officials manifested considerable concern over the rapid growth of the Knights in the ranks of their employees. One official from Galesburg indicated that he had heard that the Knights had a "heavy" membership in Creston. "I would not be surprised if such were the case," he went on, "as the farther west we go, the stronger the rolls of these 'Communist' societies seem to be." A local newspaper published by the Republican banker J. B. Harsh estimated that the Knights had 125 members in Creston by the spring of 1885. Master Mechanic C. W. Eckerson believed that one-third of the Q. shopmen were members of the Knights as well. He also reported that the Knights were led by the mayor, an alderman, two justices, a newspaper editor, and "quite a number of the same stripe." Superintendent of Motive Power G. W. Rhodes, in his summary of the investigation of the Knights, noted that politicians, merchants, and petty officials seemed to join the organization for political reasons. He found that laboring men reaped some benefit from such alliances within the Knights; "in the case of any mandates [strikes] they are bolstered by the sympathy of those they aid in politics."[104]

When members of Typographical Union No. 131 struck the *Creston Advertiser* in 1885 because it had employed a scab printer from Kansas City, the Knights of Labor as well as the Railroad Brotherhoods, the Cigarmakers, and the Farmers' Alliance from neighboring townships rallied to their support. The local divisions of the brotherhoods of engineers and firemen proclaimed that "being laboring organizations" they would support the striking printers by boycotting the *Advertiser*. When the striking printers started up their own local weekly, *The Workingmen's Advocate*, which rapidly became recognized as the largest "Knights of Labor" newspaper in the state, the railroad brotherhoods declared it their official organ as well.[105]

The publisher of the *Advertiser*, S. A. Brewster, was the object of the strike. He was also the loudest voice in the community decrying the effects of the Chicago, Burlington, & Quincy "monopoly" on the city's growth. While vowing to beat the printers—theirs was not a strike of labor against capital, but of labor against labor, he claimed—he argued for labor organizations which would strike for "elevating the laboring classes and for mutual aid and protection and for insurance." He insisted that all citizens would benefit from a restoration of the railroad competition for which he so assiduously worked, but "especially the laboring people as a class."[106]

Brewster poured unflagging energy into his campaign to build an "antimonopoly" coalition that might secure the city's future prosperity. The city was not marked by fundamental class divisions, he asserted with some exaggeration in the midst of his own printers' strike, "All people in this city with but very few exceptions are working people. We have but two or three capitalists. Some of this latter class today class themselves with the laboring people, belong to labor organizations."[107] This apparent classlessness only thinly disguised serious schisms within the community. Not only did the action of the printers alienate Brewster from many laboring men, whom he patronizingly referred to as some of his "best friends," but the boycott of the *Advertiser*, which they initiated and enforced along with their trade union and business allies, polarized the community.

Brewster found unity sadly lacking even among Creston's businessmen and property owners. When a party of Chicago, Burlington & Quincy officials visited the city on a tour of the line in August 1885, the beleaguered publisher bemoaned their cool reception. He quoted the *Ottumwa Democrat* approvingly when it described a meeting of local businessmen that had resolved "to take action relative to the meeting with the officials of the Burlington." By contrast, in Creston, the visiting officials of the railroad encountered no organized committee of businessmen prepared to lay their grievances before them and "ask for redress." In fact, Brewster reported, "the officials were obliged to walk over the city, hunt up the businessmen and talk with them."

Brewster noted that there were at least three groups among Creston's "leading citizens." Some were under obligations to the C. B. & Q. and feared incurring its wrath. Others believed that the proper remedy for their freight rate grievances was through legislation. And, in Brewster's words, those in another group "feel that the proper thing is for us to stand up like men and ask for our rights." Brewster's views were apparently confirmed by a reporter for the *Chicago Inter-Ocean* who had been commissioned to "write up" the city in a half-column and reportedly left in disgust after a few days, declaring that he had never seen a city of Creston's size whose businessmen and property owners were so sharply divided.[108]

If the business stagnation and the high freight rates suffered by Creston in the mid-1880s left her business leaders demoralized and divided, expediency required that they defend the interest of the railroad workers whose incomes underpinned the city's economy. In defense of his record of support for the interests of the "laboring class" S. A. Brewster recalled that he and other businessmen had actively supported the "railroad boys" in their strike against the C. B. & Q. in 1877. He wrote, "Their interests and our own are identical. And at any time in the future as we would have done in the past should the employees on the Q. either in the shop, yard, offices or on the road strike for better wages, which we believe would be nothing more than they deserve, so long as they made a square and honorable stand for their request, they would find the *Advertiser* to their back and doing all it could to advance their interest."[109]

The Great Strike of 1888

On February 26, 1888, engineers and firemen on the entire length of the Burlington system walked off the job to enforce their demand for equalization of pay and for an end to classification of engineers. Although the strike was remarkably solid from one end of the line to the other, there were important differences in the patterns of strike participation and in the community support the strikers generated in various division towns. Chapter 5 analyzes the participation of railroad workers in the 1888 strike. This chapter compares levels of community support.

In Creston a large and vocal segment of the Creston community rallied to the support of the strikers, as it had in the previous strike. All five of the city's newspapers supported the men on strike (none of the newspapers in Burlington did).[110] At the urging of the men on strike, two committees of Creston citizens complained, in a petition to the State Railroad Commission, that the Chicago, Burlington & Quincy was operating its trains with incompetent men. The first petition was from seven local physicians; the second, from thirty-nine citizens, almost all in the retail trade. The commission held two days of hearings in the community and sustained the citizens' charge.[111]

At the end of the first week of the strike, Mayor F. J. Taylor, who was under intense pressure from the railroad, hired special police to assist in "maintaining the peace," in spite of the absence of disorder of any kind. On March 26, thirty-six of the special police struck, prompting the company to augment its own force of Pinkerton detectives. At a special session of the city council, Alderman John McCaffery, who was a leading member of the Knights of Labor and the Union Labor party, "arraigned the railroad company severely for inciting violence by the importation of Pinkerton toughs." Superintendent Brown of the railroad's Iowa lines was present for the special council session and warned that he was authorized by President Perkins to notify the city that if it failed to protect the road's loyal employees, the company would close its shops in Creston and move its workers to Burlington. "These men," he asserted, "are going to run engines and fire engines on the C. B. & Q. and it is for the city and council of Creston to say whether they will drive out forty, fifty or possibly a hundred families or whether they will extend to them proper protection." The superintendent's warning notwithstanding, the Creston City Council voted, with but one dissent, to instruct the mayor to notify Division Superintendent Duggan that he must keep his police force strictly on company grounds.[112]

The next day, the Advertiser's editorial page boiled with indignation "at again having this emaciated old skeleton drawn from the corporation closet and flaunted in their faces because they dare to have independent ideas which are not in sympathy with the great Q. monopoly." The editor recounted the number of times since

1877 that Creston had been threatened with the removal of its shops because it supported strikers, or appointed committees to investigate competing lines, or demanded lower freight or passenger rates.

> Now because some citizens dared to petition the governor for an investigation of the competency of the men running the engines, they are threatened by these Q. bulldozers, and lastly because our citizens sympathize with our *resident, property-owning, taxpaying, striking* brotherhood men and because some of the toughs the Q. has picked up to take the places of the strikers have been thumped for their insolence upon the street, by some of the strikers, the Q. cries that the city is not protecting its new men and property and threatens to close its shops here and remove the workmen to Burlington.
>
> Bah on such Balderdash. We are tired of it. It has retarded permanent investments and improvements in our city long enough. Our citizens owe the C. B. & Q. nothing.[113]

For several months the prospect of the Chicago, Burlington, & Quincy removing its shops from the city was a lively source of controversy. Numbers of towns in western and central Iowa petitioned the C. B. & Q. affirming their unshakeable loyalty to the road (in contrast to Creston) and requesting to be the beneficiaries of the threatened relocation. In spite of the threat, there were continuing manifestations of community support for the strikers, including boycotts against merchants who opposed the strike.[114]

Burlington, however, showed virtually no evidence of popular sympathy for the men on strike. The striking railroad men kept largely to themselves. Adequately supplied with willing conductors, brakemen, and shopmen to guard company property, the local division superintendent, O. E. Stewart, did not have to rely on the city force for protection. The majority of the new men were recruited locally.[115]

Shortly after the inauguration of the strike, Superintendent Brown informed the *Burlington Hawkeye* that if the other divisions of the road "were as well off as the Eastern Iowa Division, all passenger trains and some freights would be running."[116] Throughout the first month of the strike the *Hawkeye* published a barrage of editorials and letters condemning the strikers. They reserved particular venom for the switchmen's sympathy strike in late March and the "insane demand" that the men should "assume the right to dictate to the owners whom they should employ."[117] The bitterness engendered by the strike was expressed in an exchange of letters between "A Businessman" and "A Lady Reader of all the Papers." Replying to his accusations that the striking men were trying to "cripple the road" and place a tax on the public, the lady reader challenged the businessman to have the moral courage to reveal his identity, and alluding to the possibility of a boycott, she suggested that "we would like to form his acquaintance; we would like to know whether he wears brass buttons or flour dust on his coat, or threads and ravelings from a dry goods store." She closed her letter with the wish that he and his business might "rest in peace."[118]

The editor of the *Hawkeye* waded into the fray by reminding readers of Martin Irons, the "dictator" of the Southwest strikes, "who is now tending a peanut stand in St. Louis." The newspaper saved its harshest reprimands for Burlington's sister city, Creston, which "has been conducting itself in a disgraceful manner from the first."[119] Echoing the words of President Perkins, the *Hawkeye* urged communities to welcome the new Chicago, Burlington & Quincy employees "who have come into our family. . . . It should be understood by all that these men are here to stay with us and become part of us." Along with Pinkerton detectives, strikebreakers brought into Burlington from outside the community were housed temporarily in the company hospital, which was dubbed by the strikers the "Casino." Its inmates were visited by a welcoming committee of prominent businessmen and loyal trainmen.[120]

As the strike wore on through the summer months and into the fall, Creston opinion leaders feared for the "moral and social scars" of the strike. The editor of the *Advertiser* renewed his agitation for making Creston a major manufacturing and wholesaling center. He reported a reassuring conversation with General Manager Stone during the latter's tour of the Chicago, Burlington & Quincy system in late June 1888. Stone had expressed the company's continued interest in Creston, despite concern for the manifest lack of protection for loyal railroad men. "So long as things move on in Creston as they are now moving there is no cause for any such removal."[121]

Early in January 1889 a special committee of the Brotherhood of Locomotive Engineers negotiated an unsatisfactory end to the strike. The terms of the settlement were bitterly denounced by a number of Creston engineers as an outrageous sellout. The company declared itself willing to accept but did not feel obliged to honor applications for work from the old engineers and firemen. One hundred men on the Western Iowa Division at Creston reapplied; only fifty-three in Burlington did so. None were rehired in either town.[122]

With the strike settled, leading citizens turned to the task of healing the wounds opened during the conflict. The *Creston Daily Advertiser* had already argued that those who had taken the places of the strikers must be accepted as residents of the community, "to mingle as such in our social and business life." Looking ahead, the newspaper urged citizens to accept the results of the strike. "Let the scars made in the heat of the conflict be healed, let the hatchet be buried." The crucial matter was Creston's future welfare and prosperity, which should occupy all its citizens' attention "to the exclusion of personal bickerings or unavailing discussion of past events." And discussion did turn to other topics—the possibility of another railroad through Creston, the prospect that the C. B. & Q. would expand its shops in the city to construct locomotives, and the general "building up" of the city as the "future metropolis of southwestern Iowa."[123]

By the early months of 1889, the Chicago, Burlington, & Quincy Railroad was well on its way to creating a tractable work force. The men who had struck in Burlington and Creston were barred from future employment on the road and with few exceptions left the communities to search for other work. With them went the economic and social force of brotherhood organization in the communities. Most of the new men joined the Burlington Voluntary Relief Association, a company-sponsored insurance scheme designed to replace the shattered brotherhoods. This was but one of several organizations in Creston that formed in the wake of the strike to harmonize class interests.

Industrial peace revived Creston's urban ambitions. Community solidarity was as much the basis for the realization of those ambitions as it had ever been. Railroad men and their purchasing power still provided the economic foundations of the city's commercial trade. But now this community solidarity led to accommodation rather than resistance to the C. B. & Q. In spite of lingering anti-monopoly sentiment, Creston's leading citizens and her railroad men identified their interests more with those of the railroad than in the days before the strike. The "recent unpleasantness," as it was referred to, and Creston's heritage of insolence to the railroad monopoly were put aside for the time being. Illusory though Creston's ambitions may have been, the town pursued them with a diehard pragmatism that sought to emulate the social and economic development bequeathed by historical and geographical forces to her rival, Burlington. Such pragmatism could again conceivably lead to sympathy for her workers in another confrontation with the distant railroad corporation. But it would come only when an organized and assertive local labor movement demanded it. In the absence of an effective labor movement, the community pursued other alliances in behalf of its own development.

Summary

Railroad division towns were a particular species of the genus of industrial communities. They had common characteristics because of their role within the railroad service network. Differences among them were a function of the differences in the timing and pattern of their settlement, the extent of prerailroad economic development and their ability to transcend the economic limitations of servicing railroad operations. These differences produced differences in class structure and contrasting community behavior in response to the conflicts between railroad labor and capital.

Railroad division towns have been classed as either market cities or railroad towns. The analysis of Burlington and Creston suggests how structural differences help to explain differences in the way these communities responded to industrial conflict. In general, market cities, which were older and more economically diversified and which enjoyed comparatively steady growth and a more unified elite, supported railroad capital. Railroad towns, which were newer communities whose economies were more concentrated in servicing railroad operations, whose growth was less stable, and whose elites were smaller and more divided, more often supported their fellow citizens who were railroad men.

Even in communities that provided substantial support for striking railroad men there was an underlying ambivalence which surfaced in the face of the strikers' defeat. Long-term economic growth inevitably meant alliances with railroad corporations, even though, in the short run, communities might find it necessary to support the class interests of politically and economically powerful railroad workers.

"Producers' consciousness" and agitation against the railroad's "monopoly" power over rates and land allowed residents of these railroad towns to see the world divided into two classes— producers and monopolists. But the distinction between class and community interest was blurred. Producerism masked sharpening class divisions. To the extent that communities supported the more narrowly defined "class interest" of railroad men against their corporate managers, that support was lent in the name of "community interest." But when railroad men lost their power to enforce their class interest as community interest (because of lost strikes, the blacklist, elimination of the brotherhoods, and migration out of the community), that community interest resurfaced in another form. Producers' consciousness could also applaud the initiatives of *productive* capital when it promised to benefit the community through the construction of new facilities, timely donations to public insti tutions, and a reduction of freight rates.

The instincts of economic self-preservation dictated different responses to railroad strikes in different situations. Smaller railroad towns were no less "modern" or market-oriented than their larger and more diversified competitors. The structure of their economies and the barriers to further growth shaped their perception of their interests. The plight of victimized railroad men was readily fused with the frustrated ambitions of town promoters in an antimonopoly coalition that promoted progress, independence, and community solidarity.

The defeat of the C. B. & Q. strikers in 1888 and the introduction of a labor force loyal to the railroad corporation were important elements in the disintegration of that antimonopoly coalition in towns such as Creston. In again welcoming the proffered patronage of the railroad and in reaffirming their own urban ambitious, the people of Creston found that their differences with the railroad, which had been so manifest during the recent strike, seemed to dissolve. Just as citizens of Burlington welcomed their new "scab" neighbors, the people of Creston came around to "burying the hatchet" with theirs. In so doing they inaugurated a new era in railroad-community relations, which was quickened by their metropolitan ambitions

5

Persistence, Promotion, and the Solidarity of Railroad Labor

Perhaps you wouldn't take me for an old enough man to have done railroading twenty-seven years ago, but it's true. I worked steadily on one train for nine years from 1852. I left the road several times and tried to better myself and when I went back I always found a place ready for me.[1]

—Barney J. Donahue
Hornellsville, New York
Interview in jail,
July 31, 1877

The railroad companies have a well-defined purpose in hounding men from place to place, persecuting them from lodgment to lodgment, driving them, on account of some old score—some part in the great A. R. U. strike perhaps, or some small falsification in a personal record—at last out of the vocation they have grown into and followed until their minds are molded around it and their hands cunning in its ways. . . . The larger this floating, discontented, almost desperate element, the better for the railroads in time of need.[2]

—William John Pinkerton
His Personal Record

Work on the railroad was a powerful magnet to nineteenth-century workers. In spite of the enormous personal risks, the irregular hours, and wide fluctuations in income, men flocked to the service. They were drawn by the promise of comparatively high wages, the opportunities for promotion, the prestige of the industry, and the popular image of railroad work.

Although at first the recruitment of railroad labor was haphazard and unsystematic, relying on the whim of local officials and shaped by the ebb and flow of business, clear and consistent social patterns within the railroad labor force emerged early. Ethnic stratification by department and trade was noticeable from the outset. Trackmen and shopmen may have been predominantly Irish and German in certain areas and Chinese or Swedish in others, but their departments always had a higher proportion of foreign-born workers in the nineteenth century than other branches of railroad employment. Brakemen, firemen, and switchmen were almost always younger, frequently single, more likely to be boarders, and more transient than their skilled counterparts—engineers and conductors. The men in these operating trades were overwhelmingly native born.[3]

Ethnicity, labor market demand, and the enforcement of work discipline defined the range of opportunities open to railroad men. The structure of opportunity in railroad work was also a function of the peculiarities of the local labor market in railroad towns. Differences in the size, economic diversity, and timing of settlement also shaped the opportunities available in particular towns. The level of social solidarity among railroad men was a product of both the general condition of their trades and the class relations in their communities. Chapter 4 noted the relationship between patterns of community development and the level of community support for railroad strikes. This chapter explores the social basis of railroad workers solidarity, their participation in strikes, and the viability of their unions in specific local settings.

In spite of fairly high population turnover in railroad communities, a stable core of workers remained from one decade to the next. In any given community this core grew larger over time. As the community aged, the age profile of its labor force rose. This process might be termed the life cycle of a local labor force. Where a community stood in its labor-force life cycle had some impact on how fast men in the running trades could expect to be promoted. If congestion on the local occupational ladder coincided with an economic decline and a generally swollen labor supply, men in the running trades were likely to perceive themselves as being faced with a serious crisis. The labor-force life cycle helps to account for differences in the rate of promotion and persistence. It is directly related to community differences in strike participation.

In the late nineteenth century there were two social processes at work in communities servicing railroads that affected workers' propensities to strike and to migrate. One will be described as a process of "normal" social development in which the social solidarity among workers was great. High levels of population turnover and rapid occupational mobility did not inhibit the formation of such communities. These were most commonly new and relatively isolated railroad towns. Men might come and go in pursuit of occupational advancement, "to better themselves," as Barney Donahue said; they might even move up to supervisory positions, but their sense of social solidarity remained strong. That solidarity was built on the risks they shared, their trade unions, and other fraternal and associational ties. It was fed by a strong sense of self-respect rooted in the scarcity of their skills and in the power they exercised over the conditions of their work. This social solidarity persisted in communities of railroad workers even when many individual workers did not. It was nourished to some extent by the ease with which highly mobile railroad workers could sustain ties over long distances. Railroad workers traveled more easily than other members of the working class. The counterpart of the free passes that companies handed out to legislators and other men of influence was the unofficial system by which brotherhood members provided free transportation to one another.

A second social process, which we will term "abnormal," led to the disintegration of such stable worker communities through the disruptive influence of involuntary migration resulting from wholesale discharges and the blacklist, systematic layoffs during cyclical and seasonal declines, and the adoption of strict seniority and internal promotion that deprived mobile railroad workers of the prerogatives of skill. The critical blow to the social solidarity of railroad communities was the loss of strikes, and with such defeats came the discharge of large numbers of men and the banning of brotherhood lodges and Knights of Labor assemblies. The solidarity of railroad workers was rooted in the strength of their economic organizations. Without those organizations and with the sudden scattering of their most active members, social solidarity could not easily be sustained. This process was abnormal because it was not the product of natural market forces and voluntary migration but frequently the direct consequence of deliberate managerial initiatives aimed at undermining trade union organization.

Out of the disruption of stable worker communities emerged two streams of migratory railroad workers. One was a group of veterans of one or more such struggles who became bearers of the traditions of worker organization and social solidarity. The other was a group of men who, having experienced defeat, were prepared to shed their brotherhood loyalty as the price for continued employment in their trades. These men were willing to accept the terms of employment offered, to substitute the security of company insurance and favoritism for brotherhood insurance and the pride of independent organization. They were prepared on occasion to scab their way back into railroad employment.

In the wake of lost strikes many worker communities underwent a transformation. The lives of new workers brought in as scabs or hired at the end of a major strike were regulated to a great extent by their employers and the employers' community allies. Without trade unions and their benevolent services, in a labor market increasingly saturated with other would-be scabs, and faced with an array of fraternal and political associations dominated by a less-sympathetic middle class, these new railroad men found themselves isolated and unable to resist the domination of the railroad corporation.

Militancy and Mobility—Theoretical Considerations

Since the path-breaking work of Stephan Thernstrom on Newburyport, Massachusetts, the historical study of social and geographical mobility in the United States has carried with it the provocative hypothesis that high levels of geographical mobility inhibited the development of class consciousness. "An adequate model of the conditions which promote working class solidarity must presume not only relative permanence of membership in the class—that is, low levels of upward mobility—but also some continuity of class membership in one setting, so that workers come to know one another and to develop bonds of solidarity and common opposition to the class above them."[4] Thernstrom has described a large proportion of the urban working class in nineteenth-century America as "permanently transient," legally disenfranchised because of their high volatility, and "psychologically and socially inert," because of their failure "to sink roots and to form organizations."[5]

The mass of data supporting the contention of high geographical mobility, which has been generated by Thernstrom and scores of other urban social historians, is impressive. Comparing the findings of thirty other case studies of nineteenth- and twentieth-century urban communities with his own for Boston, Thernstrom notes that the persistence rate for Boston in the 1880–90 decade—64 percent of urban males present in 1880 remained to be counted in 1890—was actually the *highest* of all the studies. "There was a striking consistency of pattern. In more than three-quarters (twenty-four of thirty-one) of all the cases, the ten-year persistence rate ranged from 40 percent to 60 percent. Rather surprisingly, there does not seem to have been any systematic variation between time periods or community types."[6]

Thernstrom acknowledges that certain highly mobile occupational groups still manifested "labor militancy." He argues, however, that these are special cases and do not apply to the general labor turnover experienced by American workers in nineteenth-century cities.[7] Yet he does not provide case studies that specify this relationship between turnover and labor militancy or determine the level at which turnover becomes too high to sustain organization in one place at one time.[8]

Other studies of nineteenth-century communities have suggested that migration, though it involved substantial numbers of people, was more like "island hopping" and that "high population turnover may well have enhanced the stability of certain groups in a community while encouraging an overall appearance of extreme fluidity."[9] The ability of persistent groups of workers, even if they formed only a minority of the working-class population, to sustain organization and militancy is a phenomenon to which we will return in our discussion of railroad workers.

Imbedded in Thernstrom's argument is the assumption that it takes time for "workers to come to know one another and to develop bonds of solidarity. . . ."[10] This definition of the process of class formation relies heavily on a bourgeois conception of social relations and the way these relations are formed. It rests on the dubious notion that class involves nothing more than individual workers "getting to know each other" rather than the mutual recognition of a position within an economic hierarchy defined by ownership and control of the means of production. If class consciousness does imply some sense of mutualism, it may not be bounded by time and place. Those who are new to industrial work—farmers, peasants, and downwardly mobile small proprietors and professionals—may take some time to establish their class bearings, not because friendships are slow to form, but because such individuals persist in defining their work and occupational status in other than industrial-class terms. By contrast, seasoned industrial workers, either from their own experience or as their inheritance from a previous generation of workers, require little time to define themselves in relation to their fellow workers.[11] Their perception of class is *facilitated* by the ease with which they move from community to community, with or without a union traveling card, and find a place for themselves. Their sense of class is highly portable, particularly when they move from place to place within an industry and only slightly less so when they move from one industry to another, where the prescriptive organization of work might vary but the underlying distribution of authority is readily identifiable.

An essential aspect of geographical mobility is its variation from one industry and occupational group to another. In the work of Thernstrom and many other urban social historians, the level of aggregation is so high—a cornucopia of trades and industries, albeit in one city at a time—that it is virtually impossible to sort out the experiences of particular groups of workers and relate levels of mobility to collective protest. While it is of some interest to compare the mobility of different status groups in a population—skilled workers and lower white-collar workers for instance—the dynamics of population movement are more directly affected by "sector of employment," by structural changes in different segments of the labor force, and by the effects of cyclical patterns of expansion and contraction in the economy.[12] Clearly industry-specific changes in levels of employment, technology, and recruitment had a direct effect on both social and geographical mobility. What we have with metropolis-wide data on persistence and occupational mobility, classified by status, is a net change in persistence, or the sum of the experience of groups of workers subjected to very different industrial and occupational pressures.

This study seeks to locate industry- and occupation-specific variables that determined rates of geographical mobility and strike participation. It suggests that because of the nature of the railroad industry and the structure of trade unionism, fairly high levels of geographical mobility were compatible with the formation of worker communities. Such communities became bases for labor militancy in the late nineteenth century, not because workers were more persistent but because of a particular convergence of industrial conditions—an oversupply of labor, an age structure that promoted congestion on the occupational ladder, and a high degree of social solidarity based on the strength of trade union organization. Militancy increased even in the face of rapid population turnover. In fact the evidence suggests that workers were less militant in those situations where there was greater persistence—in the larger, more "integrated" communities and in the scab communities that came into being in the aftermath of major strikes in worker communities.

Men in Motion, Men in Place

Even in the midst of the enormous population movements of nineteenth-century America, railroad workers might be considered the preeminent "men in motion." Certainly the image of boomer railroad men crisscrossing the country moving from job to job was widely held. Working in a national industry with a high degree of integration, they had access to transportation and information about job opportunities. The combination of regional labor scarcities and an employment cycle highly sensitive to seasonal and cyclical fluctuations caused a substantial number of men to look regularly for new jobs.

The relative attractiveness of railroad work—its high wages and prestige—inclined some railroad men, when placed on the "extra board" or laid off, to travel in search of another railroad job rather than accept alternative employment in the same community. Railroad unions—the brotherhoods, the Knights of Labor, and the American Railway Union—made it possible for many itinerant men to move easily from one community to another by means of the "traveling card." The columns of brotherhood journals were filled with "intelligence" about the state of the labor market. The letters from lodges throughout the country that appeared in these journals were largely filled with long reports of members' travels and of the visits of friends and former associates.

In spite of widely diffused information and the use of traveling cards to facilitate movement, railroad workers do not appear to have been significantly more mobile than other workers or segments of the population. A comparison of rates of persistence for railroad workers in different regions during the decades of the late nineteenth century reveals rates that fell generally within the range found by Thernstrom and other urban historians who have studied geographical mobility. The rates of persistence varied by occupational group, with as many as 60 percent of the engineers in a community staying from one decade to the next and as few as 10 percent of the switchmen in one community staying to the next decade. (An average of persistence rates for the studies of nineteenth-century population turnover that Thernstrom cites is 46 percent.)* A comparison of the numbers of traveling cards issued to locomotive engineers and printers indicates that engineers were the more persistent of the two.[13]

*Data on the persistence of shopmen and section hands are difficult to systematize because of variations in occupational notation from one census year to another. With the exception of seasonal crews of trackmen that were recruited in large urban centers and transported long distances on a contract basis, section hands and most shopmen were probably more persistent than men in the running trades. They did not have access to the same kind of job information. They had neither highly organized brotherhood networks nor the opportunity in their job to travel over a large area, interconnecting with men from other roads.

The popular image of railroad workers notwithstanding, there were a number of factors that limited their geographical movement. It was noted in an earlier chapter that an increase in the supply of railroad labor spread from east to west in the late nineteenth century. As the railroads "made" more men in the skilled trades and promoted from within, workers who might have considered a voluntary change in order to better themselves thought longer about it. The spread of seniority systems further discouraged migration. If a move meant beginning again at an entry level position, such as a wiper or a brakemen, a skilled engineman did so with some hesitation. Seniority was most often applied on a divisional basis, limiting movement even within the same railroad system.

Because of the relatively high incomes of certain grades of railroad workers, rates of home ownership were also comparably high. Railroad men, like other workers, formed attachments of place that inhibited movement. As Mr. Dean, a locomotive engineer, said to T. J. Potter, vice-president of the Chicago, Burlington & Quincy Railroad, when he was told to look for a better job if he did not like his wages, "I have been here a good while; I live in Aurora and that has been my home, and a man does not always like to pull up a good place after being in a place so long."[14]

Although many railroad workers' lives were disrupted by work schedules that made laying down roots and regular participation in community life difficult, these were often relatively brief episodes in movement along the occupational ladder. In expansionary phases of nineteenth-century railroad work, time spent on the extra board or on irregular runs might be exceedingly brief, as men moved rapidly into regular runs and secure employment. With a more congested labor market and, in the twentieth century, a larger proportion of irregular traffic, men lingered longer in these unstable niches with more disruptive consequences to their social and family life.

During much of the nineteenth century it had been possible and, indeed, common for railroad men to move in and out of railroad employment with relative ease, while maintaining their skilled status. Faced with an unacceptable transfer or an assignment to an undesirable run, an engineer or firemen could move into another trade as a kind of holding pattern until he could sell his services under more favorable conditions. Thus many railroad men who went to farming, operating stationary machinery, or keeping a store eventually returned to railroading. In 1883 engineers on the New Haven & Hartford Railroad resisted an order changing the runs in a way that would have required their moving from New Haven to either Hartford or the Harlem River. The *Locomotive Engineers Journal* pointed out that the men resisted moving because "most of them owned their own homes and have their friends and associations of twenty-five and thirty years standing and it was natural for them to oppose any change that required the severing of such ties."[15]

Some sociological literature suggests that railroad workers in the twentieth century were more persistent than their nineteenth-century counterparts, and that they inhabited a world that was more closed. The irregularity of work schedules, the lack of promotional opportunities, relatively high wages in some grades of employment, and the unique language and ethos of the trades combined to separate the worlds of railroad men along departmental lines (most notably shopmen from running trades) and bred an aloofness to civic affairs and wider community participation.[16]

For the nineteenth century, such a description of the social relations of railroad men appears dubious. At a time of industrial expansion, the railroads seemed anything but a closed world. New recruits daily filled the ranks of unskilled employees and quickly moved up as the demand for skilled labor accelerated. These new recruits, often from nearby villages and farms, brought with them a web of familial and social connections that counterbalanced the "boomer" culture of itinerant railroad men. Those work schedules that were most disruptive to the organized social life of railroad men were the extra board and the irregular freights. While twentieth-century enginemen and trainmen might find their lives disrupted for many years by highly irregular work schedules as they waited for promotion, movement from grade to grade in the expansionary years of the nineteenth century was so rapid that men did not have to wait long to begin laying down roots in a community.

Evidence that nineteenth-century railroad men joined in the social and civic life of their communities abounds. Fraternal and beneficial associations, in addition to their own brotherhoods, linked them to the rest of the community as well as to other railroad workers. The obituaries of railroad workers killed in the line of duty typically listed membership in one or more fraternal associations. Itinerant railroad men used their fraternal memberships, as well as their brotherhood ties, to get established in a new community. A brakemen, for instance, who moved from Creston, Iowa, wrote back to his brothers in the trade to say that he had no difficulty finding his way into the new community of La Junta, Kansas, thanks to the assistance of his lodge brothers in the Ancient Order of United Workmen.[17]

That railroad workers held their share of offices in local associations is attested to by evidence from city directories in railroad towns. Even an itinerant work history did not prevent Martin Irons, leader of the Knights of Labor in the Great Southwest strike and a machinist by trade, from being elected to offices in the Odd Fellows, the Ancient Order of United Workmen (A. O. U. W.), and the Knights of Pythias in different cities.[18] The protective organizations of railroad workers were important institutions in the life of new railroad towns; their lodge rooms, their bands, their numerical strength in local parades and festivities lent an important measure of stability to community life. Members of the Knights of Labor working on the Union Pacific in Evanston, Wyoming, reported in June 1886 that the Knights band was in much demand to play at the affairs of other organizations in the community. The local chapter of the Grand Army of the Republic (G. A. R.) had asked the Knights to assist in the recently held Decoration Day ceremonies, and a gymnasium room added to the Knights hall was being well used by the community.[19]

Worker Communities: A Model

The expansion of the railroad network into successive regions led to the formation of new communities and the transformation of older rural hamlets. Such railroad towns shared a number of characteristics. Railroad operations were their dominant economic activity. They enjoyed an initial spurt of growth during the first or second decade after acquiring a railroad connection. A network of social and fraternal organizations in which railroad workers played an important part quickly sprang to life in such communities. The brotherhoods were esteemed by the community as an anchor and a symbol of the self-respect and prosperity of railroad workers. Neither rapid promotion nor relatively high turnover inhibited the development of social solidarity in such communities, where the organized running trades formed the core of the population.

The process of community formation varied widely. It was noted in chapter 4 that railroad towns appeared in the West almost overnight, and workers frequently played a decisive role in organizing and governing the affairs of such new towns. But, even in the East, an analogous process had occurred in previous decades with the location of railroad divisional operations in small rural towns and the rapid transformation of those towns into bustling railroad centers. One such example of the development of a worker community is a town previously discussed in this work, Hornellsville, New York, between 1850 and 1880.

Hornellsville was a comparatively late-blooming and rather slow-growing agricultural village in the southern tier of New York until the Erie Railroad projected its route west to intersect with the village. Fifteen years of anticipatory speculation and local promotion actually preceded the first locomotive, which arrived on September 1, 1850. As the headquarters of three divisions on the Erie, Hornellsville was transformed during the next three decades from a quiet village to a bustling industrial town of nearly 10,000.[20]

Although Hornellsville's development was retarded somewhat by the panic of 1857 and by the Civil War, it sported a railroad labor force of 743 men by 1875. (The next largest employer in town was a shoe manufacturer with 150 hands.) The railroad labor force experienced two major bursts of growth—the second more decisive than the first. The first occurred before the panic of 1857, and the second, immediately after the Civil War. Each period of growth saw rapid turnover, the appearance of a more youthful labor force, and an increase in the number of boarders. Each was followed by a period of settling in, during which persistence grew, the age profile rose, and more workers established their own households, purchased property, and married.[21]

Railroad workers in the running trades organized in Hornellsville some of the earliest lodges of their respective brotherhoods in the country. Division No. 47 of the Brotherhood of Locomotive Engineers was organized there in 1864 during the founding year of that organization. Firemen organized Lodge No. 2 of their organization in 1873, and that same year the first national convention of firemen was hosted by the men of Hornellsville. The town's brakemen were not far behind. They organized the first lodge of the Brakemen's Brotherhood in 1874 and sent organizers across the country to promote the new organization.[22]

The social and fraternal interstices in the community were densely filled by the late 1870s, but much of that organization was of recent vintage, a product of the community's postwar growth. Lodges of the Ancient Order of United Workmen, the Odd Fellows, and particularly of Saint Ann's Catholic and Total Abstinence Society overlapped the railroad brotherhoods.[23]

The early 1870s were a critical time for railroad workers in Hornellsville. Rates of persistence for most trades reached their highest levels during that five-year period, though turnover was still substantial. Seventy-five percent of the engineers and 56 percent of the firemen who were in the community in 1870 were still there in 1875. A larger proportion of men in every trade were heads of households than in any previous period. Brotherhoods were formed among firemen and brakemen, and an unprecedented series of strikes involving diverse trades was initiated. These strikes—of brakemen in 1869, 1870, 1871, and 1874 and of other trades in 1870 and 1874—were all won by the railroad workers. They struck for regular payment and to secure back pay, to resist reductions in the size of crews, and to prevent wage reductions; and they struck for equitable distribution of free passes and for a wage increase. By the summer of 1877 it had become routine in Hornellsville for railroad workers on the Erie to act under the auspices of a joint grievance committee. The Brakemen's Brotherhood, whose membership included men from a wide range of trades, had assumed the character of an industrial union, complementing, but not displacing, the various brotherhoods.[24]

The strike of 1877 at Hornellsville was more than a visceral act of resistance to repeated wage cuts. Instead, it was a test of power, invited by the company's discharge of the entire joint grievance committee. As Assistant Receiver Sherman told a reporter, "The company will not make any concessions whatever [on this issue] to the men, and if it is necessary to close the road until the company's authority is re-established then the road will be closed."[25] Successful strike tactics that had been tested in previous encounters were used again. But the strike took a grimmer turn. With more than fifteen hundred soldiers occupying the town, strike leaders were arrested and sent out of the community to jail in New York City.[26] Professional and business leaders who had supported the men in previous strikes or remained neutral began to pressure the men to settle the strike without reinstatement of the grievance committee.

The settlement, once achieved, set in motion a process that significantly eroded the solidarity that had been built in the town over the previous decade.[27] In a defensive reaction to the 1877 strikes, the brotherhoods of engineers and firemen expelled large numbers of their Hornellsville members who had joined the unauthorized strike. The Brakemen's Brotherhood became a highly secret organization (eventually linking up with the Knights of Labor, it is presumed). The leaders of the grievance committee were not reinstated, though there were no more disciplinary firings.

Turnover among railroad workers was rising by 1880 and rose even more by 1884. An ineffective strike in 1881 was easily crushed.[28]

The threat to the integrity of the worker community posed by the strike in 1877 was acutely noted by strike leader Barney Donahue in an interview from his jail cell in New York City, where he watched the strike collapse from a distance. The issue extended beyond a wage cut, even beyond the reinstatement of the workers' grievance committee, to the very nature of the worker community they had built.

> It seemed to me that the officers of the road were bound to break the spirit of the men, and any and all organizations they belonged to. The company had a fixed policy to pursue in common with other trunk lines, and they were making the experiment then and there—all of their movements were and are well understood. . . . They [the workers] also knew by bitter experience that all organizations among themselves, for mutual improvement, were opposed, as thousands of men on railroads in the United States can testify to. They were to be squeezed out of all organizations they belonged to. Many of the men belong to Masonic and Odd Fellowship societies and also various societies belonging to the Catholic Church, so if the men had not the money to pay their dues, of course they would have to withdraw from all these associations, from all fellowship for mutual aid with fellow men, *leaving them a heterogeneous mass, without civil or social aid.*[29]

The formation of worker communities in which railroad men experienced the power of their collective organization and under certain conditions exercised that power with great, if transitory, benefits was a phenomenon of the expansionary periods of railroad growth in the late nineteenth century. It was compatible with high levels of voluntary turnover, occupational mobility, and cross-class alliances characteristic of the antimonopoly culture of smaller industrial communities. These were not so much communities of class-conscious workers as they were communities of workers whose commitment to collective self-help led them inevitably into conflict with their employers.

Worker communities provided the crucibles in which a generation of railroad workers learned the harsh lessons of class relations. The communities were fractured with great regularity as employers sought to create a more malleable work force. They yielded up a rivulet of seasoned veterans of industrial struggle who saw the world more clearly in class terms and were prepared to act on that basis.

Labor-Force Life Cycles

Unlike many other industrial workers, railroad men in the running trades expected to move up a rather clearly defined and regulated occupational ladder. Occupational mobility infrequently carried them out of the working class, but it did hold out for them the hope of securing a stable niche as an engineer or conductor on a regular run. Persistence among railroad men was directly related to promotion. And the rate of promotion bore heavily on their satisfaction and the inclination of railroad workers lower on the occupational ladder to move.

Promotion was a way of life for men in the running trades. Not only did firemen, brakemen, and some switchmen anticipate moving into positions such as engineer or conductor, they routinely experienced a whole range of more modest promotions—from extra to regular runs, from branch line to mainline, and from freight to passenger service. Promotion was governed by a number of factors. The rate of expansion of the railroads and the number of additional runs or new branch lines that were put into operation affected the rate of advancement of men in the running trades. The business cycle directly affected the volume of freight and, consequently, the number of men required to move it. Improving economic conditions meant rapid advancement; poor harvests and a sluggish business climate meant little advancement, none at all, or even demotion. Favoritism continued to vie with seniority as the mechanism for regulating promotion. Whether railroads promoted strictly from within to fill skilled positions or continued to hire engineers and conductors from outside had a direct bearing on the opportunities for less-skilled men. Finally, the age of skilled men and their rate of retirement and mortality also governed the number of positions that opened up for promotion.

The geographical mobility of firemen, brakemen, and switchmen was directly influenced by the rate at which they could expect promotion and by the availability of better opportunities elsewhere. A Kansas brakemen in 1888 commented that he would not wait nine years for the chance to become a conductor on any road.[30] Firemen commonly expected to be promoted to the right side of the cab in no more than five years if all things went well. Engineers on the Eastern Iowa Division of the Chicago, Burlington and Quincy Railroad who struck in 1888 had worked an average of just under four years as firemen during the previous three decades.[31] In the 1880s the length of time served by firemen and brakemen before promotion was already growing in the East.[32] By the twentieth century it was not uncommon for firemen and brakemen to serve as many as fifteen to twenty years before earning promotion.[33] Even in the 1890s many firemen were coming to view their work as permanent.

The persistence of 50 percent to 60 percent of skilled men in the operating trades from decade to decade posed something of a crisis for younger men in lower-skill positions. The crisis deepened with each decade and was made particularly acute as the railroads exhausted their frontiers of expansion in the late 1880s and early 1890s. In order to understand the nature of this crisis, it is useful to think of the changing age structure of the railroad labor force in terms of a "life cycle." Let us imagine for the moment a division headquarters in western Iowa which was established as a new center of railroad operations in 1870 and which acquired at that time a full complement of men in the operating trades. Let us assume further that the average age of the engineers was twenty-eight. They included men in their early to middle twenties, older men recruited from positions as firemen at more settled points along the line, and experienced men from more distant points attracted by higher wages and the opportunity for more rapid promotion to preferred runs.

If there were no out-migration during the next decade and no expansion of railroad service to change the makeup of the work force, the average age of the engineers would have been thirty-eight in 1880 and forty-eight in 1890—still within the working age for engineers. Under these assumptions, no firemen would have been promoted. The work force would have aged in the way an individual moves through the life cycle. Attrition as the result of accidents or early death would have opened up some positions, but not until the 1890s or the early twentieth century would mortality have taken a substantial toll and opportunities for occupational movement been created.

Now assume, more realistically, that an average of 50 percent of the engineers disappeared from the division town in each decade as the result of out-migration. By 1880, 50 percent of the engineers would have been new men and presumably younger as a group than those they replaced. Two factors limited the impact of this population turnover on the opportunities for promotion. First, migrants tend to be younger than nonmigrants within a population.[34]

Therefore, although the older engineers who remained from 1870 to 1880 were ten years older, they were joined by new recruits whose average age was considerably younger. If 50 percent of the new recruits stayed during the next decade, they and successive cohorts of new workers would tend to retard movement through the labor-force life cycle. A second factor also contributed to increasing congestion in the local labor market. For workers who persisted for some period of time in a locality—usually three to five years—their subsequent rate of persistence rose significantly.[35] Of the 50 percent of engineers who remained until 1880, probably 75 percent to 80 percent would be expected to remain until 1890 and beyond. This would also hold true for the 50 percent of the new recruits who remained from 1880 through 1890.

What you then have, under the somewhat more realistic conditions of an assumed 50 percent rate of persistence, is a labor force that is aging but at a somewhat slower rate than if there were no out-migration. While some positions are opening up each decade—50 percent after the first decade and 37.5 percent after the second decade—opportunities for promotion are becoming progressively fewer as that portion of the labor force which persists grows older, that is, until the point at which mortality begins to take its toll on the original and successive groups of persisters. But that point occurs at least twenty years and quite possibly forty years after the original labor force in a community was put together.

As this model suggests, the labor force in every community was at a different point in the labor-force life cycle, depending on when railroad operations commenced. The fortunes of men lower on the occupational ladder varied accordingly. The expansive climate of dynamic communities, where labor was scarce and workers were relatively youthful, gave way to a situation in which promotional channels were choked with men persisting in the skilled positions. Opportunities for upward movement were constricted as compared with just a few years earlier. If, in addition, the supply of labor in the region was swollen, if troughs in the business cycle were forcing some men back down the occupational ladder, and if companies were showing an interest in lowering wages by restrictive measures like classification, the crisis would have been perceived by men in these circumstances as acute indeed.

Simultaneously, older towns whose railroad history in 1880 already stretched back twenty or thirty years felt the first effects of a demographic transition as the death or retirement of older, skilled men made way for younger men. Relative to men in newer communities, their opportunities for promotion were considerably less constricted; the impact of a tightening labor market, business downturns, and restrictive company policies were less harsh.

Such differences in position in the labor-force life cycle relate directly to differences in the way workers reacted to corporate policies that further limited opportunities for occupational advancement. A growing supply of skilled railroad workers in the region made migration a less-viable route to occupational advancement. This was never absolute, of course. Real or illusory opportunities could always be found in some corner of railroad expansion, which drew off numbers of less-skilled men. But to the extent that firemen, brakemen, and switchmen perceived that things were little better any place else, they were forced either to accept relatively permanent low-skilled status or to attempt to better their condition where they were.

Railroadmen and Mobility: a Social Analysis

The labor-force life cycle offers a basis for describing and comparing the experience and the expectations of railroad workers in various community settings. The convergence of two factors, congestion on the local occupational ladder and a growing regional labor surplus, could and did produce a powerful basis for working-class militancy. The incidence of strikes migrated during the late nineteenth century as these conditions converged in successive regions.

Two communities, already familiar from chapter 4, illustrate different stages of the labor-force life cycle. Their railroad development was separated by more than fifteen years, though they lay no more than a few hundred miles apart. Burlington, Iowa, developed as a railroad center five years before the Civil War. Creston's development did not begin until the 1870s. Both communities of railroad workers participated in the period of tumultuous industrial relations from 1877 through the great strike in 1888. For more than a decade, the issue of classification was of paramount importance to enginemen and, indirectly, to other railroad workers. However, strike participation and the solidarity of other railroad trades differed noticeably in these two communities. The differences were related in part to the nature of the communities—a railroad town and a market city—and to the life-cycle positions of their railroad labor forces. Workers in one community (Creston) saw in the classification issue more of a threat to their livelihood than workers in the other.

Birthplace and Recruitment

The railroad labor force in the two communities was drawn from essentially the same general sources, in spite of the fifteen years separating the coming of the railroad to them. The running trades in both were overwhelmingly native born—86 percent in Creston and 89 percent in Burlington. Shopmen and laborers included more foreign born—in 1885, 46 percent of the shopmen and 75 percent of the laborers in Burlington. The proportions of foreign born are roughly comparable to those found in eastern railroad towns during the decade before, but the foreign born shopmen and laborers in the East had been predominantly from the British Isles, whereas in the Middle West they were more frequently Germans and Swedes.[36]

A closer look at the birthplaces of men in the running trades reveals interesting differences in recruitment patterns. In general, Creston's railroad labor force was less local than Burlington's; Creston had more foreign born, more men born in other midwestern states, and fewer Iowa-born men (table 10).

Most of the native-born workers in the running trades of the two towns had been born in the Midwest, particularly the younger men

Table 10. Birthplace of Men in the Running Trades—Creston and Burlington, Iowa—by Percentage of Total within Each Trade, 1880

		Engineer	Fireman	Switchman	Conductor	Brakeman
Foreign:	Creston	16	26	22	8	7
	Burlington	14	15	14	9	4
Midwest:	Creston	42	49	22	44	59
	Burlington	32	23	19	32	37
East:	Creston	35	15	22	36	15
	Burlington	29	15	39	32	29
Iowa:	Creston	5	7	33	12	18
	Burlington	22	43	19	26	26
Other:	Creston	2	3	1	—	1
	Burlington	3	4	8	1	4

Source: U.S. Department of the Interior, Tenth Census (1880) Population Schedules, Des Moines and Union Counties, Iowa.

in the entry trades of brakemen, firemen, and switchmen. About 30 percent to 40 percent of the engineers and conductors in both towns hailed from New England or Middle Atlantic states. Considering railroad men born in the Midwest, we find a salient contrast: in every trade, the proportion of men born in other midwestern states was higher in Creston than in Burlington. Burlington had a higher proportion of Iowa-born engineers, firemen, conductors, and brakemen. Of the Iowa-born, 46 percent of the railroad men in Creston came from its immediate congressional district, but an incredible 96 percent of those in Burlington did.[37]

Data on the place of birth of railroad men in the two communities offer a contrast indicative of different patterns of labor-force recruitment. Burlington had a more settled hinterland than Creston in 1880, which yielded a larger labor pool in the immediate area. Creston, the newer town, and in a more sparsely settled area of the state, had to recruit its railroad workers from farther afield, and fewer Iowa-born men from the immediate area turned up in the ranks of its railroad workers. More foreigners and men from other midwestern states filled the jobs, particularly in the less-skilled running trades. The composition of Creston's labor force makes even more noteworthy the level of solidarity achieved. There was not an organic sense of community deriving from longstanding face-to-face relationships. The solidarity that railroad men achieved was built on a breadth of experience brought from other places; the community support they won was pragmatic, a consequence of their organization and of the economic and political power they wielded in the community.

Age and Persistence

In a previous section it was argued that the persistence of railroad workers in the running trades was directly related to their rate of promotion. The extent of the opportunities for firemen to become engineers and for switchmen and brakemen to become conductors was an important determinant of their job satisfaction. Two factors, among others, affected the rate of promotional opportunity. The first was the age and mortality or retirement of workers in skilled positions. Large numbers of older workers in skilled positions meant increasing opportunities for promotion as death and retirement took their toll. The other factor was the size and diversity of the community and the extent to which skilled workers were inclined to move into other pursuits.

An examination of the ages of workers in the running trades in

Burlington and Creston in 1880 reveals a sharp contrast. Burlington, the older town, had a higher proportion of older engineers and conductors. In spite of the constant erosion of geographical mobility, some portion of Burlington's skilled engine and trainmen persisted and occupied niches in the occupational hierarchy. Thirty-seven percent of the engineers and 49 percent of the conductors were in their twenties. Creston's skilled engineers and conductors were younger; fully 47 percent of her engineers and 70 percent of her conductors were in their twenties in 1880. By contrast, Burlington's firemen and to a lesser extent her switchmen were younger in 1880 than were Creston's.

These figures suggest that Creston was a community that, by virtue of its youthfulness, was experiencing congestion in the ranks of its skilled running trades. Relative to Burlington, the larger number of younger men in skilled positions left diminished prospects for the future promotion of Creston's firemen, switchmen, and brakemen. The ages of the latter indicated that men were lingering longer in these positions as they waited for promotion. The contrasting situations in the two communities stand in bold relief when the data on persistence are incorporated.

The decisions of railroad workers to remain in a community or leave were influenced, as they are for all individuals, by a complex of factors touching many elements of their sense of well-being. While family, community, and ethnic attachments weigh in the balance, they rarely weigh as heavily as current and anticipated economic fortunes. The hardship of unemployment and low wages sent many individuals in search of opportunities, leaving behind at least temporarily family, countrymen, and the safe haven of a known community. For railroad workers, the factor of promotion was a central part of the formula by which men measured their well-being. To linger too long on the lower rungs of the occupational ladder in the railroad running trades was unacceptable to most men as long as expanding opportunities beckoned elsewhere. As those opportunities contracted, either because of a depression or because the limits of expansion within the current levels of technology and investment had been reached, many men remained in one place longer than they might have expected. Such conditions, representing as they did a collision between established expectations and changing economic conditions, were ripe for producing sharply drawn conflict over issues related to recruitment and promotion. This was the situation in the upper Midwest when the Burlington strike of 1888 broke out.

For the eight-year period preceding the great Burlington strike, the persistence patterns for engineers and firemen in the two communities show opposite configurations.[38] Approximately 40 percent of the engineers in Burlington in 1880 were still in the community at the time the strike broke out in 1888. In Creston, engineers were more persistent during the same period, with 53 percent remaining in the community. However, virtually all of Creston's more youthful engineers remained engineers, while in Burlington nearly one-third of the engineers who remained had moved into other occupations or retired by the end of the eight-year period (table 11). The difference between the two communities was not simply the relative age of their engineers but also the other opportunities for employment available in a larger and more diversified town.

During the same period Burlington's firemen were more persistent than Creston's. In Burlington, nearly 50 percent of the firemen remained in the community for the eight-year period (a considerably higher persistence rate than that for Burlington's engineers), while in Creston only 33 percent of the firemen stayed. In both communities virtually all firemen who stayed (95 percent) moved into other railroad occupations, usually becoming engineers. It would appear that few firemen were prepared to stay in a community for eight years without promotion. Where the persistence of engineers was higher (Creston), a larger proportion of firemen moved on; where engineers' persistence was lower and op-

Table 11. Persistence of Engineers and Firemen in Burlington and Creston, Iowa, 1880–88

	Rate of Peristence (percent)	Same Occupation (percent)	Different (percent)
Engineers			
Burlington	39.6	27.5	12.1
Creston	53.1	50.1	2.5
Firemen			
Burlington	48.3	1.8	46.6
Creston	33.3	1.5	31.8

Source: U.S. Deparment of the Interior, *Tenth Census* (1880), Population Schedules, Des Moines and Union Counties, Iowa; and "List of Enginemen . . . who struck, February 28, 1888," Strike Papers (33 1880 9.51), Burlington Archives.

portunities for promotion greater (Burlington), more firemen remained in the community.

Although it is not possible to track the mobility of firemen and engineers *within* their occupational groups, the movement between occupational groups suggests that similar differences in intraoccupational mobility would also have been at work. The higher numbers of departing engineers and upwardly mobile firemen in Burlington would also have produced a rippling movement of men within those occupations from extra to regular runs and from less-favorable to more-favorable runs than would have been found in Creston.

The model of the labor-force life cycle does seem pertinent to explaining differences in the persistence and age of railroad workers in the communities of Burlington and Creston. Those differences created very different conditions with which workers, particularly firemen, had to contend in the 1880s. As the supply of skilled railroad labor grew and as men were kept in less-skilled positions longer, it is not surprising that railroad workers turned their attention to those corporate policies that seemed to exacerbate the problem. The classification of engineers was such a policy. It not only caused engineers to be paid discounted wages for a period of two years before promotion to "first-class" status, but it was perceived by railroad workers as a device for swelling the supply of qualified engineers. It was claimed that men were regularly discharged before they reached their third year and that their positions were then filled by newly promoted men.[39] An oversupply of skilled engineers was seen as a threat to the earnings and promotional opportunities of engineers and firemen.

The conditions described for enginemen in Creston and Burlington produced some differences in the perception of how acute the crisis of a labor surplus was. In Creston the channels of promotion were choked, in part because there was less attrition among more youthful engineers. By contrast, in Burlington a significant number of engineers, most of them older, moved into other less-arduous occupations, retired, or died, creating in the short run more opportunities for the promotion of firemen to the right side of the cab and engineers to more-favored runs. It is not surprising that a higher proportion of men who were firemen in 1880 were still in Burlington in 1888 and that virtually all of them had become engineers.

Both communities of railroad workers experienced the same company practices of classification and promotion from within.

Both were also subjected to the generally increasing supply of available railroad labor. But for firemen and engineers in Burlington and other older market cities, conditions did not appear so grim. The situation was more fluid; opportunity seemed more likely to knock. In Creston and probably in other new western railroad towns, conditions were worse. Promotion was slowed by the congestion of younger men in the skilled positions. Compounding the problem were company policies that further slowed promotion. Feeling the acuteness of the problem, Creston's firemen and engineers were more determined to resist the erosion of wages and the classification system that threatened to further flood the market with skilled railroad labor.

The Limits of Opportunity

To summarize our findings based on the social data, railroad workers in the running trades in Burlington were older (at least in the more skilled trades), more settled, and more often of local origin than were railroad workers in Creston. Creston, the new town, had a railroad labor force that was generally younger, more transient, and from farther away. A larger proportion had been born outside of Iowa and in other countries.

In Creston, rising levels of persistence and household formation among the skilled trades—characteristics that are common to any community after the initial years of high turnover—coincided with a saturated regional labor market that further restricted opportunities for promotion. The relatively scarce opportunities for promotion and limited nonrailroad employment fostered an intense resistance to company practices that were perceived to be responsible for the oversupply of railroad men.

In Burlington, an older labor force had achieved comparative stability with high levels of householdership, local and familial patterns of recruitment, and comparatively rapid promotion. These social characteristics tended to mute the effects of labor market congestion and to dampen the spirit of resistance on the part of men in the running trades. For many firemen, promotion seemed a distinct and not-too-distant prospect as older engineers left railroad service. Employees loyal to the company could expect their sons to find openings in railroad work. The local economy held open sufficient nonrailroad opportunities to reduce the anxiety about upward occupational movement still further. Men recruited locally for railroad work did not bring with them a wide experience in the world of labor.

Strike Participation

Such differences in the social backgrounds of railroad men in the two communities might be expected to have produced quite different levels of strike participation during the Great Strike in 1888. To a large extent this presumption is borne out by the available evidence.

On February 26, 1888, engineers and firemen on the entire length of the Burlington system walked off the job to enforce their demand for equalization of pay and an end to the classification of engineers. It was a long-standing grievance—one that lay behind the participation of these trades in the nationwide strikes of 1877. It was the central issue in the negotiations between the brotherhood and the company that had been going on since 1886. The negotiations had been conducted on behalf of the men by a committee of the Brotherhood of Locomotive Engineers, with representatives from each operating division. It was, however, western men who took the lead in the negotiations, selecting as their chairman S. E. Hoge, an engineer from the Western Nebraska Division at McCook.

Initially, the strike was remarkably solid from one end of the line to the other, a testimony to the thoroughness with which the brotherhoods had organized enginemen. Only 29 engineers and 28 firemen on various divisions of the Chicago, Burlington & Quincy failed to join the strike at the outset; 1,030 engineers and 1,062 firemen turned out. An additional 45 engineers and 23 firemen returned to work during the course of the strike—still a small proportion of defections considering the length of the strike. The differences in participation between divisions, however, were significant. Twenty-two of the engineers who failed to strike were employed on divisions east of Creston; only seven worked on the western Iowa or Nebraska divisions. Nine engineers and nine firemen in Burlington either refused to strike or returned to work while the strike was still on; only three engineers and five firemen did so in Creston.[40]

In early July 1888 a negotiating committee representing engineers and firemen agreed to poll the members on a settlement proposed by the company. With the strike already more than four months old, support among the enginemen appeared to be ebbing. The vote took place against a backdrop of arrests of some local brotherhood officials on charges of planning to dynamite trains. When strike leaders toured division towns of Illinois, Iowa, and Nebraska to sample sentiment for an agreement based on terms offered by the company, they found opinion sharply divided along geographical lines. East of Creston, workers favored acceptance of the terms or were narrowly divided. From Creston west, there was unanimous opposition to the proposal. The vote in Burlington was 43 favoring settlement, 32 against. In Creston, 160 men opposed the settlement; none favored it. This vote is one of the best measures we have of the differences in levels of support for the strike among enginemen in the two communities and on the eastern and western ends of the line.[41]

The solidarity of other railroad men in support of the strike was a function not only of the extent to which they too felt threatened by the classification issue, but of the social solidarity that extended across craft lines. On both counts, railroad workers in Creston drew behind their striking enginemen with greater unity than did railroad workers in Burlington.

Initially confident that their places could not be filled, the proud Chicago, Burlington & Quincy engineers and firemen gradually saw their jobs taken by men from other grades of employment on the railroad and by fellow townsmen and imported workers. Service resumed unevenly through the system and was a function of how much replacement labor could be recruited locally. The percentage of full service that the railroad was able to muster during March differed at various division points in Iowa and Illinois (table 12).[42]

On March 11, 1888, two weeks after the onset of the strike, Creston still lagged significantly behind other divisions in the level of

Table 12. Percentage of Railroad Service Resumed on the Chicago, Burlington & Quincy Divisions during the 1888 Strike

	March 11	March 15	March 20
Chicago	66	76	84
Galesburg	81	82	84
E. Iowa—Burlington	61	76	80
Creston	49	73	105

Source: "Statistics on Resumption of Service," Strike Papers 1888 (33 1880 9.11), Burlington Archives.

service. However, within the space of the next ten days, when large numbers of imported replacement workers were finally made available to the western divisions, railroad service in Creston caught up with and surpassed the eastern divisions.

Where possible the Chicago, Burlington & Quincy had initially relied on local loyal employees and supervisory personnel to fill engine crews needed to move the stalled traffic. During the first three days of the strike in Burlington, 53 percent of the men who operated trains were normally employed by the railroad in the running trades at that division (primarily conductors and brakemen). In Creston, 39 percent were men locally employed in the running trades. Burlington required many fewer "new men" to move basic traffic during the first three days—only 16 percent of the initial "scab" labor force was new. In Creston, however, more than twice that proportion (36 percent) were new to employment on the Chicago, Burlington & Quincy, and they were brought in from outside the community.[43]

Another index of solidarity is contained in the meticulously kept company records identifying employees who provided "good service" during the strike—that is, who worked above and beyond their normal duties—primarily as special policemen or as replacements for men in critical positions. In Burlington, virtually all of this "good service" was provided by brakemen and conductors; these two groups of workers received fully 93 percent of the citations on the Burlington division. In Creston, by contrast, only 14 percent of the citations went to brakemen and conductors. The largest group on the Western Iowa Division were section hands who usually worked outside of Creston and were brought into town for special service. They were 13 percent of all of the loyal employees on that division.[44]

The Chicago, Burlington & Quincy strike produced an epidemic of sympathy strikes in the West, particularly in the Missouri Valley. Many railroad men on roads out of Omaha and Kansas City contracted cases of the mysterious "Q. colic" and found themselves unable to handle trains with Chicago, Burlington & Quincy cars attached. The unsettling effects of the sympathy strikes were felt by the Burlington through much of March. However, by the last weeks of the month, a combination of injunctions and friendly persuasion in the board rooms of railroads that had tolerated the sympathetic actions brought an end to the epidemic.

By March 22 a potentially more ominous manifestation of railroad workers' solidarity had surfaced in a sympathy strike of Chicago, Burlington & Quincy switchmen. Switchmen had demonstrated their strategic position in the strikes of the early 1880s. Chicago was thoroughly organized by the Switchmen's Mutual Aid Association, and the power of the organization radiated outwards. Its roots struck deeper in some locations than in others. In Burlington, switchmen resisted the call for a strike for several days after the Chicago men had gone out, and their wavering was faithfully recorded in the daily journal of the division superintendent at Burlington. Finally, on March 30, after the strike had spread farther west, a handful of switchmen walked off the job in support of the engineers and firemen, followed on several succeeding days by a few more. Altogether, twenty out of thirty-six switchmen in Burlington eventually struck.[45]

Switchmen in Creston struck earlier than in Burlington and almost to a man. Only three out of thirty-two refused to go out. As early as March 20 a Pinkerton operative in Creston had noted the switchmen's support for the strikers: "The switchmen in the yards are making it very unpleasant for the new engineers. There has [sic] been two or three engines off the track in the yards that were let off the track by the switchmen. The switchmen also refuse [sic] after the engines were off the track to help put them on again. Instead of helping to get the engines on the track they went to the shanty and went to sleep."[46]

The end of the Great Burlington Strike was negotiated nearly ten months after it had begun by a committee of engineers appointed at the annual convention of the Brotherhood of Locomotive Engineers. Differences in the implementation of the settlement from one division to the next were a further reflection of differences in the intensity and solidarity of the strike in different locations.

One of the few concessions won by the engineers' negotiating committee was a commitment by the company not to discriminate against strikers in filling future openings. It was agreed that this did not apply to men whose actions during the strike made them particularly "objectionable" to the company.

In conformity with the settlement, H. B. Stone, general manager of the road, solicited lists from his division superintendents of all employees who had reapplied for work on their respective divisions. Interestingly, there were significant differences in the numbers of men who remained in various division towns to apply for the positions they felt to be rightfully theirs. In Burlington, less than one-half of the men who struck reapplied for their jobs at the end of the strike. Most had left the community or found other employment. In Creston, however, only a handful of the striking engineers, firemen, and switchmen had left the community. Their presence after nearly a year on strike is testimony to the solidarity of the strike and the community support it enjoyed in Creston.[47]

In addition to providing lists of strikers who had reapplied for positions, division superintendents were asked to indicate which strikers had made themselves objectionable. The activities cited that earned men this label ranged from Joel West's observation that Burlington engineer J. D Hawksworth was "very prominent in getting subscribers and corresponding with strike papers. He was a leading correspondent for strikers," to the description of Ottumwa firemen J. G. Johnson, who "made himself as obnoxious as he possibly could by calling our new men scabs and other names. He insulted one of the old men that staid [sic] with us, Engineer Thos Walker's wife, by running against her on the street and pushing her off the sidewalk. . . ."[48]

Company officials tried to keep the proportion of "objectionables" in any given division in the neighborhood of 15 percent of those who had reapplied in order to demonstrate their good faith in abiding by the agreement reached with the brotherhoods. This proved somewhat difficult in certain divisions where hard feelings between local officials and strikers ran very deep, indeed. It is consistent with what we know about community support and solidarity in the two Iowa division towns to assume that the strike would have been most divisive where community support was most fragmented and where railroad workers were most often pitted against each other. Relatively few men were declared objectionable by local officials of the Chicago, Burlington & Quincy in Creston—a mere 5 percent—whereas in Burlington, 19 percent were classified as objectionable even after the company forced local officials to reduce their number.[49]

What was the net effect of this elaborate scheme for screening applicants? As far as it can be determined, it was largely an exercise in public relations. Although men not declared objectionable were theoretically eligible for reemployment on the railroad, statistics kept by the road for the next one and one-half years indicate that only a handful on the entire line were ever rehired, and in some divisions not one striker was employed again. In both the Burlington and Creston divisions the only strikers rehired were those who regained their positions *before* the end of the strike by forswearing loyalty to their fellow strikers. From January 1889 through March 1890, not one engineer or firemen who had struck was rehired on the Iowa divisions. A spot check of the payrolls for those divisions in the 1890s bears out the conclusion that a virtual companywide blacklist, not restricted to the so-called objectionables, was instituted after the 1888 strike.[50]

Community Differences

Workers in Burlington and Creston, Iowa, responded differently to the strike of 1888 and the issues that lay behind it. In Burlington, more engineers and firemen refused to join the strike or returned to work before it was over. A majority were prepared to settle on the company's terms after four months. During the course of the conflict more than half of the men on strike in Burlington moved away or took other jobs and ceased to participate actively in it. In Creston fewer men refused to join, none voted for an early settlement on the company's terms, and, almost to a man, they remained active in the strike to the very end.

This evidence suggests that enginemen in the two communities viewed the strike and its issues differently. Differences in age and persistence seem to have led to more congestion on the occupational ladder in one community than in the other. Creston firemen and engineers on the less-favored runs had more reason to be concerned about their prospects for promotion. The general economic climate of the mid-1880s, the leveling off of expansion, continuing immigration, and the contraction of employment opportunities only reinforced the sense that railroad men faced a crisis. The issue of classification—and the flooding of the labor market with engineers, which many workers saw as its direct result—became a symbol not only for engineers but for railroad workers generally who aspired to more skilled positions in the running trades.

Other railroad workers in the two communities did not provide equivalent levels of support to the men on strike. In Burlington, switchmen joined the sympathy strike reluctantly and in smaller numbers. Brakemen and conductors in that community more readily took out engines or guided scab engineers over the road. Most of the company citations for good service as special policemen and for other duties went to men in these two occupations. These acts contributed to the bitterness of the strike in Burlington and to the demoralization of the strikers. With a vengeance company officials in Burlington sought to exclude strikers from any future employment on the road. In Creston, switchmen had covertly supported the strikers well before the onset of the sympathy strike and went out almost to a man. The company had greater difficulty recruiting local scabs and was forced to import larger numbers of new workers. Conductors and brakemen showed more reluctance to take out engines and to act as special policemen. The strikers had more support not only from the community at large but from their fellow railroad men in town. Morale remained high, and fewer men were cited for "objectionable" acts at the end of the strike.

The different ranges of opportunity that shaped the perceptions of engineers and firemen in the two communities also affected other men in the running trades, but to a lesser degree. The promotion of brakemen or switchmen to positions of conductor were less automatic. The ratio of unskilled to skilled in these trades was three or four times that for enginemen. Brakemen and switchmen were highly mobile workers. They were more likely to move in and out of railroad employment. They were also more vulnerable to injury and death on the job. Classification and the crisis generated by a growing labor supply were perceived as an issue, but not with the same intensity that firemen and engineers saw it.

The social cohesiveness of railroad towns was also a factor in determining the level of solidarity and support which striking enginemen enjoyed from other railroad trades. Highly mobile though switchmen and brakemen may have been, their sympathy actions were reinforced by the sense of working-class solidarity, which emerged in the smaller, more homogeneous, railroad towns not having a dominant local elite intimately bound to the railroad corporation. Social and fraternal organizations, political parties, and local businesses all reflected to a greater degree the dominant interests of the resident railroad workers. That influence was more diluted and fragmented in larger, older, more-diversified communities. [51]

The New Order

In the space of a few months the communities of railroad workers in Burlington and Creston underwent a rather dramatic transformation. Certain occupational groups—engineers, firemen, and switchmen— many of whom had worked in their respective towns for many years, were displaced by new workers. The displacement was most complete in Creston, where virtually all workers in these trades were imported from other places. These new workers were drawn from a number of sources: (1) under-employed enginemen from the East, recruited by Pinkerton agents; (2) veterans of previous strikes who bore grudges against the Brotherhoods—most notably Knights of Labor from the Reading strike; and (3) upwardly mobile shopmen, clerks, brakemen, and conductors who saw opportunities opening before them as enginemen. This sudden "mortality" of skilled railroad workers on the Chicago, Burlington & Quincy created a short-term labor shortage, which was quickly filled by anxious applicants, despite the social pressure and militant strike action that made that process both more difficult and more dangerous.

The strikebreakers entered a world of employment that was very different in some respects from that which their predecessors had left. Enginemen and switchmen now lacked any organized representation of their interests; the brotherhoods and the Switchmen's Mutual Aid Association were gone. In their place the company had set up the Burlington Voluntary Relief Association to satisfy the insurance needs of their employees. In communities like Creston, a wide gulf initially separated them from many of the townspeople who had so actively supported the strike. Classification and unequal pay were now unchallenged company policy. As the promotion of firemen slowed down in the 1890s, initially because the new engineers were younger and later because of the depression, firemen and switchmen became accustomed to waiting for unheard-of lengths of time in what now appeared to be more permanent rungs on the occupational ladder. C. E. Perkins continued to reiterate the importance of the "object lesson of 1888" in keeping industrial peace. He attributed the Chicago, Burlington & Quincy's comparatively good fortune in the Pullman boycott of 1894 to that lesson. "The men had found out how serious it might be for them to give up their places."[52]

A comparison of the social backgrounds of strikers and strikebreakers who inhabited the same community within a short space of time illuminates the impact of corporate policies aimed at more thorough control of the labor force. The linkage of several types of records makes such a comparison for the town of Creston possible.[53]

Creston did not outwardly manifest dramatic changes from 1880 to 1895. Its growth had reached a plateau. The diversity of its economic activities did not increase significantly in those years. It remained a railroad town, dependent on the traffic and payroll of the Chicago, Burlington & Quincy for its economic vitality. On closer examination, however, there were significant differences in the social composition of its railroad labor force, differences whose roots lay not only in the life cycle of its labor force but also in the impact of the Great Strike of 1888.

Men in the ranks of Creston's running trades in 1895 were, generally speaking, a much more home-grown lot than men in the same trades in 1880 had been. In every trade, except switchmen, there was an increase in the proportion of Iowa-born men and a decline in the proportions of men from other midwestern states. The recruitment of Iowa-born men was most noticeable among firemen, where the proportion rose from 7 percent in 1880 to 39 percent in 1895. The strike unquestionably offered opportunities for young men from the surrounding rural counties to enter railroad work for the first time in the 1880s. And by the decade of the 1890s the surrounding western Iowa counties were more densely settled and had more sons to give up to industrial life. Evidence of the company's active recruitment of engineers and switchmen in the East during the 1880 strike is shown in the higher proportions of men in these trades who were born in the Middle Atlantic states. In every occupational category there was a decline in the proportion of foreign-born workers.

We have noted the impact of the labor-force life cycle on the age profile of workers in a community at different times. This aging process was disrupted in the operating trades directly affected by the strike. Numbers of men, somewhat younger than the striking engineers they replaced, were recruited. Some were men stalled on the promotional ladder in other places who saw opportunities for advancement opening up with the strike. Others, as some contemporaries suggested, may have been young men, displaced in a previous strike, who saw the opportunity to reenter the profession.

The most dramatic differences between the groups of strikers and strikebreakers in Creston before and after the strike of 1888 were their rates of persistence and occupational mobility. As we have previously noted, 53 percent of the engineers in Creston in 1880 remained in the community until the time of the strike in 1888, and 32 percent of the firemen stayed. Virtually all of the persistent engineers remained in the same occupation and almost none of the firemen did so. If we examine the persistence of the group of workers who entered these same occupations in 1888, a different pattern is evident. Approximately the same proportion of scab engineers persisted for an equivalent period of time in the 1890s. A slightly higher proportion moved into other occupations. The major difference was with firemen. A much higher proportion of scab firemen (52 percent) were persistent. It was a rate of persistence more typical of engineers than of firemen. It was still more surprising that at the end of the eight-year period more than half of the scab firemen were still working as firemen, whereas among the earlier, striking group of firemen only one of those who stayed in the community during the 1880s was still a firemen.

Strikebreaking firemen entered employment with expectations and values different from their predecessors. They also faced different conditions and a different range of options in the years after the 1888 strike. The rate of promotion to engineer slowed somewhat in the 1890s. About 26 percent as opposed to 32 percent of the firemen moved to the right side of the cab. But clearly most of the difference in the rate of persistence of firemen was accounted for by those firemen who chose to remain in the community without promotion rather than to move on. This provides further evidence of the changing state of the railroad labor market. As the supply of labor grew and more companies promoted from within, the opportunities for rapid advancement elsewhere diminished. Men in the lower occupational rungs were forced to wait longer for promotion. And, at least in Creston, they did so under conditions that made it difficult to voice dissatisfaction. They enjoyed neither community support nor brotherhood organization to give voice to whatever grievance they may have felt. As strikebreakers, they were employed under conditions that in the short run undermined whatever basis for collective resistance they might have had.

Boomers: Voluntary and Involuntary Migration

The sharp increase in labor conflict on the railroads during the mid-1880s signaled important changes. There was growing congestion in the railroad labor market, particularly in the upper Midwest and Great Plains states. The effects of that congestion were felt with particular force in newer railroad towns like Creston that had been settled in the 1870s. At the same time, railroad managers sought to increase the labor supply further through active recruitment, internal promotion, and revisions of wages and work rules.

The migration of railroad workers was, as noted earlier, peculiarly responsive to their rate of promotion. The comparison of Burlington and Creston in the 1880s provides testimony on that point. But, as the case study of the Iowa divisions on the Chicago, Burlington & Quincy also suggests, there was an important shift during the 1880s to a new type of migration. If the former migrations of railroad men might be termed generally voluntary or normal, the latter migrations were increasingly involuntary or abnormal.

Normal migrations of railroad workers may be defined as those that were essentially voluntary and represented. Clearly railroad corporations always engaged in some attempts to manipulate the supply of labor through wage policies and recruitment practices, but the general movement of workers in response to changing opportunities generated by the growth of the industry and the shifts in demand for labor from one region to another were, in one sense, normal. Normal, voluntary migration was gradual. It was sensitive to economic cycles, the information available to workers, and their perception of opportunities. Above all, it was individually initiated.

For organized railroad workers the instrument of normal migration was the brotherhood traveling card. It symbolized an era in which skills were portable, and a skilled worker was a skilled worker wherever he went. Normal migration left in its wake normal persistence—that is, rates of persistence consistent with those that generally characterized nineteenth-century America. Such normal levels of persistence not only led to an aging labor force but created the minimum conditions necessary for effective organization through a network of brotherhood and fraternal organizations. The free movement of labor under such conditions, regulated by individual choice and facilitated by the collective organization of working men, did not disrupt the social solidarity of railroad men in particular communities, but rather reinforced it.

By contrast, abnormal or involuntary migration was the movement of railroad workers in response to specific management initiatives designed to discipline and restructure the labor force. These initiatives included measures such as classification and internal promotion, as well as disciplinary discharge and the blacklist. Abnormal migration bore little relationship to the economic push-and-pull factors that generated normal migration. It was a product of specific management policies designed to control and discipline the labor force, the use of which became more widespread as the supply of labor increased. In contrast to voluntary migration, involuntary migration of railroad workers was sudden and disruptive. For many railroad workers it was precipitated by a layoff or discharge. Brotherhood members in good standing may have still carried a traveling card in their search for employment, but they were also burdened by a "personal record." Migration under such conditions often meant being stripped of the benefits of skill and beginning again at the bottom of the occupational ladder, where promotion from within was the rule.

One index of abnormal migration is the wholesale displacement of railroad strikers in the aftermath of major strikes. The labor commissioner's strike statistics for the period 1887–94 reveal growing numbers of railroad men displaced during that period, reaching flood tide with the Pullman boycott of 1894.[54]

Such abnormal migration had a number of effects. It disrupted the social solidarity that had developed in many communities and usually destroyed, at least for a time, local trade unions. By releasing large numbers of strikers into an already swollen migration stream, it increased the labor supply even further. For many skilled railroad men it was a personal calamity, often entailing the sacrifice of a home and community ties, as well as movement down the skill ladder in search of new railroad employment. If a discharge involved skilled railroad workers, as it did in the Burlington strike, it created conditions that, in demographic terms, were comparable to the sudden mortality of the more skilled segment of the labor force, which might normally have occurred over thirty to forty years. It created the opportunity for very rapid promotion of some less-skilled men, who previously saw their fortunes stalled in the occupational hierarchy. In so doing it fractured the social solidarity built in some railroad towns over many years. It enabled railroad companies to restructure their labor relations by handpicking a skilled labor force more loyal to company interests and enmeshing those men in work rules and relief associations, which would continue to ensure their loyalty.

If the traveling card was the symbol of normal migration, the infamous "personal record" was the symbol of abnormal migration. The personal record of employment recorded not only the work experience of railroad workers but the date and cause of their discharge. It came into use in the 1880s and after the Pullman boycott was required virtually without exception. Its use served to eliminate from future railroad employment a substantial segment of those men who struck in 1894 and before.[55]

During the 1880s and early 1890s, as more and more companies promoted exclusively from within, as seniority by division became more regularized, and as the labor market became more saturated even in the expansive West, fewer workers voluntarily pulled up stakes to better themselves. Forced to deal with the conditions of their employment by organization rather than by movement, frustrated by slower rates of promotion and stagnating wages resulting from a labor surplus, and emboldened by the formation of class-based labor organizations, railroad workers challenged the management initiatives that were undermining their opportunities and their control over the conditions under which they sold their labor. That challenge resulted in increased strikes over noneconomic issues even as the chances of their success diminished. As the success rate of those strikes plummeted, the migration of discharged railroad workers increased.

Before 1888, Creston, like Hornellsville before the Great Railroad Strike of 1877, might be described as a worker community in which voluntary migration did not significantly inhibit the development of a social solidarity, characteristic of new railroad towns. Brotherhood organization was strong; many unskilled shopmen and laborers belonged to the Knights of Labor. The social and economic hegemony of railroad men was exercised through their purchasing power, their participation in the social and fraternal life of the community, and through political activity, a significant channel for which in the mid-1880s was the Union Labor Party. The tensile strength of their solidarity and the extent of community support they enjoyed had been tested in the 1877 strike. As conflict with the Chicago, Burlington & Quincy over classification and other forms of management labor control continued during the 1880s, members of the running trades were welded into even closer alliance. The migration of individual railroad workers did not diminish. If anything, it increased for men who perceived themselves as stalled on the promotional ladder. But that migration did not erode social solidarity that had been built.

The strike of 1888 and the subsequent wholesale discharge of engineers, firemen, and switchmen thoroughly disrupted the worker community that had developed over the previous fifteen years. Overnight, as it were, striking workers were forced to disperse involuntarily. In their place a large group of strikebreakers was introduced. The strike fractured the social solidarity in the community; community leaders went to great editorial lengths urging residents to put aside their differences and continue with the important work of building the community. The diaspora of railroad workers was an abnormal migration indeed.

What happened to the men who struck and for whom there remained little prospect of employment again on the C. B. & Q.? As a correspondent to the *Switchmen's Journal* wrote in February 1889, "The greater number of our men are scattered to the four winds. . . . "[56] The scattering, however, appears to have followed a distinctly westward pattern. A switchman from Ottumwa accounted for the whereabouts of his lodge brothers in March 1889: "B. Dempsey is in Green River [Wyoming] doing the old act; Brother Hart is doing New Mexico, blistering his feet tying up cars; Brothers Workland and Vreeland are in Sioux City; Brother Lonshire is doing the night act in Chillicothe, Mo.; Brother Shader is over in Peoria doing something; I learn that Brother Vaughn and several others are in the region of Kansas City." One had gone back to Chicago, a couple of others were somewhere in Iowa, B. Smith was running a popcorn stand, and a half-dozen remained in Ottumwa looking for work.[57] The *Creston Advertiser* regularly published news of the whereabouts and fortunes of firemen and engineers forced to leave the community in search of work. The vast majority had moved westward to places such as Jamestown, North Dakota, Pocatello, Idaho, Ogden, Utah, and Denver and Truckee, Colorado. A sizeable contingent landed positions on the Northern Pacific, though their presence and divisional locations were carefully noted by that railroad. A complete listing of all of the former Chicago, Burlington & Quincy enginemen hired after 1889 was kept in the Northern Pacific corporate records for the Pullman boycott of 1894.[58] Some Creston enginemen, the local newspaper noted, had left railroading but remained in the area: firemen C. A. Flint went to his farm to "lead the rural life," A. A. McGregor joined an implement business in nearby Afton, and J. B. Kirsch solicited life insurance business (probably among railroad men) for the Mutual Reserve Life Fund.[59]

The end of the strike happened to coincide with another expansionary phase of the railroad industry in the Great Northwest. That expansion offered the opportunity for some men to remain in their profession. Although the Chicago, Burlington & Quincy strikers were effectively blacklisted on that railroad and its subsidiaries, it is not known whether an attempt was made to blacklist the men on other roads. General Superintendent G. W. Holdredge of the Burlington & Missouri (Nebraska) adopted the practice of giving strikers letters "stating the length of their service on our road, and that they left on account of the strike of February 26, 1888. We have given no further recommendation than this to any of the old men, but we have given letters of this kind to all who have applied."[60] If other railroad companies chose to ignore the warning implied in this personal record because of an acute demand for labor or other reasons, that was their business. The procedure for effective, industrywide blacklisting was in place.

Migration and Class Consciousness

Involuntary migration resulting from a disciplinary discharge or blacklisting after a lost strike produced two very distinctive groups of migrants. One was a group of men whose sense of class loyalty was broken and who were prepared to reenter railroad employment under any conditions, even as scabs in the next strike. The other was a group of workers whose class consciousness was heightened with each strike, who entered an agitational circuit that was of increasing importance in the general organization of railroad labor leading up to the Pullman boycott.

The first group perceived their loss of a job (and a position on the occupational hierarchy) as a *personal calamity*. They sought an individual solution that would ensure their return to the good graces of railroad employment. In some cases they harbored great bitterness for brotherhood leaders or members who they felt were responsible for the loss of the strike. They were ripe for duty as scabs and for reintegration into a permanent, less-mobile, and more loyal work force. Sandy Burrell was a striking engineer on the Burlington in 1877 who was subsequently discharged and who returned to scab in 1888 after running a hotel in Missouri for several years. He told a reporter during the latter strike that he had gotten enough strike in 1877 to last a lifetime.[61] No one has described more poignantly the way former strikers were lured to scab than William J. Pinkerton, a peripatetic agitator in his own right.

> Hardship and persecution break the manhood of the bravest. The railroad man who has been blacklisted, hunted from place to place, forced to abandon the name of his father . . . loses faith in the potency of unionism. He grows bitter in time, and resentful. He argues: "My union has done nothing for me in the hour of my extremity; it has not interceded between my unjust employer and me; it has not reached out its hand to stay the lash; it has not comforted me. In the strength of my youth, the confident morning of my life, I was faithful to it, and now, like a wanton mistress, it turns from me when the luster is dying from my hair and the footprints of experience track my brow." It is to this reasoning the railroads desire to bring him. Then, when the strike comes, their agents seek him. He takes out the abandoned engine, or makes up the train in the congested yards. Chance, fortune, circumstances have favored him again. He sees the pathway he has followed the better part of his life again opening to him, even though he must begin it anew at a reduced wage. But, he believes he has been wronged more deeply than he can wrong. It is an individual struggle, as it appears to him, each man for himself. So he turns deaf ears to entreaties, threats, slanders. He becomes a scab. . . . The outcast "scab"

is used until some student, innocent of a past and of
experience, can be persuaded, under protection of the United
States militia, to take his place. Then, its purpose
accomplished, the corporation relaxes its hold upon the
broken tool. . . .[62]

The other group of workers discharged for strike participation
and thrown involuntarily into the migratory stream was best
represented by Pinkerton himself. They were dispossessed, class-
conscious, often "nameless" (many had long since forsaken their
real names in order to gain employment), moving usually within
the lower grades of railroad work—commonly as switchmen, brakemen, or shop laborers—and carrying on agitation wherever they
went. Switchmen, it was said, always carried, tucked away with
their rabbit's foot and toothbrush, a neatly folded list of grievances
as they moved from job to job.[63] A correspondent to the
Brakemen's Journal described approvingly the role of outside agitators in a brakemen's strike on the Central Pacific Railroad in 1887.
"Agitators, chronics and dynamiters" they might be, "but they
leave their footprints on the payrolls of time, . . . they make unfit
places or divisions, good divisions for civilized men to work."[64]

Pinkerton's own career provides an exceptional sketch of the agitational circuit followed by one class-conscious railroad man. After
being fired from a position as a coal heaver at Williams, California,
for leading a strike and from a job as a fireman on the Southern
Pacific for "abusing" a master mechanic over a wage reduction,
Pinkerton was faced with the harsh reality of the personal record
system which, according to his account, was beginning to make itself felt in 1889. Drifting in and out of railroad employment in the
West, he was continually conscious of the threat posed by the
blacklist. Even Pocatello, Idaho, which he described as "that Mecca
of black-listed and outlawed railroad men . . . was rapidly settling
down to a solid working basis, and it was almost impossible to
secure a position."[65] His condition was made worse by his participation as a delegate in the American Railway Union meeting on the
Union Pacific that declared the Pullman boycott on that road. He
struck, was arrested, and was tried. After the strike, despite name
changes, he was hounded from one road to another as he tried to
put together a work record that made it appear that he had not been
doing railroad work during the period of the 1894 strike. Faced
with stool pigeons, chance encounters with officials who had
known him on the Union Pacific, belied by his own experienced

hands, and confronted with a more rigorous physical examination with each new prospective employer, he found the circuit narrower and narrower.[66] His experience was shared by innumerable veterans of the railroad strikes from 1884 through 1894.

Summary

During the late nineteenth century not all railroad workers were equally affected by the changing conditions of work in their industry. Geographical region and the age and economic diversity of the communities where they worked were factors. As the railroads expanded, they created temporary islands of labor scarcity, but with increasing settlement and economic development that scarcity disappeared and with it the automatic privileges of high wages and liberal work rules. At any given time, workers in different regions were in very different bargaining positions.

Because of the uneven rate of railroad expansion, different divisions on the same system were often built and a labor force recruited decades apart. Differences in the age of the work force of communities made for differences in the promotional opportunities. Among the running trades, rapid promotion was a major index by which railroad workers measured their satisfaction. By the mid-1880s it was, ironically, in some of the newer towns that workers found the channels of promotion most congested and consequently perceived their opportunities as in most jeopardy.

It was in these very communities—newer, more homogeneous railroad towns—that the social solidarity characteristic of worker communities was most likely to be developed. As the effects of a growing labor supply on wages and work rules were felt with particular acuteness, workers resisted. The instruments of that resistance were lodges of their brotherhoods, local federations, and the social solidarity characteristic of their communities. Strikes ultimately turned on the issue of the maintenance of that social solidarity and the unions that were its backbone.

The loss of strikes, the increase in punitive discharges and blacklisting, combined with congestion and segmentation in the labor market, effectively disrupted the social and economic solidarity in worker communities. Class-conscious, nameless railroad labor activists discharged in previous strikes searched the corners of the railroad network for employment. Some dropped out of this agitational circuit and took the next opportunity to reenter railroad work—as scabs. Others were driven out of the new world of tightened management control over personnel matters.

The development of this management control was less the result of grand design than the by-product of intensifying industrial conflict. Railroad labor conflict was precipitated by the competitive logic of the industry that produced overexpansion and the necessity for draconian measures of cost reduction. Railroad managers found that conditions of labor surplus enabled them to more effectively reduce wages, revise work rules, and undermine labor organization. Gradually, they fabricated a "system" for managing labor and sustaining control. But these measures were contested every step of the way, as the strikes of the 1880s and 1890s illustrate.

6

A Search for Order: Railroad Management and the Labor Crisis

A great deal can be done by pinching, long hours, short grub time, some cussin' and a fair amount of praying.[1]
    —James Clarke,
        President, Illinois Central Railroad, 1883

In the first place, he who had passed through his period of probation and whose name was enrolled in the permanent service would naturally feel that his interests were to a large extent identified with those of the company; and that he on the other hand had rights and privileges which the company was bound to respect. . . . Once let the growth of associations like these begin, and it proceeds with almost startling rapidity. . . . Every man who was so fortunate as to become a permanent employee of the company would then be assured of provision in case of sickness or disability, and his family would be assured of it in case of his death.[2]
    —Charles Frances Adams, Jr.,
        President, Union Pacific Railroad, 1889

Railroad managers in the last decades of the nineteenth century were men of widely varying experience and temperament. Their fields of operation were diverse, from New England roads, small enough to be a single division of a large system, to vast transcontinental lines. As many railroad systems expanded in size and as the density of operations grew, managers were forced to adapt the rather simple and straightforward management structures that had been appropriate for a single division or a small road to larger systems. The pressures toward centralized authority and systematic management were felt in many areas of operation, such as the standardization of gauges, rate making, and purchasing. Similar pressures, though coming from a different source, were felt in the management of the railroad labor force. Local autonomy in the areas of recruitment, wage determination, discipline, and discharge was a source of conflict in railroad labor relations that general officers and brotherhood officials alike sought to curtail.[3] More fundamental divisions over wages, control of the labor supply, and recognition also infected railroad labor relations at all levels.

Railroad management's attention to labor relations was not consistent. Managers may have been pioneers in corporate consolidation and in the development of cost accounting and other techniques essential to the smooth operation of large firms, as Alfred D. Chandler, Jr., has argued, but in labor relations the dead weight of tradition retarded innovation. Major strikes or prolonged conflict over wages and work rules generated great concern among railroad managers. That concern produced serious debate over and experimentation with new techniques for managing men. But whenever labor conflict subsided, the attention of railroad managers drifted away from labor matters and back to concerns such as rate making and financing new construction. The aftermath of the 1877 railroad strikes saw a flurry of discussion and specific proposals ventured by railroad leaders and others for ameliorating the relations between labor and capital. Counterproposals insisted on firm discipline and the free operation of the iron law of supply and demand in setting wages. In the expansive atmosphere of the 1880s, as western railroads busied themselves with building into new territory and filling out existing networks, proposals for new initiatives in railroad labor relations withered from inattention or lack of interest. Not until the labor crisis of the middle 1880s did railroad managers turn their attention again to the schemes of the late depression.

By the end of the 1880s, it is possible to see the outlines of a "system" for managing railroad labor. The elements included: (1) centralized payrolls and discharge lists, (2) the use of the "personal record" system to screen employees, (3) the "Brown system" of discipline by record, (4) the widespread adoption of seniority as a means of reducing labor turnover, (5) a variety of company welfare schemes, and (6) a system of corporate cooperation to meet the threat of strikes, insure adequate supplies of workers, and standardize wages. During the 1880s most of the elements of this system for managing railroad labor were developed on one road or another, although no road permanently instituted all of them. Each element continued to be the subject of vigorous debate, and many managers, even at the end of the decade, viewed most of the schemes with great skepticism. Each major strike or wave of strikes

created a more favorable climate within railroad management circles for the adoption of management reforms. Even Charles E. Perkins, the most vigorous opponent of company welfare schemes, accepted in practice what one historian has termed the elements of a
"reluctant paternalism" after the strike of 1888.[4]

The crisis of 1893–94, which erupted finally in the Pullman boycott, proved the most profound challenge yet to management authority. It welded together a new consensus among railroad
managers that systematic attention to the management of workers
was needed. Drawing on the experiences of the previous decade,
the General Managers' Association of Chicago was reinvigorated
and provided leadership in forging that consensus.[5] As the dust
settled from that momentous strike, key leaders in government and
among railroad corporations set about creating a more lasting
framework for labor-management cooperation in which a place for
the brotherhoods, acting on behalf of the various operating trades,
was prepared. The framework essentially provided for the prohibition of national railroad strikes through arbitration and, when
necessary, the liberal use of the injunction. It provided guarantees
to organized labor by outlawing the blacklist and prohibiting companies from excluding unions. Significant elements were written
into the Erdman Act of 1898, whose author, Richard Olney, had
also designed the federal suppression of the Pullman boycott and
devised the legal basis for prohibiting disruptive railroad strikes.[6]
The framework for labor-management cooperation on the railroads
emerged in the context of widespread adoption by railroad
managers of various elements of a more systematic personnel
management.

Local and Centralized Management Authority

The divisional system of railroad organization was a logical structure adopted as railroads expanded from local single division
operations into larger territories with multiple divisional units. Expansion in this way did not require structural innovation but rather
a simple increase in the number of divisional units. Although some
central staff positions were required to integrate and standardize
certain aspects of the system's operations, a great deal of authority
remained with local division officials. Particularly in the area of labor relations, the division master mechanic reigned supreme in the
recruitment, assignment, and dismissal of engine crews and the
railroad shop force. The favoritism and arbitrariness with which lo-

cal division officials exercised their considerable authority over workers under their jurisdiction was endemic. These officials could be a source of considerable good or bad fortune. The uncertainty and inequity experienced by railroad workers at the hands of local officials contributed directly to their efforts to organize.

From the perspective of a locomotive engineer or a railroad shop machinist, the centralization of authority in management may have proceeded at too leisurely a pace. The "old time Master Mechanic," as he was referred to in later years with a mixture of nostalgia and lingering fear, was the central figure in the work lives of most men in the transportation departments. His authority was absolute within his domain. His word on hiring, firing, and the distribution of work was unchallengeable. He might delegate some of that authority on occasion, or even routinely, to foremen, but it never diminished his own potential power. In the reminiscences of railroad men there are references to master mechanics, foremen, division superintendents, and other local officials who were held in great affection and whose authority was dispensed in judicious measures. But there are also numerous references to officials who were perceived as vindictive and arbitrary in assigning runs, in granting promotions, and in disciplining workers with suspensions, fines, and ultimately with dismissal.[7]

The arbitrariness of local management authority did not sit well with railroad workers. As the *Railway Service Gazette* claimed in an 1886 editorial, "It is certain that one of the most prolific sources of trouble between employers and employees results from incompetency of subordinates who are vested with authority over their fellow employees."[8] A spokesman for the locomotive engineers on the Northern Pacific argued vehemently to the general manager of the road in the 1893 wage negotiations that "the trouble with us has never been in the general office. All the trouble there is has been local—someone trying to take technical advantage of a schedule. It is what has brought these various rulings about."[9] And even Grand Chief Peter M. Arthur, surveying the previous several decades of turmoil on the railroads, reminded the Industrial Commission in 1900 that men in supervisory positions had "in a little heat" commonly dismissed or suspended men without just cause. "That is really what caused the brotherhood to establish these general committees."[10]

Time and experience illustrated to railroad workers the advantages to be gained by forming grievance committees and demanding equitable treatment from an authority higher than the divisional level. A circular of the Brotherhood of Railway Carmen written in 1892 instructed members on the advantages of such a procedure. "We would say, let every lodge appoint its grievance committee at once—and they will be surprised at what they can do. Meet and discuss your troubles; settle on your demands; carry them if necessary to the highest official on the road. . . ."[11]

Many railroad officials were displeased with railroad workers' success in pushing the authority over labor management out of the hands of local officials into the hands of general officers. The general manager of the Northern Pacific, J. W. Kendrick, complained to the road's receivers that too much of his time was taken up with labor negotiations. He noted that it had become customary to allow workers to go over the heads of their superiors to the general manager of the road. As a result, the general manager spent more than half his time "listening to complaints, which were to a considerable extent fictitious." The effect of this problem was more serious, however, because such meetings inevitably led to compromise—"certain claims have been allowed and certain disallowed, with the net result that the men have continually gained ground."[12] At the same time Kendrick acknowledged that "unequal treatment" existed between the divisions and "more than any other factor has led to the growth of labor organizations." His solution was to reassert management authority over the grievance procedure, creating an orderly system of appeal that did not undermine the necessary authority of local officials but balanced it with the standardizing influence of general officers.[13]

Even as some railroad workers perceived advantages in dealing with general officers and more centralized authority, others saw such advantages as illusory. From their point of view, the only thing worse than arbitrary exploitation was systematic exploitation. The general officers, and particularly those who advocated local autonomy for divisions and subsystems, had created conditions that encouraged local exploitation. In advocating this system, Perkins himself insisted that it stimulated "local responsibility and an interest in results."[14] John T. Wilson, leader of the Brotherhood of Railroad Trackmen, described to the Industrial Commission the results of this system from the point of view of the trackmen. A roadmaster desiring recognition and promotion drives the men under him "from daylight to dark" to keep down costs. "As the higher officials are on the lookout for men who can produce the greatest results at the least cost, he becomes a favorite and is held up as an example for all other roadmasters to follow. . . ."[15]

Ultimately the general officers bore responsibility for the way in which authority was exercised, whether by local officials or by themselves. "If a foreman of a small gang of men is mean and over-bearing," a track laborer from the Dalles, Oregon, wrote, "We must consider that it was just this disposition that won him his promotion. . . . Let us find fault with those who seek such men to promote."[16]

After the Great Strike of 1877, railroad men perceived an even greater threat from the general labor policies of railroad corporations promulgated at the highest levels. The irritant of inequitable treatment at the hands of local officials continued and precipitated many local strikes, but the major confrontations between labor an management were the result of deliberate and generalized efforts by management to impose new rules or wage levels on labor. Further, managers of many roads actively cooperated to increase the supply of labor at critical times, to standardize wage rates at levels reflecting the increased supply, and to enlist the government and the public in limiting the influence of organized labor. The development of a wide range of welfare and relief schemes on many roads was likewise an innovation by general managers to restrict the scope of organized labor and ultimately deprive unions of their appeal.

1877: Crisis and Response among Railroad Managers

The 1877 strikes produced a sense of crisis in railroad management circles. The unity that lay behind the wage cuts introduced on one road after another was shattered as managers assessed the immensity of labor's response. Two schools of thought on labor relations emerged. Nowhere were they reflected more clearly than in the views of Robert Harris and Charles Perkins, president and vice-president of the Burlington.

When the 1877 strikes spread to the Burlington, Harris urged prudence and conciliation. He was concerned that the Burlington would not be able "to stock this road" with men as good as they had, and at the conclusion of the strike he insisted that the "old men who are reemployed should be reemployed at the old rate—that is—let the amnesty be a real and thorough amnesty." He feared that the pauperization of labor would inevitably lead to "the result of pauperized labor"—inferior workers.[17] Together with many other managers after the 1877 strikes, he looked to insurance schemes, support of reading rooms and YMCAs, and the general promotion of employee welfare as an answer to strikes. He was prepared to deal with committees of the men and to consider formal contracts; he was even taken with the notion of a sliding scale of wages tied to the net earnings of the company. [18]

This general orientation to labor was shared by some railroad officials, even before the outbreak of the 1877 strikes. William K. Ackerman, vice-president of the Illinois Central, proposed in April 1877 a company welfare scheme which, though not implemented at the time, reflected the thinking of some managers. Western railroad companies should agree to offer the engineers the same or better advantages than they obtained from their brotherhood. First-class engineers might be offered a life appointment, some "consideration" in the event of sickness or injury, and a "gratuity" for their families should they be killed. Second-class men would have these benefits to look forward to, and in both cases the cause for some of "their present feeling of insecurity and restlessness" would be removed. [19] In spite of scattered participation by Illinois Central employees in the 1877 strikes, Ackerman claimed that his men were "loyal" and ordered them paid for the strike days. He lent his support to the organizing efforts of the YMCA along his line, serving on YMCA boards in Chicago and subsidizing evangelists in Cairo and Amboy. [20]

When open conflict erupted within the Burlington management during the 1877 strikes, it was not simply over the way the company was managing the strike nor the relative authority of local versus central officials. Instead, a major philosophical difference in the area of labor relations divided Harris from his chief antagonist, Charles Perkins. A similar division erupted between Ackerman and James Clarke on the Illinois Central during the 1880s. Perkins believed fervently in the natural law of supply and demand as the governing principle in the relations between an employer and his employees. Harris perceived employers and employees as bound by a more complex set of reciprocal loyalties and obligations. Such paternalism, Perkins argued, confused employees about "the true character of business relations." When an unsigned article entitled "The Care of Railroad Employees" appeared in the Nation in 1880 arguing for more attention by railroads to the welfare of their employees, Perkins wrote a stinging rejoinder. He was particularly irritated to learn that the author of the article was his own general manager on the Burlington & Missouri (Nebraska), A. E. Touzalin. [21]

Touzalin agreed with Charles Francis Adams, Jr., that railroad corporations should concern themselves with the welfare of their employees. Such closer ties, he argued, would also "pay the own-ers of the western roads." Corporations must consider the employ-ees' welfare *"beyond their working hours and outside their duties for which they are paid."* Schemes for helping the men "in their private lives," he believed, could be accomplished for a trifling outlay. As an example he suggested a company-sponsored loan fund to help employees purchase houses. The result would be a higher esprit de corps, which would remove the "possibility of strikes and riots."[22]

Two weeks later under the pseudonym "Gradgrind," Charles E. Perkins replied to his own general manager's paternalism. Perkins attacked the specific scheme of loans to employees and the general philosophy of management it implied.

> The doctrine now generally accepted as sound is that
> personal service is a commodity worth the market price, good
> and zealous service always commanding a better price than
> poor or indifferent in the long run; that great railroads are
> peculiarly dependent upon the general labor market for their
> supply; and that whatever disarranges it is to their detriment.
> Paternalism, however well meant on the part of railroad
> companies, will weaken the conviction in the minds of
> working people that wages are solely dependent upon the law
> of supply and demand, and there will be substituted the
> feeling that the owners of the property are adding, can add,
> will add, and soon that they *should* add something
> "reasonable" as a reward of merit, as if a man were not
> employed and paid good wages to do his duty.[23]

As railroad managers entered the 1880s, they were sharply divid-ed over fundamental questions of management structure and labor policy. The scale of operations undertaken in the expansion of the early 1870s and of the early 1880s raised serious questions about adequacy of autonomous operating divisions. The unprecedented revolt of railroad labor in 1877 caused some managers to rethink the labor relations on their roads. They groped for conciliatory measures, for ways to build employee loyalty that would reduce the appeal of unionism.

Railroad operations expanded into new territory in the early 1880s. The threatening labor crisis of just a few years before seemed to recede, and with it interest in management reform. The fractious atmosphere of competitive building and rate making was not conducive to building consensus among managers on the proper distribution of management authority nor on the appropriateness of company welfare measures. Indeed, to the extent that welfare programs represented additional cost, they came to be viewed by most as expendable. The building of durable organizations for cooperation between railroad managers, even toward such a universally acceptable goal as limiting organized labor's influence, had to await another crisis.

Building a Labor Relations System

Although the level of interest in management circles was not generally conducive to innovation in labor relations during the early 1880s, the decade was not without some important developments in this area. By the end of the decade, it was still not possible to speak of systematic labor relations, but the major elements of a system were available and being practiced to different degrees on various roads. Innovations in personnel records, disciplinary procedures, seniority, and company welfare programs were providing railroad officials with new instruments for managing employees within their jurisdictions. While far from comprehensively applied, these new measures altered the environment of railroad labor relations and helped to undermine the growth of general unionism in the 1890s.

Railroad Personnel Records

Railroad personnel records reflected the decentralized nature of railroad operations until the 1880s. A division superintendent and his local department heads might know who was employed during any given month in their division, but the general officers had little idea. When the pay car appeared in the division, the paymaster was told whom to pay, and how much. Overall costs for each division were scrutinized by general officials, and pressure was applied to reduce costs, but specific decisions on whom to hire and at what rates were rarely centralized.

During the mid-1880s, General Manager T. J. Potter of the Chicago, Burlington, & Quincy expressed growing concern with escalating costs and instituted a system of payroll surveillance. Payrolls were scrutinized by his office prior to payment. All wage increases after 1884 had to have prior approval of the general manager.[24] When the engineers' strike occurred on the Burlington, the general office still found it necessary to have divisions submit lists of employees who had struck and those who had remained loyal. From these divisional lists they were able to compile a roster of strikers for the entire system.[25] Ironically, since most engineers and firemen struck, this was probably the company's first general census of employees in those occupations.

In the aftermath of the 1888 strike, centrally kept payroll records, based on data submitted by the divisions, were instituted. The payrolls recorded the number of days worked, the rates of pay, special charges and deductions including payment to the Burlington Voluntary Relief Association, and gross and net pay.[26]

Payroll records were not the only type of personnel data developed by railroads in the nineteenth century. Records of discipline and discharge of employees were created, at least on the Burlington, before 1880. As early as 1870, Chicago, Burlington, & Quincy division superintendents submitted lists of discharged employees, which were circulated throughout the other divisions in order to prevent the reemployment of a discharged individual. Beginning in 1877, this system was extended by having the general superintendent maintain a master list and circulate it among divisions. This discharge book was actively maintained between 1877 and 1892, during which time 8,093 names were entered, along with the offenses for which they had been discharged.[27] It should be noted, however, that a separate list was maintained of those employees discharged for participation in the 1888 strike. (They numbered 2,092 engineers and firemen, plus several hundred switchmen).[28]

Paul Black, a historian of Burlington personnel policies, argues that alcohol was far and away the most important cause of discharge during the period covered by the Chicago, Burlington & Quincy discharge list and that strikes and labor agitation were relatively minor compared to their usual reputation. Black, however, fails to note that the more than 2,000 strikers of 1888 were never recorded in the discharge book, and few were ever rehired. If their numbers were added to the discharges due to strike activity that are listed, then this cause would rank only slightly behind alcohol. And if discharges for "disobedience," "insolence," and "insubordination" were considered as even partly related to labor agitation, then these two labor-related causes for discharge (strike activity and labor agitation) would be the most important, surpassing even alcohol.

Even as the general superintendent was maintaining a central list of discharges, some division superintendents kept detailed records of other infractions that led to less drastic forms of employee discipline. In 1888, O. E. Stewart, division superintendent on the Eastern Iowa Division, submitted a list of striking employees which detailed the work history of each on his division of the Chicago, Burlington, & Quincy system and their infractions, large and small.[29] For example, Stewart gave a summary account of John Nason's career on the Burlington division.

> JOHN NASON, Locomotive Engineer
> Commenced as Loco. Fireman, February, 1879.
> November, 1879, to Hostler.
> January, 1880, set up to Engineer.
> October, 1880, suspended 10 days for not giving proper
> signals after breaking in two on Fairfield grade.
> January, 1881, suspended 10 days, running on short time to
> Ketchams station against passenger train.
> December, 1881, suspended 5 days pulling engine 227
> through switch in Burlington yard.
> Quit February 27th, 1888, account of Strike. Put in
> application on Form 1608, January 12th, 1889.
> Record since strike: A bad Striker, trying to get our new
> men drunk, got so himself, was noisy calling our
> conductors scabs, etc.[30]

Other roads maintained centralized lists of discharged employees for internal use during the 1880s. Such a list existed on the Illinois Central as early as 1885 but was not provided to other employers.[31] The Union Pacific Employees Magazine refers to such an internal discharge list circulated among Union Pacific divisions in 1889.[32]

By the early 1890s changes were underway in record keeping on employee performance. In 1892 the Chicago, Burlington & Quincy discontinued the central discharge list kept by the general superintendent. The alternative system of requiring letters of reference from all prospective employees was working more effectively than a list of discharged employees. George B. Harris expressed confidence that it was better to require "good men to produce good credentials" than to attempt to keep "a blacklist of the dissolute and vicious."[33] The Illinois Central developed printed forms for providing references.[34] Some roads, such as the Chesapeake & Ohio, maintained a central discharge list past the turn of the century.[35]

The system of requiring references from previous employers provided a much more comprehensive control over recruitment. Frank

P. Sargent explained to the Industrial Commission in 1900 that the practice of requiring a formal statement of previous work experience and the inquiries with former employers as to the reasons for termination, had "the effect of the old blacklist, while at the same time it does not render those who follow it amenable to the law."[36] William J. Pinkerton described in meticulous detail the workings of this "personal record system" in his own reminiscences, ironically titled *His Personal Record*. "It is not generally known," he wrote, "that all the great railway companies of the United States maintain systems of espionage and bureaus of information, interchangeable and unlimited in scope." Every action of an employee's life is "traced, tabulated, and in time arrayed against him." Together with his official personal record of employment, the employee must file a tintype photograph—"a tintype because it will show, therefore, all facial marks and blemishes that surgery might, at some future time, remove."[37]

The elimination of general discharge lists by many roads in the early 1890s did not mean the end of the blacklist, even in its old and cruder form. After the Pullman boycott many roads developed and circulated comprehensive lists of discharged employees. The numbers were so large and the interest of the companies in preventing their reemployment was so great that lists were widely used. The most famous case was that of the Illinois Central.

Chicago Attorney William J. Strong was persuaded to take on the case of Fred Ketcham, formerly a conductor on the Chicago & Northwestern, who claimed to have been blacklisted. Through the Ketcham case Strong discovered scores of other men who had been blacklisted. He uncovered a list circulated by the Illinois Central not only to their own divisions but to the other twenty-three member roads of the General Managers' Association, identifying employees who had struck, were discharged, and should not be considered for reemployment.[38]

Evidence exists of blacklists on other roads as well. As noted in an earlier chapter, the Northern Pacific put together a comprehensive list of striking ARU workers who had been discharged, a duplicated copy of which survives.[39]

Discipline

The 1890s also saw dramatic changes in the attitude of many railroads toward disciplining their employees. Traditionally, discipline had taken the form of suspension, fines, or outright dismissal by local and supervisory employees. Decisions were final and there was no right of appeal. As noted earlier, even by the 1880s the absolute authority of local officials was being challenged by organized railroad workers. Appeals of decisions were made to higher officials. Strikes were undertaken for the removal of particularly arbitrary local officials. Even as the appeal process was being regularized and limited through special boards of inquiry on some roads, a new system of discipline, known as "discipline by record" or the "Brown system," was adopted with increasing regularity on many roads. By 1900, fifty-seven railroad systems were using it.[40]

George R. Brown, general superintendent of the Fall Brook Railway, devised a system of record keeping that did away with immediate dismissal or suspension except for very flagrant offenses, such as intemperance or insubordination. In the words of Marshall Kirkman, a widely read railroad management theorist of the nineteenth century, it was "so aimed and adjusted as to correct the errors and mistakes of employes without unnecessary friction." Brown described how he recorded every infraction of the rules that a man committed. This record replaced the disciplinary discharge but was equally dreaded. He went to work with no disruption and only the supervisory personnel knew. When several such incidents had been recorded, he was warned, and "when the page is full of irregular circumstances the judgement is usually written at the bottom in two words, 'discharged, incompetent.'"[41] The system was widely adopted by the end of the 1890s, and it was a major step toward the internalization of discipline on an individual basis. Together with the personal record of employment, readily available to any prospective employer, discipline by record tended to define employment as strictly a matter between an individual employee and his employer.

Discipline by record was a way of strengthening the bonds between an individual employee and his employer. Another was creating incentives for more loyal and productive labor.[42] Marshall Kirkman noted that pay premiums were demonstrating their value in improving train service on a number of roads. "A record is kept of the acts of trainmen, the number of cars moved, whether trains were on time or not, accidents, complaints against employes, errors of the latter, deportment, dress, and the condition and cleanliness of the cars, and so on. This record is made the basis for awarding a sum of money in addition to the regular pay and for making promotions."[43] In this manner, the record of discipline was inverted to build bonds of employee loyalty. But Kirkman cautioned that it should not be simply routinized. It should symbolize "a lofty appreciation" of "faithful service" and individual merit. The effect should be "to make men plan and strive to achieve high aims."[44] Railroads experimented with many other devices besides premium pay to build employee loyalty. A host of insurance and welfare schemes were developed on different roads. These schemes will be discussed later.

Seniority

The origins of seniority as a means to determine the order of promotion and layoff on the railroads is shrouded in obscurity. Available evidence indicates that it was customary on some roads at a very early date. It became in time a central element of virtually every written agreement between railroad companies and the runing trades, from the time that such agreements began to appear. One of the earliest agreements, on the Erie Railroad in 1870, included a provision for seniority. The clause stipulated that promotion to preferred engines or runs would be according to length of service, but that length of service applied only within an operating division. If a man moved from one division to another, he went to the bottom of the seniority list.[45]

The older idea that promotion should be on the basis of individual merit continued to have great appeal for many railroad managers. "The company reserves to itself entire discretion as to promotion," wrote the Chicago, Burlington, and Quincy's George Chalendar to a division superintendent. "Merit will have the precedence over seniority in all cases."[46] Charles E. Perkins was even more adamant in 1877, arguing the "the only solid rock to anchor to" was the principle "that merit and merit only shall be rewarded."[47] It was only reluctantly that this principle was sacrificed or modified to accommodate the principle of seniority. In its earliest forms seniority was applied only to promotions, and it was usually qualified by the inclusion of some standard of merit.[48]

During the period of railroad expansion from 1879 through 1883, when the railroad brotherhoods, particularly the engineers, secured their first agreements with many roads, seniority was inevitably a part of those agreements. Once the principle was accepted, its application tended to be broadened in successive agreements to cover layoff and recall.[49]

It seems clear that the pressure to allocate jobs according to length of service came primarily from workers. They sought an alternative to the arbitrary and discriminatory practices of railroad officials who used their power over job allocation for personal advantage or to exclude unions and cement employee loyalty. It was a case of employees seeking to rationalize the procedure by which their work was regulated in order to protect themselves. Ideally the brotherhoods would have appropriated the allocation of jobs to themselves. "We insist," the Engineers' Journal argued in 1881, "that it is immaterial to the officers of the road whether A or B runs their engines, so long as one is in every way as qualified as the other; of this there can be no better judge than the engineers themselves."[50] When the New York Central failed to promote according to seniority, the members of its Albany division took matters into their own hands and passed resolutions forbidding a member of the Brotherhood of Locomotive Engineers from taking an engine or a run "to which he was not entitled," on pain of expulsion.[51]

Once railroad companies accepted the notion of written agreements with their men, the principle of seniority, though still a bitter pill, was inevitably swallowed. By 1900 the principle was widely accepted by railroads in their dealing with the "Big Four" brotherhoods. It did not extend to the less well-organized railroad trades.[52]

While most railroad managers would not have chosen to abide by seniority of their own free will—they preferred the discretion of selecting and promoting whom they chose—they learned to live with it. Few, if any, strikes were precipitated over seniority alone. Indeed, seniority fit very logically with other aspects of an emerging system for better managing their labor forces. The system of classifying employees according to length of service and promoting from within were complementary with the principle of seniority. Employees objected not to classification per se but to using a classification scheme as a tool for justifying lower wages to some perfectly skilled men and as an incentive for local officials to discharge higher priced, "first-class" men.[53] Promotion from within went a step beyond seniority by excluding skilled workers from entry to their trade with a new employer and requiring that they begin at the bottom of the promotional ladder.

Both classification and promotion from within, as well as seniority, had the effect of making the penalty of discharge more severe and the prospect of losing a strike more hazardous. Both tended to encourage immobility and to some extent a more cautious attitude toward strikes.[54] The only major historical study of railroad labor seniority suggests that even in the nineteenth century railroad managers were prepared partially to abandon their prerogative over job allocation if the disruption caused by high labor turnover could be diminished.[55] Their acceptance of the principle also reflected the presence of an adequate supply of labor that could replenish the stock of skilled workers by gradual promotion from the lower ranks.

Company Welfare

If the application of seniority principles tended to reduce labor mobility, many railroad managers perceived that the introduction of company-sponsored insurance, hospital care, pensions, and even profit sharing would increase employee loyalty and reduce the appeal of unionism. What is remarkable is that these schemes received so little support from railroad managers for so long. As the reply of Charles Perkins to his own subordinate in the columns of the *Nation* revealed, company welfare measures were viewed with great skepticism by some leaders of railroad corporations. T. F. Oakes, vice-president of the Northern Pacific Railroad, in 1881 did not believe the company could afford to contribute to such schemes, and he echoed the view of the company's counsel that the plans did not provide sufficient protection from liability suits.[56] Prosperity tended to erode management's interest in such schemes, which had been stirred by the 1877 railroad strikes.[57]

Insurance and Relief Associations. For all of the flirtation with company-sponsored relief, few roads actually established plans. The most durable scheme was developed on the Baltimore & Ohio in 1880.[58] Early plans were also tried on the Illinois Central and the Philadelphia & Reading but survived only a few years. The Baltimore & Ohio plan, though instituted in 1880, was not legally incorporated until 1882. It was initiated as an independent association of railroad employees with company support; participation was voluntary. However, in 1889 the association was absorbed as a department of the company. From the outset operating expenses were paid by the company, but with the introduction of a pension system, the company shifted to making direct payments into the pension fund. Participation in the relief department was compulsory for every new or promoted employee and remained so until compulsory relief schemes were banned by the Erdman Act of 1898. In addition to the relief functions of the department, which included payment for disability, sickness, and death and a pension plan for selective retirement because of infirmity, there was also a savings plan for employees.[59]

The Baltimore & Ohio relief plan was followed by a very similar plan on the Pennsylvania in 1886. Because of growing employee opposition to the compulsory features of the schemes, the Pennsylvania plan remained voluntary. The Philadelphia & Reading reinstituted a compulsory plan in 1888, and the Chicago, Burlington & Quincy established a plan, Charles Perkins's views notwithstanding, in 1889 after the engineers' strike. The fifth major plan was developed in the 1880s on the western lines of the Pennsylvania system. A number of roads contributed toward private insurance for their employees. Toward the very end of the nineteenth century another group of major railroad systems established voluntary relief programs, among them the Plant System, the Atlantic Coast Line, and the Lehigh Valley. In lieu of insurance, some roads supported hospitals for their employees. These included the Atchison, Topeka & Santa Fe, the Illinois Central, the Southern Pacific, the Denver & Rio Grande, and the Texas & Pacific.[60]

Surveys conducted by the Interstate Commerce Commission in 1889 and 1892 provide a window on the general acceptance of company welfare programs by railroad corporations. In 1889, 85 companies responded to the survey, with 12 maintaining insurance or guaranty funds, 5 supporting hospital funds, and 5 more contributing to benefit associations run by employees.[61] A more complete survey of 350 companies in 1892 showed that 59 were supporting an insurance or guaranty fund, hospital fund, or relief association for the benefit of their employees. Nearly twice as many companies, but still a minority, indicated that disabled employees were given other work to do or provided with assistance on an individual basis. About 225 companies made no such claim.

Clearly, the support for company-sponsored welfare, though growing, was still limited. Opposition was particularly concentrated on smaller roads with limited capital, but others simply continued to view such schemes with suspicion.[62] By the end of the century, it was the view of at least one railroad president queried by the Industrial Commission that more and more railroad managers were seriously looking into insurance and pensions for their employees.[63]

Railroad employees perceived company welfarism as a direct threat to their unions. Few workers could afford to carry more than one kind of insurance, and when such insurance was made compulsory, by railroad corporations, it tended to reduce participation in the brotherhoods and their own insurance schemes. Company-sponsored relief tended to make employees more dependent by taking away "their freedom from changing employers by causing them to forfeit the benefits for which they have paid assessments." Finally, workers recognized that the insurance schemes had been designed in large part to forestall liability suits by injured employees or by the families of employees killed at work. All of the relief plans included a provision whereby, with acceptance of relief, railroad employees or their families waived the right to sue the company for damages.[64] Among the many abuses which William John Pinkerton discussed in his 1904 reminiscence, he attacked none more vehemently than relief and pension programs, or as he preferred to call them, the railroad's "self-protection fund."[65] In the event of an employee's death, the corporation first requires his widow to sign away her rights to sue the company, and then, "the munificent corporation grudgingly inserts its flabby hand into the coffers of the pension fund, the fund to which the dead man contributed all the heavy years he served, from 75 cents to $3.75 a month, and hands the widow HER OWN MONEY, while the world applauds the generosity and fatherly care of the corporation."[66]

When the Pennsylvania Railroad first announced its voluntary relief scheme in 1886, Eugene V. Debs vigorously attacked it in the pages of the *Locomotive Firemen's Magazine*. He expressed indignation and humiliation over all the patronizing talk by employers concerning employee welfare. "The question is all too often asked, what can we do for our working people? . . . They do not require the guardianship of their employers. All they demand is justice, fair play, fair wages for a day's work, the control absolutely of the money they earn without question or qualification."[67] Debs asked rhetorically if the companies by establishing relief departments intended the "disbandment" of the brotherhoods. And he answered unequivocally from his analysis of their plans, "manifestly, such is the intention."

The brotherhoods and the corporations were in direct competition to insure their members or employees. A 1906 study of the beneficiary features of the railroad brotherhoods notes that each brotherhood that instituted a compulsory feature in its insurance plan during the 1890s showed a more substantial increase in membership during the decade, and its losses during the depression of 1893–97 were less than in those organizations where membership remained voluntary. The Brotherhood of Locomotive Engineers increased its membership from 7,408 in 1890 (when the compulsory feature was added) to 18,739 in 1897, and to 46,400 in 1904. The Order of Railway Conductors grew from 13,933 in 1891 to 15,807 in 1898 and to 31,288 in 1904. The telegraphers, the firemen, and the switchmen sustained severe losses and recovered more slowly.[68] With the ban on compulsory corporation relief plans in the Erdman Act of 1898, the relative position of the voluntary plans improved somewhat.

Railroad YMCAs and Reading Rooms. Company interest in the welfare of their employees did not end with insurance and pension schemes. A broader, though equally episodic, concern had to do with the way employees spent their time off the job, in particular during layovers between runs. Company concern focused on two evils—the saloon and the brotherhood lodge—as places where men socialized and picked up bad habits. William Ackerman noted in 1882 that men used the Sunday holiday to indulge in excessive drink, especially during layovers, and as a result the company endured "the loss of their services not only for that day, but for a part or all of the following day also."[69] The Chicago, Burlington & Quincy discharge records for the 1880s confirm that excessive drinking was indeed a problem on the road.[70]

The YMCA and its railroad branches were effective at promoting themselves as an alternative to both the saloon and the brotherhood lodge rooms. In the aftermath of strikes, railroad officials found these appeals particularly persuasive. Henry L. Bauer, general secretary of the YMCA at Creston, Iowa, told Charles Perkins of the importance of Bible study in changing men who formerly "talked of nothing but what they read in their brotherhood papers."[71] A resolution from the railroad branch of the YMCA in East Saint Louis proclaimed in 1886 that their members had acted responsibly during the recent strike. It urged companies to make "temperance and morality" the basis for judging employee fitness and predicted that there would be as a result "fewer loud-mouthed agitators . . . and less labor trouble."

A report from the YMCA branch in Troy, New York, to the Interstate Commerce Commission in 1892 noted that the railroad men's taste in literature had shown a "very marked change for the better." They interested themselves largely in scientific periodicals and technical journals on railroading. "There is a social and business snap about the men with whom we come in contact that is encouraging and indicative of future results. As to promotion all are preparing themselves with that end in view."[72] The Baltimore & Ohio reported to the commission that its own attempts to provide reading rooms for its employees had been considerably less successful. At Mount Clare, West Virginia, a library of over 10,000 volumes "with all the best technical and scientific journals" was provided, "but while the library room at Mount Clare has been open at all hours for the use of employes and this fact has been liberally advertised, no one takes advantage of it." Similar facilities at Martinsburg and Keyser, West Virginia, and Garrett, Indiana, proved equally unsuccessful.[73]

Many railroad employers found long-term support of the YMCAs unappealing. As the immediate threat of industrial conflict receded, support for the YMCAs waned. On the Chicago, Burlington, & Quincy, the company made modest contributions to railroad YMCAs in Chicago after 1879, but rejected appeals from Atchison, Keokuk, and Creston, and in 1889 significantly reduced its Chicago contribution.[74]

The reception of YMCAs among railroad workers varied widely. Men in McCook, Nebraska, petitioned the company to support a railroad YMCA. The Brotherhood of Locomotive Firemen gratefully acknowledged a cordial reception at the YMCA during its 1886 convention. But when the YMCAs along the New York Central line provided hospitality to scabs during the Knights of Labor strike in 1890, they were greeted with deep hostility. The *Union Pacific Employees Magazine* noted that the YMCA club rooms "will have a deadly, unwholesome smell to honest men for a long time to come."[75]

The Interstate Commerce Commission found in 1892 that company-sponsored eating and lodging facilities and support for reading rooms or "places of resort" for employees were only slightly more popular than company relief; 52 out of 350 companies questioned provided eating or lodging facilities or subsidized room and board for their employees. Seventy-eight provided reading rooms or places of resort, and of these 44 did so in conjunction with the YMCA.[76] Although support for these forms of company welfare appears to have grown by the end of the century, many companies large and small remained aloof.

Corporate Collectivism

Competition for territory and traffic permeated the relationships among major railroad systems during the late nineteenth century. In self-protection railroad managers hammered out short-term alliances or divisions of traffic, but these were consistently undermined by the roads in their anxiety to capitalize on advantages and by the public, which correctly saw the maintenance of competition as a lever for maintaining lower rates.[77]

Railroad managers also eyed each other competitively when it came to labor recruitment. Seasonal shortages of track hands could provoke bidding wars between roads in need of the scarce commodity. Labor recruiters for expanding western roads plied the eastern lines looking for skilled enginemen. Wages in the West were pushed higher to attract men from lower-paying roads, and railroad managers anxiously gathered any wage data that could be obtained to position themselves better.[78]

Only in times of crisis when restive workers threatened major gains in wages and working conditions or when coordinated wage cuts offered greater security did railroad managers overcome their mutual distrust. The deepening depression in 1877 produced the first appearance of widespread cooperation between major railroad systems, even though managers of the eastern trunk lines later denied any collusion in the staggered wage cuts imposed on their employees that spring.[79] Encouraged by the success of the Philadelphia & Reading Railroad in ridding itself of the brotherhoods, the Baltimore & Ohio and in succeeding months the Pennsylvania, the Erie, and the New York Central cut wages, precipitating the great strikes of July 1877. Whether the product of collective design or not, the cuts and the strikes that followed forced on the roads an awareness of their common interests. In unison they demanded action by federal and state governments to protect their property. They identified and selectively eliminated troublemakers from their work forces. In some larger railroad centers they jointly supported railroad YMCAs and other measures to pacify their workers. Managers failed to develop institutional mechanisms for more permanent cooperation, but they did identify common interests and recognize a mutual vulnerability to strikes.

The expansive years of the early 1880s dulled memories of the 1877 strikes as roads reasserted their individual interests. Not until early 1886, with the loss of the Gould strikes, the explosive organizing of the Knights of Labor, and the prospect of massive eight-hour strikes, did railroad managers reaffirm their common interests and give them a specific institutional form. Strikes of freight handlers and switchmen, against the backdrop of the general eight-hour day agitation, led to daily meetings of railroad managers in Chicago from May 3 through May 12. Donald McMurry has recounted the results of the meetings, which were chaired by E. T.

Jeffrey, general manager of the Illinois Central.[80] The managers voted against altering working hours or rates of pay and resolved to discharge and blacklist employees who refused to follow orders. They agreed to disregard union membership in the employment or discharge of men and to deal with the men only as individuals. They appealed collectively for better local protection and for federal legislation to prevent railroad strikes. They pledged to seek greater uniformity in the wages they paid to labor.

Adjourning on May 12, railroad managers did not reconvene until June 25, when switchmen again struck a member road, the Lake Shore, in an action that stemmed from the as-yet-unresolved strike of April 1886. A series of meetings during the summer produced expressions of support for the Lake Shore in its ordeal and a pledge of $25,000 to relieve some of its burden. But as the crisis passed, so did the incentive to meet regularly. With no formal structure and preoccupied once again with the exigencies of running railroads in a highly competitive territory, the Chicago managers went their separate ways.[81]

The absence of enduring bonds of cooperation was most evident in the strike of enginemen against the Chicago, Burlington & Quincy in late February 1888. Several Chicago roads acquiesced to an employee boycott of that railroad's cars, with the Rock Island even going to court against the Burlington to defend its right not to handle Burlington rolling stock. Although Jeffery, of the Illinois Central, tried to mediate the dispute between the Burlington and its employees and did not condone the boycott, he also felt that the Burlington had been guilty of "injudicious conduct" in causing the strike. A member of the board of directors of the Illinois Central went even further:

> In the rivalry which now exists between railway corporations it does not seem to me that the Illinois Central is bound to consider the welfare of its competitors. If we can really improve our own condition, and elevate our own reputation, by conciliating those who are in our employ, or by conciliating labor organizations, I certainly would do it. Our object is to carry freight and passengers at a cheaper rate than our rivals. If, therefore, a policy of conciliation, and even a higher rate of wages than other railway companies pay, will bring to us a more efficient, and therefore in the end a cheaper, service, it does seem to me that good policy would prompt that line of action.[82]

Although barriers to sustained management cooperation in labor matters remained, as the Burlington strike illustrated, the elements of a personnel management system common to many roads were being assembled. During the course of the 1880s the relative shortage of labor in the West had eased, and railroad managers considered standardization of wages. They were concerned with work rules that perpetuated the advantages of scarcity under conditions that did not warrant them. On one western road after another they remedied the scarcity through active recruitment and rapid promotion, "making" skilled enginemen and trainmen from within their own ranks. Discharge records and blacklists were developed in one form or another on most roads, and improved record keeping permitted the freer exchange of information about employees. The advanced thinking of Charles Francis Adams, Jr., of the Union Pacific and other moderate railroad managers was gradually beginning to influence others in the direction of building a permanent, loyal work force through company welfare and conciliation.[83]

Reorganization of the General Managers' Association

Formal reorganization of the General Managers' Association, however, had to await the emergence of a new group of leaders and industrial conditions that again seriously disturbed relations between railroads and their employees. A constitution and bylaws of the organization were drafted during 1892 under the leadership of Everett St. John, general manager of the Chicago, Rock Island & Pacific, to whom Jeffrey had passed on the minutes of the association. They were formally adopted on January 29, 1893. During the next month—the same month in which railroad employees met to launch the American Railway Union—the General Managers' Association was called together for the first time in some years to consider a labor-related matter: Chicago switchmen were again agitating for a wage increase.[84]

The rapid response of the association to the prospect of another switchmen's strike illustrates the progress that had been made in forging a common management strategy. Three committees were instituted. The first was responsible for securing the services of switchmen from other areas. The expense of bringing them to the threatened strike center was to be charged to the roads in proportion to the number of men they used. The second committee was responsible for reviewing employee demands and approving or disapproving wage or work rule changes that were proposed by the member roads. The third committee was to manage the strike, enlist support of city and county authorities, and assess member roads to help those that suffered inordinate losses during the strike. The association pledged itself not to acquiesce in a boycott of cars (the memory of the Chicago, Burlington, & Quincy strike lingered). It proposed to formulate model rules to govern employees on any road.[85]

Faced with the threat of a citywide strike of switchmen, the Chicago general managers were prepared to consign some of their autonomy in labor matters to the collective management of the association. They fully accepted standardization of wage rates and work rules. They collectively recruited new workers and agreed to an equitable distribution of them. They accepted general financial responsibility for the welfare of each member road. And they foreswore taking competitive advantage of any roads that were struck—a temptation which had proved irresistible to some as recently as 1888.

The strike of switchmen did not materialize. The general managers exulted in the potency of their new organizational machinery. During the next few months they processed nineteen cases of changes in rules or pay rates brought in by member roads. In eight of the cases the association recommended that the demands of the employees be partially or wholly met. In only one did a strike result, and its defeat confirmed the power of the association. An additional organizational change saw the establishment of an "employment bureau" that functioned to regulate and monitor the flow of railroad labor to and within the city. Although it facilitated the exchange of information about employees, the committee insisted that this was not blacklisting. The committee asserted that it was opposed to the idea of blacklisting, but it insisted on the right of association members to know the previous employment records of prospective employees. Possessed of the desired information from the Employment Bureau, member roads were free to act as they saw fit.[86]

The association was less successful in extending its work into other major railroad centers. An insight into the efforts to do so is provided in the correspondence of J. W. Kendrick, general manager of the Northern Pacific, who was invited to attend a major recruiting meeting in Chicago on August 17, 1893. Kendrick reported at some length the substance of the discussions at the meeting of the General Managers' Association in Chicago to T. F. Oakes, a former Northern Pacific official who in 1893 became a court-appointed receiver for the road.

The sense of the papers read by Messrs Odell and Porter, and of the discussion in relation thereto, was that there should be an organization of the General Managers of all the lines in the country. That all conflicts with organized labor should be dealt with as a unit, and that the companies so organized would be very much stronger than the men; that the idea of a proper schedule is a good one, affording a line of procedure in dealing with the men which would secure uniformity of treatment and be productive of harmony between the men and the railroads; that the existing provisions in the present schedules must be greatly modified so as to afford greater latitude to the railroad companies in the management of their affairs; and that the rates of pay must of necessity be reduced.[87]

The thrust of the meeting was somewhat diverted by the general manager of the Cairo Short Line, a self-proclaimed "old fogey," who condemned any dealing with organized labor. He argued against an association that might compel him to pay more to his men than he was inclined to pay. A committee of five was appointed to canvass the roads outside of Chicago, and another meeting was called for the end of August.

Discussions with General Manager Dickinson of the Union Pacific and with James J. Hill, president of the Great Northern, encouraged Kendrick to consider some cooperative effort to align the schedules of the major transcontinental lines. Dickinson believed that at a minimum such an agreement could be reached among the Union Pacific, the Northern Pacific, the Great Northern, and the Santa Fe.

Kendrick was anxious to get the participation of Hill and the Great Northern, noting that it was a "manifest absurdity for two lines, interwoven as ours and the Great Northern are, to maintain different rates of compensation for similar service." He was particularly concerned that the Great Northern's schedules were "much more favorable than ours," but discussions with Hill showed him to be skeptical of associations. Hill stated, according to Kendrick, "that he would not care to be a member of an organization which could order his company to do thus or so, or whose action would involve his line, especially an organization the members of which were connected with roads whose interests were very diverse from those of the West and Northwest."[88]

Wary of Hill's motives, Kendrick still tried to coordinate the coming wage cuts. Just before leaving for the second Chicago meeting he voiced his continuing distrust of the Great Northern and his suspicion that Hill sought to precipitate a conflict that would benefit him in the end. Nevertheless, Kendrick remained committed to the idea of a common schedule.[89] Throughout September and October, Kendrick postponed one deadline after another for announcing changes in the Northern Pacific schedules of wages, in the hope of securing simultaneous action from the Great Northern and the Union Pacific. On October 27 he wrote that the Union Pacific wanted six more weeks and that the prospects of getting the Great Northern to join were diminishing. But on November 13 he reiterated the belief that the Northern Pacific could not afford to act alone. On November 17, W. G. Pierce, another Northern Pacific receiver, reported to Kendrick, based on a recent conversation with James J. Hill, that he believed Hill had no intention of taking simultaneous action. Apparently, Hill was convinced that different methods of "treating with the men" should be pursued by the different roads, while substantially similar but not identical rules and rates should be adopted.[90] Pierce concluded, "We can place no dependence on J. J. Hill."

With this information, Kendrick and the receivers were forced to abandon their plans for joint action by the transcontinentals. Their dreams of a national umbrella association and district organizations of roads could not yet be realized. A "national schedule of wages, graded in accordance with the arbitrary time divisions, or such other established districts as may be decided upon" was premature and would, as he correctly perceived, require "a great deal of time."[91] But the greatest disappointment was that not even a regional organization of transcontinentals could be effected.

When James J. Hill eventually did cut the wages of his employees in the spring of 1894, Kendrick, who had maneuvered carefully and astutely to avoid an earlier strike by his own employees, refused to fulfill the strike-bound Great Northern's requests for transportation and declined to receive freight routed in Great Northern cars. "The benefits we could have rendered Mr. Hill in this way," he wrote to Receiver H. C. Payne on April 21, "would in any case have resulted in saving him a very small sum of money, while the appearance of participation in his cause, by this road, would in my opinion have caused us a great deal of trouble and unknown expense."[92] Toward the very end of the same letter he waxed more self-righteous, revealing the bitterness harbored from his earlier efforts to enlist Hill in his cooperative scheme. "I find that Hill has oppressed his men," he asserted, "by reducing their wages to a shameful extent." The cost of the strike was much greater than any savings the Great Northern might gain from the reduction over a year's time.

If this episode in the Northwest reveals the continuing barriers to effective management cooperation in its dealings with labor, the role played by the General Managers' Association in the Pullman strike in Chicago reveals how far some roads had progressed toward effective cooperation. Several conditions in Chicago promoted cooperation: the association was a seasoned organization with some history of success in meeting the challenges of labor; the roads themselves had relatively well-established territories and traffic patterns; the centralization of headquarters in Chicago made communication and contact among roads easy. The solidarity of the Chicago roads during the Pullman boycott was impressive, indeed.

During the early months of 1893 the revived General Managers' Association had been tested, and it responded well. The roads had successfully resisted the demands of switchmen for increased pay; there had been no breach in the ranks. New workers had been efficiently recruited in the East and transported to Chicago; the costs had been shared. The notion of standardized wages, collectively determined (by the railroads) had gained wide acceptance. And with such unity it had been possible to appeal to public authorities for the protection needed in the event of a strike. By August 1893 the association had turned to evangelizing, and Everett St. John outlined to managers gathered from roads outside of Chicago the system of organization which he and his Chicago colleagues now regarded to be virtually strike proof.[93] Although no mass conversion of eastern and western general managers occurred, the association was undeterred in its own work. In November a massive codification and classification of wage rates was completed, and members of the association received copies to guide them in the proposed effort to standardize wages. Work on standardization of wages and rules continued in committee through March 1894.[94]

By the time the association met again to consider labor matters, it was facing an unprecedented situation. The American Railway Union, a formidable organization by the early spring of 1894, had mushroomed as a result of the court victory over the Union Pacific and the strike against the Great Northern. What was initially a rather obscure strike of Pullman car shop employees was catapulted to the nation's attention when the First Annual Convention of the ARU declared a boycott of all Pullman cars. Meeting on June 25, just before the deadline for the boycott to begin, the General Managers' Association swung into action.[95] They appointed one of their former members, John T. Eagen, as full-time strike manager. In daily sessions they hammered out a strategy for combating the boycott. The essential elements of the strategy had been formulated during previous strike threats. The appropriate committee structure was in place. Employment offices were opened and staffed in major eastern railroad centers. The managers resolved to discharge any employee who refused to handle a Pullman car, and further to ensure that no railroad worker so discharged or who struck would ever be eligible for employment on any road represented by the association. A special committee of attorneys explored legal options. A deliberate effort was made to draw the United States government into the fray when, surprisingly, the ARU appeared to have successfully brought western railroad traffic to a standstill. Faced, not with the strike on one road for which the machinery of the association had been prepared to deal, but with a strike on all of the member roads and in fact most of the roads in the West, the association found that even its resources were inadequate.

More than any previous railroad strike, the Pullman boycott brought about the broad application of federal authority in its suppression. None of the tools of federal intervention were new with this crisis: troops, injunctions, and contempt of court citations had been tried before. But never before was the scale of federal intervention as great, and never before had it been as masterfully coordinated with a well-organized association of general managers.

The internal discipline of the General Managers' Association roads was maintained during the strike. It continued to function as a single voice for railroad management in negotiations with city and federal officials. Its expenditures, though relatively modest, were shared according to an equitable formula. And available evidence suggests that the commitment of the roads not to hire back ARU strikers was maintained.[96] However, the strike was broken only through the massive intervention of the federal government and the unalloyed use of federal court injunctions, which disrupted the strike's leadership and fractured the central communications network on which far-flung strike committees depended.

A new level of corporate collectivism was ushered in by the Pullman boycott. It was a product of careful and systematic construction. It distilled the experience of the Chicago roads, during the tumultuous era of the 1880s and 1890s. Its rationalizing principles reflected a maturation of the Chicago roads, the diminishing of the harsh competitiveness of an earlier era, and the triumph of a new corporatism in which ironically, a seat for organized railroad labor had been carefully prepared. It was ultimately guaranteed by the power of the federal government and the federal courts.

A Framework of Labor-Management Cooperation

At the height of the Pullman boycott or even in its immediate aftermath, it would have been difficult to make the case that railroad management's posture toward organized labor was moderating and maturing. The General Managers' Association trumpeted its victory (largely the result of federal intervention). The leaders of the American Railway Union were vilified by railroad officials and the press. Rank-and-file members of the ARU who had struck in sympathy with the Pullman carmen found their return to gainful employment blocked, not only with their former employers but with other roads in the region. Persecuted and desperate, many changed their names and moved frequently in an attempt to find jobs. The federal government, having broken the strike by injunction, aggressively prosecuted Eugene Debs and the ARU directors in order to prevent further disruptive railroad strikes. The incremental evolution over more than a decade of corporate welfare schemes, seniority systems, standardized wages, disciplinary procedures, and even the recognition of the major brotherhoods on many roads tended to be ignored in the context of the most momentous confrontation between labor and capital of a conflict-ridden century.

If moderating forces in railroad labor relations were difficult to discern in 1894, it was also unexpected that one of the primary voices that favored moderation would be the architect of the federal government's intervention in the Pullman boycott and the chief prosecutor of Eugene Debs and ARU leaders. Richard Olney had served as a director and as corporation counsel for major railroads for more than twenty years, first with the Boston & Maine and later with the Chicago, Burlington & Quincy and others. His appointment as attorney general in the Grover Cleveland administration insured that railroads could muster substantial inside influence with the federal government in the event of a major crisis. Pullman was such a crisis, and Olney fulfilled his mission ably.[97]

Proceeding initially to insist that there be no interference with the mails during the Pullman boycott, Olney quickly found that basis too restricted to prevent what was emerging as a national general strike of railroad workers. In fact, the strikers made serious efforts to comply with the government's order regarding the mails. Olney eventually found, with the assistance of Edwin Walker, his special counsel in Chicago, a broader basis for an injunction against the strikers and for the intervention of federal troops to enforce it. That basis was the Sherman Antitrust Act, which forbade restraint of trade and interference with interstate commerce. A sympathetic federal judiciary in Chicago brought forth the broadly defined injunction needed. Armed with this and similar injunctions filed in federal courts throughout the West, authorities arrested ARU leaders and charged them with contempt of court. When these arrests of the strike's leadership and the widespread intervention of federal troops eventually broke the back of the strike, Olney and the general managers were triumphant. [98]

Olney's actions in the months after the Pullman strike are revealing, not only of the evolution of his own thinking and the impact of the strike upon it, but of the emergence of a new basis for railroad labor relations in the years to come. Olney was determined that the role of the federal government in breaking the strike should be vindicated. He sought to establish the strongest possible grounds for that vindication. But, inscrutably, he also sought to reconcile segments of the railroad labor movement.

From the beginning Olney had been uncomfortable with resting the government's case for an injunction to restrain the actions of the American Railway Union leaders on the Sherman Antitrust Act. The 1890 legislation was still regarded as experimental, and sections of it were quite probably unconstitutional. In Olney's view it provided no durable basis for preventing major disruptions of the railroad network. [99] In his arguments before the circuit court in September and more directly before the Supreme Court in March 1895, Olney sought to shift the basis of the government's contempt case away from the Sherman Antitrust Act to the historical right of the government to prevent "a great public nuisance," and even more specifically, the obstruction of a "public highway." That historical responsibility had been reinforced by the Interstate Commerce Act of 1887, which had declared all railroads to be interstate carriers and had given the federal government the exclusive responsibility to regulate and prevent interference with interstate commerce. On this foundation, Olney argued the government was wholly within its right to prevent railroad strikes that interfered with interstate commerce. [100]

When the Supreme Court ruled in May 1895 that Debs et al. had acted in contempt of a legitimate injunction, it affirmed fully and specifically the legal foundation argued by Olney in the case. Olney had vindicated the government's role in the Pullman strike, and, what was more important, he had established a formidable legal precedent for enjoining future railroad strikes. This decision, as Gerald Eggert has argued, outlawed strikes on interstate railways without specific legislation to that effect. "Any labor dispute that involved interstate commerce or the mails—and what railroad strike would not—could be enjoined, and the injunction could be enforced by the full, armed might of the United States if not obeyed."[101]

Even as he sought to prevent future railroad strikes through the power of the federal government, Olney began to move in directions that were surprising and disconcerting to some of his railroad corporation colleagues. As early as 1893, he had shown some discomfort with an injunction issued by Judge Jenkins in the Northern Pacific case—an injunction which was so broadly drawn as to prohibit strikes of any kind and which virtually proscribed the right of railroad workers to organize at all. Olney was practically concerned that such a broad ruling might be overturned in such a way as to restrict the "legitimate" use of injunctions, but as his later actions showed, he had also come to believe that unions had a place in corporate life and that workers' rights to organize had to be protected.[102]

The Origins of the Erdman Act

Olney revealed his sentiments most explicitly when he intervened on behalf of the Brotherhood of Railway Trainmen in federal circuit court in Philadelphia shortly after the Pullman boycott, at the request of Edward A. Mosely, secretary of the Interstate Commerce Commission. The trainmen on the Philadelphia & Reading Railroad had been ordered by the court-appointed receivers to quit their union or be discharged. The men appealed the ruling to the federal court. Mosely arranged an interview between Stephen Wilkinson, grand master of the Brotherhood of Railway Trainmen, and Olney. Wilkinson told Olney of his own efforts to thwart the Pullman strike, which included disguising himself and taking up arms against the strikers, and of the suspension of 20,000 men from the brotherhood for participating in the strike. Olney was by his own account interested in what Wilkinson had to say and promised to consider assisting the Brotherhood of Trainmen. The interview

took place in September, not more than two months after the collapse of the Pullman strike and at the very time Olney was
developing the argument in the government's contempt case.

In an amicus brief to Judge George M. Dallas, Olney argued that
the prohibition of union membership was "invidious, if not ille-
gal." The brotherhood had acquitted itself as a responsible union,
and its members should not be denied the benefits of membership
and their right to associate. He also felt that a favorable decision
might help to further conciliate the "employed classes." He waxed
eloquent on the broader implications of protecting labor's right to
organize.

> Whatever else may remain for the future to determine, it must
> now be regarded as substantially settled that the mass of
> wage-earners can no longer be dealt with by capital as so
> many isolated units. The time has passed when the individual
> workman is called upon to pit his feeble single strength
> against the might of organized capital . . . and the burning
> question of modern times is how shall the ever-recurring
> controversies between them be adjusted and terminated. If the
> combatants are left to fight out their battles between
> themselves by the ordinary agencies, nothing is more certain
> than that each will inflict incalculable injury upon the other;
> while, whichever may triumph, will have won a victory only
> less disastrous and less regrettable than defeat.[103]

The brief, though resoundingly rejected by Judge Dallas, reflected
the evolution of Olney's thinking. He had come to believe that arbitration, preferably compulsory arbitration, offered the best hope for
a peaceable future in railroad labor relations.

When the Strike Commission, appointed by the president to investigate the Pullman strike, recommended a more permanent
framework for arbitration, Olney was quick to second it. Olney incorporated the views of the commission into the draft of a bill. He
proposed not a permanent commission but the machinery for rapidly appointing commissions as needed to arbitrate disputes.
Though arbitration remained voluntary, an agreement once reached
through arbitration could be enforced by the courts. In the case of
threatened strikes, Olney proposed that the government be em-
powered not only to enjoin strikes but also to appoint receivers to
operate recalcitrant railroads. This provision was ultimately eliminated from the bill. Like the Strike Commission's recommenda-
tions, Olney's bill prohibited blacklisting, yellow-dog contracts,

and interference with men joining unions of their choice. Though Olney's bill had a tortuous legislative history between 1895 and 1898, it was finally enacted into law as the Erdman Act of 1898 with most of his provisions intact. The brotherhoods had swung their support behind the bill.[104]

As important as Olney's role was in developing the machinery for the government to police the relations of railroad labor and capital, it is important to recognize that these views were coming to be shared by a vocal and influential segment of railroad managers, brotherhood leaders, and government officials. In their report to the president, the strike commissioners noted that there was a growing sentiment among employers favoring organization of their employees. And they asked, rhetorically, "Is it not wise to recognize them by law; to admit their necessity as labor guides and protectors, to conserve their usefulness, increase their responsibility, and to prevent their follies and aggressions by conferring upon them the privileges enjoyed by corporations, with like proper restrictions and regulations?"[105]

Although many railroad managers were reluctant to surrender their authority over wages to an arbitration tribunal, they accepted the general notion of voluntary arbitration before a public tribunal. The chairman and secretary of the Interstate Commerce Commission, strong advocates of government regulation, found evidence not long after the passage of new legislation in 1898 that a new "era of good feeling" had been inaugurated. Secretary E.A. Mosely asserted that "since the passage of that law there has not been the slightest murmur, and it meets the approval of every railroad man I have met. There are some who predict that there will not be any more strikes."[106]

Premature though that prediction may have been, fundamental changes were underway in railroad labor relations. Other developments in the industry also made them possible. Financial instability and the bankruptcy of numerous roads had led to renewed efforts to reduce competition and to rationalize the corporate structure of the roads. Bankers, most notably J. P. Morgan, promoted consolidation of railroads into fewer major systems and fostered the development of "communities of interest" of systems operating within a region.[107] The return of prosperity and the easing of competition contributed to a more lenient attitude toward labor.

Downward adjustments in wage rates and work rules in response to changes in the labor supply had been made by most roads. With adequate numbers of workers available to staff skilled positions in most parts of the country and with the institutional machinery available to recruit and promote more if they should be needed, the major roads had taken advantage of the depression to standardize wage rates at reduced levels. Railroads managers were also rationalizing and systematizing their personnel procedures. More lines introduced discipline by record, accepted the principle of seniority, and were contributing to some form of employee welfare scheme.

Finally, railroad employers had long accepted some forms of government intervention in labor matters. They readily turned to the courts for recourse during strikes and to state and federal authorities for troops to protect their property. These principles of government intervention had received new legitimacy in the eyes of many railroad managers as they faced the most serious threat ever to their control of their roads, namely the Pullman boycott. They were prepared to accept the extension and routinization of the government's role, even the recognition of responsible labor organizations, if future such disruptions could thus be prevented.

The Erdman Act was not the perfect instrument for federal regulation of railroad labor relations. Further federal intervention during World War I and additional legislation, specifically the Railway Labor Act of 1926, would increase the government's role in policing railroad labor relations. The key arbitration provisions of the Erdman Act were voluntary and its application was sporadic during the period 1898–1906. The act's significance lies in the fact that for the first time important legal protections (some of which were later declared unconstitutional) were provided to organized railroad labor, and that it was supported by the brotherhoods.[108] Frank P. Sargent of the Brotherhood of Locomotive Firemen affirmed before the Industrial Commission his support of "the principles of conciliation, mediation and arbitration" of railroad labor disputes. "We earnestly sought enactment of the bill approved June 1, 1898, entitled 'An Act concerning carriers engaged in interstate commerce and their employees.'"[109]

On the surface it was ironic that Olney should have written the major legislation of the 1890s that protected certain basic rights of railroad labor. Certainly some of his more conservative corporate colleagues found it so. Charles Perkins wrote to John Murray Forbes in 1895 that "it is very surprising that [he] should favor legislation of this kind. . . . I do not understand what has come over Olney."[110] But on another level, having established the power of the federal government effectively to prohibit any major disruption of railroad traffic, Olney perceived that the brotherhoods could be enlisted to police a new era of industrial peace in return for a guarantee of their survival.

Revival of the Brotherhoods

As we have seen in the previous chapters, the gulf between the brotherhoods and the industrial unionists among railroad men was not opened first by the Pullman boycott. Attempts to federate the orders had collapsed in the early 1890s. Out of the wreckage of the Supreme Council of the United Orders of Railway Men had emerged the American Railway Union, inspired by the industrial organization of the Knights of Labor. The brotherhoods were not unaffected by the deepening depression in 1893 and 1894, but at least at the leadership level they accepted as inevitable some retrenchment of wage rates and revision of work rules. In fact, Frank Sargent of the Brotherhood of Locomotive Firemen expressed some sympathy for the predicament in which roads like the Northern Pacific found themselves. In August 1893, General Manager J. W. Kendrick told T. F. Oakes of a recent letter he had received from Sargent in which the union official had expressed the view that modifications in the existing rates were inevitable. Further, Sargent was certain that after a full explanation of the facts, the men of his organization "would submit gracefully to any reasonable reduction, and loyally support the interests with which they were identified." Kendrick expressed his satisfaction that this correspondence indicated where Arthur and Sargent would be found in the event of any controversy in these matters, "always provided they do not in the meantime change their minds."[111]

Intervention of the heads of the respective brotherhoods had managed to avoid a strike on the Northern Pacific in early 1894, but it also had accelerated the migration of railroad men into the American Railway Union. As the ARU grew rapidly in the West, the brotherhoods assumed a defensive posture, which categorically ruled out support of the Pullman boycott. The refusal of official support could not prevent thousands of brotherhood members from joining the boycott, if not the ARU itself. Arthur denounced engineers on the Wabash and other roads who joined the boycott, and he threatened them with expulsion.[112] The Switchmen's Mutual Aid Association and the Carmen's Union were essentially destroyed by the exodus of their members when these unions refused to support the ARU. It was noted that officials of the Brotherhood of Railroad Trainmen claimed to have expelled nearly 20,000 men after the strike and that the leadership literally participated in the suppression of the strike. Many years later, Samuel Gompers claimed that the refusal of the American Federation of Labor to sanction a call for a general strike in support of the ARU was "the biggest service that could have been performed to maintain the integrity of the Railroad Brotherhoods. Large numbers of their members had left their organizations and joined the ARU. It meant, if not disruption, weakening to a very serious extent."[113]

With the collapse of the Pullman boycott and the continuing persecution of the American Railway Union, the brotherhoods quietly began to heal their wounds, expel ARU supporters, and reestablish their own authority to represent railroad men in their trades. They found many railroad managers receptive, if not grateful for their existence. Peter M. Arthur reflected upon this changed atmosphere, in speaking to the Industrial Commission in 1900. "We did not receive for many years the assistance and cooperation of the railroad companies that we were entitled to in that direction, but of late years we have." He accounted for this change by pointing to the sincere and unremitting efforts of the brotherhoods to provide the companies with "a more reliable, trustworthy class of men." Who could be in a better position to judge these qualities in the men than the brotherhoods and their officers? "We are mingling day and night, while the officers are at home or asleep."[114] Frank Sargent also noted that the firemen had observed significant changes in the respect for their brotherhood by railroad operators. "One of the best evidences," he told the commissioners, "is the fact we are supplying a great many of our members today to the railway companies who are in need of experienced men; they telegraph our office and ask us to supply the demand."[115]

When F. J. O'Rourke, a representative of the new Switchmen's Union of North America, was asked by the Industrial Commission how he would suggest that strikes be prevented, he asserted, simply through "closer association, better understanding, more harmonious dealings between employer and employee." The union scrutinized closely would-be members in its effort not to provide shelter for agitators. "Men in making application for membership must show as good a character as any railway company has ever asked of any man."[116]

That this role for the brotherhoods was warmly approved by many railroad corporations is apparent both from their testimony and from their actions. By 1902, 102 companies had signed agreements with the Brotherhood of Locomotive Engineers. Even those companies that the historian of the brotherhood termed diehards followed in short order: the Burlington (1904), the Philadelphia & Reading (1906), and the Lehigh Valley (1908).[117] Stuyvesant Fish, president of the Illinois Central, distinguished between "organized labor" and what he termed "labor trusts," such as the ARU, which were composed of professional agitators" and had a disorganizing effect on railroad labor relations. "I am an advocate of organized labor and organized everything," he asserted.[118] He placed the Brotherhood of Locomotive Engineers squarely in the class of "organized labor." Samuel Callaway, president of the New York Central, spoke of labor unions in evolutionary terms. Originally "intoxicated with their own strength and power," the unions had attempted to regulate everything. But he noted that, in recent years, "they have become more or less reasonable" in their demands, "largely organizations looking after their injured, sick and aged."[119]

Summary

In many ways the Erdman Act symbolized the emergence of a new framework for railroad labor relations, at least for the Big Four brotherhoods of operating employees. It promoted arbitration of their disputes, but it also held out the stick of federal injunctions to prevent strikes. In return it offered new protection to labor, it prohibited compulsory company-sponsored insurance, and it formally outlawed the blacklist and the yellow-dog contract.[120] The bargain provided the brotherhoods with a kind of stability not even they had enjoyed in the era before the Pullman boycott. By asserting the government's right to prevent, through injunction, any railroad strikes that threatened interstate commerce, this legislation relegated to the scrap pile (at least for the time being) the only major weapon by which broader organizations of railroad men had been able to assert the rights of the skilled and the unskilled alike. Without the threat of the mass strike as a means of suddenly and totally reordering the relations of labor and capital, the dream of a strikeless era in which the rights of even the humblest workingmen would be guaranteed receded.

The brotherhoods had won an unprecedented level of security for the segment of the labor force that they represented. That security would be further buttressed in the early twentieth century by "concerted movements" and hard bargaining. But ironically the less-skilled railroad men, whose participation had helped fuel the dynamic power of the Knights of Labor and the American Railway Union and who had thereby contributed to securing the position of "organized labor," were left out of the bargain. Shopmen, switchmen, and track laborers enjoyed little more security than they had ever had. The bargain did not extend to them. And to the extent that major railroad strikes occurred during the first quarter of the twentieth century, they issued from the ranks of these workers.

Railroad managers made substantial progress during the last two decades of the nineteenth century toward perfecting the machinery for managing their labor force. Many of the changes were undertaken reluctantly in response to a perceived crisis in their relations with labor. As each crisis passed, there was some retrenchment, some return to older methods. By the turn of the century, however, major industrywide changes were evident. The Big Four brotherhoods were recognized by most railroad systems. The "personal record" system was widely used as a means of screening employees; on many roads it was becoming a system of personnel records. Seniority had been widely accepted as a principle for governing promotions and layoffs for the running trades. Discipline by record rather than suspension or immediate discharge had been adopted by most roads. Company welfare schemes were hardly universal, but the number of companies that adopted some form of welfare plan continued to grow. A "corporate collectivist" view governed the relations among railroad managers, at least in the area of labor relations, to a greater extent than ever before. The lessons of 1894 were clear. The spirit of business "associationism" was spreading rapidly, and other industrial sectors were discovering the benefits of a more cooperative attitude toward "organized labor." The National Civic Federation, in promoting corporate collectivism and arbitration of labor disputes, drew directly on the lessons of the railroad experience. Finally, the federal government had been enlisted as the ultimate guarantor of labor peace. Newly fabricated arbitration machinery backed by the threat of massive military and legal intervention, made plausible by the events of 1894, kept the peace in railroad labor relations by the turn of the century.

Railroad managers had moved farther and faster in the direction of systematic labor relations than management in other industrial sectors. They had done so in response to an unprecedented crisis in their relations with railroad labor between 1877 and 1894.

7

Conclusion

By the end of the nineteenth century the United States was without question a deeply class-divided society. The generation that entered the industrial labor force after the Civil War saw large corporations rise to positions of dominance in key sectors such as railroads, iron and steel, meat packing, coal and metal mining, and petroleum. They experienced in their own work lives the effects of new technologies, the deterioration of standard wages and traditional systems of wage determination, the impact of increasing numbers of immigrants in the labor market, and the controlled chaos unleashed by the cyclical pattern of growth and consolidation that governed the American economy. Coming of age in the depression of the 1870s, this generation reached the twilight of its work life in the depression of the 1890s. Its experience encompassed the most intense period of class warfare in American history.

Again and again between 1877 and 1894 railroad workers ignited a combustible working class into struggles that led to new and broader forms of organization. Their prominence in the industrial conflicts of the late nineteenth century grew directly out of their own predicament. The peculiar nature of railroad expansion created conditions that fostered conflict. The structure of the industry and the mobility of railroad workers caused that conflict repeatedly to spread beyond the confines of a single road or a single community. While the experience of railroad men during the period between the great depressions of the nineteenth century was not entirely distinct from other members of the industrial working class, and while railroad labor conflict was not confined to this period, there were conditions peculiar to these years that produced conflict of greater intensity and gave to this "boomer" generation of railroad workers a leading role within the working class.

Railroad expansion after the Civil War mirrored the sequential development of the American economy. The colonization of less densely settled areas and the integration of successive regions into the national economy were products of railroad growth. At any given time, railroads operated under very diverse economic and social conditions. While the social distance between a well-established metropolitan area, with its multiple railroad connections, and the newly constructed frontier division town was great, notable differences also existed between towns in neighboring regions, which acquired their railroad connections little more than a decade apart.

Frontiers of Labor Scarcity

The significance of regional diversity is particularly noteworthy in the sequential development of labor relations. Rapid expansion of the railroad network generated demand for labor on the perimeter of settlement. Inhospitable conditions and a scarcity of labor made it imperative for the roads to offer the high wages and extra benefits that would attract men from some distance. Limited competition from other railroads made it feasible to charge higher rates and pay premium wages. Rapid promotion and the recognition of the brotherhoods through contracts that guaranteed seniority and the integrity of craft distinctions made life on the frontier more attractive than it would otherwise have been.

Overexpansion and intensifying railroad competition made these frontier conditions relatively fleeting. The railroads, faced with inadequate revenues on the one hand and with rising labor costs on the other, sought to overcome the problem of a labor shortage and at the same time reduce operating costs. They devised numerous strategies for increasing the labor supply. They intensified recruitment, which under depression conditions was more likely to be successful at lower cost. They accelerated promotion from within to relieve the scarcity of workers at the skilled levels. They classified workers in a way that permitted the delayed payment of top wages. They maintained a large extra board of workers during slack times, and they revised work rules so that employers could assign workers to tasks with less regard for craft distinctions. Where possible, the railroads also reduced wage rates or insisted on modes of wage determination that individualized pay.

Each of these measures, designed to increase the labor supply and to reduce operating costs, met with organized resistance from railroad workers. A period of conflict and adjustment occurred in each region as management sought to create a more favorable labor supply and to alter the terms of employment in ways that would reflect the new labor market conditions. Resistance to wage reductions and revision of established work rules led to the abrogation of contracts and direct attacks by management on railroad labor organizations. Many of the major strikes of the period centered around the defense of organization itself. They were the culmination of a sequence of struggles over issues that related to the control of the labor supply.

The pattern of railroad strikes during this period reflects this sequential development of labor relations and the intensification of conflict. The westward drift of strike activity is particularly noteworthy after 1884. The Midwest and, somewhat later, the Great Plains and the northern Rocky Mountain regions led the country in the incidence of railroad strikes and the percentage of workers on strike. The role of workers lower in the job hierarchy is particularly evident in these strike-prone regions. Their perception of declining opportunities for promotion as the labor supply grew and their willingness to organize across craft boundaries contributed to the rising incidence of railroad strikes. The strike data confirm a qualitative shift in the central issues of railroad strikes. Wage strikes were overtaken in the late 1880s and early 1890s by strikes over noneconomic issues, such as union recognition, work rules, supervision, and the discharge of workers. The incidence of sympathy strikes by workers in different trades rose dramatically in two waves—between 1885 and 1888 in the Midwest and the Great Plains, and in 1893–94 throughout the territory west of Chicago.

Railroad labor conflict intensified in spite of a decline in the number of successful strikes. Even as the success rate fell and workers faced the prospect of discharges, they struck more frequently and their strikes more often enjoyed official union sanction. By 1894 this pattern of conflict, particularly in the West, was building toward a climax. For many workers the issues were no longer incremental. The deepest depression of the nineteenth century contributed to the already widespread notion that a titanic struggle between labor and capital was at hand.

Railroad labor conflict may have been predominantly the product of a set of grievances related to changes in the labor market, but when railroad workers struck, it was within the specific social setting of the towns where they lived and worked. Differences in class structure and community economic growth were essential determinants of the extent of community support for strikers and the cross-class solidarity generated during railroad strikes.

Market Cities and Railroad Towns

Towns performed two very different functions within the railroad network. As commercial entrepôts, they marketed raw materials and finished products. As division headquarters, they directly serviced railroad operations and enjoyed the direct benefits of railroad expenditures. Towns that functioned as division headquarters were not all created from the same mold. Differences in location and timing of their development in relation to railroad expansion created enormous differences in the commercial advantages they enjoyed. Market cities that antedated railroad development frequently dominated the commercial opportunities found by upstart railroad towns, whose development coincided with railroad expansion.

Burlington and Creston, Iowa, are representative of these community types. Burlington, an important market city, enjoyed the initial advantages of a river town and was an active partner in promoting railroad expansion. By contrast, Creston was a railroad town—a creature of railroad promotion, owing its very existence to the locational decisions and speculative enterprise of the Chicago, Burlington & Quincy's officers. Its economy was created and limited by the patronage of the railroad. Its very dependence bred a fierce independence.

In Burlington a visible and self-organized elite identified closely with the development of the railroad from the outset. Its dominant wholesale and manufacturing interests were able to extend their markets because of the rate advantages they received and because of the railroad's own expansion. When industrial conflict erupted, they were found on the side of the railroad. Striking railroad workers did not exercise the same kind of influence over community affairs in Burlington that they did in smaller communities. Their numbers were diluted in a larger and more diverse working population. Their sense of social solidarity was more fragile and fragmented.

Creston's elite, to the extent that one can be identified, had more parochial interests. Its leading figures were retail merchants, not wholesalers or manufactures, and they rankled under the limits imposed by their dependence on a single railroad line. Their anti-monopoly sentiments provided the basis for an alliance with the community's railroad workers in their mutual difficulties with the outside railroad corporation. Railroad workers occupied an important position in the community through their purchasing power and the strength of their numbers and organization. When they struck in Creston, they found the community much more solidly aligned with them in opposition to the railroad than did the railroad workers of Burlington.

Evidence from the two Iowa communities and other railroad towns suggests that far from being a rigid, ahistorical type, the railroad division town developed under diverse conditions and underwent important changes in its progress from frontier conditions to settled community. The relationship among classes in such communities was not static; the community solidarity that Herbert Gutman has suggested was characteristic of smaller industrial communities in the late nineteenth century could be ephemeral.[1] The evidence presented in this work suggests a model that accounts for changing class relations within railroad towns in different regions.

Labor Force Life Cycles

The historical differences between such communities influenced the patterns of railroad labor conflict in the late nineteenth century in another way. When railroad service began in each community, a cohort of workers was assembled whose age and persistence directly affected the opportunities for promotion of younger, less-skilled workers who arrived later. In the 1880s as a labor surplus developed on western railroads, the issue of promotion within the running trades surfaced with a vengeance. Railroad workers measured the seriousness of the crisis by the immediate circumstances in which they found themselves. In older market cities like Burlington in the 1880s, significant numbers of older, skilled railroad workers retired or moved into less-arduous occupations, creating some local opportunities for younger, less-skilled men to be promoted. In newer railroad towns like Creston, a more youthful labor force meant congestion in the line of promotion and less opportunity for fulfilling expectations of normal occupational mobility. It is not surprising that the extent of strike participation and the intensity of workers' concern over issues related to promotion and the supply of labor varied significantly from one type of community to the next.

In railroad towns, particularly those in the West, the social solidarity of railroad workers was high, as was their participation in and influence over community affairs. A densely woven fabric of social and fraternal associations complemented the structure of economic organizations through which they made their influence felt. Contrary to the assumptions made in much of the recent literature on urban social and geographic mobility,[2] rapid promotion and a relatively high turnover of population did not disrupt this social fabric in the early stages of a community's development. The volatility of the population that was fostered by a scarcity of labor contributed to the sense of well-being, prestige, and class pride of railroad workers.

As conditions changed, as the supply of labor grew, and as railroad workers began to feel pressure on their wages and on the rules that had guaranteed the privileges of scarcity, they resisted. A period of conflict and disruption occurred in one region after another. Resistence was frequently most determined in smaller railroad towns. Strikes in such communities that began over wages and work rules frequently became contests over the very existence of workers' economic organizations and, in turn, over the question of whether the social fabric of their worker communities was to survive or whether they were to become, a "heterogeneous mass."[3]

Railroad workers devised a variety of organizations to meet their changing needs. In periods of expansion and labor scarcity they turned to brotherhoods and other craft organizations that promised to effectively regulate entrance to their trades, maintain standard wages and work rules, and win the respect of employers as legitimate representatives. During periods of stagnation and in successive regions as labor scarcity was replaced by a labor surplus, railroad men regularly turned to broader forms of organization to protect their wages and work rules and to defend their right to organization and representation. Four discernable episodes of industrial unionism occurred during this period. Each drew directly on the lessons of previous organization and was fueled by strikes undertaken to defend and later expand the control of workers over the conditions under which they labored.

The first episode occurred in the 1870s when men in the running trades, primarily in eastern railroad centers, joined the Brakemen's Brotherhood or the Trainmen's Union, which functioned before and during the Great Strikes of 1877 as an umbrella organization for disaffected railroad workers regardless of trade. During the second episode in the mid-1880s, large numbers of railroad workers in smaller midwestern and western railroad centers joined the Knights of Labor. District assemblies were strongest among shopmen but commonly encompassed large numbers of workers in other trades. Many assemblies, formed shortly before or during bitter strikes, did not survive long, but on a few systems, notably the Union Pacific, the Knights maintained a durable and powerful industrial union presence. Deteriorating conditions for many skilled as well as unskilled railroad workers after 1888 and the disasterous defeat of enginemen on the Burlington ushered in the third episode. These events persuaded leadership elements in the major brotherhoods to move toward closer affiliation of their national unions. Hobbled by jurisdictional disputes and by continuing employer intransigence, national federation efforts collapsed in 1891. Persistent agitation within the Knights of Labor for the federation of all railroad workers at the local level, together with the failure of national federation, led directly to the fourth episode, the formation of the most ambitious industrial union of the era, the American Railway Union.

The railroad labor conflicts of the late nineteenth century precipitated the search by railroad managers for a new order to govern the relations between railroad management and labor. The shape of the new order was decisively influenced by the crisis that had preceded it. Both brotherhood leaders and corporate managers, in testimony before the U.S. Industrial Commission in 1900, looked back to the period of crisis and shuddered with relief that the disruption of railroad labor relations and a massive threat to the social order was behind them. In place was a new framework for labor-management cooperation within which the federal government loomed as an important partner and guarantor. The Erdman Act of 1898 represented a preliminary codification of that framework, which provided certain rights for labor and capital. The guarantees to labor were unprecedented. They reopened doors for the brotherhoods that allowed them to rebuild and surpass previous levels of membership. Even such old enemies as the Chicago, Burlington & Quincy Railroad were eventually persuaded to resume relations with the brotherhoods of engineers and firemen. The brotherhoods reaffirmed their opposition to entangling alliances of the sort devised by railroad workers between 1884 and 1894. This did not mean that the brotherhoods would not bargain hard for their own interests in the years to come, or even, on occasion, strike or threaten to strike. It did mean that they would again steer a separate course from other railroad workers—in the shops, on the roads, and in the offices.

The railroad labor crisis of the late nineteenth century set apart the experience of a generation of railroad workers, a generation of boomers. Boomer railroad men had been characteristic of the early phases of railroad building. They moved frequently in an effort to better themselves. Their life-style was a function of their scarcity and the extraordinary demand for their services in new, undeveloped territory. By the 1890s, large numbers of railroad men in territories that were now more settled were again on the boom. They were veterans of seasons of industrial struggle. Their mobility had a more desperate quality. Their skills were not as scarce. Many had changed their names to avoid the mark of the blacklist or of a personal record. Some found their way back into railroad employment under the new order but others were barred forever.

Legacies

This generation of boomers left three legacies for future railroad workers and for the labor movement generally. The first was a gift. The railroad struggles of the late nineteenth century created for workers in the running trades an unprecedented level of security and recognition. Most American workers had to wait until the 1930s to enjoy the guarantees that were granted to the railroad brotherhoods and their members at the very end of the nineteenth century and improved on by the Adamson Act and the Railway Labor Act of 1926. For railroad men, those benefits grew directly out of the struggles of 1884–94.

The second legacy was a lesson. The lesson was that workers' struggles take place in a political context, and that control of the instruments of state power is ultimately decisive. Eugene Debs told how he and many railroad workers who joined the American Railway Union had learned that lesson during the Pullman boycott: "Next followed the final shock—the Pullman strike—and the American Railway Union again won, clear and complete. The combined corporations were paralyzed and helpless. At this juncture there was delivered, from wholly unexpected quarters, a swift succession of blows that blinded me for an instant and then opened wide my eyes—and with the gleam of every bayonet and the flash of every rifle the class struggle was revealed."[4] The American Railway Union and the Knights of Labor before it had already espoused public ownership of the railroads as an objective. What the Pullman boycott revealed to many railroad workers and to others was that the realization of that objective required the conquest of political power. Many members of the ARU followed Eugene Debs into the Socialist Party as a logical consequence of that lesson.

Finally, this generation of boomers left a promise. It was a promise that had motivated their actions in the waning years of the century—that workers, if thoroughly and broadly enough organized, could usher in an era of industrial peace in which their rights would be protected and their lives enriched by sharing more fully in the fruits of their labor. For many, the luminescent phrase, "the cooperative commonwealth," defined that promise. It was a promise for a future generation to keep.

Appendix A

Supplementary Railroad Strike Statistics

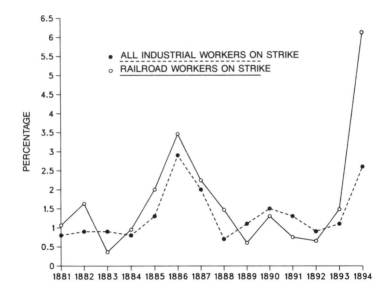

Figure A1. Percentage of railroad workers and all industrial workers on strike, 1881–94

Source: U. S. Labor Commissioner, *Third Annual Report* and *Tenth Annual Report* (Washington, D.C.: 1887, 1895).

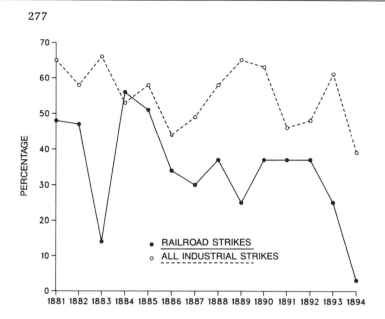

Figure A2.   Success rates—strikes on railroads and in all industries
Source: U.S. Labor Commissioner, *Third Annual Report* and *Tenth Annual Report*
(Washington, D.C.: 1887, 1895).

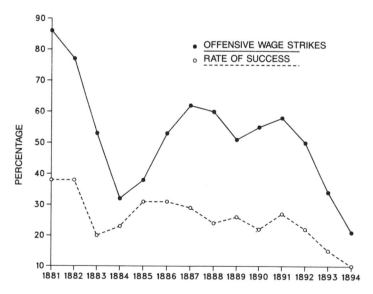

Figure A3.   Incidence and rate of success, offensive railroad wage strikes,
1881–94 (three-year moving average)
Source: U.S. Labor Commissioner, *Third Annual Report* and *Tenth Annual Report*
(Washington, D.C.: 1887, 1895).

278

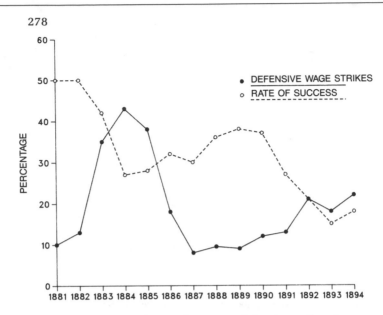

Figure A4.   Incidence and rate of success, defensive railroad wage strikes, 1881–94 (three-year moving average)

Source: U.S. Commissioner, *Third Annual Report* and *Tenth Annual Report* (Washington, D.C.: 1887, 1895).

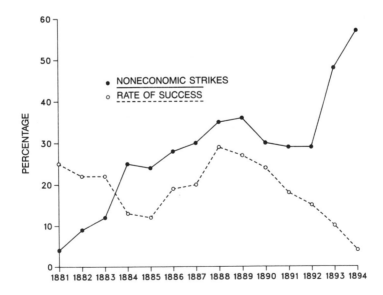

Figure A5.   Incidence and rate of success, noneconomic railroad strikes, 1881–94 (three-year moving average)

Source: U.S. Labor Commissioner, *Third Annual Report* and *Tenth Annual Report* (Washington, D.C.: 1887, 1895).

Appendix B

Regions Adopted by the Interstate Commerce Commission for the Compilation of Railway Statistics

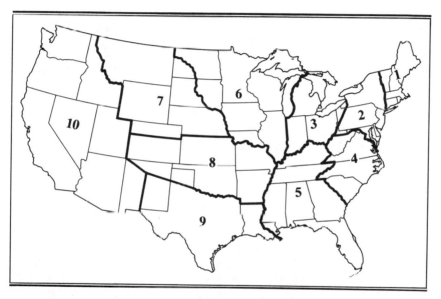

Figure B1. Regions adopted by the Interstate Commerce Commission for the compilation of railway statistics

Appendix C

Railroad Wage Data for the Nineteenth Century

Wage data for railroad workers are uneven and not very comprehensive for the late nineteenth century. Three primary sources have been used to compare sectional differences in the wage rates of railroad workers. For the 1880s, data provided by a publication of the U.S. Department of Labor, Bureau of Labor Statistics, has been consulted (*History of Wages in the United States from Colonial Times to 1928*, Bulletin No. 604 [Washington, D.C.: 1934]). This work samples the reports of state bureaus of labor statistics over a period that includes the two decades under consideration here. Average daily rates of pay for selected occupations are provided for each year. Between four and twenty-two states are sampled, depending on the year. The sectional coverage is, therefore, highly uneven. For the year 1889, the *Annual Report* of the U.S. Commissioner of Labor is largely devoted to a report on "Railway Labor," and data were gathered from sixty railroad companies that represented appproximately one-third of the railroad labor force. Again, the geographical coverage of the data is uneven, and a further problem is that the data are divided into seven regions that do not correspond to the more standard ten regions adopted by the Interstate Commerce Commission (see appendix B). The most comprehensive data are provided in the *Annual Reports* of the Interstate Commerce Commission beginning in 1892. The wage data were compiled from reports to the commission by all interstate roads. They are organized by region and give average daily compensation for each of eighteen occupational groups. The data for the period 1892–1900 are conveniently summarized in the *Report* of the U.S. Industrial Commission, volume 17 (Washington: 1901) in Exhibit 1, pp. 910–13.

Several general qualifications must be made in using wage rate data. First, as noted in chapter 2, wage *rates* were only one factor in determining railroad workers' earnings. The number of days worked or miles run, overtime, "arbitraries," and other special payments created considerable variation in actual earnings. Second, these wage rates are obviously not corrected for differences in the cost of living; they are not "real wages." A study of regional differences in real wages for the period 1851–80 indicates that real wages in the Midwest during that period were

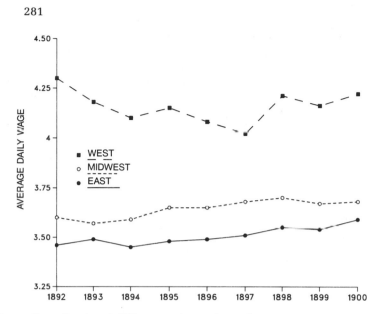

Figure C1.   Sectional differences in engineers' wages, 1892–1900

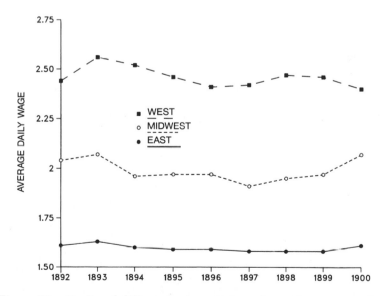

Figure C2.   Sectional differences in switchmen's wages, 1892–1900

Source: U.S. Industrial Commission, "Wages of Railway Employees, 1892–1900," Report on Labor Organizations, Labor Disputes and Arbitration, and on Railway Labor, vol. 17 (Washington, D.C.: 1901), 910–13.

higher than real wages in the East, but no attempt has been made to correct the wage data used in this study for regional differences in prices. (See Philip R. Coelho and James F. Shepherd, "Regional Differences in Real Wages: The United States, 1851–1880," *Explorations in Economic History*, vol. 13 [1976], 203–30.) Third, toward the very end of the nineteenth century, railroad managers showed less inclination to alter basic wage rates. This reflected both the changed labor market condition, but also a fear of precipitating further industrial conflict. Both factors contributed to a stabilization of wage rates in the 1890s.

Notes

Preface

1. See Robert V. Bruce, *1877, Year of Violence* (Indianapolis: 1959); Philip S. Foner, *The Great Labor Uprising of 1877* (New York: 1977); Ruth Allen, *The Great Southwest Strike* (Austin, Tex.: 1943); Donald McMurry, *The Great Burlington Strike of 1888: A Case History of Industrial Relations* (Cambridge, Mass.: 1956); Almont Lindsey, *The Pullman Strike, the Story of a Unique Experiment and of a Great Labor Upheaval* (Chicago: 1942).

2. Excellent studies of working-class communities include: Alan Dawley, *Class and Community, The Industrial Revolution in Lynn* (Cambridge, Mass.: 1976); John Cumbler, *Working Class Community in Industrial America: Work, Leisure, and Struggle in Two Industrial Cities, 1880–1930* (Westport, Conn.: 1979); Daniel J. Walkowitz, *Worker City, Company Town, Iron and Cotton-Worker Protest in Troy and Cohoes, New York, 1855–1884* (Urbana, Ill.: 1978); John W. Bennett, "Iron Workers in Woods Run and Johnston: the Union Era, 1865–1895" (Ph.D. dissertation, University of Pittsburg, 1977).

3. The work of Herbert Gutman on industrial conflict in nineteenth-century communities remains the essential starting point for any discussion. See Herbert Gutman, "Workers Search for Power: Labor in the Gilded Age," in *The Gilded Age: A Reappraisal*, ed. H. Wayne Morgan (Syracuse, N.Y.: 1963), and his collected essays, *Work, Culture, and Society in Industrializing America* (New York: 1976).

Introduction

1. On the contradictions within the "free labor" ideology, see David Montgomery, *Beyond Equality: Labor and the Radical Republicans, 1862–1872* (New York: 1967), 30–32; Eric Foner, *Free Soil, Free Labor, Free Men: The Ideology of the Republican Party Before the Civil War* (New York: 1970), 11–39.

2. See Paul G. Faler, *Mechanics and Manufacturers in the Early Industrial Revolution: Lynn, Massachusetts, 1780–1860* (Albany, N.Y.: 1981); Thomas Dublin, *Women at Work: The Transformation of Work and Community in Lowell, Massachusetts, 1826–1860* (New York: 1979); the series of articles, "Labor in New York," *Harbinger*, September 6, 1845–January 17, 1846; Sean Wilentz, *Chants Democratic: New York City*

and the Rise of the American Working Class, 1788–1850 (New York: 1984):
Bruce Laurie, Working People of Philadelphia (Philadelphia, Pa.: 1980). In
addition to Wilentz's and Laurie's excellent studies, the organization of
city centrals is chronicled in several older works: Edward Pessen, Most
Uncommon Jacksonians (Albany, N.Y.: 1967); Walter Hugins, Jacksonian
Democracy and the Working Class: A Study of the New York
Workingmen's Movement (Stanford, Calif.: 1960). The most persuasive
case for the appearance of a new class at the end of the Civil War is that of-
fered by David Montgomery, Beyond Equality, 25–44. On the impact of industrialization in the "West," see Steven J. Ross, Workers on the Edge:
Work, Leisure and Politics in Industrializing Cincinnati, 1788–1890, (New
York: 1985). David Brundage, "The Making of Working Class Radicalism
in the Mountain West: Denver, Colorado, 1880–1903" (Ph.D. dissertation,
University of California, Los Angeles, 1982), Hartmut Keil and John Jentz,
German Workers in Industrial Chicago 1850–1910: A Comparative Per-
spective (Dekalb, Ill.: 1983), and Alexander Saxton, The Indispensable
Enemy: Labor and the Anti-Chinese Movement in California (Berkeley,
Calif.: 1971).

    3. The literature on the social and economic consequences of railroad
expansion is substantial. See Alfred D. Chandler, Jr., The Railroads: The
Nation's First Big Business (New York: 1965), and his more recent book,
The Visible Hand: The Managerial Revolution in American Business
(Cambridge, Mass.: 1977). On the linkages between railroad growth and
other economic activity, see Edward Kirkland, Industry Comes of Age:
Business, Labor, and Public Policy, 1860–1897 (New York: 1961); Lance E.
Davis, Richard A. Easterlin, Richard N. Parker, et al., American Economic
Growth: An Economist's History of the United States (New York: 1972),
520–31; Peter Temin, Iron and Steel in Nineteenth-Century America (Cambridge, Mass.: 1964), 222–23. The best analyses of railroad land policies
remain the case studies of Paul Wallace Gates, The Illinois Central Railroad and Its Colonization Work (Cambridge, Mass.: 1934), and Richard C.
Overton, Burlington West: A Colonization History of the Burlington (Cambridge, Mass.: 1941). Lloyd J. Mercer, Railroads and Land Grant Policy: A
Study in Government Intervention (New York: 1982), finds the land grants
to five of the seven major railroad systems to have been economically ra-
tional.

    4. For the effects of the Civil War on economic growth, see a sum-
mary of the historiographical debate in Harry N. Scheiber, "Economic
Change in the Civil War Era: An Analysis of Recent Studies," Civil War
History 11 (December 1965): 296–411. See also the essays, especially that
of George Rogers Taylor, "The National Economy before and after the Civil
War," in David T. Gilchrist and W. David Lewis, eds,. Economic Change in
the Civil War Era (Greenville, Del.: 1965). On the impact of the Civil War
on railroad growth, see Thomas Weber, The Northern Railroads in the
Civil War, 1861–1865 (New York: 1952), 3–24.

    5. The development of American manufacturing by the end of the

Civil War was very uneven. Certain zones of industrial activity with good access to water transportation developed rapidly; others, which were poorly connected to national transportation systems, languished. See Montgomery, *Beyond Equality*, 3–25; Richard Wade, *The Urban Frontier* (Chicago: 1959); Julius Rubin, "Urban Growth and Regional Development," in *The Rise of Seaport Cities, 1790–1825*, ed. David T. Gilchrist (Charlottesville, Va.: 1967); David M. Gordon, Richard Edwards, and Michael Reich, *Segmented Work, Divided Workers: The Historical Transformation of Labor in the United States* (Cambridge, Mass.: 1982), 79–91.

6. Lance E. Davis, Jonathan R. T. Hughes, and Duncan McDougall, *American Economic History: The Development of a National Economy* (Homewood, Ill.: 1969), 283.

7. The best account of these waves of railroad expansion is in Julius Grodinsky, *Transcontinental Railway Strategy, 1869–1893: A Study of Businessmen* (Philadelphia: 1962), 15–35, 122–75, 270–307; Alfred D. Chandler, Jr., *The Visible Hand*, 159–71.

8. Grodinsky, *Transcontinental Railway Strategy*, 307; Chandler, *The Visible Hand*, 171–85 (This account of the consolidation movement in the 1890s is most helpful).

9. Paul W. Gates, "The Railroad Land Grant Legend," *Journal of Economic History* 19 (Spring 1954), 143–46; for a review of the debate over the economic significance of railroad land grants, see Vernon Carstensen, ed., *The Public Lands: Studies in the History of the Public Domain* (Madison, Wis.: 1968), 121–80.

10. The dimensions of nineteenth-century immigration are summarized in Maldwyn Jones, *American Immigration* (Chicago: 1960), and Philip Taylor, *The Distant Magnet: European Immigration to the U.S.A.* (New York: 1971), 63, 103.

11. Frederick Jackson Turner, "The Significance of the Frontier in American History" (1893); reprint, F. J. Turner, *The Frontier in American History* (New York: 1920), 12.

12. Josiah Strong, *Our Country: Its Possible Future and Its Present Crisis* (New York: 1885), 157–58.

13. Hope T. Eldridge and Dorothy S. Thomas, "Demographic Analyses and Interrelations," in *Population Redistribution and Economic Growth in the United States, 1870–1950*, vol. 3, ed. Simon Kuznets et al. (Philadelphia: 1960), 8.

14. Lance E. Davis, Richard Easterlin, William N. Parker et al., *American Economic Growth*, 509.

15. This concept is borrowed from the analysis of nineteenth-century labor processes in Gordon, Edwards, and Reich, *Segmented Work, Divided Workers*, 22–32.

16. The "leading sector" thesis is analyzed in Harold G. Vatter, *The Drive to Industrial Maturity: The U.S. Economy, 1860–1914* (Westport, Conn.: 1975), 157–62.

17. Albert Fishlow, "Productivity and Technological Change in the Railroad Sector, 1840–1910," in *Output, Employment, and Productivity in the United States after 1800*, Conference on Research in Income and Wealth, Studies in Income and Wealth, vol. 30 (New York: 1966), 628–29; Davis et al., *American Economic Growth*, 508; Vatter, *The Drive to Industrial Maturity*, 158–59.

18. Fishlow, "Productivity and Technological Change," 629–33; Davis et al., *American Economic Growth*, 502–3; Chandler, *The Visible Hand*, 130.

19. Chandler, *The Visible Hand*, 90.

20. Davis et al., *American Economic Growth*, 505–6.

21. *Ibid.*, 502, 505–8.

22. Vatter, *The Drive to Industrial Maturity*, 162; Davis et al., *American Economic Growth*, 510; for the railroads' rationale for rate differences, see Arthur T. Hadley, "Competition and Combination" and "Railroad Charges and Discriminations," in Chandler, *The Railroads*, 163–72. On state efforts to regulate railroad rates, see George H. Miller, *Railroads and the Granger Laws* (Madison, Wis.: 1971).

23. Chandler, *The Visible Hand*, 124–33, 148–71; a helpful case study is Julius Grodinsky, *The Iowa Pool: A Study in Railroad Competition* (Chicago: 1950).

24. Chandler, *The Visible Hand*, 159.

25. Davis et al., *American Economic Growth*, 521–23; Temin, *Iron and Steel in Nineteenth-Century America*, 222–23.

26. Davis et al., *American Economic Growth*, 523–26.

27. Vatter, *The Drive to Industrial Maturity*, 157–58.

28. For a vivid description of this process in the case of the Erie Railroad, see Stuart Daggett, *Railroad Reorganization* (Cambridge, Mass.: 1908), 35–39.

29. Henry Adams, *The Education of Henry Adams: An Autobiography* (Boston: 1918), 240.

30. Charles Francis Adams, Jr., *Chapters of Erie and Other Essays* (New York: 1886), 98.

31. George Rogers Taylor and Irene Neu, *The American Railroad Network, 1861–1890* (Cambridge, Mass.: 1956), 3–7.

32. See the discussion of railroad land colonization in chapter 4.

33. Gates, *The Illinois Central Railroad*, 303–7; Overton, *Burlington West*, 245–47, 268.

34. William Larrabee, *The Railroad Question: A Historical and Practical Treatise on Railroads, and Remedies for Their Abuses* (Chicago: 1898), 205–7.

35. *Ibid.*, 207–30, discusses the railroad pass system in great detail.

36. The classic analysis of railroad intervention in national politics is C. Vann Woodward, *Reunion and Reaction: The Compromise of 1877 and the End of Reconstruction* (New York: 1951). Subsequent scholarship on the Compromise of 1877 has called into question the extent to which the

terms of the bargain were met, but the evidence that such a bargain was struck remains largely unchallenged. See Allan Peskin, "Was There a Compromise of 1877?" and C. Vann Woodward, "Yes, There Was a Compromise of 1877," *Journal of American History* 60 (1973): 63–73, 215–23. Also see Michael Les Benedict, "Southern Democrats in the Crisis of 1876–77: A Reconsideration of *Reunion and Reaction*," *Journal of Social History* (1980): 489–524.

37. Albro Marin, "Railroads and Equity Receivership: An Essay in Institutional Change," *Journal of Economic History* 34 (September 1974): 686.

38. Gerald G. Eggert, *Railroad Labor Disputes: The Beginnings of Federal Strike Policy* (Ann Arbor: 1967), 68–69, 125.

39. Thomas B. Scott, letter in *North American Review* 125 (September 1877), quoted in Eggert, *Railroad Labor Disputes*, 55; Jerry M. Cooper, "The Army as Strikebreaker—the Railroad Strikes of 1877 and 1894," *Labor History* 18, no. 2 (Summer 1977): 179–96; Charles F. Ames, Jr., "Repression or Concession: Press and Party Leader Response to the Threat of Social Upheaval, 1871–1903" (Ph.D. dissertation, Boston University, 1973), 224. A more complete discussion of the use of federal troops in suppressing strikes is available in Jerry M. Cooper, *The Army and Civil Disorder: Federal Military Intervention in Labor Disputes, 1877–1900* (Westport, Conn.: 1980).

40. Gerald G. Eggert, *Richard Olney, Evolution of a Statesman* (University Park, Pa.: 1974), 52.

1. The Pattern of Railroad Strikes

1. Terence V. Powderly, *The Path I Trod* (New York: 1940), 170–71.

2. U.S. Strike Commission, *Report on the Chicago Strike of June-July, 1894*, 53rd Cong., 3rd Sess., Sen. Exec. Doc. No. 7 (Washington, D.C.: 1895), 163.

3. "Joint Letter (G. R. Blanchard and others) to Hon. H. J. Jewett in answer to allegations made in complaint of Charles Potter and others in the Supreme Court of New York," 1878, *Miscellaneous Papers of the Erie Railroad Company*, New York Public Library; Herbert Gutman, "Trouble on the Railroads in 1873–1874, Prelude to the 1877 Crisis?" *Labor History* 2, no. 2 (Spring 1961): 215–35. Gutman was the first historian to draw our attention to the precedents for the 1877 strikes in the railroad strikes of 1873–74.

4. Details of these strikes may be found in the *Hornellsville Tribune* for the respective dates. For a complete chronology of Hornellsville strikes, see Shelton Stromquist, "Class and Community in a Nineteenth Century Railroad Town, Hornellsville, New York, 1860–1880" (Master's essay, University of Pittsburgh, 1973), 105.

5. *Hornellsville Tribune*, February 27, 1874.

6. *Ibid.*, December 23, 1870.

288

7. See *Ibid.* for an early example of the soaped rails strategy.

8. *Ibid.*, March 6, 1874.

9. *Buffalo Commercial Advertiser,* July 23, 1877.

10. *New York Herald,* July 22, 1877.

11. *Buffalo Commercial Advertiser* and *New York Tribune,* July 26, 1877.

12. *New York World,* July 25, 1877.

13. *New York Tribune,* July 26, 1877.

14. *New York World,* July 28, 1877.

15. J. A. Dacus, *Annals of the Great Strikes in the U.S.* (New York: 1877), 16.

16. Ruth Allen, *The Great Southwest Strike* (Austin, Tex.: 1943); Robert V. Bruce, *1877: Year of Violence* (Indianapolis: 1959); Philip S. Foner, *The Great Labor Uprising of 1877* (New York: 1977); Almont Lindsey, *The Pullman Strike: The Story of a Unique Experiment and of a Great Labor Upheaval* (Chicago: 1942); Donald L. McMurry, *The Great Burlington Strike of 1888: A Case History of Industrial Relations* (Cambridge, Mass.: 1956).

17. For international comparisons, see strike studies by Richard Hyman, *Strikes* (London: 1972); James E. Cronin, *Industrial Conflict in Modern Britain* (London, 1979); Charles Tilly and Edward Shorter, *Strikes in France, 1830–1968* (New York: 1974); Clark Kerr and Abraham J. Siegel, "The Interindustry Propensity of Strike—An International Comparison," in *Labor and Management in Industrial Society,* ed. Clark Kerr (Garden City: 1964). For a discussion of the social significance of strikes, see Ernest T. Hiller, *The Strike: A Study in Collective Action* (Chicago: 1928).

18. The most recent analyses of aggregate strike data for the United States in the nineteenth century are: P. K. Edwards, *Strikes in the United States, 1881–1974* (New York: 1981); Sari Bennett and Carville Earle, "The Geography of Strikes in the United States, 1881–1894," *Journal of Interdisciplinary History* 13 (1982): 63–84; David Montgomery, "Strikes in Nineteenth-Century America," *Social Science History* 4, no. 1 (February 1980): 81–104. Edwards is primarily interested in long-term trends and the effects of institutionalized collective bargaining on strike activity. Bennett and Earle examine locality differences (metropolitan area versus smaller industrial towns) on strike activity. Montgomery's arguments will be taken up in some detail in this chapter. In none of these studies are the data analyzed *primarily* in terms of the industrial sector. For an analysis of strikes in the coal industry, see Jon Amsden and Stephen Brier, "Coal Miners on Strike: The Transformation of Strike Demands and the Formation of a National Union," *Journal of Interdisciplinary History* 7, no. 4 (Spring 1977): 583–616.

19. Excellent strike data for the years 1881–94 may be found in U.S. Commissioner of Labor, *Third Annual Report* (Washington, D.C.: 1887) and *Tenth Annual Report* (Washington, D.C.: 1894). During these years the staff of the U.S. Labor Commissioner's office systematically assembled a

year by year listing of strikes. Agents were assigned to districts for "active canvassing." Employers, labor organizations, local newspapers, and trade associations were consulted and interviewed. Information on particular strikes was checked against other sources. Following this method, the commissioner claimed to have secured information relating to "nearly every strike, if not every strike, which has occurred in the United States during the period covered." The two summary reports in 1887 and 1894 follow similar formats in reporting data on strikes, and, most importantly, the strike data are enumerated by individual strike. Subsequent published strike data for the early twentieth century offer only statistical summaries, which make analysis by specific occupational group and locality virtually impossible.

20. *New York Sun*, June 22, 25, 1882. For an insightful account of the freighthandlers' strike and other labor boycotts in New York City, see Michael Gordon, "The Labor Boycott in New York City, 1880–1886," *Labor History* 16 (1975): 184–229.

21. *New York Sun*, June 25, 1882.

22. *Ibid.*, July 7, 1882.

23. See enumeration in U.S. Commissioner of Labor, *Third Annual Report* (Washington, D.C.: 1887), 342–437.

24. A "matrix of sophistication" to measure the degree to which strikes were "modern, forward-looking," is developed in Peter Stearns, "Measuring the Evolution of Strike Movements," *International Review of Social History* 19 (1974): 1–27. More recent studies by Montgomery and Amsden and Brier specifically eschew such a modernization framework. A useful older work is Grover G. Huebner, "The Statistical Aspect of the Strike," *Twelfth Biennial Report of the Bureau of Labor and Industrial Statistics of Wisconsin* (Madison: 1906), 75–174.

25. *Chicago Times*, April 17, 1886.

26. *Ibid.*, April 18, 1886.

27. See various accounts of the Southwest strikes in Selig Perlman, "Upheaval and Reorganization," in John R. Commons, *History of Labour in the United States*, vol. 2 (New York: 1918); Joseph Buchanan, *The Story of a Labor Agitator* (New York: 1903); Ruth Allen, *The Great Southwest Strike* (Austin, Tex.: 1943); Norman Ware, *The Labor Movement in the United States, 1860–1895* (New York: 1929).

28. See Amsden and Brier, "Coal Miners on Strike," 605–6; for an analysis that emphasizes the influence of the business cycle, see Alvin Hansen, "Cycles of Strikes," *American Economic Review* 11 (1921): 618.

29. U.S. Industrial Commission, *Report of the Industrial Commission on Transportation*, vol. 4 (Washington, D.C.: 1900), 127 (Arthur testimony).

30. David Montgomery, "Workers' Control of Machine Production in the Nineteenth Century," *Labor History* 17 (Fall 1976): 491, 503.

31. *Chicago Times*, June 25, 1890.

32. *Irish World and Industrial Liberator*, March 22, 1890.

33. *Ibid.*, April 22, 1890.

34. *Ibid.*, June 21, 1890.

35. Philip Foner, *History of the Labor Movement in the United States*, vol. 2 (New York: 1955), 251.

36. Fred S. Hall, *Sympathetic Strikes and Sympathetic Lockouts* (New York: 1898), 79.

37. Expressions of such support for government ownership of the railroads are commonplace in publications of the Knights of Labor, The Farmers' Alliance, and the Populist Party. See *Union Pacific Employees Magazine* (August 1892): 200; U.S. Strike Commission, *Report on the Chicago Strike*, 163; *ibid.*, testimony of R. M. Goodwin, ARU director, 101–2.

38. David Montgomery has argued that a similar "audacity" was reflected in the control struggles of craftsmen in the early 1890s. These struggles were characterized by declining rates of success in spite of record levels of union support. The defeats brought greater caution, particularly about entering into sympathy strikes, after 1892. The data for railroad workers show a distinctly different pattern. See Montgomery, "Workers' Control of Machine Production in the Nineteenth Century," 505.

39. John I. Griffin, *Strikes: A Study in Quantitative Economics* (New York: 1939), 208, developed industrywide data on workers thrown out of jobs by strikes, to which the railroad industry's experience can be compared.

40. Powderly, *The Path I Trod*, 170–71.

2. Brotherhoods, "Strikers' Unions," and the Strategy of Class Organization

1. Terence V. Powderly, *The Path I Trod* (New York: 1940), 38–45.

2. Reed C. Richardson, *The Locomotive Engineer, 1863–1963: A Century of Railway Labor Relations and Work Rules* (Ann Arbor: 1963), 186–87; *Locomotive Engineers Monthly Journal* (November 1878): 498.

3. Ray Ginger, *The Bending Cross: A Biography of Eugene V. Debs* (New Brunswick, N.J.: 1949), 55; *Locomotive Firemen's Magazine* (November 1878); Nick Salvatore, *Eugene V. Debs, Citizen and Socialist* (Urbana, Ill.: 1982), 58–60.

4. Herbert Gutman, "Trouble on the Railroads in 1873–74; Prelude to the 1877 Crisis?" *Labor History* 2, no. 2 (Spring 1961): 215–35.

5. Shelton Stromquist, "Class and Community in a Nineteenth Century Railroad Town: Hornellsville, New York, 1860–1880" (Master's essay, University of Pittsburgh, 1973), 113–16.

6. *New York Times*, November 26, 1869.

7. Clipping from the *James Hogan Scrapbook*, January 1876. The source is a scrapbook kept by an engineer who worked on the Erie Railroad from the 1870s through the early twentieth century. Many of the clippings are not dated or identified as to specific newspaper source, but many can be dated approximately because they describe events known from other

sources. The scrapbook is in the possession of James Hogan's granddaughter, Rosemary Hogan, of Hornell, New York.

8. *Ibid., New York World*, October 1878.

9. *Ibid.*

10. *New York Times*, August 21, 1881. For a complete accounting of railroad strikes in Hornellsville, see Shelton Stromquist, "Class and Community," 105.

11. *Hornellsville Tribune*, March 6, 1874.

12. The latest version of the founding of the Trainmen's Union appears in Philip S. Foner, *The Great Labor Uprising of 1877* (New York: 1977), 29–32. Like all previous accounts, this one rests exclusively on Robert Ammon's testimony in the *Report of the Committee Appointed to Investigate the Railroad Riots in July, 1877* (Harrisburg: 1878), 671–74.

13. During the 1877 strikes there was direct telegraphic communication between Barney Donahue, the leader of the strike on the Erie at Hornellsville, and Ammon in Pittsburgh. Donahue made a point of refusing rail transportation that would force him to travel the northeastern corner of Pennsylvania on his return from imprisonment in New York City, because he feared additional conspiracy charges in Pennsylvania. Only additional research in other eastern railroad centers will reveal the possible connection between the organizations.

14. *New York Times*, July 27, 1878; Powderly, *The Path I Trod*, 60.

15. Albert Fishlow, "Productivity and Technological Change in the Railroad Sector, 1840–1910," in *Output, Employment, and Productivity in the United States after 1800*, Conference on Research in Income and Wealth, Studies in Income and Wealth, vol. 30 (New York: 1966), 613; Julius Grodinsky, *Transcontinental Railway Strategy, 1869–1893: A Study of Businessmen* (Philadelphia: 1862), 122–47.

16. *Locomotive Engineers Monthly Journal* (November 1882): 565. For sample agreements see *ibid.*, April, May 1883 and July, October 1884.

17. *Locomotive Firemen's Magazine* (June 1881): 169. On Debs's reaction to the 1877 railroad strikes and his views of the relations between labor and capital in the early 1880s, see Nick Salvatore, *Eugene V. Debs, Socialist and Citizen* (Urbana, Ill.: 1982), 47–49.

18. *Locomotive Engineers Monthly Journal* (October 1881): 497.

19. *Ibid.* (October 1887): 737.

20. *Ibid.* (April 1888): 176.

21. Terence V. Powderly to Peter M. Arthur, August 17, 1885, Outgoing Correspondence, Reel No. 10, Terence V. Powderly Papers.

22. *St. Louis Post-Dispatch*, March 25, 1886.

23. S. E. Hoge, "To the Officers and Members of Sub-Division ———," Strike Papers, Bundle 5 (33 1880 9.11), Burlington Archives.

24. *Locomotive Firemen's Magazine* (May 1886): 419; *ibid.* (March, 1889): 240–41.

25. *Ibid.* (February 1889): 110; *ibid.* (March 1889): 240–41.

26. *Ibid.* (October 1889): 920–21.

27. Joseph R. Buchanan, *The Story of a Labor Agitator* (New York: 1903), 70–78.

28. Selig Perlman, "Upheaval and Reorganization," in *The History of Labour in the United States*, vol. 2, ed. J. R. Commons, (New York: 1918), 368.

29. *Chicago Interocean*, February 29, 1888.

30. *Ibid.*

31. *Galesburg Tribune*, March 3, 1888.

32. Martin Irons, "My Experiences in the Labor Movement," *Lippincott's Monthly Magazine* 37 (June 1886): 626–27.

33. Perlman, "Upheaval and Reorganization," 368.

34. Jonathan Garlock, "A Structural Analysis of the Knights of Labor: Prolegomena to the History of the Producing Classes" (Ph.D. dissertation, University of Rochester, 1974).

35. *Ibid.*, 46–47. Garlock notes that many of what are conveniently termed trade assemblies of railroad workers are, in fact, assemblies of "mixed railroad trades." The *Journal of United Labor* provides such trade designations for local assemblies as: "Railroad Employees" "Railroad-men," "Mixed Railroad Trades," "Railroad Shopmen, Mixed," "Steam Railroadmen," and so forth. There were also local assemblies of a particular trade: "Switchmen," "Railroad Gatemen," "Car Inspectors, Repairers, & Locomotive Firemen." Some railroad trade assemblies explicitly mixed railroad and nonrailroad workers: "Railroad Laborers, Sawmill & Farm Hands," or less specifically, "Railroadmen and Limestone Quarrymen." It appears that among the railroad trade assemblies there were local industrial unions which were more or less inclusive, organizations of both related and unrelated railroad trades, and local general unions of workers in different industrial sectors. In some cases, they were drawn together by the fact of a common employer.

36. R. F. Trevellick to T. V. Powderly, October 18, 1885, Incoming Correspondence, Reel No. 10, Terence V. Powderly Papers.

37. D. G. Johnson to T. V. Powderly, August 21, 1885, *ibid.*

38. *Union Pacific Employees Magazine* (September 1877): 255.

39. Charles Williams to T. V. Powderly, August 27, 1885, Incoming Correspondence, Reel No. 10, Terence V. Powderly Papers.

40. "Engineers' Grievance Committee Papers, 1885–86" (33 1880 3.1), Burlington Archives.

41. R. W. Colville to G. W. Rhodes, August 25, 1885, *ibid.*

42. G. W. Holdredge to H. B. Stone, August 3, 1885, *ibid.*

43. "Strike Papers—M. L. Scudder, Jr." (33 1880 9.11), Burlington Archives.

44. "A Plea for Federation," June 5, 1885 Circular, Incoming Correspondence, Reel No. 10, Terence V. Powderly Papers.

45. U.S. Industrial Commission, *Report of the Industrial Commission on Transportation*, vol. 4 (Washington: 1900), 221.

293

46. U.S. Circuit Court, Nebraska District, Oliver Ames, II, et al. v. Union Pacific Railway Company, et al., *Record in the Matter of the Petition of the Receivers in Reference to Wage Schedules of Employees* (Omaha: 1894), 568.

47. *Union Pacific Employees Magazine* (August 1892): 203.

48. Robert G. Athearn, *Union Pacific Country* (Lincoln: 1971), 342–53.

49. *Union Pacific Employees Magazine* (August 1886): 206–7.

50. *Ibid.* (January 1887): 4.

51. *Ibid.* (April 1888): 92; *ibid.* (August 1888): 215.

52. *Topeka Commonwealth*, March 6, 1888 and *Minneapolis Tribune*, March 9, 1888, in "Newspaper Clippings About Strike, 1888" (33 1880 9.23), Burlington Archives.

53. C. H. Salmons, *The Burlington Strike* (Aurora, Ill.: 1889), 323–24.

54. "Pinkerton Reports, 1888–89" (33 1880 9.23), Burlington Archives.

55. *Ibid.*

56. *Chicago Tribune*, July 24, 1888.

57. *Switchmen's Journal* (June 1888): 52.

58. Quoted in *Switchmen's Journal* (August 1888): 152.

59. "Pinkerton Reports of the Annual Convention of the Brotherhood of Locomotive Engineers, Richmond, Virginia, October–November 1888" (33 1880 9.31), Burlington Archives.

60. *Union Pacific Employees Magazine* (May 1888): 102; *ibid.* (September 1888): 255.

61. *Locomotive Firemen's Magazine* (November 1888): 810–11.

62. *Ibid.* (March 1891): 251–53.

63. *Union Pacific Employees Magazine* (August 1889): 218; *ibid.* (September 1889): 255; *ibid.* (October 1889): 280.

64. *Ibid.* (May 1890): 120.

65. *Ibid.* (November 1889): 297.

66. *Ibid.* 296.

67. *Ibid.*

68. *Ibid.* (April 1890): 71.

69. *Switchmen's Journal* (February 1890): 438–39.

70. *Ibid.* (June 1891): 83–89; *ibid.* (July 1891): 208–12; see also Philip Foner, *History of the Labor Movement in the United States*, vol. 2 (New York: 1955), 250–53.

71. *Union Pacific Employees Magazine* (April 1890): 91.

72. *Ibid.* (July 1893): 178.

73. *Ibid.* (July 1890): 184.

74. Samuel Gompers, *Seventy Years of Life and Labor: An Autobiography* (New York: 1925), 218.

75. *Union Pacific Employees Magazine* (November 1892): 302.

76. *Ibid.* (September 1892): 226.

77. Donald L. McMurry, "Federation of the Railroad Brotherhoods, 1889–1894," *Industrial and Labor Relations Review* 7 (October 1953): 88.

78. Samuel McCune Lindsay, "Railway Employees in the United States," *Bulletin of the Department of Labor*, No. 37 (November 1901): 1103.

79. McMurry, "Federation of the Railroad Brotherhoods," 74; Foner, *History of the Labor Movement*, 247–57.

80. *Union Pacific Employees Magazine* (June 1893): 153.

81. ARU, "Declaration of Principles" (Terre Haute, Ind.: n.d.), 5.

82. ARU, "Constitution, adopted June 20, 1893" (Terre Haute, Ind.: n.d.), 10.

83. ARU, "Declaration of Principles," 8.

84. *Ibid.*, 8–9.

85. ARU, "Address of Eugene V. Debs at the Convention of the American Railway Union at Chicago, Illinois, June 12, 1894" (Terre Haute, Ind.: 1894), 11.

86. ARU, "Declaration of Principles," 9–10.

87. ARU, "Constitution, adopted June 20, 1893," 24.

88. ARU, "Proceedings of the 1st Annual Convention of the American Railway Union, Chicago, June 12, 1894" (Terre Haute, Ind.: 1894), 70; Ginger, *The Bending Cross*, 116; Philip S. Foner, *Organized Labor and the Black Worker, 1619–1973* (New York: 1974), 103–5.

89. ARU, "Proceedings of the 1st Annual Convention", 70–71.

90. U.S. Strike Commission, *Report on the Chicago Strike of June-July, 1894*, 53rd Cong., 3rd Sess., Sen. Exec. Doc. 7 (Washington, D.C.: 1895), 26–27, 52–57.

91. ARU, "Declaration of Principles," 9.

92. ARU, "Address of Eugene V. Debs," 16.

93. U.S. Strike Commission, *Report*, 172.

94. Salvatore, *Eugene V. Debs*, 108–117. Salvatore perceptively discusses the evolution of Debs' views during this period.

95. T. V. Powderly, "Government Ownership of Railways," *The Arena* 7 (December 1892): 58–63.

96. Richard T. Ely, "Natural Monopolies and the Workingman," *North American Review* 158 (March 1894): 294–303.

97. ARU, "Address of Eugene V. Debs," 13–14.

98. U.S. Strike Commission, *Report*, 102.

99. *Union Pacific Employees Magazine* (October 1893): 286.

100. Ginger, *The Bending Cross*, 100–101.

101. *Union Pacific Employees Magazine* (October 1893): 286.

102. U.S. Industrial Commission, *Report*, vol. 4, 526–28; *Machinists' Monthly Journal* 21, no. 2 (February 1909): 165; U.S. Strike Commission, *Report*, 152–53.

103. *Union Pacific Employees Magazine* (November 1893): 316,319.

104. *The Railway Times*, January 1, 1894.

295

105. *Ibid.*, July 2, 1894.

106. Almont Lindsey, *The Pullman Strike* (Chicago: 1942), 235.

107. *Great Falls Tribune*, April 17, 18, 20, 1894.

108. *Ibid.*, May 1, 17, 22, 1894.

109. Secretary's Department, Receivers' Correspondence Pads, 1893–1894, in the Northern Pacific Archives, contain scattered references to pre 1893 labor relations.

110. J. W. Kendrick to T. F. Oakes, August 18, 1893, General Manager's Correspondence Files (unprocessed), Box 2264, Northern Pacific Archives.

111. J. W. Kendrick to T. F. Oakes, September 4, 1893, *ibid.*

112. J. W. Kendrick to E. Dickinson, December 15, 1893, *ibid.*

113. P. M. Arthur to J. W. Kendrick, February 2, 1894, General Manager's Correspondence Files, Box 2265, *ibid.*

114. *The Railway Times*, May 1, 1894; ARU Committee to J. W. Kendrick, April 16, 1894, General Manager's Correspondence Files, Box 2266, Northern Pacific Archieves; W. P. C. Adams, ARU Director to Employees of Northern Pacific, April 22, 1894, *ibid.*

115. W. G. Pierce to J. W. Kendrick, April 20, 1894, Northern Pacific Archives.

116. J. W. Kendrick to T. F. Oakes, May 15, 1894, Receivers' Correspondence Pads, Box 8, n. 388, *ibid.*

117. J. W. Kendrick to T. F. Oakes, May 25, 1894, *ibid.*

118. J. W. Kendrick to T. F. Oakes, July 26, 1894 "Report of the Strike," Box 2266, *ibid.*; J. W. Kendrick to T. F. Oakes, June 28, 1894, *ibid.*; J. W. Kendrick to Ainslie, June 28, 1894, *ibid.*; J. W. Kendrick to T. F. Oakes, July 9, 1894, *ibid.*

119. J. W. Kendrick to T. F. Oakes, July 11, 13, 1894, *ibid.*

120. J. W. Kendrick to A. J. McCabe and A. A. Sharpe, June 29, 1894, Receivers' Correspondence Pads, Box 8, n. 388, *ibid.*

121. J. W. Kendrick to T. F. Oakes, July 12, 1894, General Manager's Correspondence Files, Box 2266, *ibid.*

122. "Classified Statement, by Division, of Number of Men Not Re-Employed at Close of Strike," *ibid.*

123. U.S. Department of the Interior, "Railway Labor" (Washington, D.C.: 1893), from *Eleventh Census of the United States* (1890).

124. James H. Ducker, "Men of the Steel Rails: Workers on the Atchison, Topeka and Santa Fe Railroad, 1869–1900" (Ph.D. dissertation, University of Illinois, 1980), 316–17.

125. *Burlington Hawkeye*, July 3, 1894.

126. *Ibid*, July 4, 1894.

127. Payroll Ledgers, Galesburg, East and West, Iowa Divisions, July 1894 (unprocessed), Burlington Archives.

128. Names from payroll were compared with *Burlington City Directory*, 1888.

129. *The Railway Times*, June 1, October 15, 1895.

130. Ginger, *The Bending Cross*, 195–99.

131. William John Pinkerton, "Debs Treachery to the Working Class" (Washington, D.C.: 1911), 2–3. This enigmatic pamphlet was written in response to an article by Debs in the *Appeal to Reason*, which attacked recent positions taken by the railroad brotherhoods. Though highly polemical, the positions taken on the ARU would seem to have some credibility, given Pinkerton's own work history and particularly in the light of his impressive volume, *His Personal Record* (1904).

132. Carlos A. Schwantes, *Radical Heritage, Labor, Socialism and Reform in Washington and British Columbia, 1885–1917* (Seattle: 1979), 142–49; W. Thomas White, "From Class to Community: Varieties of Radical Protest in the Railroad Industry of the Pacific Northwest, 1894–1917" (Paper presented at the annual meeting of the American Historical Association, Washington, D.C., 1982).

133. *Railway Employees Journal*, August 27, 1903.

3. Wages, Work Rules, and the Supply of Labor

1. "Grievance Committee Meeting with T. J. Potter, March 20, 1886," Engineers' Grievance Committee Papers, 1885–86 (33 1880 3.1), Burlington Archives.

2. Comments on the high cost of living in areas of new settlement abound in the journals of railroad labor organizations. A "critic" from Cheyenne, Wyoming, wrote that "no man of ability can live in the West for the same wages he received in the East, simply because the conditions of living are not the same." *Union Pacific Employees Magazine* (August 1886): 222.

3. Julius Grodinsky, *Transcontinental Strategy, 1869–1893: A Study of Businessmen* (Philadelphia: 1962), 226–55, 319–32, provides graphic description of the downward pressure of railroad freight rates. See also W. Z. Ripley, *Railroads, Rates, and Regulation* (New York: 1912).

4. On the diffusion of the automatic coupler and the air brake, see Emory R. Johnson and Truman W. Van Metre, *Principles of Railroad Transportation* (New York: 1903), 64; John Stover, *The Life and Decline of the American Railroad* (New York: 1970), 227; Henry G. Prout, *A Life of George Westinghouse* (New York: 1921), 32.

5. *Railroad Brakemen's Journal* (April 1887); *ibid.* (October 1887); *Locomotive Engineers Monthly Journal* (February 1886).

6. Albert Fishlow, "Productivity and Technological Change in the Railroad Sector, 1840–1910," in *Output, Employment, and Productivity in the United States after 1800* Conference on Research in Income and Wealth, Studies in Income and Wealth, vol. 30 (New York: 1966), 635–36.

7. *Ibid.*, 635.

8. U.S. Circuit Court, Nebraska District, Oliver Ames, II, et al. v.

297

Union Pacific Railway Company, et al., *Record in the Matter of the Petition of the Receivers in Reference to Wage Schedules of Employees* (Omaha: 1894), 573–74; Fishlow, "Productivity and Technological Change," 628; James Reed Golden, *Investment Behavior by United States Railroads, 1870–1914* (New York: 1975), 16–17.

9. See Harold G. Vatter, *The Drive to Industrial Maturity: The U.S. Economy, 1860–1914* (Westport, Conn.: 1975), 161; P. J. Conlon, "Past, Present, and Future of Our Association," *Machinists' Monthly Journal* 21, no. 1 (July 1909): 627; and Harold M. Groves, "The Machinist in Industry: A Study of the History and Economics of His Craft" (Ph.D. dissertation, University of Wisconsin, 1927), 29.

10. For an example of the individualizing impact of revisions in wage-related work rules, see "Transcript of Wage Negotiations, December 30, 1893," General Manager's Correspondence Files, Box 2263, Northern Pacific Archives. A portion of the Northern Pacific Railroad Company's records are now available at the Minnesota Historical Society.

11. U.S. Industrial Commission, *Report of the Industrial Commission on Transportation*, vol. 4 (Washington, D.C.: 1900), 22 (the testimony of Samuel Callaway).

12. U.S. Circuit Court, Nebraska Division, Oliver Ames, II, et al. v. Union Pacific Railway Company, et al., 568.

13. See Western Iowa Division, Payroll Ledger, 1889 (unprocessed), Chicago, Burlington & Quincy Railroad, Burlington Archives.

14. Reed C. Richardson, *The Locomotive Engineer, 1863–1963: A Century of Railway Labor Relations and Work Rules* (Ann Arbor: 1963), 143–47.

15. Alfred D. Chandler, Jr., *The Visible Hand: The Managerial Revolution in American Business* (Cambridge, Mass.: 1977), 104–7, 175–81; Paul V. Black, "The Development of Management Personnel Policies on the Burlington Railroad, 1860–1900" (Ph.D. dissertation, University of Wisconsin, 1972), 527–28.

16. See Payrolls, 1889–1900, Chicago, Burlington & Quincy Railroad (unprocessed), *Burlington Archives*.

17. Black, "The Development of Management Personnel Policies," 528–29, 532–34; also see, Walter M. Licht, "Nineteenth-Century American Railwaymen: A Study in the Nature and Organization of Work" (Ph.D. dissertation, Princeton University, 1977).

18. Transcript of Wage Negotiations, December 30, 1893, General Manager's Correspondence Files, Box 2263, Northern Pacific Archives.

19. John T. Wilson testimony, "On almost every large system of railway, someone is put in charge of a division in the capacity of roadmaster who is ambitious to excel all other roadmasters on the system, and in order to have it said that he is the best roadmaster on the system, he becomes a very hard taskmaster, drives the men under him from daylight till dark, and maintains his division at minimum cost. As the higher officials are on the lookout for men who can produce the greatest results at the least cost,

he becomes a favorite and is held up as an example for all other roadmasters to follow. . . ." U.S. Industrial Commission, *Report*, vol. 4, 45.

20. *Locomotive Engineers Monthly Journal* (March 1881): 132.

21. *Ibid.* (June 1880): 275.

22. William John Pinkerton, *His Personal Record: Stories of Railroad Life* (Kansas City, Mo.: 1904), 212–16.

23. U.S. Industrial Commission, "Wages of Railway Employees, 1892–1900," in *Reports of the Industrial Commission on Labor Organizations, Labor Disputes and Arbitration, and on Railway Labor*, vol. 17 (Washington, D.C.: 1901), 322. For a comparison of wages paid to railroad men on the Atchison, Topeka & Santa Fe and workers in selected nonrailroad occupations, see James Howard Ducker, "Men of the Steel Rail: Workers on the Atchison, Topeka and Santa Fe, 1869–1900" (Ph.D. dissertation, University of Illinois, 1980), 19.

24. E. J. Hobsbawm, "The Labour Aristocracy in Nineteenth Century England," in *Labouring Men: Studies in the History of Labour* (New York: 1964), 322.

25. Samuel McCune Lindsay, "Railway Employees in the United States," U.S. Department of Labor Bulletin, No. 37 (November 1901), 1054; *Locomotive Engineers Monthly Journal* (March 1881): 132.

26. Richardson, *The Locomotive Engineers*, 122.

27. *Locomotive Engineers Monthly Journal* (November 1886): 801.

28. *Locomotive Firemen's Magazine* (July 1888): 438.

29. Burlington, Iowa, *Saturday Evening Post*, March 10, 1888.

30. Emory R. Johnson, "Brotherhood Relief and Insurance of Railway Employees," U.S. Department of Labor, Bulletin No. 17 (Washington, D.C.: 1898), 557.

31. Ray Ginger, *The Bending Cross: A Biography of Eugene V. Debs* (New Brunswick, N.J.: 1949), 28; Salvatore, *Eugene V. Debs, Citizen and Socialist* (Urbana, Ill.: 1982), 18.

32. For example, see Joseph Bromley, *Clear the Tracks: The Story of an Old Time Locomotive Engineer* (New York: 1943), 1–143.

33. Shelton Stromquist, "Class and Community in a Nineteenth Century Railroad Town, Hornellsville, New York: 1860–1880" (Master's essay, University of Pittsburgh, 1973), 88–90.

34. William Z. Ripley, "Railway Wage Schedules and Agreements," in *Report of the Eight-Hour Commission* (Washington, D.C.: 1918), 287, House of Representatives, 65th Cong., 2d Sess.

35. U.S. Commissioner of Labor, *Fifth Annual Report*, 1889, 86–89; also Interstate Commerce Commission, *Annual Reports*, 1892–1900.

36. Ripley, "Railway Wage Schedules and Agreements," 286.

37. Joel Seidman, *The Brotherhood of Railroad Trainmen: The Internal Political Life of a National Union* (New York: 1962), 8.

38. Victor S. Clark, "Employment Conditions in Road and Yard Service," in *Report of the Eight-Hour Commission* (Washington, D.C.: 1918),

299

387; House of Representatives, 65th Cong., 2d Sess., Pinkerton, *His Personal Record*, 258–71; Chauncey Del French, *The Railroadmen* (New York: 1938), 15–20.

39. Ripley, "Railway Wage Schedules and Agreements," 287.

40. See in this respect the *Switchmen's Journal*, vols. 1–9, 1886–94. The *Journal* was modeled on that of the firemen, as were their balls and other social events. See chapter 2.

41. Interstate Commerce Commission, *Thirteenth Annual Report, 1901* (Washington, D.C.: 1901), 910–13.

42. P. J. Conlon, "Past, Present and Future of Our Association," *Machinists' Monthly Journal* 21, no. 7 (July 1909): 1627.

43. Railroad labor force data are taken from U.S. Industrial Commission, "General Conditions of Railway Employees," *Report*, vol. 17 (Washington, D.C.: 1901), 719–21.

44. Department of the Interior, "Report on the Agencies of Transportation in the United States." *Tenth Census of the United States*, vol. 4 (Washington, D.C.: 1883), 257; Interstate Commerce Commission, "Statistics of Railways in the United States—Railway Employees" *Annual Reports*, 1889–1905 (Washington, D.C.: 1889–1905).

45. Interstate Commerce Commission, "Statistics of Railways"; on the introduction of air brakes, see Johnson and Van Metre, *Principles of Railroad Transportation* 64–66, and Fishlow, "Productivity and Technological Change," 635–36.

46. Ripley, "Railway Wage Schedules and Agreements," 274.

47. Richardson, *The Locomotive Engineer*, 170.

48. *Locomotive Engineers Monthly Journal* (April 1880): 177. "On nearly all roads the engineer is required to carefully inspect the machinery under his charge, to report all defects and breakages, and indicate the repairs necessary to be made: clean, trim and fill the headlight and do all the hemp packing, together with such odd jobs as are necessary to keep the machinery in such a condition as will enable him to make his trip without unnecessary detention and in doing so from two to five hours are readily taken up."

49. Ripley, "Railway Wage Schedules and Agreements," 275 (Ripley says that day rates do not disappear until 1887).

50. *Ibid.*, 276.

51. *Ibid.*, 276, 277.

52. "Grievance Committee meeting with T. J. Potter, March 20, 1886," Engineers' Grievance Committee Papers, 1885–86 (33 1880 3.1), Burlington Archives.

53. Ripley, "Railway Wage Schedules and Agreements," 277–78.

54. *Ibid.*, 276–77.

55. "Transcript of Wage Negotiations, December 1893," General Manager's Correspondence Files, Box 2263, Northern Pacific Archives.

56. Ripley, "Railway Wage Schedules and Agreements," 277.

57. Donald L. McMurry, *The Great Burlington Strike of 1888: A Case History in Labor Relations* (New York: 1956), 40–41.

58. Richardson, *The Locomotive Engineers*, 211.

59. Ripley, "Railway Wage Schedules and Agreements," 290.

60. Richardson, *The Locomotive Engineers*, 218–19.

61. *Ibid.*, 219.

62. Ripley, "Railway Wage Schedules and Agreements," 290.

63. U.S. Circuit Court, Nebraska Division, Oliver Ames, II, et al. v. Union Pacific Railway Company et al., 500–505.

64. Ripley, "Railway Wage Schedules and Agreements," 270–72.

65. *Burlington Hawkeye*, Iowa, March 11, 1888.

66. Quoted in David L. Lightner, *Labor on the Illinois Central Railroad, 1852–1900: The Evolution of an Industrial Environment* (New York: 1977), 23; see also Paul W. Gates, *The Illinois Central and Its Colonization Work* (Cambridge, Mass.: 1934), 94–98.

67. *Union Pacific Employees Magazine* (September 1886): 253.

68. Hope T. Eldridge and Dorothy S. Thomas, "Demographic Analyses and Interrelations," in *Population Redistribution and Economic Growth in the United States, 1870–1950*, vol. 3, ed. Simon Kuznets et al. (Philadelphia: 1960), 65.

69. *Ibid.*, 8–9.

70. Richard A. Easterlin, "Regional Growth of Income: Long Term Tendencies," in *Population Redistribution and Economic Growth*, vol. 2, ed. Kuznets et al., 145; see also Stanley Lebergott, *Manpower in Economic Growth: The American Record since 1800* (New York: 1964), 131–37, 147, 172.

71. Scott Nearing, *Wages in the United States, 1908–1910* (New York: 1914), 149–53, found little evidence for significant regional variation in wages of railroad workers (or other workers, for that matter) in 1908. His data, taken from the 1908 Interstate Commerce Commission *Annual Report*, were from a period in which the railroad labor market had to a large extent stabilized; relatively uniform wages reflected that stability. He notes that wages were slightly higher in the West, and more varied for unskilled than for skilled railroad men. Paul Douglas, *Real Wages in the United States* (New York: 1930), 167–68, demonstrates that real earnings of railroad workers during the first twenty years of the twentieth century were consistently lower than the average for the years 1880–99. Not until after the First World War did real earnings move beyond the level of the 1890s. The smoothing out of regional wage differentials apparently meant declines in real earnings for most railroad workers.

72. *Union Pacific Employees Magazine* (August 1886): 222.

73. Black, "The Development of Management Personnel Policies" 201–2; Gates, *The Illinois Central*, 94; Pinkerton National Detective Agency, "Reports of Operatives, 1888–1889, Eastern Points," Strike Papers, 1888 (33 1880 9.3),1, Burlington Archives.

301

74. *Railroad Brakemen's Journal* (May 1888): 223; Order of Railway Conductors, *Proceedings, 20th Annual Convention,* 1888 (Cedar Rapids, Iowa: 1888), 192.

75. O. E. Steward, "Strike Notes, February 26–April 16th, 1888," Strike Papers, 1888 (33 1880 9.83), Burlington Archives.

76. See chapter 5 for a more complete discussion of involuntary turnover.

77. See, for example, *Locomotive Firemen's Magazine* July 1888: 520.

78. Quoted in Lightner, *Labor on the Illinois Central Railroad,* 180.

79. *Locomotive Engineers Monthly Journal* (February 1886): 77.

80. *Locomotive Engineers Monthly Journal* (January 1886): 21–22; see also Harold M. Groves, "The Machinist in Industry: A Study of the History and Economics of His Craft" (Ph.D. dissertation, University of Wisconsin, 1927), 29.

81. Eastern Iowa Division, Payroll Ledgers, 1894–1900, (unprocessed), Chicago, Burlington & Quincy Railroad, Burlington Archives.

82. *Machinists' Monthly Journal* 21, no. 2 (February 1909): 164–65.

83. L. S. Stanley, "The Machinist Union Story," *New Leader,* January 19, 1927, 6.

84. U.S. Department of Labor, Bureau of Labor Statistics, *History of Wages in the United States from Colonial Times to 1928,* Bulletin No. 604 (Washington, D.C.: 1934).

85. U.S. Commissioner of Labor. "Railway Labor," *Fifth Annual Report* (Washington, D.C.: 1889), 86–106.

86. *Locomotive Engineers Monthly Journal* (June 1880): 274.

87. "Strike Notes, M. L. Scudder, Jr.," Strike Papers, 1880–89 (33 1880 8.1), Burlington Archives.

88. "Miscellaneous Papers, 1866–1881," Decade File, 1880–89 (33 1880 8.1), Burlington Archives.

89. Richardson, *The Locomotive Engineer,* 155.

90. *Railroad Brakemen's Journal,* (May 1888): 212.

91. Dan H. Mater, "The Development and Operation of the Railroad Seniority System," *The Journal of Business* 12 (April 1939): 399–400; Ripley, "Railway Wage Schedules and Agreements," 307.

92. *Locomotive Firemen's Magazine* (June 1886): 353.

93. *Railroad Brakemen's Journal* (November 1887): 167.

94. *Locomotive Firemen's Magazine* (March 1886): 167.

95. Clark, "Employment Conditions in Road and Yard Service," 390–91.

96. Quoted in Ripley, "Railway Wage Schedules and Agreements," 305.

97. *Locomotive Firemen's Magazine* (June 1886): 352.

98. *Locomotive Engineers Monthly Magazine* (May 1885): 276.

99. Ripley, "Railway Wage Schedules and Agreements," 311;

Richardson, *The Locomotive Engineer*, 156; *Locomotive Firemen's Magazine* (June 1886): 353.

100. Peter Doeringer and Michael J. Piore, *Internal Labor Markets and Manpower Analysis* (Lexington, Mass.: 1971), 40.

101. *Railroad Brakemen's Journal* (November 1887): 492; Walter F. McCaleb, *The Brotherhood of Railroad Trainmen, with Special Reference to the Life of Alexander P. Whitney* (New York: 1936), 33–34.

102. "Schedule of Wages of Apprentice Locomotive Engineers, July 10, 1877," Miscellaneous Papers, 1876–77 (33 1880 8.1), Burlington Archives; *Locomotive Firemen's Magazine* (January 1888): 7.

103. *Locomotive Firemen's Magazine* (September 1886): 514.

104. *Railroad Brakemen's Journal* (April 1888): 174.

105. Pennsylvania General Assembly, *Report of the Committee Appointed to Investigate the Railroad Riots in July, 1877* (Harrisburg: 1878). (testimony of A. J. Cassett)

106. C. E. Perkins to Robert Harris, December 1876, (undated) Miscellaneous Papers, 1866–81 (33 1880 8.1), Burlington Archives.

107. *Chicago Tribune*, February 28, 1888.

108. *Locomotive Engineers Monthly Journal* (August 1886): 552; *Chicago Times*, February 28, 1888.

109. Ripley, "Railway Wage Schedules and Agreements," 306–7.

110. George Chalender to Joel West, September 1, 1876, Miscellaneous Papers, 1866–81 (33 1880 8.1), Burlington Archives.

111. *Locomotive Firemen's Magazine* (July 1886): 412.

112. *Locomotive Engineers Monthly Journal* (June 1886): 395–96.

113. Clark, "Employment Conditions in Road and Yard Service," 388.

114. *Ibid.*, 394.

115. *Kansas City Star*, April 17, 1893.

116. *Railway Age*, March 3, 1888, "Newpaper Clippings about Strike, 1888," Strike Papers (+33 1880 9.23), Burlington Archives.

117. William H. Buckler, "The Minimum Wage in the Machinists' Union," in *Studies in American Trade Unionism*, ed. Jacob Hollander and George E. Barnett (New York: 1905), 150.

118. Charles E. Perkins to Robert Harris, December 15, 1877, "Papers Concerning Employees, 1877–1898—Strike of 1877" (33 1880 3.6), Burlington Archives.

119. *New York Times*, February 28, 1888.

120. *Locomotive Engineers Monthly Journal* (November 1882): 565.

121. *Ibid.* (September 1880): 410.

122. *Union Pacific Employees Magazine* (June 1888): 130.

4. Town Development, Social Structure, and Industrial Conflict

1. The literature on the urbanizing effects of railroad development is substantial. See, for instance, Paul W. Gates, *The Illinois Central and Its*

Colonization Work (Cambridge, Mass.: 1934); Albert Fishlow, *American Railroads and the Transformation of the Ante-Bellum Economy* (Cambridge, Mass.: 1965); Richard C. Overton, *Burlington West: A Colonization History of the Burlington* (Cambridge, Mass.: 1941); Richard Wade, *The Urban Frontier: The Rise of Western Cities, 1790–1830* (Cambridge, Mass.: 1959); Julius Rubin "Urban Growth and Regional Development," in David T. Gilchrist, *The Growth of Seaport Cities, 1790–1825* (Charlottesville, Va.: 1967), 1–21 provides a useful framework for understanding pre-railroad urban economic development.

2. Historical geographers have shown some interest in the railroad's impact on settlement patterns. See Chauncey D. Harris and Edward L. Ullman, "The Nature of Cities," *Annals of the American Academy of Political and Social Science* 242 (1945): 7–17; Edward L. Ullman, "The Railroad Pattern of the United States," *Geographical Review* 39 (1949): 242–56; John Hart Fraser, "The Middle West," *Annals of the Association of American Geographers* 62 (June 1972): 258–82; Howard J. Nelson, "Town Founding and the American Frontier," *Association of Pacific Coast Geographers Yearbook* 36 (1974): 7–23; D. W. Meinig, "American Wests: Preface to a Geographical Interpretation," *Annals of American Geography* 62 (June 1972): 159–84; Michael P. Conzen, "A Transport Interpretation of the Growth of Urban Regions: An American Example," *Journal of Historical Geography* 1 (1975): 361–82. For the most part these studies examine the impact of the railroad on urban location and economic growth in relation to marketing functions. The service functions of railroad division towns are only sporadically mentioned in the literature and nowhere systematically classified. Gunnar Alexandersson, *The Industrial Structure of American Cities: A Geographic Study of Urban Economy in the United States* (Lincoln, Neb.: 1956), mentions these service functions, as does Robert L. Wrigley, Jr., "Pocatello, Idaho, as a Railroad Center," *Economic Geography* 21 (1943): 325–36.

3. The distribution of railroad workers as a proportion of the local labor force is based on an analysis of all towns in Iowa with over 100 employees in 1895 (see below). The 2 percent figure is for Dubuque with 685 railroad men, and the 35 percent is for Creston with 596 railroad men. Secretary of State, *Census of Iowa for the Year 1895* (Des Moines: 1896).

A few other studies using twentieth-century data have identified "transportation and communication" towns that have from 6 percent to 14 percent of their workers in that industrial class. J. F. Hart, "Functions and Occupational Structure of Cities in the American South," *Annals of the Association of American Geographers* 45 (1955): 269–86; C. D. Harris, "A Functional Classification of Cities in the United States," *The Geographical Review* 33 (1943): 86–99.

4. R. W. Colville to G. W. Rhodes, August 25, 1885, Engineers' Grievance Committee Papers, 1885–86 (33 1880 3.1), Burlington Archives.

5. J. W. Kendrick to T. F. Oakes, July 13, 1894, General Manager's Correspondence, (unprocessed), Box 2266, Northern Pacific Archives.

6. *Ibid.*

7. Amos Flaherty, "The Great Northern Strike of 1894: When Gene Debs Beat Jim Hill," in *The People Together*, ed. Meridel LeSueur et al. (Minneapolis: 1958), 21–23.

8. See Joseph F. Tripp, "Kansas Communities and the Birth of the Labor Problem, 1877–1883," *Kansas History* 4, no. 2 Summer 1981): 114–29, and James H. Ducker, "Workers, Townsmen and the Governor: The Santa Fe Enginemen's Strike, 1878," *Kansas History* 5, no. 1 (Spring 1982): 23–32.

9. *New York Tribune*, July 26, 1877; *New York World*, July 28, 1877; *Hornell Daily Times*, May 11, 1881. See also Shelton Stromquist, "Class and Community in a Nineteenth Century Railroad Town: Hornellsville, New York, 1860–1880" (Master's essay, University of Pittsburgh, 1973) 125–27, 177–79; Michael J. Cassity, "Modernization and Social Crisis: The Knights of Labor and a Midwest Community, 1885–1886." *Journal of American History* 66, no. 2 (February 1979): 41–61, argues that a similar change in community support occurred in Sedalia, Missouri.

10. Nick Salvatore, *Eugene V. Debs, Citizen and Socialist* (Urbana, Ill.: 1982), 85–87, 181–82, is particularly sensitive to the changing relationships between local business leaders and an emerging militant leader of the working class in the context of a developing midwestern industrial city; also, Nick Salvatore, "Railroad Workers and the Great Strike of 1877: The View from a Small Midwestern City," *Labor History* 21 (Fall 1980): 522–45. On the impact of racial and ethnic changes in the railroad towns of the Northwest, see W. Thomas White, "From Class to Community: Varieties of Radical Protest in the Railroad Industry of the Pacific Northwest, 1894–1917" (Paper presented at the Annual Meeting of the American Historical Association, Washington, D. C., 1982), and W. Thomas White, "A History of Railroad Workers in the Pacific Northwest, 1883–1934" (Ph.D. dissertation, University of Washington, 1981).

11. W. P. C. Adams to Employees of the Northern Pacific, April 22, 1894, General Manager's Correspondence Files, Box 2265, Northern Pacific Archives.

12. "Lists of Newspapers . . . for and against Strike," Strike Papers, 1888 (33 1880 9.11), Burlington Archives.

13. W. G. Pierce to (unnamed), Bozeman, Montana, December 12, 1893, General Manager's Correspondence Files, Box 2264, Northern Pacific Archives.

14. The best theoretical statement of Gutman's views on the response of nineteenth-century communities to industrial struggles appears in Herbert Gutman, "Workers Search for Power: Labor in the Gilded Age," in *The Gilded Age: A Reappraisal*, ed. H. Wayne Morgan (Syracuse, N.Y.: 1963). See also his other essays in *Work, Culture, and Society in Industrializing America* (New York: 1977).

15. Gutman stresses the need for further study of this problem in relation to the changing structure and economy of smaller industrial cities in

his essay "Class, Status, and Community Power in Nineteenth-Century American Cities: Paterson, New Jersey: A Case Study," in Gutman, Work, Culture and Society in Industrializing America, 259–60.

16. See Jeremy W. Kilar, "Community and Authority: Response to the Saginaw Valley Lumber Strike of 1885," Journal of Forest History 20 (April 1976): 67–79, for an analysis of absentee ownership and industrial concentration as factors in community support of strikes. Another useful analysis of community class differences and behavior in strikes is John Foster, Class Struggle and the Industrial Revolution: Early Industrial Capitalism in Three English Towns (London: 1974).

17. The most widely accepted theory of urban location is "central place hierarchy" developed in a south German setting by Walter Christaller. See August Lösch, The Economics of Location (New Haven, Conn.: 1954). In the American setting, it is most closely associated with the work of Allan Pred, The Spatial Relations of Cities in the United States (Cambridge, Mass.: 1966), and Brian J. L. Berry, Geography of Market Center and Retail Distribution (Englewood Cliffs, N.J.: 1967).

18. Edward K. Muller, "The Development of Urban Settlement in a Newly Settled Region: The Middle Ohio Valley, 1800–1860" (Ph.D. dissertation, University of Wisconsin, 1972), classifies towns tributary to Cincinnati in the middle Ohio valley in relation to stages of agricultural and transportation growth.

19. Ibid., 27–28, 387, 389.

20. Fishlow, American Railroads, 165–71, has demonstrated that ante-bellum railroads were not generally built ahead of demand. However, for the post–Civil War era, more recent work by Lloyd J. Mercer shows that most western trunk lines were built ahead of existing demand. See Lloyd J. Mercer, "Building Ahead of Demand: Some Evidence for the Land Grant Railroads," Journal of Economic History 34 (June 1974): 492–500.

21. James E. Vance, Jr., The Merchant's World: The Geography of Wholesaling (Englewood Cliffs, N.J.: 1970), 82.

22. William Z. Ripley, Railroads, Rates and Regulation (New York: 1920), 124–27.

23. See Berry, Geography of Market Centers and Retail Distribution, 7, on railroads' influence on the development of retail trade centers.

24. Ripley, Railroads, Rates and Regulation, 163.

25. Sam Bass Warner, The Urban Wilderness: A History of the American City (New York: 1973), 71–72.

26. Wilbur Thompson, A Preface to Urban Economics (Baltimore: 1965), 22.

27. Wilbur Thompson, "Urban Economic Growth and Development in a National System of Cities," in The Study of Urbanization, ed. Philip M. Hauser and Leo F. Schnore (New York: 1965), 468.

28. Pred, The Spatial Relations of Cities, 52.

29. Warner, The Urban Wilderness, 104; Alan Pred, The Spatial Relations of Cities, 54–57.

306

30. Gates, *The Illinois Central*, 122.

31. *Ibid.*, 127.

32. Overton, *Burlington West*, 286.

33. Gates, *The Illinois Central*, 126.

34. *Ibid.*, 127.

35. A recent survey of the planning of western urban communities in the nineteenth century provides additional descriptions of how western railroad towns developed but does not offer an analysis of differences in their growth patterns; see John Reps, *Cities of the American West: A History of Frontier Urban Planning* (Princeton: 1979), 524–631.

36. John W. Clampitt, *Echoes from the Rocky Mountains* (Chicago: 1889), 133–34.

37. Archibald R. Adamson, *North Platte and Its Associations* (North Platte, Neb.: 1910), 26–27, 32.

38. *Ibid.*, 118–19, 123.

39. E. H. Saltiel and George Barnett, *History and Business Directory of Cheyenne and Guide to the Mining Regions of the Rocky Mountains* (Omaha: 1868), 30–31.

40. Saltiel and Barnett, *History and Business Directory*, 30; Robert C. Morris, *Cheyenne Illustrated: Report of the Cheyenne Board of Trade* (Cheyenne: 1888), pages unnumbered.

41. Morris, *Cheyenne Illustrated*.

42. Richard J. Bonney, "The Pullman Strike of 1894: Pocatello Perspective," *Idaho Yesterdays* (Fall 1980): 24.

43. Almon Gunnison, *Rambles Overland: A Trip Across the Continent* (Boston: 1884), 19–20.

44. Lenora Koelbel, *Missoula the Way It Was: A Portrait of an Early Western Town* (Missoula, Mont.: 1972), 29–42; Helena Board of Trade, *Helena Illustrated* (Helena, Mont.: 1885), pages unnumbered; Charles D. Warner, *Studies in the South and West with Comments on Canada* (London: 1890), 147–50.

45. Helena Board of Trade, *Helena Illustrated*.

46. Marie MacDonald, *Glendive: The History of a Montana Town* (Glendive, Mont.: 1968), 14.

47. *Ibid.*, 15.

48. Berry, *Geography of Market Centers and Retail Distribution*, 5–9.

49. On the development of Iowa railroads, see Julius Grodinsky, *The Iowa Pool* (Chicago: 1950); Iowa Board of Immigrants, *Iowa: The Home for Immigrants* (Des Moines: 1870), 40–46; Sidney Halma, "Railroad Promotion and Economic Expansion at Council Bluffs, Iowa, 1857–1869," *Annals of Iowa* 42 (Summer 1974): 371–89; Herman C. Nixon, "The Economic Basis of the Populist Movement in Iowa," *Iowa Journal of History and Politics* 21, no. 3 (July 1923): 381–83; William Larrabee, *The Railway Question: A Historical and Practical Treatise on Railroads, and Remedies for Their Abuses* (Chicago: 1898).

307

50. George H. Miller, *Railroads and the Granger Laws* (Madison, Wis.: 1971), 97–116; Frank H. Dixon, *State Railroad Control with a History of Its Development in Iowa* (New York: 1896).

51. Iowa's exceptional record of census-taking during the nineteenth century makes it possible to compare the growth patterns of a large number of cities. From as early as 1850—biennially until 1875, and thereafter at five-year intervals—Iowa recorded village, town, and hamlet populations over one hundred persons. The 1895 state census published not only aggregated populations but, for all towns of one thousand or more, provided a detailed occupational breakdown. On the basis of these census data, it is possible to identify with certainty all towns having large concentrations of railroad employees and to sketch the occupational and industrial structure of these towns.

52. Secretary of State, *Census of Iowa for the Year 1895* (Des Moines: 1896).

53. Iowa Bureau of Labor Statistics, *Seventh Biennial Report, 1895–96* (Des Moines: 1897), 19–55. The Iowa Bureau of Labor Statistics conducted annual surveys of businesses (manufacturing, wholesale, and retail) for a number of years in the 1890s. The figures for 1895 were used in order to complement the data on population growth and occupational distribution from the 1895 census. Because of the focus on the distribution of manufacturing and wholesaling between towns rather than counties, and because the Bureau of Labor Statistics data were tabulated by county, two railroad towns (Marion and Belle Plaine) and four market cities (Cedar Rapids, Clinton, Fort Madison, and Keokuk) were dropped from consideration because they were in counties with multiple urban centers of more than 2,000 population. As one consequence of the elimination of these towns, the relative share of manufacturing and wholesaling of the market cities is understated, which only strengthens the conclusions being drawn here. Those towns that remained under consideration were the only towns with more than 2,000 people in their respective counties. It was assumed that all manufacturing and wholesaling enterprises in those counties were in those towns.

54. *Portrait and Biographical Album of Des Moines County* (Chicago: 1880), 713–14.

55. Department of the Interior, Census Office, *Statistics of Population of the United States at the Tenth Census, June 1, 1880* (Washington, D.C.: 1883). Interconnecting roads were the Burlington, Cedar Rapids & Northern, the Burlington & Western, the Burlington & Northwestern, and the Keokuk & Northern. The last three were subsidiaries of the Chicago, Burlington & Quincy.

56. H. H. Hartley and L. G. Jeffers, *Business Directory and Review of the Trade, Commerce, and Manufactures of the City of Burlington, Iowa* (Burlington: 1856), 6, 14–15. *Portrait and Biographical Album of Des Moines County*, 762.

57. George A. Boeck, "A Decade of Transportation Fever in Burling-

ton, Iowa, 1845–1855." in *Patterns and Perspectives in Iowa History*, ed. Dorothy Schweider (Ames, Iowa: 1973), 135–52.

58. *Ibid.*, 146.

59. Overton, *Burlington West*, 15–24, 39–52; Boeck, "A Decade of Transportation Fever," 148–52.

60. *Ibid.*, 153–56; Overton, *Burlington West*, 57–60.

61. *Census of Iowa, 1895; Business Directory* (Burlington: 1856), 8, 13.

62. *Ibid.*, 8, 13.

63. *Portrait and Biographical Album of Des Moines County*, 769.

64. *Burlington Weekly Hawkeye*, May 11, 1858, quoted in Overton, *Burlington West*, 101.

65. *Burlington Weekly Hawkeye*, April 13, 1857, quoted in Overton, *Burlington West*, 115.

66. Overton, *Burlington West*, 218.

67. *Ibid.*, 275.

68. Augustus M. Antrobius, *History of Des Moines County, Iowa, and Its People* (Chicago: 1915), 455.

69. Miller, *Railroads and the Granger Laws*, 97–116; Ripley, *Railroads, Rates and Regulations*, 163, 242–43.

70. Antrobius, *History of Des Moines County*, 148; Federal Writers' Project, *Iowa: A Guide to the Hawkeye State* (New York: 1949), 522.

71. Clara B. Rouse, *Iowa Leaves: Six Chapters* (Chicago: 1891), 238.

72. David L. Lightner, *Labor on the Illinois Central, 1850–1900*, (New York: 1977); *Portrait and Biographical Album of Des Moines County*, 769.

73. *Portrait and Biographical Album*, 771.

74. James Maitland, *Historical Sketches of Burlington, Iowa* (Burlington: n.d.), 18–19.

75. *Biographical and Historical Record of Ringgold and Union Counties, Iowa* (Chicago: 1887), 722.

76. C. J. Colby, *Illustrated Centennial Sketches, Map, and Directory of Union County* (Creston: 1876), 17.

77. J. L. Tracey, *Guide to the Great West* (Saint Louis: 1870), 197.

78. *The Prairie Farmer*, December 14, 1875, quoted in Colby, *Illustrated Centennial Sketches*, 20–21.

79. Colby, *Illustrated Centennial Sketches*, 20.

80. U.S. Department of the Interior, Census Office, *Manufacturing Schedules*, Des Moines County, Iowa, 1880.

81. *Iowa State Gazetteer, Business Directory, and Farmers' List* (Dubuque, Iowa: 1892).

82. *Creston Daily Advertiser*, January 7, 1885.

83. *Ibid.*

84. *Biographical and Historical Record of Ringgold and Union Counties, Iowa* (Chicago: 1887), 725.

85. *Ibid., Creston City Directory* (Creston: 1889).

309

86. *Burlington Hawkeye*, March 1, 1888.

87. *Creston Daily Advertiser*, March 2, 1888.

88. *Biographical and Historical Record of Ringgold and Union County*, 468.

89. Colby, *Illustrated Centennial Sketches*, 60–66.

90. The use of subscription biographies as a means of identifying community elites is not without its potential problems. As the product, at least in part, of self-selection, they are open to the bias of those who would promote their social position beyond their real stature in the community. Likewise, some substantial men in the community might have disdained contributing their biographies. The value of the biographies is in the richness of the information conveyed about individuals, including in most cases very specific accounts of their migrations, their education, their various business ventures, their associational and political affiliations. We have checked the membership list of the Burlington Board of Trade against the biographies and found that, with the exception of those who died or left the community, the coverage is nearly universal. On the other hand, there were a few obvious cases of individuals whose biographies were very brief and whose occupational and associational affiliations were very humble, who appeared to be using the biographies as a vehicle for social mobility. These cases were few and readily identifiable. The richness of the source and its accessibility have persuaded us to use it for the limited purpose of identification of elites, taking into account the exceptions noted above.

91. Colby, *Illustrated Centennial Sketches*, 93–96; *Biographical and Historical Record of Ringgold and Union Counties*; C. W. Eckerson to C. W. Rhodes, July 23, 1885, Engineers' Grievance Committee Papers (33 1880 3.1), Burlington Archives; Fred Haynes, *Third Party Movements Since the Civil War, with Special Reference to Iowa* (Iowa City: 1916); Nixon, "The Economic Basis of the Populist Movement," 3–107.

92. *The History of Des Moines County, Iowa* (Chicago: 1879); Maitland, *Historical Sketches of Burlington*, 18.

93. *Portrait and Biographical Album of Des Moines County, Iowa.*

94. *Burlington Daily Gazette*, July 23, 25, 1877; Charles E. Perkins to Robert Harris, July 23, 1877, Strike Papers, 1877 (33 1870 3.1), Burlington Archives.

95. G. W. Beymer to C. E. Perkins, July 25, 1877, *Ibid.*; C. E. Perkins to Mr. Walker, July 22, 1877, *Ibid.*

96. C. E. Perkins to Robert Harris, July 26, 27, 28, 1877, *Ibid.*; *Burlington Daily Gazette*, July 27, 1877.

97. *Burlington Daily Gazette*, July 27, 1877; *Burlington Hawkeye*, July 27, 1877; Robert Harris to C. E. Perkins, July 28, 1877 (33 1870 3.1), Burlington Archives.

98. *Burlington Daily Gazette*, July 31, 1877.

99. C. E. Perkins to Robert Harris, July 28, 1877, Strike Papers, 1877 (33 1870 3.1) Burlington Archives.

100. *Burlington Daily Gazette,* July 28, 29, 30, 1877; *Burlington Hawkeye,* July 28, 29, 30, 1877.

101. T. J. Potter to C. E. Perkins, July 24, 1877, Strike Papers, 1877 (33 1870 3.1), Burlington Archives; W. A. Chatterton to T. J. Potter, July 30, 1877, *Ibid.;* J. W. Chapman to C. E. Perkins, July 31, 1877, *Ibid.;* C. E. Perkins to R. P. Smith, A. D. Temple, and William Scott, July 30, 1877, *Ibid.;* R. P. Smith to C. E. Perkins, July 31, 1877, *Ibid.;* T. J. Potter to W. B. Strong, August 1, 1877, *Ibid.*

102. C. H. Salmons, *The Burlington Strike* (Aurora, Ill.: 1889), 29–100, and Donald L. McMurry, *The Great Burlington Strike of 1888: A Case History in Labor Relations* (New York: 1956).

103. *Creston Daily Advertiser,* February 11, 1888.

104. *Creston Gazette,* March 30, 1885; R. W. Colville to G. W. Rhodes, August 25, 1885, "Engineers' Grievance Committee Papers, 1885–86" (33 1880 3.1), Burlington Archives; G. W. Rhodes to H. B. Stone, August 25, 1885, *Ibid.;* C. W. Eckerson to G. W. Rhodes, July 23, 1885, *Ibid.*

105. *Creston Daily Advertiser,* March 12, 1885; *Creston Daily Gazette,* April 23, 1885.

106. *Creston Daily Advertiser,* March 30, April 21, 1885.

107. *Ibid.,* December 14, 1885.

108. *Ibid.,* August 12, 21, 1885.

109. *Ibid.,* March 30, 1885.

110. "Lists of Newspapers," Strike Papers, 1888 (33 1880 9.11), Burlington Archives.

111. "Testimony Regarding the Strike before the Iowa Board of Railway Commissioners," Strike papers, 1888 (33 1880 9.11), Burlington Archives.

112. *Creston Daily Advertiser,* April 3, 1888.

113. *Ibid.,* April 4, 1888; some evidence of a similar antimonopoly basis for community support for striking railroad workers in Sedalia, Missouri, in 1885 is offered by Michael J. Cassity, "Modernization and Social Crisis," 47.

114. *Creston Daily Advertiser,* August 21, September 4, December 20, 1888.

115. O. E. Stewart, "Strike Notes" (33 1880 9.83), Burlington Archives; "Clippings from Burlington Papers" (+ 33 1880 9.22), *Ibid.*

116. *Burlington Hawkeye,* February 28, 1888.

117. *Ibid.,* March 30, 1888.

118. *Ibid.,* March 29, 30, April 1, 1888.

119. *Ibid.,* April 3, 14, 1888.

120. *Ibid.,* April 6, 18, 1888.

121. *Creston Daily Advertiser,* July 3, 1888.

122. "Lists of Enginemen who struck," Strike Papers, 1888 (33 1880 9.51), Burlington Archives.

123. *Creston Daily Advertiser,* March 2, 1888, January 7, 16, 1889.

5. Persistence, Promotion, and the Solidarity of Railroad Labor

1. *New York World,* July 31, 1877.
2. William John Pinkerton, *His Personal Record* (Kansas City, Mo.: 1904), 12, 14.
3. Paul W. Gates, *The Illinois Central and Its Colonization Work* (Cambridge, Mass.: 1934), 95–97; *Switchmen's Journal* (July 1890): 144; U.S. Industrial Commission, Testimony of John T. Wilson, *Report of the Industrial Commission on Transportation,* vol. 4 (Washington, D.C.: 1900), 51–53. See also Shelton Stromquist, "Class and Community in a Nineteenth Century Railroad Town: Hornellsville, New York, 1860–1880" (Masters essay, University of Pittsburgh, 1973), 66–69.
4. Stephan Thernstrom, "Working Class Social Mobility in Industrial America," in *Essays in Theory and History,* ed. Melvin Richter (Cambridge, Mass.: 1970), 225.
5. *Ibid.;* also Stephan Thernstrom, "Urbanization, Migration, and Social Mobility in Late Nineteenth-Century America," in *Towards a New Past: Dissenting Essays in American History,* ed. Barton J. Bernstein (New York: 1967). The thesis is more cautiously ventured in Thernstrom's important work, *Poverty and Progress: Social Mobility in a Nineteenth Century City* (Cambridge, Mass.: 1964), 84–90, 158–59. One of the primary sources that Thernstrom acknowledges for this theory of the effects of population turnover on labor militancy is an important essay by Clark Kerr and Abraham Siegel, "The Inter-Industry Propensity to Strike—An international Comparison," in *Labor and Management in Industrial Society,* ed. Clark Kerr (Garden City, N.Y.: 1964). In the essay the authors attempt to explain why certain industries are more strike prone in the twentieth century. They point to the "location of the worker in society" as the primary explanatory variable and suggest that workers who form an "isolated mass" are most likely to be strike prone. By isolated mass, they mean workers living in communities that set them apart from others—a mining town, a logging camp, or a waterfront district. These workers "have their own codes, myths, heroes and social standards." There are no neutrals in such settings. The employer is usually an absentee owner, and grievances against him are broadly shared. They contrast such isolation with "integrated groups" of workers who live in multi-industry, multi-class settings and whose associations are heterogeneous. In their discussion of these community types, Kerr and Siegel only fleetingly use the phrase out of which Thernstrom has made so much—that workers in an isolated mass not only "have the same grievances, but have them at the same time, *at the same place* and against the same people." There is no direct suggestion made by the authors about the effects of high population turnover on groups of workers and their propensity to strike; there is no hint of what would constitute high turnover.

6. Stephan Thernstrom, *The Other Bostonians: Poverty and Progress in the American Metropolis, 1880–1970* (Cambridge, Mass.: 1973), 221–24; also Peter Knights, *Plain People of Boston, 1830–1860* (New York: 1971); Clyde Griffin and Sally Griffin, *Natives and Newcomers: The Ordering of Opportunity in Mid-Nineteenth Century Poughkeepsie* (Cambridge, Mass.: 1978); Stephan Thernstrom and Peter Knights, "Men in Motion: Some Data and Speculations about Urban Population Mobility in Nineteenth-Century America," *Journal of Interdisciplinary History* 1, no. 1 (Autumn 1970): 7–36.

7. Thernstrom, "Working Class Social Mobility in Industrial America," 225.

8. Joan Scott, *The Glassworkers of Carmaux* (Cambridge, Mass.: 1974), 84–85, identifies a growth in the persistence of French glassworkers from 34 percent to 57 percent in successive decades in the late nineteenth century. She relates this increasing settledness of the glassworkers to the militant defense of their craft traditions and their support for socialism. But this change in levels of persistence falls entirely within the range of what Thernstrom defines as *high* turnover in the thirty-one American case studies he cites.

9. Richard S. Alcorn, "Leadership and Stability in Mid-Nineteenth Century America: A Case Study of an Illinois Town," *Journal of American History* 61 (December 1974): 686. See also Clyde Griffin, "Workers Divided: The Effects of Craft and Ethnic Differences in Poughkeepsie, New York, 1850–1880," in *Nineteenth-Century Cities*, ed. Stephan Thernstrom (New Haven, Conn.: 1969).

10. Stephan Thernstrom, "Urbanization, Migration, and Social Mobility in Late Nineteenth-Century America," 168.

11. For a very perceptive discussion of the differences between peasants and seasoned industrial workers in response to working-class mobilization, see Leopold Haimson, "The Problem of Social Stability in Urban Russia, 1905–1917," *Slavic Studies* 23, no. 4 (December 1964); *ibid.* 24, no. 1 (March 1965).

12. Roberta Balstead Miller, "The Historical Study of Social Mobility: A New Perspective," *Historical Methods Newsletter* 8, no. 3 (June 1975): 92–93; Stanley Engerman, "Up or Out: Social and Geographic Mobility in the United States, A Review Essay," *Journal of Interdisciplinary History* 3 (Winter 1975): 487. For other useful critical analyses of mobility and the American working class, see Paul Worthman, "Working Class Mobility in Birmingham, Alabama, 1880–1914," in *Anonymous Americans: Explorations in Nineteenth Century Social History*, ed. Tamara Hareven (Englewood Cliffs, N. J.: 1971); James Henretta, "The Study of Social Mobility: Ideological Assumptions and Conceptual Bias," *Labor History* 18 (Spring 1977): 165–78; John T. Cumbler, *Working Class Community in Industrial America: Work, Leisure, and Struggle in Two Industrial Cities,*

313

1880–1930 (Westport, Conn.: 1979). Helpful studies of worker mobility in other countries are William H. Sewell, Jr., "Social Mobility in a Nineteenth Century City: Some Findings and Implications," *Journal of Interdisciplinary History* 7, no. 2 (Autumn 1978): 217–33, and J. S. MacDonald, "Agricultural Organization, Migration, and Labour Militancy in Rural Italy," *Economic History Review* 16 (August 1963): 61–75.

13. Persistence data are available for Hornellsville, N. Y., 1860–1880, and for Burlington and Creston, Iowa, in the 1880s and 1890s. James Ducker's analysis of persistence rates for a sample of "old-time employees" on the Santa Fe shows significant differences between trades—the most persistent being shopmen and the most mobile being operating employees. See James Ducker, "Men of the Steel Rails: Workers on the Atchison, Topeka and Santa Fe Railroad, 1869–1900" (Ph.D. dissertation, University of Illinois, 1980), 23–24. Data on traveling cards for printers are in Lloyd Ulman, *The Rise of the National Union* (Cambridge, Mass.: 1955), 64–65, and for engineers in the monthly reports on admissions and withdrawals by card, *Locomotive Engineers Monthly Journal* (1878–94).

14. "Grievance Committee Meeting with T. J. Potter, March 20–21, 1886," Engineers' Grievance Committee Papers, 1885–86 (33 1880 3.1), Burlington Archives.

15. *Locomotive Engineers Monthly Journal* (January 1883): 29.

16. This argument is made by Fred Cottrell, *The Railroader* (Stanford, Calif.: 1940), 38–39.

17. *Creston Daily Advertiser*, March 3, 1888.

18. See, for example, Hough's *Hornellsville Directory*, 1075, and *Centennial Sketches: Map and Directory of Union County, Iowa*, 1876; Martin Irons, "My Experiences in the Labor Movement," *Lippincott's Magazine* (June 1886): 625–26.

19. *Union Pacific Employees Magazine* (June 1886): 157.

20. I. W. Near, *History of Steuben County and Its People* (Chicago: 1911), 324; Hon. Harlo Hakes, ed., *Landmarks of Steuben County, New York* (Syracuse, N.Y.: 1890), 282.

21. New York State, *Population Schedules*, 1865, 1875, Steuben County; U.S. Census Office, *Population Schedules*, 1860, 1870, 1880, Steuben County, New York.

22. *Locomotive Engineers Monthly Journal* (November 1874): 556; Hough's *Hornellsville City Directory*, 1875 (Hornellsville, N.Y.: 1875); *Locomotive Firemen's Magazine* (July 1874): 17.

23. See for example accounts of these organizations in *Hornellsville Tribune*, May 17, 1872, and *Hornell Daily Times*, April 2, 1879.

24. Accounts of the various strikes appeared in the local Hornellsville press; see, for instance, *Hornellsville Tribune*, December 23, 1870, August 29, 1873, February 27, 1874. On the character of the Brakemen's Brotherhood, see *James Hogan Scrapbooks*, January 1876.

25. *New York World,* July 22, 1877.

26. *Ibid.*

27. *New York Tribune,* July 26, 27, 28, 1877; *New York World,* July 25, 1877.

28. See *Locomotive Engineers Monthly Journal* (February-May 1878), for lists of expelled engineers; *Smith's Hornellsville Directory,* 1884; *Hornell Daily Times,* August, 18, 1881.

29. *Irish World,* August 18, 1877.

30. *Railroad Brakemen's Journal* (November 1887): 510.

31. O. E. Stewart, "Strike Notes, February 26–April 16, 1888" (33 1880 9.83), Burlington Archives.

32. *Locomotive Firemen's Magazine* (March 1886): 166–67.

33. Victor S. Clark, "Employment Conditions in Road and Yard Service," in *Report of the Eight-Hour Commission* (Washington, D.C.: 1918), 390–91, House of Representatives, 65th Cong.

34. See Thernstrom, *Poverty and Progress,* Griffin, *Natives and Newcomers;* also Michael Katz et al., "Migration and Social Order in Erie County, New York, 1855," *Journal of Interdisciplinary History* 8, no. 4 (Spring 1978): 669–701.

35. See Stromquist, "Class and Community," 91.

36. U.S. Census Office, *Population Schedules,* 1880, Des Moines and Union Counties.

37. State of Iowa, Census, *Population Schedules,* 1885, Des Moines County.

38. Persistence for the 1880–88 period was calculated using manuscript returns for the federal census of 1880 and employment lists by division compiled by the Chicago, Burlington & Quincy Railroad at the onset of the strike in 1888.

39. Donald L. McMurry, *The Great Burlington Strike of 1888: A Case History in Labor Relations* (New York: 1956), 38–39.

40. "Lists of enginemen. . . who struck, February, 1888," Strike Papers, 1888 (33 1880 9.11). Burlington Archives.

41. McMurry, *The Great Burlington Strike,* 228.

42. "Meeting the Strike," Burlington Archives.

43. *Ibid.*

44. *Ibid.*

45. O. E. Stewart, "Strike Notes. . . . " (33 1880 9.83), Burlington Archives.

46. Pinkerton National Detective Agency, "Report of Operative J. M., Creston, March 20, 1888" (33 1880 9.3), *Ibid.*

47. "Lists of Enginemen" (33 1880 9.51), *Ibid.*

48. *Ibid.*

49. *Ibid.*

50. "Strike Papers—Miscellaneous, 1888–1897" (33 1880 9.81), Payroll Ledgers, East and West Iowa Divisions, 1889–1900 (unprocessed), *Ibid.*

315

51. Here the contrast between an "isolated mass" and an "integrated group" may be illuminating. See Kerr and Siegal, "The Inter-Industry Propensity to Strike," 109–13.

52. Richard C. Overton, *The Burlington Route* (New York: 1965), 238.

53. Social data on railroad workers in Creston after the 1888 strike were compiled from several sources. For 1895, the Iowa state census was used, but because of generic occupational notation, the Chicago, Burlington & Quincy payrolls and city directories were also compared. Persistence from 1889 to 1895 was calculated by comparing payroll ledgers for the same months in 1889 and 1895. (An incomplete run of payroll ledgers prevented the same comparison for Burlington.)

54. See chapter 1.

55. William J. Strong, "Blacklisting: The New Slavery," *The Arena* 21, no. 3 (March 1899): 273–92.

56. *Switchmen's Journal* (February 1889): 455.

57. *Ibid.* (November 1888:299; *ibid.* (April 1889).

58. "List of C. B. & Q. Strikers, 1889," General Manager's Correspondence Files, Box 2262, Northern Pacific Archives.

59. *Creston Daily Advertiser*, January 25–October 5, 1889.

60. "Correspondence, Memos, Circulars, etc., Concerning the Strike, 1886–1889" (33 1880 9.74), Burlington Archives.

61. *Saturday Evening Post* (Burlington, Iowa), March 24, 1888.

62. Pinkerton, *His Personal Record*, 12–14.

63. *Switchmen's Journal* (January 1889): 409.

64. *Brakemen's Journal* (December 1887): 560.

65. Pinkerton, *His Personal Record*, 188.

66. *Ibid.*, 169–209.

6. Railroad Management and the Labor Crisis

1. James Clarke to William K. Ackerman, October 12, 1883, quoted in David L. Lightner, *Labor on the Illinois Central Railroad, 1852–1900: The Evolution of an Industrial Environment* (New York: 1977), 280.

2. Charles Francis Adams, Jr., "The Prevention of Railway Strikes," in *The American Railway: Its Construction, Development, Management and Appliances* (New York: 1889), 376, 378–79.

3. See Thomas C. Cochran, *Railroad Leaders, 1845–1890: The Business Mind in Action* (New York: 1965), 173–83; Alfred D. Chandler, Jr., *The Railroads: The Nation's First Big Business* (New York: 1965), 99; Walter Licht, "The Dialectics of Bureaucratization: The Case of Nineteenth Century Railwaymen, 1830–1877" (Paper presented at the annual meeting of the Organization of American Historians, New York, 1978), and "Nineteenth Century Railwaymen: A Study in the Nature and Organization of Work" (Ph.D. dissertation, Princeton University, 1977); Paul V. Black, "The Development of Management Personnel Policies on the Burlington Railroad, 1860–1900" (Ph.D. dissertation, University of Wisconsin, 1972).

316

4. Black, "The Development of Management Personnel Policies," 268.

5. On the efforts of the roads in Chicago to build a multi-road framework to limit labor's effectiveness, see Donald L. McMurry, "Labor Policies of the General Manager's Association of Chicago, 1886–1894," *Journal of Economic History* 13, no. 2 (Spring 1953): 160–79.

6. See Gerald G. Eggert, *Railroad Labor Disputes: The Beginnings of Federal Strike Policy* (Ann Arbor: 1967), 192–225.

7. "The Old Time Master Mechanic," *Locomotive Engineers Monthly Journal* (January 1907): 116; Walter Licht, "The Dialectics of Bureaucratization," offers substantial evidence to support the general contention that local officials in the early years of railroad development acted very arbitrarily.

8. Quoted in the *Union Pacific Employees Magazine* (December 1886): 338.

9. "Transcript of Wage Negotiations, December 26, 1893," General Manager's Correspondence Files, Box 2263, Northern Pacific Archives.

10. U.S. Industrial Commission, *Report on Transportation*, vol. 4 (Washington, D.C.: 1900), 118.

11. Leonard Painter, *Through Fifty Years with the Brotherhood of Railway Carmen* (Kansas City, Mo.: 1941), 29.

12. J. W. Kendrick to T. F. Oakes, August 18, 1893, General Manager's Correspondence Files, Box 2264, Northern Pacific Archives.

13. J. W. Kendrick to H. C. Payne, January 23, 1894, General Manager's Correspondence Files, Box 2263, Northern Pacific Archives.

14. Charles E. Perkins to G. B. Harris, December 1, 1890, cited in Black, "The Development of Management Personnel Policies," 115.

15. U.S. Industrial Commission, John T. Wilson testimony, *Report*, vol. 4, 45.

16. *Union Pacific Employees Magazine* (September 1889): 252.

17. Richard C. Overton, *The Burlington Route: A History of the Burlington Lines* (Cambridge, Mass.: 1965), 158–60; Cochran, *Railroad Leaders*, 176.

18. Cochran, *Railroad Leaders*, 178, 181.

19. Ackerman to Osborn, Chicago, 28 April 1877, cited in Lightner, *Labor on the Illinois Central*, 182.

20. *Ibid.*, 202, 276.

21. Black, "The Development of Management Personnel Policies," 332.

22. "The Care of Railroad Employees," *Nation*, February 19, 1880, 134–35.

23. "Railroad Companies and Their Employees," *Nation*, March 18, 1880, 211–12.

24. Black, "The Development of Management Personnel Policies," 268.

317

25. "List of Striking Enginemen, February, 1888" (33 1880 9.51), Burlington Archives.

26. C. B. & Q. Payrolls, 1889–1900 (unprocessed), Burlington Archives.

27. Paul V. Black, "Experiment in Bureaucratic Centralization: Employee Blacklisting on the Burlington Railroad, 1877–1892," *Business History Review* 51, no. 4 (Winter 1977): 444–47; "Record of Discharged Employees. . . February, 1877-June, 1892" (33 1870 3.4), Burlington Archives.

28. "List of Striking Enginemen, February, 1888," (33 1880 9.51), Burlington Archives; see also Donald McMurry, *The Great Burlington Strike of 1888* (New York: 1956), 75; Black, "Experiment in Bureaucratic Centralization," 451–55.

29. O. E. Stewart, "Strike Notes, February 26-April 16th, 1888," Strike Papers, 1888 (33 1880 9.83), Burlington Archives.

30. *Ibid.*

31. Lightner, *Labor on the Illinois Central*, 252.

32. *Union Pacific Employees Magazine* (March 1889): 34.

33. George B. Harris to G. W. Holdrege, October 4, 1895, cited in Black, "Experiment in Bureaucratic Centralization," 458.

34. Lightner, *Labor on the Illinois Central*, 351–52.

35. U.S. Industrial Commission, testimony of Melville E. Ingalls, *Report*, vol. 4, 288.

36. *Ibid.*, testimony of F. P. Sargent, 65; *ibid.*, testimony of Aldace F. Walker, 772.

37. William John Pinkerton, *His Personal Record* (Kansas City, Mo.: 1904), 8.

38. U.S. Industrial Commission, testimony of William J. Strong, *Report*, vol. 4, 516; William J. Strong, "Blacklisting: The New Slavery," *The Arena* 21 (March 1899): 276–77, 285.

39. "List of Striking Employees, July, 1894," General Manager's Correspondence Files, Box 2266, Northern Pacific Archives.

40. Samuel McCune Lindsay, "Railway Employees in the United States," *Bulletin of the Department of Labor*, No. 37 (November 1901), 1051–52, 1054.

41. *Ibid.*, 1055, James H. Ducker, "Men of the Steel Rail: Workers on the Atchison, Topeka and Santa Fe, 1869–1900" (Ph.D. dissertation, University of Illinois, 1980), 74–78, discusses the implementation of the Brown system of discipline on the Santa Fe system during the 1890s.

42. See, for instance, *The Railroad Gazette*, April 2, 1886, 232–33.

43. Marshall M. Kirkman, *The Science of Railways: Operation of Trains* (Chicago: 1894), 56–57.

44. *Ibid.*, 58.

45. Dan H. Mater, "The Development and Operation of the Railroad Seniority System," in *The Railroad Seniority System: History, Description,*

and Evaluation, ed. Dan H. Mater (Chicago: 1941), 390–97; Reed C. Richardson, *The Locomotive Engineer, 1863–1893: A Century of Railway Labor Relations and Work Rules* (Ann Arbor: 1963), 155.

46. George Chalendar to Joel West, n.d. (1876) (33 1880 8.1), Burlington Archives.

47. Charles E. Perkins to Robert Harris, December 15, 1877 (33 1870 3.6), Burlington Archives.

48. Richardson, *The Locomotive Engineers,* 156; *Locomotive Engineers Monthly Journal* (March 1883): 138–39.

49. For representative agreements, see *Locomotive Engineers Monthly Journal* (March 1883): 138; *ibid.* (May 1883): 248–49; illustration of the broadening of seniority provisions in Chicago, Milwaukee, St. Paul & Pacific agreements for the years 1880, 1883, 1887, 1891, and 1902 is offered by Mater, "The Development and Operation of the Railroad Seniority System," 405–7.

50. *Locomotive Engineers Monthly Journal* (May 1881): 221.

51. *Ibid.*

52. Mater, "The Development and Operation of the Railroad Seniority System," 408–9, 417.

53. *Locomotive Engineers Monthly Journal* (July 1887): 495.

54. Sumner Slichter, *Union Policies and Industrial Management* (Washington, D.C.: 1941), 154–55.

55. Mater, "The Development and Operation of the Railroad Seniority System," 403.

56. T. F. Oakes to General Manager Haupt, November 4, 1881, General Manager's Subject Files, Telegrams Received, 1881–84, Northern Pacific Archives.

57. Cochran, *Railroad Leaders,* 178, notes the interest of Harris, Griswold, Forbes, Ackerman, Ledyard, and Oakes in "mutual benefit plans" after 1877.

58. Emory R. Johnson, "Railway Departments for the Relief and Insurance of Employees," *Annals of the American Academy of Political and Social Sciences* 6 (1895): 69–71.

59. Lindsay, "Railway Employees," 874–75.

60. *Ibid.,* 875–77, 868.

61. Interstate Commerce Commission, *Third Annual Report* (Washington, D.C.: 1889), 342.

62. Interstate Commerce Commission, *Sixth Annual Report, 1892* (Washington, D.C.: 1892), 326.

63. U.S. Industrial Commission, testimony of Melville Ingalls, *Report,* vol. 4, 290.

64. A discussion of employee objections to company-sponsored relief is contained in Johnson, "Railway Departments," 457–61, and in Lindsay, "Railway Employees," 880–83; see also U.S. Industrial Commission, testimony of H. R. Fuller, *Report* vol. 9, 8–71.

319

65. Pinkerton, *His Personal Record*, 256–57.

66. *Ibid.*, 253.

67. *Locomotive Firemen's Magazine* (April 1886): 196.

68. J. B. Kennedy, "The Beneficiary Features of the Railway Unions," in *Studies in American Trade Unionism*, ed. Jacob Hollander and George E. Barnett (New York: 1906), 342.

69. Ackerman to Jeffrey, Chicago, June 3, 1881, *Illinois Central Archives*; cited in Lightner, *Labor on the Illinois Central*, 276.

70. Black, "Experiment in Bureaucratic Centralization," 451–53.

71. Black, "The Development of Management Personnel Policies," 355.

72. Interstate Commerce Commission, *Sixth Annual Report, 1892*, 335.

73. *Ibid.*, 326.

74. Black, "The Development of Management Personnel Policies," 355.

75. *Locomotive Firemen's Magazine* (December 1886): 714–15; *Union Pacific Employees Magazine* (October 1890): 264.

76. Interstate Commerce Commission, *Sixth Annual Report, 1892*, 324.

77. See Julius Grodinsky, *The Iowa Pool: A Study in Railroad Competition, 1870–1884* (Chicago 1950), for the most detailed study.

78. Paul Gates, *The Illinois Central and Its Colonization Work* (Cambridge, Mass.: 1934), 94–98; see also Pinkerton National Detective Agency, "Reports of Operatives, 1888–1889, Eastern Points," Strike Papers, 1888 (33 1880 9.3), Burlington Archives.

79. See Robert V. Bruce, *1887: Year of Violence* (Chicago: 1959), 40, on the timing of wage cuts in 1877.

80. McMurry, "The Labor Policies of the General Managers' Association of Chicago, 1886–1894," 161. McMurry draws heavily on the minutes of the General Managers' Association, which at one time were housed at the John Crerar Library in Chicago. The Crerar Library has subsequently disposed of some of its holdings, including these minutes, which have not since been located.

81. *Ibid.*, 162–65.

82. Lightner, *Labor on the Illinois Central*, 258; see also Donald L. McMurry, *The Great Burlington Strike of 1888*, 101–13.

83. Adams, Jr., "The Prevention of Railway Strikes," 376–80.

84. McMurry, "The Labor Policies," 167–68.

85. *Ibid.*, 68.

86. *Ibid.*, 172–73.

87. J. W. Kendrick to T. F. Oakes, August 18, 1893, General Manager's Correspondence Files, Box 2264, Northern Pacific Archives.

88. *Ibid.*

89. J. W. Kendrick to T. F. Oakes, August 28, 1893, *ibid.*

90. W. G. Pierce to J. W. Kendrick, November 17, 1893, *ibid.*

91. J. W. Kendrick to T. F. Oakes, August 18, 1893, *ibid.*

92. J. W. Kendrick to H. C. Payne, April 21, 1894, *ibid.*, Box 2265.

93. McMurry, "The Labor Policies," 176–77.

94. Almont Lindsey, *The Pullman Strike* (Chicago: 1942), 118–19.

95. This account of the General Managers' Association is drawn from the descriptions of Almont Lindsey and Donald L. McMurry, both of whom had access to the minutes of the association (see note 80, above).

96. See Strong, "Blacklisting," 188.

97. See Gerald G. Eggert, *Richard Olney: Evolution of a Statesman* (University Park, Pa.: 1974), 13–32.

98. *Ibid.*, 137–42.

99. Eggert, *Railroad Labor Disputes*, 194–95.

100. Eggert, *Richard Olney*, 154–55, 164–68.

101. Eggert, *Railroad Labor Disputes*, 202.

102. Eggert, *Richard Olney*, 154–55, 164–68.

103. *Ibid.*, 156–68.

104. *Ibid.*, 161–64; Richardson, *The Locomotive Engineer*, 265.

105. U.S. Strike Commission, *Report on the Chicago Strike of June-July, 1894*, 53rd Cong., 3rd Sess., Sen. Exec. Doc. No. 7 (Washington, D.C.: 1895), xlviii.

106. U.S. Industrial Commission, *Report*, vol. 4, 37.

107. Alfred D. Chandler, Jr., *The Visible Hand: The Managerial Revolution in American Business* (Cambridge, Mass.: 1977), 172–75.

108. Leonard A. Lecht, *Experience under Railway Labor Legislation* (New York: 1955), 17–20.

109. U.S. Industrial Commission, testimony of F. P. Sargent, *Report*, vol. 4, 68–69.

110. Eggert, *Richard Olney*, 163.

111. J. W. Kendrick to T. F. Oakes, August 18, 1893, General Manager's Correspondence Files, Box 2264, Northern Pacific Archives.

112. Lindsey, *The Pullman Strike*, 264.

113. Samuel Gompers, *Seventy Years of Life and Labor: An Autobiography* (New York: 1925), 223.

114. U.S. Industrial Commission, testimony of P. M. Arthur, *Report*, vol. 4, 327.

115. *Ibid.*, testimony of F. P. Sargent, 87.

116. *Ibid.*, testimony of F. J. O'Rourke, 528–29.

117. Richardson, *The Locomotive Engineer*, 285.

118. U.S. Industrial Commission, testimony of Stuyvesant Fish, *Report*, vol. 4, 327.

119. *Ibid.*, testimony of Samuel Callaway, 222.

120. U.S. Industrial Commission, *Report of the Industrial Commission on Labor Organizations, Labor Disputes and Arbitration, and on Railway Labor*, vol. 17 (Washington, D.C.: 1900), 875. At the time that the Erd-

321

man Act became law, more than half of the company-sponsored relief programs were compulsory.

7. Conclusion

1. Herbert Gutman, "Workers Search for Power: Labor in the Gilded
Age," in *The Gilded Age. A Reappraisal*, ed. H. Wayne Morgan (Syracuse,
N.Y.: 1963)

2. See especially Stephan Thernstrom, "Working Class Social Mobility in Industrial America," in *Essays in Theory and History*, ed. Melvin
Richter (Cambridge, Mass.: 1970), 221–40.

3. *Irish World*, August 18, 1877.

4. Eugene V. Debs, "How I Became a Socialist," in *Writings and
Speeches of Eugene V. Debs*, ed. Arthur M. Schlesinger (New York: 1948).

Bibliography

Manuscripts

Burlington Archives. The Newberry Library. A guide/catalog to the corporate archives of the Chicago, Burlington & Quincy Railroad and its subsidiaries is available. Elisabeth Coleman Jackson and Carolyn Curtis. *Guide to the Burlington Archives in the Newberry Library, 1851–1901.* Chicago: The Newberry Library, 1949.

Erie Railroad Company Papers, Miscellaneous. New York Public Library.

Great Northern Railroad Archives. Minnesota Historical Society. Saint Paul, Minn.

Hogan, James. Scrapbooks. In the possession of Rosemary Hogan, Hornell, New York.

Iowa. Secretary of State. Population Schedules, 1885. Des Moines County. Iowa Division of History and Archives, 1885. Des Moines, Iowa.

———. Population Schedules, 1895. Des Moines and Union Counties. Iowa Division of History and Archives. Des Moines, Iowa.

Knights of Labor Data Bank. Inter-University Consortium for Political Research. Ann Arbor. A guide to the use of this computer data bank is, Jonathan Garlock. *The Knights of Labor Data Bank: User's Manual and Index to Local Assemblies.* Ann Arbor, Mich.: Inter-University Consortium for Political Research, 1973.

New York. Secretary of State. Population Schedules, 1865. Steuben County. Steuben County Courthouse. Bath, New York.

———. Population Schedules, 1875. Steuben County. Steuben County Courthouse. Bath, New York.

Northern Pacific Railroad Archives. Minnesota Historical Society. Saint Paul, Minn.

Terence Vincent Powderly Papers. Catholic University of America. Available in a microfilm edition at the State Historical Society of Wisconsin, John A. Turcheneske, Jr., ed. *A Guide to the Microfilm Edition.* Glen Rock, N.J.: Microfilming Corporation of America, 1975.

United States. Department of the Interior. Census Bureau. Manufacturing Schedules. Des Moines and Union Counties, Iowa. 1880, 1890.

———. Population Schedules. Des Moines and Union Counties, Iowa. 1880.

———. Population Schedules. Steuben County, New York. 1860, 1870, 1880.

Government Publications

Colorado. Bureau of Labor Statistics. *Third Biennial Report, 1891–92.* "The Rio Grande Strike." Colorado Springs: The Gazette Printing Company, 1892.

———. *Fourth Biennial Report, 1893–94.* "The Great 'Sympathetic Strike' of Members of the American Railway Union." Denver: Smith-Brooks Printing Company, 1894.

Iowa. Board of Immigrants. *Iowa: The Home for Immigrants.* Des Moines: n.p. 1870.

———. Bureau of Labor Statistics. *Seventh Biennial Report, 1895–96.* Des Moines: F. R. Conaway, 1897.

———. Secretary of State. *Census of Iowa for the Year 1885.* Des Moines: George E. Roberts, 1885.

———. *Census of Iowa for the Year 1895.* Des Moines: F. R. Conaway, 1896.

———. *Iowa Official Register.* 1889–97. Des Moines: F. R. Conaway, n.d.

Pennsylvania. General Assembly. *Legislative Document,* vol. 5, Doc. 29, 1878. *Report of the Committee Appointed to Investigate the Railroad Riots in July, 1877.* Harrisburg: Lane S. Hart, 1878.

United States Circuit Court, Nebraska District. *Oliver Ames, II, et al., v. Union Pacific Railway Company, et al. Record in the Matter of the Petition of the Receivers in Reference to Wage Schedules of Employees.* Omaha: 1894.

United States. Commissioner of Labor. "Strikes and Lockouts." *Third Annual Report, 1887.* Washington, D.C.: GPO, 1887.

———. "Railroad Labor." *Fifth Annual Report, 1889.* Washington, D.C.: GPO, 1889.

———. "Strikes and Lockouts." *Tenth Annual Report, 1894.* Washington, D.C.: GPO, 1895.

United States. Department of Commerce. *Historical Statistics of the United States, Colonial Times to 1970.* Washington, D.C.: GPO, 1975.

United States. Department of the Interior. *The Statistics of Population of the United States Compiled from the Original Returns of the Ninth Census.* Washington, D.C.: GPO, 1872.

———. Department of the Interior. *Statistics of Population of the United States at the Tenth Census, June 1, 1880.* Washington, D.C.: GPO, 1883.

———. "Report on the Agencies of Transportation in the United States." *Tenth Census of the United States, 1880.* Vol. 4. Washington, D.C.: GPO, 1883.

———. *Report on the Population of the United States at the Eleventh Census: 1890.* Part 1. Washington, D.C.: GPO, 1895.

———. *Report on Transportation Business in the United States at the Eleventh Census, 1890.* Washington, D.C. GPO, 1893.

———. *Twelfth Census of the United States.* Vol. 1. Population. Part 1. Washington, D.C.: GPO, 1901.

324

United States. Department of Labor. Bureau of Labor Statistics. Bulletin No.8, January 1897. Emory R. Johnson. "Railway Relief Departments." Washington, D.C.: GPO, 1897.

———. Bulletin No. 17, July 1898. Emory R. Johnson. "Brotherhood Relief and Insurance of Railway Employees." Washington, D.C.: GPO, 1898.

———. Bulletin No. 37, November 1901. Samuel McCune Lindsay. "Railway Employees in the United States." Washington, D.C.: GPO, 1901.

———. Bulletin No. 604. *History of Wages in the United States from Colonial Times to 1928*. Washington, D.C.: GPO, 1934.

———. Bulletin No.651. Florence Peterson. *Strikes in the United States, 1880–1936*. Washington, D.C.: GPO, 1938.

United States. House of Representatives. William Z. Ripley. "Railway Wage Schedules and Agreements." Victor S. Clark. "Employment Conditions in Road and Yard Service." *Report of the Eight-Hour Commission*. 65th Cong., 2d sess. Washington, D.C.: GPO, 1918.

United States Industrial Commission. *Report of the Industrial Commission on Transportation*. Vol. 4. Washington, D.C.: GPO, 1900.

———. *Report of the Industrial Commission on Labor Organizations, Labor Disputes and Arbitration, and on Railway Labor*. Vol. 17. Washington, D.C.: GPO, 1901.

United States. Interstate Commerce Commission. "Relations Existing Between Railway Corporations and Their Employees." *Third Annual Report, 1889*. Washington, D.C.: GPO, 1890.

———. "Relations between Railway Corporations and Their Employees." *Sixth Annual Report, 1892*. Washington, D.C.: GPO, 1893.

———."Railway Departments for the Relief and Insurance of Employees." *Tenth Annual Report, 1896*. Washington, D.C.: GPO, 1897.

———. "Comparative Summary of Average Daily Compensation of Railway Employees for the Years Ending June 20, 1892 to 1900, by Groups." *Statistics of Railways in the United States*. Washington, D.C.: GPO, 1900.

United States Strike Commission. *Report on the Chicago Strike of June-July, 1894*. 53rd Cong. 3rd sess. Sen. Exec. Doc. No. 7. Washington, D.C.: GPO, 1895.

Wisconsin. Bureau of Labor and Industrial Statistics. "The Statistical Aspect of the Strike." *Twelfth Biennial Report, 1905–06*. Madison, Wis.: n.p., 1907.

Trade Union Periodicals and Other Publications

American Railway Union. "Address of Eugene V. Debs at the Convention of the American Railway Union at Chicago, Illinois, June 12, 1894." Terre Haute, Ind.: Moore & Langen, 1894.

———. "Constitution, adopted June 20, 1893." Terre Haute, Ind.: Moore & Langen, n.d.

————. "Declaration of Principles." Terre Haute, Ind.: Moore & Langen, n.d.

————. "Proceedings of the 1st Annual Convention of the American Railway Union, Chicago, June 12, 1894." Terre Haute, Ind.: Moore & Langen, 1894.

Locomotive Engineers Monthly Journal. 1874–1900, 1907.

Locomotive Firemen's Magazine. 1878–94.

Machinists' Monthly Journal. 1889–97, 1909.

Order of Railway Conductors. *Proceedings of the 20th Annual Convention, May, 1888.* Cedar Rapids, Iowa: Standard Company, 1888.

Railroad Brakemen's Journal. 1887–92.

Railway Employees Journal. (United Brotherhood of Railway Employees) 1902–1903.

Railway Times. (American Railway Union.) 1894–97.

Switchmen's Journal. (Switchmen's Mutual Aid Association) 1886–94.

Union Pacific Employees Magazine. (D.A. No. 82, Knights of Labor) 1886–94.

Newspapers

Buffalo Commercial Advertiser, 1877.
Burlington Daily Gazette, 1877, 1888–89.
Burlington Daily Hawkeye, 1877–78.
Burlington Hawkeye, 1882–94.
Chicago Interocean, 1888.
Chicago Mail, 1888.
Chicago Times, 1886–90, 1894
Chicago Tribune, 1888.
Creston Daily Advertiser, 1885–89.
Creston Daily Gazette, 1885, 1888.
Creston Weekly Advertiser, 1890–94.
Creston Weekly Gazette, 1885.
Daily Argus (Fargo), 1888.
Detroit Free Press, 1886.
Galesburg Tribune, 1888.
Great Falls Tribune (Montana), 1894.
Harbinger (New York), 1845–46.
Hornell Daily Times (New York), 1878–81.
Hornellsville Tribune, 1869–78.
Iowa State Register (Des Moines), 1871, 1878, 1888.
Irish Standard (Minneapolis), 1887–94.
Irish World and Industrial Liberator, 1877, 1890–91.
Kansas City Star, 1893.
Knights of Labor (Chicago), 1886–89.
Labor Enquirer (Chicago), 1887–88.

New York Sun, 1877, 1882.
New York Times, 1869, 1877–78, 1881, 1887–88.
New York Tribune, 1877.
New York World, 1877–78.
Omaha Daily Bee, 1877, 1888.
Omaha Daily Herald, 1888.
The Railroad Gazette, 1886.
Railway Age, 1888, 1893–94.
St. Louis Post-Dispatch, 1886.
Saturday Evening Post (Burlington, Iowa), 1888.

City Directories

Burlington City Directory (Burlington, Iowa).
    1881–82
    1887
    1888
    1890
    1892
Colby, C.J. *Centennial Sketches, Map and Directory of Union County, Iowa, 1889*. Creston, Iowa: C. J. Colby, 1876.
A Directory of Creston and Other Cities and Towns of Union County, Iowa, 1889. Creston, Iowa: Nixon Waterman, 1889.
Hough's Hornellsville Directory, 1875. Hornellsville, N.Y.: Hough & Co., 1875.
Smith's Hornellsville Directory (Hornellsville, N.Y.).
    1877
    1880
    1884

Autobiographies

Adams, Henry. *The Education of Henry Adams*. Boston: Houghton Mifflin, 1918.
Bromley, Joseph. *Clear the Tracks: The Story of an Old-Time Locomotive Engineer, as told to Page Cooper*. New York: McGraw-Hill, 1943.
Buchanan, Joseph. *The Story of a Labor Agitator*. New York: The Outlook Company, 1903.
Dodge, "Jack." *The Friend of Everyman, His Life and Times, as told to William H. Whitcomb*. Los Angeles: Sherman Dabney, 1937.
French, Chauncey del. *The Railroadmen*. New York: Macmillan, 1938.
Gompers, Samuel. *Seventy Years of Life and Labor: An Autobiography*. New York: E. P. Dutton, 1925.
Pinkerton, William John. *His Personal Record: Stories of Railroad Life*. Kansas City, Mo.: The Pinkerton Publishing Co., 1904.

Powderly, Terence V. *The Path I Trod.* New York: Columbia University Press, 1940.

Reed, J. Harvey. *Forty Years an Engineer: Thrilling Tales of the Rail.* Prescott, Wash.: C. H. O'Neil, 1915.

Books—Primary Sources

Adams, Charles Francis, Jr. *Chapters of Erie and Other Essays.* New York: Holt, 1871.

Andreas, A. T. *An Illustrated Historical Atlas of Des Moines County, Iowa.* Chicago: A. T. Andreas, 1873.

————. *History of the State of Nebraska.* 2 vols. Chicago: Western Historical Publishing Co., 1882.

Antrobius, Augustus M. *History of Des Moines County, Iowa and Its People.* Chicago: S. J. Clarke, 1915.

Biographical and Historical Record of Ringgold and Union Counties, Iowa. Chicago: Lewis Publishing Co., 1887.

Carwardine, William H. *The Pullman Strike.* Chicago: C. H. Kerr, 1894.

Clampitt, John W. *Echoes from the Rocky Mountains.* Chicago: Belford, Clarke & Co., 1889.

Clark, E. E., and P. H. Morrissey. *Rates of Pay and Regulations Governing Employees in Train and Yard Service on the Principal Railroads of the United States, Canada, and Mexico.* Cedar Rapids, Iowa: T. S. Metcalfe Co., 1900.

Dacus, J. A. *Annals of the Great Strikes in the United States.* Chicago: L. T. Palmer, 1877.

Davis, Richard H. *The West from a Car Window.* New York: Harper, 1892.

Feick, Fred L. *The Life of Railwaymen.* Chicago: H. O. Shepard, 1905.

Flower, F. G. *Descriptive Illustrated Review of Ottumwa, Iowa: Trade, Commerce, and Manufactures.* Ottumwa, Iowa: n.p., 1890.

Fulton, Justin D. *Sam Hobart, The Locomotive Engineer: A Workingman's Solution of the Labor Problem.* New York: Funk & Wagnalls, 1882.

Gunnison, Almon. *Rambles Overland: A Trip across the Continent.* Boston: Universalist Publishing House, 1884.

Hadley, Arthur T. *Railroad Transportation: Its History and Laws.* New York: G. P. Putnam's Sons, 1885.

Haines, Henry S. *American Railroad Management: Addresses Delivered before the American Railway Management Association.* New York: John Wiley & Sons, 1897.

Hair, James T. *Iowa State Gazetteer.* Chicago: Bailey & Hair, 1865.

Hakes, Hon. Harlo. *Landmarks of Steuben County, New York.* Syracuse, N.Y.: D. Mason & Co., 1896.

Hall, John A. *The Great Strike on the Q, with a History of the Organization and Growth of the B. of L. E., B. of L. F., and the Switchmen's Mutual Aid Association of North America.* Chicago: Elliott & Beezley, 1889.

Hartley, H. H., and L. G. Jeffers. *Business Directory and Review of the Trade, Commerce, and Manufactures of the City of Burlington, Iowa.* Burlington, Iowa: C. M. Wilcox & Co., 1856.

Helena Board of Trade. *Helena Illustrated: Capital of the State of Montana: A History of Early Settlement and Helena Today.* Minneapolis: Frank L. Thresher, 1890.

History of Des Moines County, Iowa. Chicago: Western Historical Publishing Co., 1879.

Huebinger, M. *Map of the City of Burlington, Iowa.* Des Moines: Iowa Publishing Co., 1910.

Iowa Directory Company. *Iowa State Gazetteer, Business Directory, and Farmers List.* Dubuque, Iowa: Dubuque Telegraph, 1892.

Kirkman, Marshall M. *The Operation of Trains.* Vol. 3, *The Science of Railways.* Chicago: The World Publishing Co., 1894.

Larrabee, William. *The Railroad Question: A Historical and Practical Treatise on Railroads and Remedies for their Abuse.* Chicago: Schulte Publishing Co., 1898.

Lummis, Charles F. *A Tramp across the Continent.* New York: Charles Scribner's Sons, 1892.

Maitland, James. *Historical Sketches of Burlington, Iowa.* Burlington, Iowa: n.p. 1881.

Morris, Robert C. *Cheyenne Illustrated: Report of the Cheyenne Board of Trade.* Cheyenne, Wyo.: Daily Sun Printing House, 1888.

Near, I. W. *History of Steuben County and Its People.* Chicago: The Lewis Publishing Co., 1911.

Portrait and Biographical Album of Des Moines County, Iowa. Chicago: Acme Publishers, 1888.

Roberts, Cecil. *Adrift in America, or Work and Adventure in the States.* London: Lawrence & Bullen, 1891.

Roberts, Morley. *The Western Avernus, or Toil and Travel in Further North America.* London: Smith, Elder & Co., 1887.

Rouse, Clara B. *Iowa Leaves, Six Chapters.* Chicago: Illinois Printing & Binding Co., 1891.

Salmons, C. H. *The Burlington Strike.* Aurora, Illinois: Bunnell & Ward, 1889.

Saltiel, E. H., and George Barnett. *History and Business Directory of Cheyenne and Guide to the Mining Regions of the Rocky Mountains.* Omaha: L. B. Joseph, 1868.

Stanton, G. Smith. *When Wildwood was in Flower: A Narrative Covering the Fifteen Years Experiences of a New Yorker on the Western Plains.* New York: J. S. Ogilvie Publishing Co., 1910.

Stead, W. T. *Chicago Today, or The Labour War in America.* London: Review of Reviews, 1894.

Strong, Josiah. *Our Country: Its Possible Future and Its Present Crisis.* New York: Baker & Phelps, 1885.

Swinton, John. *A Momentous Question: The Respective Attitudes of Labor and Capital.* Philadelphia: Keller Publishing Co., 1895.

Thayer, William M. *Marvels of the West.* Norwich, Conn. Henry Bill Publishing Co., 1888.

Tracey, J. L. *Guide to the Great West.* Saint Louis: Tracey & Eaton, 1870.

Warner, Charles Dudley. *Studies in the South and West with Comments on Canada.* London: T. Fisher Unwin, 1890.

Watkins, H. K. *A Souvenir of Burlington, Iowa.* Burlington, Iowa: Journal Co., 1896.

Wolfe, J. M. *Guide, Gazetteer, and Directory of Nebraska Railroads.* Omaha: J. M. Wolfe, 1872.

Articles—Primary Sources

Adams, B. B., Jr. "The Everyday Life of the Railroad Men." In *The American Railway: Its Construction, Development, Management, and Appliances,* 383–424. New York: Charles Scribner's Sons, 1889.

Adams, Charles Francis, Jr. "The Prevention of Railroad Strikes." *Scribner's Magazine* 5 (April 1889): 424–30.

Barnard, Dr. W. T. "The Relations of Railway Managers and Employees." *Popular Science* 27 (1885): 768–85.

Conlon, P. J. "Past, Present and Future of Our Association." *Machinists' Monthly Journal* 21 (July 1909).

Debs, Eugene V. "How I Became a Socialist," In *Writings and Speeches of Eugene V. Debs.* New York: Hermitage Press, 1948.

Ely, Richard T. "Natural Monopolies and the Workingman." *North American Review* 158 (March 1894): 294–303.

Hitchcock, Ripley. "At the Head of the Rails."*Chautauquan* 9 (June 1889): 540–43.

Holst, Heinrich von. "Are We Awakened?" *Journal of Political Economy* 2 (1893–94): 485–516.

Irons, Martin. "My Experiences in the Labor Movement." *Lippincott's Magazine* 37 (June 1886): 618–26.

Molineaux, E. L. "Riots in Cities and Their Suppression." Paper read before the Military Service Institution of the United States, October 11, 1883.

[Perkins, Charles E.] "Railroad Companies and Their Employees." *Nation,* March 18, 1880, 211–12.

Pinkerton, William John. "Debs Treachery to the Working Class." Chicago: William J. Pinkerton, 1911.

Powderly, Terence V. "Government-Ownership of Railways." *The Arena* 7 (December 1892): 58–63.

Robinson, H. P. "The Lessons of the Recent Strikes." *North American Review* 159 (August 1894): 195–201.

Scott, Thomas B. "The Recent Strikes." *North American Review* 125 (September 1877): 351–62.

330

Strong, William J. "Blacklisting: The New Slavery." *The Arena* 21 (March 1899): 273–92.
Taussig, F.W. "The Southwestern Strikes." *Quarterly Journal of Economics* 1:184–222.
(Touzalin, A. E.) "The Care of Railroad Employees." *Nation*, February 19, 1880, 134–35.

Books—Secondary Sources

Adamson, Archibald. *North Platte and Its Associations*. North Platte, Nebr.: The Evening Telegraph, 1910.
Alexandersson, Gunnar. *The Industrial Structure of American Cities: A Geographic Study of Urban Economy in the United States*. Lincoln: University of Nebraska Press, 1956.
Allen, Ruth. *The Great Southwest Strike*. Austin: University of Texas Press, 1943.
Athearn, Robert G. *Union Pacific Country*. Lincoln: University of Nebraska Press, 1971.
Baldwin, W. W. *Chicago, Burlington & Quincy Railroad: A Documentary History*. 2 vols. Chicago: R. R. Donnelly & Sons, 1929.
Barger, Harold. *The Transportation Industries, 1889–1946: A Study of Output, Employment, and Productivity*. New York: National Bureau of Economic Research, 1951.
Berry, Brian J. L. *Geography of Market Centers and Retail Distribution*. Englewood Cliffs, N. J.: Prentice-Hall, 1967.
Botkin, B. A., and Alvin F. Harlow. *A Treasury of Railroad Folklore*. New York: Crown Publishers, 1953.
Brody, David. *Steelworkers in America: The Nonunion Era*. New York: Harper, 1969.
Bruce, Robert V. *1877: Year of Violence*. Indianapolis: Bobbs-Merrill, 1959.
Byers, M. L. *Economics of Railway Operations*. New York: Engineering News Publishing Co., 1907.
Campbell, Edward G. *The Reorganization of the American Railroad System, 1893–1900: A Study of the Effects of the Panic of 1893*. New York: Columbia University Press, 1938.
Carstensen, Vernon, ed. *The Public Lands: Studies in the History of the Public Domain*. Madison: University of Wisconsin Press, 1968.
Chandler, Alfred D., Jr. *The Railroads: The Nation's First Big Business*. New York: Harcourt, Brace & Co., 1965.
———. *The Visible Hand: The Managerial Revolution in American Business*. Cambridge: Harvard University Press, 1977.
Chudacoff, Howard P. *Mobile Americans: Residential and Social Mobility in Omaha, 1880–1920*. New York: Oxford University Press, 1972.
Cochran, Thomas C. *Railroad Leaders, 1845–1900: The Business Mind in Action*. Cambridge: Harvard University Press, 1953.
Cooper, Jerry M. *The Army and Civil Disorder: Federal Military Interven-*

tion in Labor Disputes, 1877–1900. Westport, Conn.: Greenwood Press, 1980.

Cottrell, Fred. The Railroader. Stanford, Calif.: Stanford University Press, 1940.

Cumbler, John. Working Class Community in Industrial America, 1880–1930: Work, Leisure, and Struggle in Two Industrial Communities. Westport, Conn.: Greenwood Press, 1979.

Daggett, Stuart. Railroad Reorganization. Cambridge: Harvard University Press, 1908.

Davis, Lance, Richard Easterlin, Richard Parker, et al. American Economic Growth: An Economist's History of the United States. New York: Harper & Row, 1972.

Dawley, Alan. Class and Community: The Industrial Revolution in Lynn. Cambridge: Harvard University Press, 1976.

Dixon, Frank H. State Railroad Control, with a History of Its Development in Iowa. New York: Thomas Crowell, 1896.

Doeringer, Peter, and Michael Piore. Internal Labor Markets and Manpower Analysis. Lexington, Mass.: Lexington Books, 1971.

Douglas, Paul H. Real Wages in the United States. New York: Houghton Mifflin, 1930.

Doyle, Don Harrison. The Social Order of a Frontier Community: Jacksonville, Illinois, 1825–1870. Urbana: University of Illinois Press, 1978.

Dublin, Thomas. Women at Work: The Transformation of Work and Community in Lowell, Massachusetts, 1826–1860. New York: Columbia University Press, 1979.

Ducker, James H. Men of the Steel Rails: Workers on the Atchison, Topeka & Sante Fe, 1869–1900. Lincoln: University of Nebraska Press, 1983.

Dykstra, Robert. Cattle Towns. New York: Alfred A. Knopf, 1960.

Edwards, P. K. Strikes in the United States, 1881–1974. New York: St. Martin's Press, 1981.

Eggert, Gerald G. Railroad Labor Disputes: The Beginnings of Federal Strike Policy. Ann Arbor: University of Michigan Press, 1967.

———. Richard Olney: Evolution of a Statesman. University Park: Pennsylvania State University Press, 1974.

Emmons, David M. Garden in the Grasslands: Boomer Literature of the Central Great Plains. Lincoln: University of Nebraska Press, 1971.

Faler, Paul G. Mechanics and Manufacturers in the Early Industrial Revolution: Lynn, Massachusetts, 1780–1860. Albany, N.Y.: State University of New York Press, 1981.

Federal Writers Project. Iowa: A Guide to the Hawkeye State. New York: Hastings House, 1946.

Fels, Rendigs. Wages, Earnings, and Employment on the Nashville, Chattanooga & St. Louis Railroad. Nashville: Vanderbilt University Press, 1953.

Fishlow, Albert. American Railroads and the Transformation of the Ante-Bellum Economy. Cambridge: Harvard University Press, 1965.

Foner, Eric. *Free Soil, Free Labor, Free Men: The Ideology of the Republican Party before the Civil War*. New York: Oxford University Press, 1970.

Foner, Philip S. *The Great Labor Uprising of 1877*. New York: Monad Press, 1977.

————. *History of the Labor Movement in the United State*. Vol. 2. New York: International Publishers, 1955.

————. *Organized Labor and the Black Worker, 1619–1973*. New York: Praeger, 1974.

Foster, John. *Class Struggle and the Industrial Revolution: Early Industrial Capitalism in Three English Towns*. London: Weidenfeld & Nicholson, 1974.

Gates, Paul. *The Illinois Central Railroad and Its Colonization Work*. Cambridge: Harvard University Press, 1934.

Gillen, Paul B. *The Distribution of Occupations as a City Yardstick*. New York: King's Crown Press 1951.

Ginger, Ray. *The Bending Cross: A Biography of Eugene V. Debs*. New Brunswick, N. J.: Rutgers University Press, 1949.

Gitelman, Howard M. *Workingmen of Waltham: Mobility in American Urban Industrial Development, 1850–90*. Baltimore: Johns Hopkins University Press, 1974.

Glaab, Charles N. *Kansas City and the Railroads: Community Policy in the Growth of a Regional Metropolis*. Madison: State Historical Society of Wisconsin, 1962.

Golden, James Reed. *Investment Behavior of United States Railroads, 1870–1914*. New York: Arno, 1975.

Gordon, David M., Richard Edwards, and Michael Reich. *Segmented Work, Divided Workers: The Historical Transformation of Labor in the United States*. New York: Cambridge University Press, 1982.

Griffin, Clyde, and Sally Griffin. *Natives and Newcomers: The Ordering of Opportunity in Mid-Nineteenth Century Poughkeepsie*. Cambridge: Harvard University Press, 1978.

Griffin, John I. *Strikes: A Study in Quantitative Economics*. New York: Columbia University Press, 1939.

Grodinsky, Julius. *The Iowa Pool: A Study in Railroad Competition, 1870–1884*. Chicago: University of Chicago Press, 1950.

————. *Transcontinental Strategy, 1869–1893: A Study of Businessmen*. Philadelphia: University of Pennsylvania Press, 1962.

Gutman, Herbert G. *Work, Culture, and Society in Industrializing America*. New York: Alfred A. Knopf, 1976.

Hall, Fred S. *Sympathetic Strikes and Sympathetic Lockouts*. New York: Columbia University Press, 1898.

Haynes, Fred S. *Third Party Movements since the Civil War, with Special Reference to Iowa*. Iowa City, Iowa: State Historical Society, 1916.

Hertel, D. W. *History of the Brotherhood of Maintenence of Way Employees: Its Birth and Growth, 1887–1955*. Washington, D.C.: Ramsdell, 1955.

Hiller, Ernest T. *The Strike: A Study in Collective Action*. Chicago: University of Chicago Press, 1928.

Hugins, Walter E. *Jacksonian Democracy and the Working Class: A Study of the New York Workingmen's Movement, 1829–1837*. Stanford, Calif.: Stanford Unversity Press, 1960.

Hyman, Richard. *Strikes*. London: Fontana, 1972.

Johnson, Emory R., and Truman Van Metre. *Principles of Railroad Tran sportation*. New York: D. Appleton, 1916.

Jones, Maldwyn. *American Immigration*. Chicago: University of Chicago Press, 1960.

Jordan, Philip D. *Catfish Bend: River Town and County Seat*. Burlington, Iowa: Craftsman Press, 1975.

Keil, Hartmut, and Jentz, John. *German Workers in Industrial Chicago, 1850–1910: A Comparative Perspective*. Dekalb, Ill.: Northern Illinois University Press, 1983.

Kirkland, Edward C. *Industry Comes of Age: Business, Labor, and Public Policy, 1860–1897*. New York: Holt, Rinehart & Winston, 1961.

Knights, Peter R. *Plain People of Boston, 1830–1860*. New York: Oxford University Press, 1971.

Koelbel, Leonora. *Missoula The Way It Was: A Portrait of An Early Western Town*. Missoula, Mont.: Gateway Print & Litho, 1972.

Kolko, Gabriel. *Railroads and Regulation, 1877–1916*. Princeton, N. J.: Princeton University Press, 1965.

Laurie, Bruce. *Working People of Philadelphia*. Philadelphia: Temple University Press, 1980.

Lebergott, Stanley. *Manpower in Economic Growth: The American Record since 1800*. New York: McGraw-Hill, 1964.

Lecht, Leonard A. *Experience under Railway Labor Legislation*. New York: Columbia University Press, 1955.

Licht, Walter. *Working for the Railroad: The Organization of Work in the Nineteenth Century*. Princeton, N. J.: Princeton University Press, 1983.

Lightner, David L. *Labor on the Illinois Central Railroad, 1852–1900: The Evolution of an Industrial Environment*. New York: Arno, 1977.

Lindsey, Almont. *The Pullman Strike: The Story of a Unique Experiment and of a Great Labor Upheaval*. Chicago: University of Chicago Press, 1942.

Long, Clarence D. *Wages and Earnings in the United States, 1860–1890*. Princeton, N. J.: Princeton University Press, 1960.

MacDonald, Marie. *Glendive: The History of a Montana Town*. Glendive, Mont.: Gateway Press, 1968.

Mater, Dan H. *The Railroad Seniority System: History, Description, and Evaluation*. Chicago: University of Chicago Press, 1940.

McCaleb, Walter F. *Brotherhood of Railroad Trainmen, with Special Refer ence to the Life of Alexander F. Whitney*. New York: Albert & Charles Boni, 1936.

McMurry, Donald L. *The Great Burlington Strike of 1888: A Case History of Industrial Relations*. Cambridge: Harvard University Press, 1956.

McPherson, James Alan, and Miller Williams, eds. *Railroads: Trains and People in American Culture*. New York: Random House, 1976.

Mercer, Lloyd J. *Railroads and Land Grant Policy: A Study in Government Intervention*. New York: Academic Press, 1982.

Miller, George. *Railroads and the Granger Laws*. Madison: University of Wisconsin Press, 1971.

Montgomery, David. *Beyond Equality: Labor and the Radical Republicans, 1862–1872*. New York: Alfred A. Knopf, 1967.

———. *Workers' Control in America: Studies in the History of Work, Technology, and Labor Struggles*. New York: Cambridge University Press, 1979.

Nearing, Scott. *Wages in the United States,1908–10: A Study of State and Federal Wage Statistics*. New York: Macmillan, 1914.

Overton, Richard C. *Burlington Route: A History of the Burlington Lines*. New York: Alfred A. Knopf, 1965.

———. *Burlington West: A Colonization History of the Burlington*. Cambridge: Harvard University Press,1941.

Ozanne, Robert. *Wages in Theory and Practice*. Madison: University of Wisconsin Press, 1968.

Painter, Leonard. *Brotherhood of Railway Carmen of America*. Kansas City, Mo.: Brotherhood of Railway Carmen, 1941.

Perlman, Mark. *The Machinists: A Study in American Trade Unionism*. Cambridge: Harvard University Press, 1961.

Pessen, Edward. *Most Uncommon Jacksonians*. Albany: State University of New York Press, 1967.

Porter, Glenn C., and Harold C. Livesay. *Merchants and Manufacturers: Studies in the Changing Structure of Nineteenth-Century Marketing*. Baltimore: Johns Hopkins University Press, 1971.

Pred, Allan R. *The Spatial Dynamics of United States Urban-Industrial Growth, 1800–1914*. Cambridge: MIT Press, 1966.

Prout, Henry G. *A Life of George Westinghouse*. New York: American Society of Mechanical Engineers, 1921.

Reinhardt, Richard, ed. *Workin' on the Railroad: Reminiscences from the Age of Steam*. Palo Alto, Calif.: American West Publishing Co., 1970.

Reps, John. *Cities of the American West: A History of Frontier Urban Planning*. Princeton, N. J.: Princeton University Press, 1979.

Reynolds, Lloyd G. *The Structure of Labor Markets, Wages, and Labor Mobility in Theory and Practice*. New York: Harper, 1951.

Richardson, Reed C. *The Locomotive Engineer, 1863–1963: A Century of Railway Labor Relations and Work Rules*. Ann Arbor: Bureau of Industrial Relations, Graduate School of Business Administration, University of Michigan, 1963.

Ripley, William Z. *Railroads, Rates, and Regulations*. New York: Longmans, Green, 1920.

Robbins, Roy M. *Our Landed Heritage: The Public Domain, 1776–1936.* Princeton, N. J.: Princeton University Press, 1942.

Ross, Steven J. *Workers on the Edge: Work, Leisure and Politics in Industrializing Cincinnati, 1788–1890.* New York: Columbia University Press, 1985.

Salvatore, Nick. *Eugene V. Debs: Citizen and Socialist.* Urbana: University of Illinois Press, 1982.

Saxton, Alexander. *The Indispensable Enemy: Labor and the Anti-Chinese Movement in California.* Los Angeles and Berkeley: University of California Press, 1971.

Schlegel, Marvin W. *The Ruler of the Reading: The Life of Franklin B. Gowen, 1836–1889.* Harrisburg: Archives Publishing Co. of Pennsylvania, 1947.

Schwantes, Carlos. *Radical Heritage: Labor, Socialism, and Reform in Washington and British Columbia, 1885–1917.* Seattle: University of Washington Press, 1979.

Scott, Joan W. *The Glassworkers of Carmaux.* Cambridge: Harvard University Press, 1974.

Seidman, Joel. *The Brotherhood of Railway Trainmen: The Internal Political Life of a National Union.* New York: John Wiley & Sons, 1962.

Sharpless, John B., II. *City Growth in the United States, England, and Wales, 1820–1861: The Effects of Location, Size, and Economic Structure on Inter-Urban Variations in Demographic Growth.* New York: Arno, 1977.

Slichter, Sumner. *Union Policies and Industrial Management.* Washington, D.C.: The Brookings Institution, 1941.

Stover, John. *The Life and Decline of the American Railroad.* New York: Oxford University Press, 1970.

Taylor, George Rogers, and Irene Neu. *The American Railroad Network, 1861–1890.* Cambridge: Harvard University Press, 1956.

Taylor, Philip. *The Distant Magnet: European Immigration to the U.S.A.* New York: Harper & Row, 1971.

Temin, Peter. *Iron and Steel in Nineteenth Century America.* Cambridge: MIT Press, 1964.

Thernstrom, Stephen. *The Other Bostonians: Poverty and Progress in the American Metropolis, 1880–1970.* Cambridge: Harvard University Press, 1973.

––––––. *Poverty and Progress: Social Mobility in a Nineteenth-Century City.* Cambridge: Harvard University Press, 1964.

Thernstrom, Stephen, and Richard Sennett, eds. *Nineteenth-Century Cities: Essays in the New Urban History.* New Haven, Conn.: Yale University Press, 1969.

Thompson, Wilbur R. *A Preface to Urban Economics.* Baltimore: Johns Hopkins University Press, 1965.

Tilly, Charles, and Edward Shorter. *Strikes in France, 1830–1968.* New York: Cambridge University Press, 1974.

Turner, Frederick Jackson. *Frontier and Section: Selected Essays of Frederick Jackson Turner*. Englewood Cliffs, N. J.: Prentice-Hall, 1961.

————. *The Significance of Sections in American History*. New York: Henry Holt, 1932.

Ulman, Lloyd. *The Rise of the National Union*. Cambridge: Harvard University Press, 1955.

Vance, J. E. *The Merchant's World: The Geography of Wholesaling*. Englewood Cliffs, N. J.: Prentice-Hall, 1970.

Vatter, Harold G. *The Drive to Industrial Maturity: The U.S. Economy, 1860–1914.*Westport, Conn.: Greenwood Press, 1975.

Wade, Richard. *The Urban Frontier: The Rise of Western Cities, 1790–1830*. Cambridge: Harvard University Press, 1959.

Walkowitz, Daniel J. *Worker City, Company Town: Iron- and Cotton-Workers' Protest in Troy and Cohoes, New York, 1855–1944*. Urbana: University of Illinois Press, 1978.

Ware, Norman. *The Labor Movement in the United States, 1860–1895: A Study in Democracy*. New York: D. Appleton, 1929.

Warner, Sam Bass, Jr. *The Urban Wilderness: A History of the American City*. New York: Harper & Row, 1972.

Weber, Thomas. *The Northern Railroads in the Civil War, 1861–1865*. New York: King's Crown Press, 1952.

Wellington, Arthur M. *The Economic Theory of the Location of Railways*. New York: John Wiley, 1891.

Wilentz, Sean. *Chants Democratic: New York City and the Rise of the American Working Class, 1788–1850*. New York: Oxford University Press, 1984.

Woodward, C. Vann. *Reunion and Reaction: The Compromise of 1877 and the End of Reconstruction*. Garden City, N.Y.: Doubleday, 1956.

Wright, Carroll D. *The Battles of Labor*. Philadelphia: George W. Jacobs, 1906.

Wyman, Walker D. *The Missouri River Towns in the Westward Movement*. Iowa City, Iowa: Iowa University Abstracts in History, 1938.

Articles—Secondary Sources

Alcorn, Richard S. "Leadership and Stability in Mid-Nineteenth Century America: A Case Study of an Illinois Town." *Journal of American History* 61 (December 1974): 685–702.

Amsden, Jon, and Stephen Brier. "Coal Miners on Strike: The Transformation of Strike Demands and the Formation of a National Union." *Journal of Interdisciplinary History* 7, no. 4 (Spring 1977): 583–616.

Benedict, Michael Les. "Southern Democrats in the Crisis of 1876–77: A Reconsideration of Reunion and Reaction." *Journal of Social History* (1980): 489–524.

Bennett, Sari, and Carville Earle. "The Geography of Strikes in the United

States, 1881–1894." *Journal of Interdisciplinary History* 8, no. 1 (Summer 1982): 63–84.

Black, Paul V. "Experiment in Bureaucratic Centralization: Employee Blacklisting on the Burlington Railroad, 1877–1892." *Business History Review* 51, no. 4 (Winter 1977): 444–59.

Boeck, George A. "A Decade of Transportation Fever in Burlington, Iowa, 1845–1855." In *Patterns and Perspectives in Iowa History*, edited by Dorothy Schwieder. Ames: Iowa State University Press, 1973.

Bonney, Richard J. "The Pullman Strike of 1894: Pocatello Perspective." *Idaho Yesterdays* (Fall 1980): 23–28.

Buckler, William H. "The Minimum Wage in the Machinists' Union." In *Studies in American Trade Unionism*, edited by Jacob Hollander and George E. Barnett. New York: Henry Holt & Co., 1905.

Cassity, Michael J. "Modernization and Social Crisis: The Knights of Labor and a Midwest Community, 1885–1886." *Journal of American History* 66, no. 2 (February 1979): 41–61

Clark, D. E. "The Westward Movement in the Upper Mississippi Valley during the Fifties." Mississippi Valley Historical Association. *Proceedings* 7 (1913–14).

Coelho, Philip R., and James F. Shepherd. "Regional Differences in Real Wages: The United States, 1851–1880." *Explorations in Economic History* 13 (1976): 203–30.

Conzen, Michael P. "A Transport Interpretation of the Growth of Urban Regions: An American Example." *Journal of Historical Geography* 1, no. 4 (October 1975): 361–82.

Cooper, Jerry M. "The Army as Strikebreaker—The Railroad Strikes of 1877 and 1894." *Labor History* 18, no. 2 (Spring 1977): 179–94.

Dancis, Bruce. "Social Mobility and Class Consciousness: San Francisco's International Workmen's Association in the 1880s." *Journal of Social History* 11, no. 1 (Fall 1977): 75–98.

Davis, T. M. "Building the Burlington through Nebraska." *Nebraska History* 30 (1949): 317–47.

———. "Lines West—The Story of G. W. Holdredge." *Nebraska History* 31 (1950): 25–47, 107–25, 204–25.

Douglas, Paul H. "An Analysis of Strike Statistics, 1881–1921." *Journal of the American Statistical Association* 18 (1922–23): 866–77.

Ducker, James H. "Workers, Townsmen, and the Governor: The Santa Fe Enginemen's Strike, 1878." *Kansas History* 5, no. 1 (Spring 1982): 23–32.

Easterlin, Richard. "Interregional Differences in Per Capita Income, Population, and Total Income, 1840–1950." In *Trends in the American Economy in the Nineteenth Century*. National Bureau of Economic Research. Princeton, N. J.: Princeton University Press, 1960.

———. "Regional Growth of Income: Long Term Tendencies." In *Population Redistribution and Economic Growth in the United States*,

338

1870–1950, Vol. 3, edited by Simon Kuznets et al. Philadelphia: American Philosophical Society, 1964.

Engerman, Stanley L. "Up or Out: Social and Geographic Mobility in the United States." *Journal of Interdisciplinary History* 5 (Winter 1974–75): 469–90.

Farnham, W. D. "The Weakened Spring of Government: A Study in Nineteenth Century American History." *American Historical Review* 68, no. 3 (April 1963): 662–80.

Fishlow, Albert. "Productivity and Technological Change in the Railroad Sector, 1840–1910." In *Output, Employment, and Productivity in the United States after 1800*. Conference on Research in Income and Wealth: Studies in Income and Wealth. New York: Columbia University Press, 1966.

Flaherty, Amos. "The Great Northern Strike of 1894: When Gene Debs Beat Jim Hill." In *The People Together*, edited by Meridel LeSueur et al. Minneapolis: n.p. 1958.

Fleisig, Heywood. "The Union Pacific Railroad and the Railroad Land Grant Controversy." *Explorations in Economic History* 2, no. 2 (Winter 1973–74): 155–72.

Fraser, John Hart. "The Middle West." *Annals of the Association of American Geographers* 62 (June 1972), 258–82.

Gallman, Robert. "Commodity Output, 1839–1899." In *Trends in the American Economy in the Nineteenth Century*. National Bureau of Economic Research. Princeton, N. J.: Princeton University Press, 1960.

Gates, Paul W. "Railroads of Missouri, 1850–1870." *Missouri Historical Review* 26, no. 2 (January 1932): 126–41.

———. "The Railroad Land Grant Legend." *Journal of Economic History,* 19 (Spring 1954): 143–46.

Gordon, Michael A. "The Labor Boycott in New York City, 1880–1886." *Labor History* 16, no. 2 (Spring 1974): 184–229.

Griffin, Clyde. "Workers Divided: The Effect of Craft and Ethnic Differences in Poughkeepsie, New York, 1850–1880." In *Nineteenth Century Cities*, edited by Stephen Thernstrom. New Haven, Conn.: Yale University Press, 1969.

Gutman, Herbert. "Class, Status, and Community Power in Nineteenth-Century American Cities: Paterson, New Jersey: A Case Study." In *Work, Culture, and Society in Industrializing America*, edited by Herbert Gutman. New York: Alfred Knopf, 1976.

———. "Trouble on the Railroads, 1873–74: Prelude to the 1877 Crisis?" *Labor History* 2, no. 2 (Spring 1961): 215–35.

———. "Workers Search for Power: Labor in the Gilded Age." In *The Gilded Age: A Reappraisal*, edited by H. Wayne Morgan. Syracuse, N. Y.: Syracuse University Press, 1963.

Haimson, Leopold. "The Problem of Social Stability in Urban Russia, 1905–1907." *Slavic Review* 23, no. 4 (December 1964): 619–42; 24, no. 1 (March 1965): 1–22.

Halma, Sidney. "Railroad Promotion and Economic Expansion at Council Bluffs, Iowa, 1857–1869." *Annals of Iowa* 42 (Summer 1974): 371–89.

Hamburg, James F. "Railroads and the Settlement Process of South Dakota during the Great Dakota Boom, 1878–1887." *South Dakota History* 5 (Spring, 1975): 165–78.

Hansen, Alvin H. "Cycles of Strikes." *The American Economic Review* 11 (1921): 616–21.

Harris, Chauncey D. "A Functional Classification of Cities in the United States." *The Geographical Review* 33, no. 1 (January 1943): 86–99.

Harris, Chauncey D., and Edward L. Ullman. "The Nature of Cities." *Annals of the American Academy of Political and Social Science* 242 (1945): 7–17.

Hart, J. F. "Functions and Occupational Structure of Cities of the American South." *Annals of the Association of American Geographers* 45 (1955): 269–86.

Hedges, James B. "The Colonization Work of the Northern Pacific Railroad." *Mississippi Valley Historical Review* 13 (December 1929): 311–42.

Henretta, James. "Families and Farms: Mentalité in Pre-Industrial America." *William and Mary Quarterly* 35, no. 1 (January 1978): 3–32.

———. "The Study of Social Mobility: Ideological Assumptions and Conceptual Bias." *Labor History* 18 (1977): 165–78.

Hobsbawm, E. J. "Class Consciousness in History." In *Aspects of History and Class Consciousness*, edited by Istvan Meszaros. London: Routledge & Kegan Paul, 1971.

———. "The Labour Aristocracy in Nineteenth-Century England." In *Labouring Men: Studies in the History of Labour*, edited by E. J. Hobsbawm. Garden City, N.Y.: Doubleday, 1964.

Jebsen, Harry, Jr. "The Role of Blue Island in the Pullman Strike of 1894." *Journal of the Illinois State Historical Society* 67, no. 3 (June 1974): 275–93.

Johnson, Emory R. "Railway Departments for the Relief and Insurance of Employees." *Annals of the American Academy of Political and Social Science* 6 (1895): 424–67.

Katz, Michael, Michael Doucet, and Mark Stern. "Migration and Social Order in Erie County, New York, 1855." *Journal of Interdisciplinary History* 8, no. 4 (Spring 1978): 669–702.

Kennedy, J. B. "The Beneficiary Features of the Railway Unions." In *Studies in American Trade Unionism*, edited by Jacob Hollander and George E. Barnett. New York: Henry Holt & Co., 1905.

Kerr, Clark, and Abraham J. Siegel. "The Interindustry Propensity to Strike—An International Comparison." In *Labor and Management in Industrial Society*, edited by Clark Kerr. Garden City, N.Y.: Doubleday, 1964.

Kilar, Jeremy W. "Community and Authority: Response to the Saginaw

Valley Lumber Strike of 1885." *Journal of Forest History* 20 (April 1976): 67–79.

Kirk, Gordon, Jr., and Carolyn Tyirin Kirk. "Migration, Mobility, and the Transformation of the Occupational Structure in an Immigrant Community: Holland, Michigan, 1850–1880." *Journal of Social History* 7, no. 2 (1973): 142–64.

MacDonald, J. S. "Agricultural Organization, Migration, and Labour Militancy in Rural Italy." *Economic History Review* 16 (August 1963): 61–75.

Martin, Albro. "Railroads and Equity Receivership: An Essay on Institutional Change." *Journal of Economic History* 34 (September 1974): 685–709.

———. "The Troubled Subject of Railroad Regulation in the Gilded Age—A Reappraisal." *Journal of American History* 61 (September 1974): 339–71.

McKenna, Frank. "Victorian Railway Workers." *History Workshop Journal* 1, no. 1 (Spring 1976).

McMurry, Donald L. "Federation of Railroad Brotherhoods, 1889–1894." *Industrial and Labor Relations Review* 7 (October 1953): 73–92.

———. "Labor Policies of the General Managers' Association of Chicago, 1886–1894." *Journal of Economic History* 8, no. 2 (Spring 1953): 160–79.

Meinig, D. W. "American Wests: Preface to a Geographical Interpretation." *Annals of American Geography* 62 (June 1972): 159–84.

Mercer, Lloyd J. "Building Ahead of Demand: Some Evidence for the Land Grant Railroads." *Journal of Economic History* 34 (June 1974): 492–500.

Miller, Roberta Balstead. "The Historical Study of Social Mobility: A New Perspective." *Historical Methods Newsletter* 8, no. 3 (June 1975): 92–97.

Montgomery, David. "Labor and the Republic in Industrial America." *Le Mouvement Social* 111 (April-June 1980): 201–15.

———. "Labor in the Industrial Era." In *U.S. Labor Department Bicentennial History of the American Worker*, edited by Richard B. Morris. Washington, D. C.: GPO, 1976.

———. "Strikes in Nineteenth-Century America." *Social Science History* 4, no. 1 (February 1980): 81–100.

Morgan, John M. "The Ann Arbor Strike of 1893." *Northwest Ohio Quarterly* 30, no. 3 (Summer 1958): 164–76.

Muller, Edward K. "Regional Urbanization and Selective Growth of Towns in North American Regions." *Journal of Historical Geography* 3, no. 1 (January 1977): 21–40.

Nelson, Howard J. "Town Founding and the American Frontier." *Association of Pacific Coast Geographers' Yearbook* 36 (1974): 7–23.

Nixon, Herman Clarence. "The Economic Basis of the Populist Movement in Iowa." *Iowa Journal of History and Politics* 21, no. 3 (July 1923): 373–96.

———. "The Populist Movement in Iowa." *Iowa Journal of History and Politics* 24, no. 1 (January 1926): 2–107.

Parsons, Stanley B. "Who Were the Nebraska Populists?" *Nebraska History* 44, no. 2 (June 1963): 83–100.

Perlman, Selig. "Upheaval and Reorganization." In *The History of Labour in the United States,* vol. 2, edited by John R. Commons. New York: Macmillan, 1918.

Peskin, Allan. "Was There a Compromise of 1877?" *Journal of American History* 60 (1973): 63–73.

Rubin, Julius. "Urban Growth and Regional Development." In *The Rise of Seaport Cities, 1790–1825,* edited by David T. Gilchrist. Charlottesville: University of Virginia Press, 1967.

Salvatore, Nick. "Railroad Workers and the Great Strike of 1877: The View from a Small Midwestern City." *Labor History* 21 (Fall 1980): 522–45.

Scheiber, Harry N. "Economic Change in the Civil War Era: An Analysis of Recent Studies." *Civil War History* 11 (December 1965): 396–411.

Sewell, William H., Jr. "Social Mobility in a Nineteenth-Century City: Some Findings and Implications."*Journal of Interdisciplinary History* 7, no. 2 (Autumn 1978): 217–33.

Shannon, David A. "E. V. Debs: Conservative Labor Editor." *Indiana Magazine of History* 47 (December 1951): 357–64.

Sieber, George W. "Railroads and Lumber Marketing, 1858–1878: The Relationship Between an Iowa Sawmill Firm and the Chicago & Northwestern Railroad." *Annals of Iowa* 3rd Ser. 39, no. 1 (Summer 1967): 33–46.

Siegel, Abraham J. "Method and Substance in Theorizing about Worker Protest." In *Aspects of Labor Economics.* National Bureau of Economic Research. Princeton, N. J.: Princeton University Press, 1962.

Spann, Robert M., and Edward W. Erickson. "The Economics of Railroading: The Beginning of Cartelization and Regulation." *The Bell Journal of Economics and Management Science* 1, no. 2 (Autumn 1970): 227–44.

Stanley, L. S. "The Machinist Union Story." *New Leader* 29, January 1927).

Stearns, Peter. "Measuring the Evolution of Strike Movements." *International Review of Social History* 19 (1974): 1–27.

Taylor, George Rogers. "The National Economy before and after the Civil War." In *Economic Changes in the Civil War Era,* edited by David T. Gilchrist and W. David Lewis. Greenville, Del.: Eleutherian Mills-Hagley Foundation, 1965.

Thernstrom, Stephan. "Urbanization, Migration, and Social Mobility in Late Nineteenth Century America." In *Toward a New Past: Dissenting Essays in American History,* edited by Barton J. Bernstein. New York: Pantheon, 1968.

———. "Working Class Social Mobility in Industrial America." In *Essays in Theory and History: An Approach to the Social Sciences,* edited by Melvin Richter, 221–40. Cambridge: Harvard University Press, 1970.

Thernstrom, Stephan, and Peter Knights. "Men in Motion: Some Data and Speculations about Urban Population Mobility in Nineteenth-Century

America." *Journal of Interdisciplinary History* 1, no. 1 (Autumn 1970): 7–36.

Thompson, Wilbur R. "Urban Economic Growth and Development in a National System of Cities." In *The Study of Urbanization*, edited by Philip M. Hauser and Leo F. Schnore. New York: John Wiley & Sons, 1965.

Tripp, Joseph F. "Kansas Communities and the Birth of the Labor Problem, 1877–1883." *Kansas History* 4, no. 2 (Summer 1981): 114–29.

Turner, Frederick Jackson. "The Significance of the Frontier in American History." In *The Frontier in American History*, edited by Frederick Jackson Turner. New York: Holt, 1920.

Ullman, Edward L. "The Railroad Pattern of the United States." *Geographical Review* 39 (1949): 242–56.

Varg, Paul A. "The Political Ideas of the A.R.U." *The Historian* 9 (Spring 1948): 85–100.

Wetzel, Kurt. "Railroad Management's Response to Operating Employee Accidents, 1890–1913." *Labor History* 21, no. 3 (Summer 1980): 351–68.

Woodward, C. Vann. "Yes, There Was a Compromise of 1877." *Journal of American History* 60 (1973): 215–23.

Worthman, Paul. "Working Class Mobility in Birmingham, Alabama, 1880–1914." In *Anonymous Americans: Explorations in Nineteenth-Century Social History*, edited by Tamara Hareven. Englewood Cliffs, N. J.: Prentice-Hall, 1971.

Wrigley, Robert L., Jr. "Pocatello, Idaho, as a Railroad Center." *Economic Geography* 21 (1943): 325–36.

Dissertations and Unpublished Papers

Ames, Charles F. "Repression or Concession: Press and Party Responses to the Threat of Social Upheaval, 1871–1903." Ph.D. dissertation, Boston University, 1973.

Bennett, John W. "Iron Workers in Woods Run and Johnstown: The Union Era, 1865–1895." Ph.D. dissertation, University of Pittsburgh, 1977.

Black, Paul V. "The Development of Management Personnel Policies on the Burlington Railroad, 1860–1900." Ph.D. dissertation, University of Wisconsin, 1972.

Boeck, George A. "An Early Iowa Community: Aspects of Economic, Social and Political Development in Burlington, Iowa, 1833–1866." Ph.D. dissertation, University of Iowa, 1961.

Brundage, David. "The Making of Working Class Radicalism in the Mountain West: Denver, Colorado, 1880–1903." Ph.D. dissertation, University of California, Los Angeles, 1982.

Caldwell, Henry H. "Plattsmouth, Nebraska: A Study in Urban Geography." Master's thesis, University of Nebraska, 1946.

Conzen, Michael P. "Metropolitan Dominance in the American Midwest during the Late Nineteenth Century." Ph.D. dissertation, University of Wisconsin, 1972.

Ducker, James Howard. "Men of the Steel Rail: Workers on the Atchison, Topeka and Santa Fe Railroad, 1869–1900." Ph.D. dissertation, University of Illinois, 1980.

Dyle, Prosper Lee. "An Early History of Beatrice, Nebraska." Master's thesis, University of Nebraska, 1941.

Ermisch, John F. "Quantitative Analysis of the Differential Growth of American Cities in the Late Nineteenth Century." Ph.D. dissertation, University of Kansas, 1974.

Friedberger, Mark W. "Cornbelt and River City: Social Change in a Midwest Community, 1885–1930." Ph.D. dissertation, University of Illinois, Chicago Circle, 1973.

Garlock, Jonathan. "A Structural Analysis of the Knights of Labor: Prolegomena to the History of the Producing Classes." Ph.D. dissertation, University of Rochester, 1974.

Graves, Carl Russell. "Scientific Management and the Santa Fe Railway Shopmen of Topeka, Kansas, 1900–1925." Ph.D. dissertation, Harvard University, 1980.

Groves, Harold M. "The Machinist in Industry: A Study of the History and Economics of his Craft." Ph.D. dissertation, University of Wisconsin, 1927.

Higgs, Robert Larry. "Location Theory and the Growth of Cities in the Western Prairie Region, 1870–1900." Ph.D. dissertation, Johns Hopkins University, 1968.

Licht, Walter M. "The Dialectics of Bureaucratization: The Case of Nineteenth-Century Railwaymen, 1830–1877." Paper presented at annual meeting of the Organization of American Historians, April 1978, New York.

————. "Nineteenth-Century American Railwaymen: A Study in the Nature and Organization of Work." Ph.D. dissertation, Princeton University, 1977.

McClelland, Marion. "The Early History of McCook, Nebraska." Master's thesis, University of Nebraska, 1942.

Muller, Edward K. "The Development of Urban Settlement in a Newly Settled Region: The Middle Ohio Valley, 1800–1860." Ph.D. dissertation, University of Wisconsin, 1972.

Ross, Steven J. "Workers on the Edge: Work, Leisure and Politics in Industrializing Cincinnati. 1788–1890." Ph.D. dissertation, Princeton University, 1980.

Shields, Roger Elwood. "Economic Growth with Price Deflation, 1873–1896." Ph.D. dissertation, University of Virginia, 1969.

Stromquist, Shelton. "Class and Community in a Nineteenth-Century Railroad Town: Hornellsville, New York, 1860–1880." Master's essay, University of Pittsburgh, 1973.

White, W. Thomas. "From Class to Community: Varieties of Radical Protest in the Railroad Industry of the Pacific Northwest, 1894–1917." Paper presented at annual meeting of the American Historical Association, December 1982, Washington, D.C.

———. "A History of Railroad Workers in the Pacific Northwest, 1883–1934." Ph.D. dissertation, University of Washington, 1981.

Index

A Note on the Author

Shelton Stromquist was graduated cum laude from Yale University. He received both his M.A. and Ph.D. in history from the University of Pittsburgh. A former coordinator of the Office of Local History, the State Historical Society of Wisconsin, he has held fellowships from the NDEA, the Newberry Library, and the Andrew W. Mellon Foundation. Mr. Stromquist is a member of the faculty at the University of Iowa.

Books in the Series The Working Class in American History